Human Capital, Innovation, and Executive Decision-Making in Pharma and Medical Device Industries

Stéphanie Monteiro
Institute for Systems and Robotics, Portugal

IGI Global
Scientific Publishing
Publishing Tomorrow's Research Today

Vice President of Editorial	Melissa Wagner
Director of Acquisitions	Mikaela Felty
Director of Book Development	Jocelynn Hessler
Production Manager	Mike Brehm
Cover Design	Jose Rosado

Published in the United States of America by
IGI Global Scientific Publishing
701 East Chocolate Avenue
Hershey, PA, 17033, USA
Tel: 717-533-8845 | Fax: 717-533-7115
Website: https://www.igi-global.com E-mail: cust@igi-global.com

Library of Congress Cataloging-in-Publication Data

LCCN: 2026011375 (CIP Data Pending)
ISBN13: 979-8-3373-9410-7
Isbn13Softcover: 979-8-3373-9411-4
EISBN13: 979-8-3373-9412-1
British Cataloguing in Publication Data
A Cataloguing in Publication record for this book is available from the British Library.

Table of Contents

Detailed Table of Contents

The pharmaceutical industry plays an essential role in the health and well-being of modern societies. However, this sector faces considerable criticism regarding its ethics and transparency. The objective of this work was to deepen the analysis of the concept of "Reputation", specifically in the pharmaceutical sector, with the aim of evaluating whether this would be a determining factor in the intention to purchase medicines. Thus, a study was carried out with a sample of 133 individuals that, through structural equations, sought to identify the impact of reputation on consumer behavior. As results obtained, this study was not able to confirm whether there is a direct influence between the two phenomena, since the numbers are not relevant in this aspect. However, other relevant analyzes were obtained for advances in the understanding of the pharmaceutical sector and the behavior of its consumers. In that regard, new suggestions for future investigations are presented, as well as the replication of this work in other countries to carry out new analyzes of the tested hypothesis.

Digital transformation is reshaping healthcare through the rapid expansion of HealthTech solutions, including telemedicine, artificial intelligence, and data-driven diagnostics. In this context, digital marketing has evolved into a strategic function that supports user engagement, adoption, and value creation, while facing regulatory and ethical constraints. This paper examines how digital marketing strategies can be integrated into strategic planning within the global HealthTech ecosystem. Using a qualitative approach that combines literature review and a case study of Knokcare, the study identifies key strategic dimensions for success. The findings highlight the importance of personalization, privacy-first communication, community engagement, localization, and value-based messaging. The study contributes by proposing an integrated framework that aligns digital marketing with the specific challenges of HealthTech.

Executive decision-making in regulated innovation environments demands a nuanced convergence of strategic leadership, regulatory intelligence, and organisational adaptability. This chapter examines how pharmaceutical and medical device executives navigate complex regulatory frameworks—including FDA pathways, EU MDR, and evolving AI-specific guidelines—to drive sustainable innovation. Drawing on recent empirical and conceptual literature, the chapter presents a framework integrating top management team competencies, risk governance, and digital transformation imperatives. . Key themes include the role of regulatory affairs in shaping pipeline strategy, leadership capabilities required for Industry 4.0 adoption, and the organisational enablers of innovation performance. The chapter contributes actionable insights for executives, policymakers, and scholars concerned with optimising the intersection of human capital, compliance, and value-creation in highly regulated industries.

This chapter per the authors examines the critical role of Human Resources in the development of medical devices, a sector characterized by high technical complexity, stringent regulatory requirements, and rapidly evolving healthcare needs. The purpose is to analyze how HR practices contribute to organizational success in this environment. The content discusses how multidisciplinary collaboration, deep technical and regulatory expertise, and ethical awareness are essential for effective product development. It further highlights HR as a strategic partner beyond administrative functions, focusing on recruitment, continuous professional development, and talent retention to ensure highly skilled and adaptable teams. The chapter also explores knowledge management as a key mechanism for preserving institutional expertise, fostering collaboration, and supporting innovation. Finally, it emphasizes aligning HR strategies with industry-specific demands to enhance quality, safety, and competitiveness.

This chapter attempts to discuss the role of strategic leadership on human capital management by focusing on the mediating effect of organisational culture in the

This chapter explores the synergistic relationship between workforce development and strategic decision-making in regulated drug development. It highlights how pharmaceutical organizations operate within a regulatory paradox that demands rapid innovation while ensuring compliance, quality, and patient safety. The discussion emphasizes future-ready workforce capabilities, including regulatory literacy, data integrity, cross-functional collaboration, and adaptive learning, as drivers of successful outcomes. Strategic frameworks such as portfolio management, risk-adjusted decision models, Target Product Profiles, and model-informed drug development are examined to demonstrate their role in improving success probabilities. Ultimately, integrating human capital with strategic governance creates resilient, agile, and innovation-driven systems capable of navigating complex regulatory environments.

This chapter explores the strategic importance of human capital and executive decision-making in regulated pharmaceutical and MedTech innovation. It examines how specialized talent, leadership capability, and knowledge management systems drive sustainable competitive advantage in highly regulated healthcare environments. The discussion highlights the role of executive leadership in portfolio strategy, risk governance, compliance integration, and cross-functional coordination. Emphasis is placed on managing uncertainty arising from regulatory shifts, clinical trial unpredictability, and market volatility. By aligning workforce development, ethical standards, and structured decision frameworks, organizations can enhance innovation effectiveness while safeguarding patient safety and regulatory trust.

The medical device industry is one of the most technologically advanced sectors within the global healthcare ecosystem, requiring not only scientific innovation but also strategic planning that integrates engineering, regulatory compliance, clinical validation, and business development. Medical device startups face significant challenges due to long development cycles, strict regulatory frameworks, and high

Preface

INTRODUCTION

The healthcare, pharmaceutical, and medical technology sectors are currently experiencing one of the most transformative periods in modern history. Digital transformation, artificial intelligence, organizational innovation, strategic leadership, and human capital development are redefining the way healthcare systems, pharmaceutical organizations, MedTech firms, and healthcare professionals operate across the globe. Simultaneously, organizations are increasingly challenged by complex regulatory frameworks, ethical expectations, sustainability concerns, workforce shortages, and the growing demand for patient-centered and value-based healthcare solutions. Within this evolving landscape, organizations are expected not only to remain compliant and operationally efficient but also to become adaptive, innovative, resilient, and ethically responsible.

This book, *Human Capital, Innovation, and Strategic Transformation in Healthcare, Pharma, and MedTech Organizations*, emerges as a multidisciplinary contribution that explores the intersection between strategy, leadership, innovation, human capital management, organizational culture, digital transformation, and healthcare governance. The chapters included in this volume collectively examine how organizations and professionals are adapting to rapidly evolving technological, organizational, and social environments. The book brings together perspectives from scholars, researchers, and professionals representing different countries, institutions, and disciplinary backgrounds, offering readers an international and multidimensional understanding of contemporary healthcare and pharmaceutical management challenges.

The subject matter of this book is especially relevant in a world where healthcare systems increasingly rely on strategic leadership, digital innovation, and human-centered organizational models to maintain competitiveness and sustainability.

Pharmaceutical companies and MedTech organizations are no longer evaluated solely based on product effectiveness or financial performance. Instead, stakeholders now expect organizations to demonstrate ethical responsibility, social accountability, organizational transparency, innovation governance, employee well-being, and strategic adaptability. Human capital has become a central organizational asset, while organizational culture, strategic management, and digital transformation have evolved into critical determinants of organizational resilience and long-term success.

The COVID-19 pandemic accelerated many of these transformations and exposed structural vulnerabilities within healthcare systems worldwide. Since then, organizations have intensified investments in digital healthcare solutions, artificial intelligence, workforce development, organizational innovation, and strategic governance. At the same time, healthcare professionals continue to face operational pressure, burnout risks, and growing performance expectations within highly regulated and technologically complex environments. Consequently, the relationship between human capital management, innovation, leadership, organizational culture, and technological transformation has become one of the most important research and managerial topics within healthcare and life sciences.

This book contributes to this discussion by exploring how organizations can strategically align human capital, leadership, innovation, ethics, organizational culture, and digital transformation to create sustainable organizational ecosystems capable of responding to future healthcare and business challenges. The chapters included in this volume address practical and theoretical issues associated with healthcare management, pharmaceutical reputation, workforce development, digital transformation, strategic decision-making, ethical leadership, organizational culture, professional competency development, and innovation governance.

The target audience for this book is broad and interdisciplinary. The book is particularly relevant for academics, researchers, doctoral students, healthcare professionals, healthcare managers, organizational leaders, pharmaceutical executives, MedTech professionals, human resource specialists, public administrators, policymakers, and postgraduate students interested in healthcare management, innovation, organizational behavior, digital transformation, and strategic leadership. Additionally, the book may serve as a valuable resource for professionals involved in healthcare operations, regulatory affairs, organizational development, strategic planning, workforce management, and technology implementation within healthcare and pharmaceutical environments.

From an academic perspective, this book contributes to the advancement of knowledge by integrating multiple disciplines, including management, healthcare administration, organizational behavior, human resource management, digital transformation, strategic management, innovation studies, healthcare governance, ethics, and competitive strategy. From a professional perspective, the book provides insights that may support decision-making processes, organizational restructuring initiatives, workforce development strategies, and innovation management practices within healthcare-related organizations.

CHAPTER OVERVIEW

The opening chapter, *Cure or Conflict: The Weight of the Pharmaceutical Reputation on the Intention to Purchase Pharma Products*, examines the growing importance of pharmaceutical reputation and its influence on consumer purchasing behavior. In an era characterized by increasing public scrutiny and digital information accessibility, pharmaceutical organizations are increasingly evaluated according to ethical practices, transparency, social responsibility, and organizational trustworthiness. This chapter explores how corporate reputation affects consumer confidence and purchasing intentions, contributing to a broader understanding of pharmaceutical marketing and organizational legitimacy within highly regulated healthcare markets.

Chapter Two, *Digital Marketing Strategy in the Global HealthTech Ecosystem: Aligning Innovation, Trust, and Value-Based Healthcare*, explores the role of digital marketing strategies within the rapidly expanding HealthTech ecosystem. The chapter highlights the importance of trust, technological innovation, patient engagement, and value-based healthcare approaches within digital healthcare environments. It further discusses how organizations can strategically integrate digital transformation and communication strategies to strengthen organizational positioning and improve stakeholder engagement across international healthcare markets.

Chapter Three, *Executive Decision-Making in Regulated Innovation Environments*, investigates the complexities associated with executive decision-making in highly regulated sectors. Pharmaceutical and MedTech industries operate within environments where innovation must coexist with strict compliance, risk management, and governance requirements. This chapter examines how executives navigate strategic decisions under regulatory pressure while maintaining innovation capacity and organizational competitiveness.

Chapter Four, *Human Resources Strategies to Support the Development of Medical Devices*, focuses on the role of human resource management in supporting innovation and development within medical device organizations. The chapter explores how organizations can strategically manage talent, competencies, collaboration, and organizational knowledge to support research, development, and innovation processes in highly specialized and regulated MedTech environments.

Chapter Five, *Impact of Strategic Leadership on Human Capital Management Mediating Role of Organizational Culture in Ethiopia's Healthcare Sector*, examines the relationship between strategic leadership, organizational culture, and human capital management within healthcare institutions. The chapter provides valuable insights into leadership effectiveness and organizational behavior in emerging healthcare environments, emphasizing the mediating role of organizational culture in shaping workforce performance and organizational outcomes.

Chapter Six, *Innovation Leadership Effect on Human Capital Management Mediating Role of Organizational Culture in Healthcare Sector*, continues the discussion surrounding leadership and organizational culture by focusing specifically on innovation leadership within healthcare organizations. The chapter explores how leadership approaches influence workforce engagement, innovation capacity, and organizational adaptability within dynamic healthcare environments.

Chapter Seven, *Leadership, Organizational Culture, and Innovation Governance in Pharmaceutical and Medical Device Firms*, investigates the relationship between organizational culture, governance mechanisms, and innovation management within pharmaceutical and MedTech firms. The chapter highlights how governance structures and leadership strategies influence organizational innovation, operational effectiveness, and long-term strategic sustainability.

Chapter Eight, *Leading Digital Transformation in Healthcare: Ethical Responsibility, Innovation, and Executive Accountability*, addresses the growing importance of digital transformation leadership within healthcare organizations. The chapter examines how healthcare executives manage technological transformation initiatives while balancing ethical responsibilities, organizational accountability, innovation goals, and patient-centered priorities.

Chapter Nine, *Marketing Strategy in Cross-National Pharmaceutical Campaigns: Ethics, Regulation, and Digital Transformation*, explores the complexities associated with international pharmaceutical marketing campaigns. The chapter discusses how organizations navigate ethical considerations, regulatory differences, digital communication strategies, and cultural adaptation within cross-national healthcare markets.

Chapter Ten, *Mindfulness as a Strategic Resource for Workplace Performance in Healthcare*, introduces mindfulness as a strategic organizational resource capable of improving employee well-being, workplace performance, resilience, and organizational effectiveness. Given the high-pressure nature of healthcare environments, the chapter emphasizes the growing importance of psychological well-being and emotional resilience within healthcare workforce management.

Chapter Eleven, *Performance Appraisal Tools: Perspectives of Healthcare Professionals in Portugal*, investigates healthcare performance evaluation systems through the perspectives of healthcare professionals. The chapter discusses performance appraisal methodologies, workforce evaluation challenges, and organizational implications associated with performance management within healthcare institutions.

Chapter Twelve, *Pharmaceutical Workforce Development and Strategic Decision-Making in Regulated Drug Development*, explores workforce development strategies within pharmaceutical organizations involved in regulated drug development processes. The chapter highlights the importance of strategic human capital management, organizational learning, and regulatory awareness in supporting effective pharmaceutical development activities.

Chapter Thirteen, *Strategic Human Capital and Executive Decision-Making in Regulated Pharma and MedTech Innovation*, further develops the discussion surrounding strategic decision-making and human capital management within pharmaceutical and MedTech sectors. The chapter examines how organizations align workforce capabilities, leadership strategies, and innovation management practices within highly regulated and technologically evolving environments.

Chapter Fourteen, *Strategic Roadmapping for Medical Device Startups*, addresses the challenges associated with strategic planning and organizational development within medical device startups. The chapter explores how emerging organizations can structure innovation roadmaps, manage uncertainty, align business strategy, and navigate regulatory complexity while pursuing sustainable growth.

The final chapter, *Talent Development, Knowledge Management Effect on Executive Decision-Making Through Change Management in Pharma and MedTech Industries*, examines the relationship between talent development, knowledge management, organizational change, and executive decision-making. The chapter highlights how organizations can leverage knowledge-sharing practices and workforce development initiatives to improve organizational adaptability and strategic performance within rapidly changing healthcare and pharmaceutical sectors.

CONCLUSION

Collectively, the chapters included in this volume demonstrate that the future of healthcare, pharmaceutical, and MedTech organizations will increasingly depend on the strategic integration of human capital, innovation, leadership, organizational culture, ethics, and digital transformation. Organizations capable of effectively balancing technological advancement with human-centered management approaches will likely be better positioned to respond to future organizational and societal challenges.

This book contributes to both academic research and professional practice by offering interdisciplinary perspectives capable of supporting future studies, strategic initiatives, and organizational decision-making processes. The diversity of contributors and thematic approaches reflects the global relevance of healthcare transformation and the growing importance of collaborative and multidisciplinary solutions.

It is our expectation that this volume will stimulate further academic discussion, encourage innovative organizational practices, and contribute to the development of more resilient, ethical, innovative, and strategically aligned healthcare ecosystems. We hope that readers will find this book both intellectually enriching and professionally valuable as they navigate the ongoing transformation of healthcare, pharmaceutical, and MedTech organizations in the twenty-first century.

This book is dedicated to my daughter, Camila Monteiro e Marcão, whose presence inspires every vision of a better future.

Chapter 1
Cure or Conflict:
The Weight of the Pharmaceutical Reputation on the Intention to Purchase Pharma Products

Pedro Manuel do Espírito Santo
http://orcid.org/0000-0001-8924-7912
Centre of Applied Research in Management and Economics (CARME), Polytechnic University of Leiria, Portugal

Patricia Milene AZinheira Cardoso
Polytechnic University of Coimbra, Portugal

ABSTRACT

The pharmaceutical industry plays an essential role in the health and well-being of modern societies. However, this sector faces considerable criticism regarding its ethics and transparency. The objective of this work was to deepen the analysis of the concept of "Reputation", specifically in the pharmaceutical sector, with the aim of evaluating whether this would be a determining factor in the intention to purchase medicines. Thus, a study was carried out with a sample of 133 individuals that, through structural equations, sought to identify the impact of reputation on consumer behavior. As results obtained, this study was not able to confirm whether there is a direct influence between the two phenomena, since the numbers are not relevant in this aspect. However, other relevant analyzes were obtained for advances in the understanding of the pharmaceutical sector and the behavior of its consumers. In that regard, new suggestions for future investigations are presented, as well as the replication of this work in other countries to carry out new analyzes of the tested hypothesis.

DOI: 10.4018/979-8-3373-9410-7.ch001

INTRODUCTION

The pharmaceutical industry plays an essential role in the health and well-being of modern societies. The distribution of medicines and the constant development of new technologies are crucial for combating diseases, alleviating symptoms and improving the quality of life of thousands of people around the world. However, the pharmaceutical industry faces considerable criticism regarding its ethics and transparency. More specifically, a few decades ago, pharmaceutical companies were highly respected. Now, due to corporate crises and social pressures, the industry is contested and its reputation reflects these impacts (Van den Bogaert et al., 2018).

An industry's reputation is shaped by a number of factors, including past experiences, social influences, and communication with stakeholders. The "Global Pharma 2023" study, conducted by the consulting firm Caliber, shows that the pharmaceutical industry has an average reputation globally.

Even after confidence in the sector improved following the COVID-19 pandemic, the report indicates that a lack of transparency regarding research and development practices, the excessive influence of marketing on drug prescriptions, and rising prices are some examples of issues that still affect the industry's reputation. These concerns have led consumers to question the reliability and ethics behind pharmaceutical companies, which can have a direct impact on consumers' perception and intention to purchase medicines.

It is well known that a company's reputation is unique. However, in practice, in sectors such as pharmaceuticals, a company's reputation can be the reputation of an entire sector that is attributed to a company (Busby, 2019). This is also indicated by the Global Trustworthiness Monitor, a study conducted in 2022 by Ipsos, which states that one of the many benefits generally associated with a strong reputation is strong industry regulation. Thus, the study suggests that if we believe the narrative that trust is in crisis, we should be seeing large-scale concerns about levels of regulation around the world and calls for greater government intervention. However, the study indicates that trust is not necessarily in crisis – on the contrary, it is low and always has been – and like most things, the relationship between one thing (trust) and another (regulation) is not that simple.

The reputation of the pharmaceutical industry is therefore a relevant issue that requires critical and balanced analysis. In this article, we will explore the different aspects that shape the reputation of the pharmaceutical industry and examine whether these perceptions actually influence consumers' intention to purchase medicines.

In addition, we will discuss strategies that pharmaceutical companies can adopt to improve their reputation and regain public trust. Therefore, the study seeks to contribute to the investigation of which brands shape this perceived reputation of the sector. Understanding this scenario is essential to improving the relationship between the pharmaceutical industry and consumers, with the aim of leveraging the sector's growth.

LITERATURE REVIEW

The Conceptual Model

The conceptual model defined for the study followed the S-O-R structure (Mehrabian & Russell, 1974). The theory states that a stimulus (S) influences people's internal affective evaluations (O), which, in turn, lead to approaches or responses (R).

Figure 1 represents the model, in which the central concept is the "Reputation of pharmaceutical brands". Based on the literature reviewed, it is concluded that the central concept is constituted from concepts I, II, and III – "Communication," "Personal Experiences & Perception," and "Social Influences," respectively. As a consequence of the central concept, we will investigate the direct impact on consumption, represented by concept IV – "Intention to purchase medicines."

Figure 1. Conceptual model

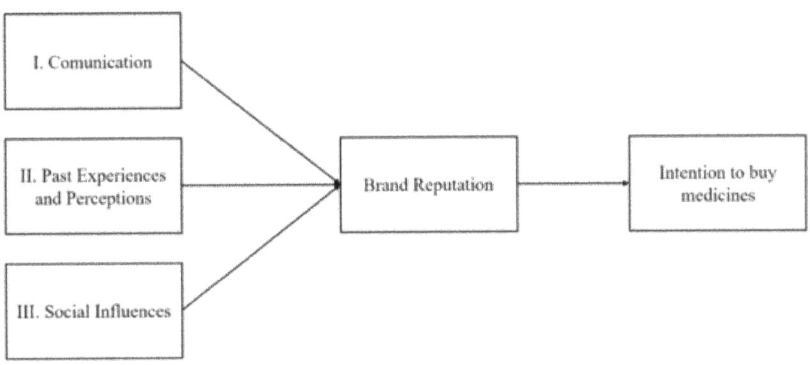

Database Selection

The bibliographic research on the reputation of pharmaceutical brands was conducted on the Web of Science platform. This bibliographic research platform focuses on multidisciplinary research and therefore offers better coverage of articles as it provides access to more than 182 million records and more than 30,000 publications appear within the search radius of the Web of Science platform. In addition, this platform allows you to search for articles in the social sciences that have been published since 1900.

The Search Formula

The literature on the reputation of pharmaceutical brands was investigated to create a search formula on the Web of Science platform. Thus, it was found that, in addition to the keyword "reputation," another term is more assertive and comprehensive in searching for articles within the field of Communication, namely "corporate reputation." Additionally, the term "pharma" was also included in the search in order to segment the investigation exclusively within this universe.

Thus, Boolean operators were used to search for publications with the keywords previously identified in the pharmaceutical sector. To this end, it was decided that the search should be carried out in all fields searchable by Web of Science, making it possible to easily find the search terms in any field. In this sense, the following formula was constructed:

((ALL=(reputation)) OR ALL=(corporate reputation)) AND ALL=(pharma*)

DATA COLLECTION

The formula created for the search returned 5,938 documents. However, these documents were related to various areas of research, so it was necessary to limit the documents found to the following areas:

- Communication;
- Business;
- Management;
- Ethics;
- Green Sustainable Science Technology.

From this procedure, articles that did not belong to these areas were excluded, so the search was reduced to 26 documents.

Of these documents, the search was limited to scientific articles, and other types of documents such as conference papers, books, and book chapters were excluded. Consequently, 21 articles remained. Figure 1 shows the data collection method used.

Figure 2. Steps for collecting and selecting scientific articles (Prisma Model)

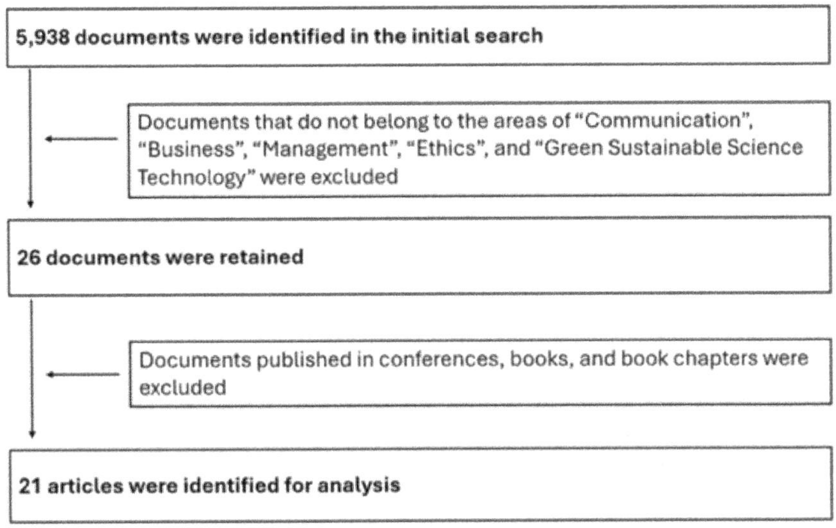

In addition, the 10 articles with the most citations in Web of Science were identified, and this result is reflected in Table 1.

Table 1. Articles with the most citations in the field of pharmaceutical brand reputation

Documents	Number of citations
Villena, V.H. and Gioia, D.A. (2018). On the riskiness of lower-tier suppliers: Managing sustainability in supply networks. Journal of Operations Management, 64: 65-87. https://doi.org/10.1016/j.jom.2018.09.004	79
Cheah, E.T., Chan, W.L. & Chieng, C.L.L. (2007). The Corporate Social Responsibility of Pharmaceutical Product Recalls: An Empirical Examination of U.S. and U.K. Markets. J Bus Ethics 76, 427–449. https://doi.org/10.1007/s10551-006-9292-1	79
Singh, V. (2007). Ethnic diversity on top corporate boards: A resource dependency perspective. The International Journal of Human Resource Management, 18(12), 2128– 2146. https://doi.org/10.1080/09585190701695275	58
Biloslavo, R. and Trnavčevič, A. (2009). "Web sites as tools of communication of a "green" company", Management Decision, Vol. 47 No. 7, pp. 1158-1173. https://doi.org/10.1108/00251740910978359	53
Min, M., Desmoulins-Lebeault, F. and Esposito, M. (2017). "Should pharmaceutical companies engage in corporate social responsibility?", Journal of Management Development, Vol. 36 No. 1, pp. 58-70. https://doi.org/10.1108/JMD-09-2014-0103	38

continued on following page

Table 1. Continued

Documents	Number of citations
Peter K.C. Lee, Antonio K.W. Lau, T.C.E. Cheng (2013). Employee rights protection and financial performance, Journal of Business Research, Volume 66, Issue 10, Pages 1861- 1869. https://doi.org/10.1016/j.jbusres.2013.02.007.	34
Hemphill, T.A. (2010). Extraordinary Pricing of Orphan Drugs: Is it a Socially Responsible Strategy for the U.S. Pharmaceutical Industry?. J Bus Ethics 94, 225–242. https://doi.org/10 .1007/s10551-009-0259-x	25
Balmer, J.M.T. and Chen, W. (2017). "Corporate heritage brands, augmented role identity and customer satisfaction", European Journal of Marketing, Vol. 51 No. 9/10, pp. 1510-1521. https://doi.org/10.1108/EJM-07-2017-0449	19
Stevens, B. (2004). The Ethics of the US Business Executive: A Study of Perceptions. Journal of Business Ethics 54, 163–171. https://doi.org/10.1007/s10551-004-9464-9	19
J.S. Busby (2019). The co-evolution of competition and parasitism in the resource-based view: A risk model of product counterfeiting, European Journal of Operational Research, Volume 276, Issue 1, Pages 300-313, https://doi.org/10.1016/j.ejor.2018.12.039.	12
Swoboda, B., Huber, C., Schuster, T. et al. Corporate Reputation Effects Across Nations: The Impact of Country Distances and Firm-Specific Resources. Manag Int Rev 57, 717– 748 (2017). https://doi.org/10.1007/s11575-017-0313-3	12

In addition to these, the article identified in Table 2 was also selected, with a lower number of citations, but directly related to the study topic linked to the pharmaceutical industry's discourse on the impact of the sector's reputation.

Table 2. Supplementary article relevant to the area of pharmaceutical brand reputation

Document	Number of citations
Van den Bogaert, S., Declercq, J., Christiaens, T., Jacobs, G., & Bracke, P. (2018). In the land of pharma: A qualitative analysis of the reputational discourse of the pharmaceutical industry. Public Relations Inquiry, 7(2), 127–147. https://doi.org/10.1177/2046147X18774588	4

From the annual evolution of the number of articles on the concept, it was found that, over the entire period, approximately 33% of the articles were published in 2017 and 2021. There is a lack of annual regularity in publications on the topic, given that from 2004, the year in which the first article on the topic was identified, until 2023, there were periods without new publications, as is the case for the years: 2005, 2006, 2008, 2011, 2012, 2014, 2015, 2022, and 2023.

It can be concluded that the topic under study is still in the early stages of discussion within the field of communication, given that the first article was published less than 20 years ago, which may mean there is room for new research and discoveries.

Figure 3. Annual comparison of the number of articles in the area of pharmaceutical brand reputation

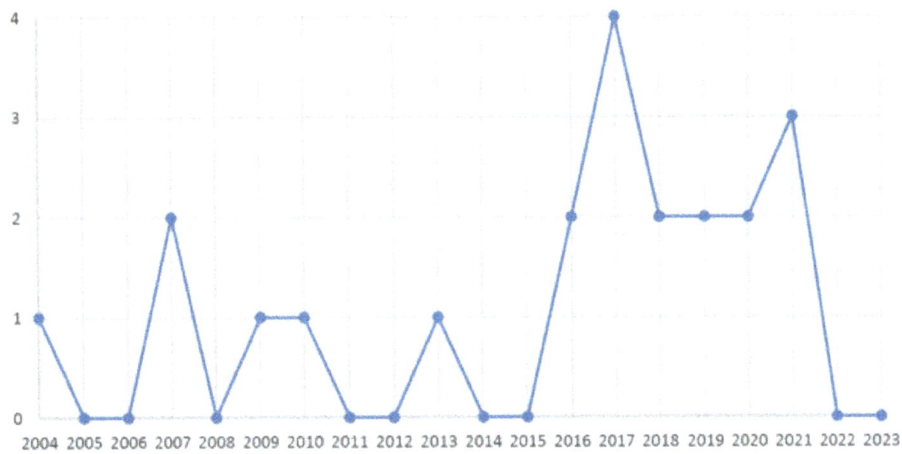

After the literature search of articles in the field of pharmaceutical brand reputation, the following chapter presents the definition of the concept, its dimensions, and its benefits for business management. Finally, suggestions for future research derived from the contributions of the reviewed articles are presented.

Concepts Definitions

Reputation

Reputation is nothing more than the result of how others perceive and evaluate a company (Van den Bogaert et al., 2018). This perception is formed from a social memory associated with a given organization, based on all previous experiences and what we have already heard or read about the organization (Biloslavo & Trnavčevič, 2009). In other words, reputation is a perceptual representation of a company's past actions and its future prospects (Hemphill, 2010).

Biloslavo and Trnavčevič (2009) explain that the formation of reputation is enabled by two interrelated processes: perception and communication. Additionally, according to Van den Bogaert et al. (2018), due to self-inflicted wounds and changes within pharmaceutical companies, the industry is increasingly contested and pressured by strong social influences.

Perceptions

According to Kunsch (2016), each individual possesses their own cognitive universe and receives, interprets, and assigns meaning to messages in their own way and within a particular context. In the same line of thought, Iasbeck (2007) adds that the impression created by organizational discourse in the minds of those who receive it tends to be strongly iconic and, therefore, filled with emotions, moods, sensations, aesthetic qualities, and affective elements. Thus, when discussing the formation of reputation, an individual's perception merges with elements of their imagination, resulting in the impression formed in the interpreter's mind.

This perception, as described by the authors analyzed, is influenced by the different forms of communication used by an organization, as explained by Biloslavo and Trnavčevič (2009). Communication is defined by Reis (2009) as the construction of organizational contexts and processes, while Balmer and Gray (2000) state that it is the means through which stakeholders perceive the company. According to Van Riel (1995), communication is the orchestration of all instruments within the field of an organization's identity.

Communication

All these communications and messages received are influenced by the social context to which the individual belongs. In the complexity of the external world, from Lippmann's (2010) perspective, we rely on what our culture has already defined for us and tend to perceive what we capture in stereotypical forms. Therefore, Secord and Backman (1965) describe social influence as occurring when the actions of one person become a condition for the actions of another. In other words, someone's behavior or thinking has been socially influenced when it changes in the presence of others.

Purchase Intention

In the pharmaceutical sector specifically, Lee et al. (2013) argue that corporate reputation is directly related to better financial performance, as it helps negotiate contracts with suppliers and governments, mitigate reputational risks, increase customer identification, and obtain better human and capital resources.

Therefore, according to Wu and Hsiao (2011), purchase intention serves as a kind of metric for evaluating consumer behaviors and attitudes. Oliver (1980) understands purchase intentions as initially being a function of an individual's attitude toward a product or service, but subject to change based on their prior expectations regarding the company's performance.

Given this phenomenon, Park and Han (2007) state that as consumer satisfaction increases, purchase intention also increases. The authors argue that in the case of high-involvement products, such as medications, this process may be influenced by the quality of the information received about the product, since consumers tend to focus on the key messages of the evaluations.

RESEARCH OBJECTIVES

Based on the literature review conducted, reputation is understood as a type of social memory linked to a specific organization (Biloslavo & Trnavčevič, 2009). However, in certain sectors—such as the pharmaceutical sector—the reputation of a company may actually reflect the reputation of the entire sector attributed to a specific company (Busby, 2019). Therefore, this study aims to analyze the reputation of the pharmaceutical sector and identify which brands contribute to shaping this perception, whether negative or positive.

With regard to the pharmaceutical sector, the literature indicates that reputational discourse is shaped by attributes that highlight how a pharmaceutical company should behave, particularly in relation to governance and product quality (Van den Bogaert et al., 2018). For this reason, this research also seeks to confirm whether these criteria described in the literature are determinant factors for the public when deciding whether a pharmaceutical brand is trustworthy.

Finally, the literature associates reputation with a strong signal that guides decision-making and affects consumer behavior (Swoboda et al., 2017). Thus, this research proposes to study the main hypothesis: the reputation of the pharmaceutical sector is a determining factor in the intention to purchase medicines.

METHODOLOGICAL APPROACH

Data Collection

Data collection for this research was based on an online questionnaire distributed through social media between April 18 and May 9, 2025. The questionnaire was divided into three parts: the first aimed at collecting the respondents' sociodemographic variables, the second focused on the concept of reputation in the pharmaceutical sector, and the third addressed the investigation of the central hypothesis, focusing on the concept of purchase intention.

In this context, for the development of the questionnaire, items from the Global Pharma Study 2023—a study on reputation in the global pharmaceutical industry conducted by the consulting firm Caliber—were adapted in order to measure the industry's reputation, identify drivers of trust, and explore the reputational ranking of pharmaceutical brands.

In the first part of the research, to identify the concept and measure the level of "Reputation" in the pharmaceutical sector, the average of items Q1, Q2, Q3, Q4, Q5, and Q6 of the questionnaire was calculated. These items were measured using 5-point Likert scales, ranging from (1) strongly disagree to (5) strongly agree (Table 3).

Table 3. Items to identify the concept of "Reputation" in the pharmaceutical sector

Item	Statement
Q1	The pharmaceutical industry is trustworthy and keeps its promises
Q2	The pharmaceutical industry is good at what it does and delivers high quality
Q3	The pharmaceutical industry is transparent and acts responsibly
Q4	The pharmaceutical industry does not try to take advantage of consumers
Q5	The pharmaceutical industry is environmentally responsible
Q6	My perception of the pharmaceutical industry changed positively after seeing the sector's efforts to deal with the COVID-19 pandemic

Source: Own Elaboration, based on literature review

Next, in order to identify the most important attributes that determine trust in a pharmaceutical brand, a multiple-choice question was included with the following options: Product safety; Research & Development; Rigorous processes and regulation; Good governance and compliance; Price and fair competition; Innovation; Humanitarian access to medicines and treatments; Low environmental impact; Green chemistry and sustainable raw materials; Employee health and safety; Diversity and Inclusion; Information security and personal data protection.

As explained previously, the final stage of the questionnaire focused on the analysis of the concept of "Purchase Intention" and sought, above all, to explore the hypothesis of whether the reputation of the pharmaceutical sector is a determining factor in the intention to purchase medicines.

To this end, participants were asked to select up to five pharmaceutical brands, from the options listed in Table 4, that they considered to be the most trustworthy. The brands selected for analysis were drawn from the "Global Pharma Study 2023" ranking by Caliber, with the aim of exploring brands with the best reputations (Haleon, Takeda, AbbVie, STADA, and Amgen) and the worst reputations (Novartis, J&J, Moderna, Pfizer, and AstraZeneca) in the sector, as well as those considered neutral or less known.

The brands were presented in alphabetical order to avoid influencing the respondents' answers. In addition, an open-ended option ("other") was provided so that participants could indicate another brand not included in the study that might potentially represent a trend within the survey sample.

Table 4. List of pharmaceutical brands analysed in the study

Pharmaceutical brands under review
AbbVie
Amgen
AstraZeneca
Bayer
BioNTech
Boehringer Ingelheim
Eli Lilly
Gilead Sciences
GlaxoSmithKline (GSK)
Haleon
Johnson & Johnson (J&J)
Merck & Co (MSD)
Merck KGaA
Moderna
Novartis
Novo Nordisk
Pfizer
Roche
Sanofi
Sinopharm
STADA
Takeda Pharma
Teva

Source: own elaboration, based on research data

Next, based on the selected brands, we sought to identify the level of "Purchase Intention" among companies that, in the participants' view, have positive reputations. The average of items Q7, Q8 and Q9 of the questionnaire was calculated, measured using 5-point Likert scales, ranging from (1) strongly disagree to (5) strongly agree (Table 5).

Table 5. Concept of "purchase intention" in relation to "trusted" pharmaceutical brands

Item	Statement
Q7	I would say something positive about the company(ies) to other people if I had the chance
Q8	I would buy, or continue buying, products and services from the company(ies) if I had the chance
Q9	I would recommend the company(ies) to other people if I had the chance

Source: Own Elaboration, based on literature review

The final stage of the questionnaire asked participants to select up to five pharmaceutical brands from the options listed in Table 4 that they considered to be the least trustworthy. Based on the selected brands, the questionnaire then sought to identify the level of "purchase intention" among companies that, in the participants' view, had negative reputations. The average of items Q10 and Q11 of the questionnaire was calculated, measured using 5-point Likert scales, ranging from (1) strongly disagree to (5) strongly agree (Table 6).

Table 6. Concept of "purchase intention" in relation to "untrustworthy" pharmaceutical brands

Item	Statement
Q10	Regarding the selected brands, if you received a medical prescription for a product from the company(ies), would you consume it?
Q11	Regarding the selected brands, if you received guidance from the government or the World Health Organization (WHO) to consume a product from the company(ies), would you consume it?

Source: Own Elaboration, based on literature review

Sample

The sample for this study, consisting of 133 individuals, reveals that 71.4% are female and the majority are under 30 years of age (63.9%). In terms of country of residence, 60.9% of respondents are in Brazil. In addition, 96.2% of participants report having at least a higher education degree. (Table 7).

Table 7. Sample

Variable	Category	N	%
Gender	Female	95	71.4
	Male	38	28.6
Age	20 years or less	4	3
	21 to 30 years	81	60.9
	31 to 40 years	27	20.3
	41 to 50 years	10	7.5
	51 to 60 years	9	6.8
	60 years or more	2	1.5
Country of residence	Portugal	35	26.3
	Brazil	81	60.9
	Mexico	16	12
	Italy	1	0.8
Educational level	Primary education	0	0
	Secondary education	5	3.8
	Higher education	83	62.4
	Postgraduate	45	33.8

Souce: Research data

RESULTS

REPUTATION ANALYSIS IN THE PHARMACEUTICAL SECTOR

As described in the previous chapter, the level of reputation in the pharmaceutical sector is being assessed based on the average of questions Q1, Q2, Q3, Q4, Q5 and Q6, described in Table 3. Considering the 133 survey participants, the overall average obtained was 3.0, suggesting a neutral perception of the sector. Next, we will analyse this reputation level based on each of the respective variables: gender, country of residence, age and educational qualifications.

Gender

The analysis of the interpretation of reputation in the sector based on different genders has begun. This involved a comparison between two different genders: male and female.

Na análise verificou-se igualdade de interpretações em ambos os gêneros. Todavia, entende-se que o público masculino (3,1) está um pouco mais propenso a considerar que o setor tem uma boa reputação, em comparação ao público feminino (2,9).

Country of Residence

As a second analysis of the concept under study, individuals were divided according to their place of residence. Two relevant groups were formed: group 1 (residents in Brazil) and group 2 (residents in other countries). We sought to statistically infer the differences between the sample and the population. The results obtained show that Brazil (2.9) presents a lower level of perception of the reputation of the pharmaceutical sector compared to the average of the other countries participating in the study (3.5).

Age

The study continued by dividing the individuals according to their age. Two distinct groups were created, considering that 60.9% of the sample profile collected is between 21 and 30 years old, and 20% are between 31 and 40 years old. Group 1 consists of individuals up to 30 years old, and group 2 of individuals over 31 years old. The results obtained show that the reputation of the pharmaceutical sector is very similar in the perception of individuals from both age groups.

Educational Level

As the last variable identified, the analysis of the study data was conducted according to the different perceptions based on the educational level of the individuals. Based on the characterization of the collected sample, the respondents were divided into two main groups: group 1 (secondary education) and group 2 (higher education or postgraduate studies).

The results indicate that the reputation of the sector decreases as the level of education increases. Individuals with secondary education (3.6) show, on average, greater trust in the sector compared to individuals with higher education or postgraduate studies (3.1). This result indicates that the variable educational level may be relevant to consider in the analysis of purchase intention, which will be presented later in this study.

Trust Attributes in the Pharma Industry

At this stage of the study, the aim was to verify the most relevant attributes for building a positive reputation for a pharmaceutical company.

It is understood that the three main attributes that should be prioritized by the sector are: product safety (78.2%), research & development (47.4%), and rigor of processes and regulation (41.4%). Price and fair competition (36.8%) and humanitarian access to medicines (27.8%) are also highlighted. The results show that governance (3%) was the attribute least considered by the sample. In addition, this study indicates that low environmental impact (10.5%) and sustainable raw materials (11.3%) are not relevant drivers for consumers when determining whether they will trust pharmaceutical companies.

Purchase Intention in the Pharmaceutical Sector

"Trusted" and "Untrusted" Brands

As the final stage of the study, the concept of purchase intention in the pharmaceutical sector was explored by comparing "trusted" and "untrusted" brands (Figure 4).

Figure 4. Trusted and untrusted brands

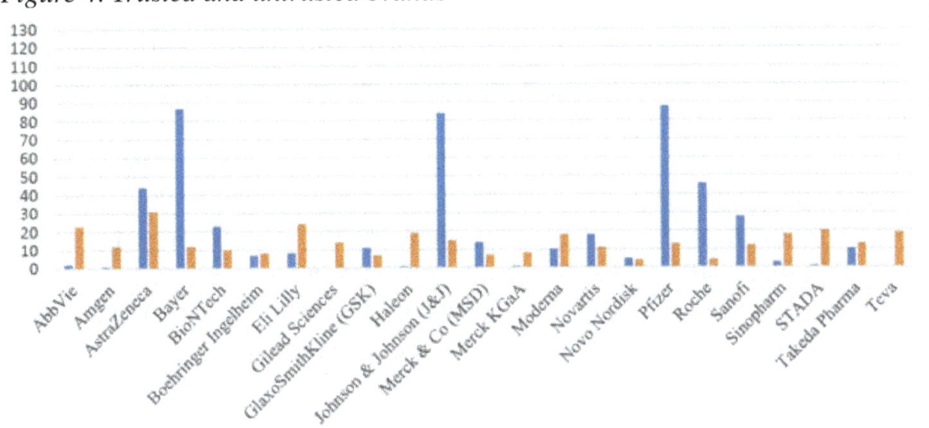

In this regard, based on the pharmaceutical brands listed for individuals to indicate those they trust the most, the following results were obtained: Pfizer (66.2%), Bayer

(65.4%), Johnson & Johnson (62.4%), Roche (34.6%), and AstraZeneca (33.1%). Regarding the brands that individuals considered "untrustworthy," the results were: AstraZeneca (23.3%), Eli Lilly (18%), AbbVie (17.3%), STADA (15%), Haleon (14.3%), and Teva (14.3%). It is noteworthy that AstraZeneca appeared among the five most relevant brands in both analyses, being the most frequently selected as "untrustworthy."

The percentages for brands selected as "untrustworthy" are lower. In addition, more brands were selected in this category, since all of them were selected at least four times. This does not occur with the "trusted" brands, where some brands received no votes at all, such as Gilead Sciences and Teva. This suggests a possible decentralization of distrust in the sector, without it being strongly associated with a specific brand.

Another relevant factor in the results is related to the open-ended option "Other," where a possible trend emerged concerning "untrustworthy" brands. In this available field, 12 individuals indicated the response "none," suggesting that there are no pharmaceutical brands they consider untrustworthy. Additionally, seven individuals responded "I don't know how to answer," "I don't know pharmaceutical brands," or "I selected the brands I do not know." Although this number of responses is not sufficient to support a definitive conclusion, it may represent an important insight for understanding the relationship between distrust and lack of knowledge about the companies that make up this sector.

Purchase Level Intention for Pharmaceutical Brands

Based on this selection, the study sought to investigate the level of purchase intention for brands considered "trusted" and "untrustworthy," in order to analyze the real impact of the sector's reputation on the consumption of medicines. As presented earlier, items Q7, Q8, and Q9 evaluate the purchase intention for "trusted" brands (Table 5), while items Q10 and Q11 evaluate the purchase intention for "untrustworthy" brands (Table 6). In other words, the analysis examines whether, in the pharmaceutical sector specifically, people would consume—or refrain from consuming—products if they did not trust the brands in question.

In the overall analysis of the 133 respondents, there was equality of interpretations regarding the level of Purchase Intention, both for brands considered "reliable" (3.58) and for "unreliable" brands (3.53).

Therefore, we then considered analysing this Purchase Intention from the perspective of the survey variables. However, as with the concept of Reputation analysed previously, only the variable of Educational Qualifications presented results relevant to the study. Figure 5 shows these results.

Figure 5. Purchase intention: Comparison between trusted and untrusted brands based on the variable of participants' educational qualifications

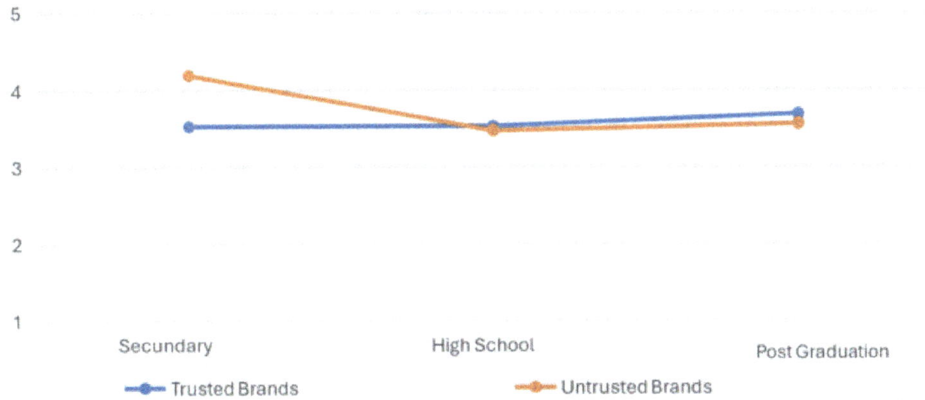

The results show that, as the level of education increases, people tend to have a stronger intention to purchase brands they "trust." When we analyse the brands that people consider "untrustworthy," this result is inversely proportional.

Furthermore, the study sought to measure the degree of influence of health experts and institutions on consumers' purchase intentions. The results indicate that, in the case of brands that people "do not trust," the influence of medical prescriptions or the World Health Organisation (WHO) remains more relevant among people with lower levels of education, as they show higher levels of purchase intention in this scenario.

Correlations

Finally, an analysis was conducted to examine the correlation between the concepts of Reputation and Purchase Intention, considering both trusted and untrusted pharmaceutical brands. The correlation was calculated using a scale ranging from -1 to 1, where 0 indicates no correlation and values above 0.5 are considered relevant correlations. This analysis aimed to determine whether the perceived reputation of the pharmaceutical sector significantly influences consumers' intention to purchase medicines.

The results indicate a correlation of 0.3249 between reputation and purchase intention for trusted companies, and a correlation of 0.3182 for untrusted companies. In both cases, the values are below the 0.5 threshold, indicating a weak relationship between the two variables. Therefore, the findings suggest that the reputation of the pharmaceutical sector does not present a statistically relevant influence on consumers' purchase intention within the scope of this study.

CONCLUSION

The literature review conducted in this study allowed for further investigation of the concept of "Reputation" in the pharmaceutical sector. However, when analysing the concept within the industry context, only two pieces of literature found in this review, Busby (2019) and Van den Bogaert et al. (2018), specifically address "Reputation" in the pharmaceutical sector. There is also a lack of consistency in research on the topic, evidenced by the irregularity of annual publications, in addition to being considered recent research for academia, with the first study published in 2004.

Regarding the seven definitions found for the concept of "Reputation" in this review, which are not necessarily exclusive to the pharmaceutical sector, it can be concluded that there is an overlap of definitions and, when this occurs, they are interconnected by the other related concepts that were also analysed, namely: "Communication", "Personal Experiences & Perception" and "Social Influences".

Furthermore, with regard to the pharmaceutical sector, the literature states that the discourse of pharmaceutical companies should prioritise pillars such as governance and product quality in order to build a good corporate reputation (Van den Bogaert et al., 2018). In this sense, as contributions from this study, the results demonstrate that companies should invest in attributes related to product performance and regulation, as evidenced by the strong trend of trust in this sector linked to product safety, research and development, and process rigour. These considerations corroborate the literature presented. However, in the perception of this sample, Governance was not identified as a relevant factor, being the least selected attribute, with only four votes among the 133 participants. Furthermore, contrary to the trend in other sectors, this study suggests that Sustainability is not a relevant driver for consumers to determine whether or not they will trust pharmaceutical companies.

Based on the principle that reputation is a strong signal that guides decision-making and affects consumer behaviour (Swoboda et al., 2017), this study is based on the main hypothesis that the reputation of the pharmaceutical sector is a determining factor in the intention to purchase medicines.

Analysis of the sample revealed that the general perception of reputation in the pharmaceutical sector is considered average and does not show significant differences based on individual variables such as gender or age. However, this distinction is more evident when comparing individuals with higher levels of education. Participants who have at least a higher education degree have lower levels of perception regarding the sector's reputation. This analysis is complemented by individuals living in Brazil, who also have lower levels of perception of reputation compared to individuals from other locations in this sample.

Regarding this reputation perceived by the sample, the literature suggests that the reputation of the entire sector can be attributed to the reputation of a specific company (Busby, 2019). Thus, the study seeks to contribute to the investigation of which brands shape this perceived reputation.

The results demonstrate a centralised perception of "trustworthy" brands, since the percentages presented were concentrated in certain companies. The same is not true for brands identified as "untrustworthy". Furthermore, it is noted that three of the top five companies with "trustworthy" ratings were involved in COVID-19 vaccine programmes and, consequently, have been more prominent in the media and other communications channels in recent years.

Therefore, this study allows for a possible interpretation related to the lack of knowledge about the brands that make up the sector, which may trigger a feeling of distrust among individuals. In this regard, new lines of research are suggested focusing on the relationship between lack of knowledge and distrust, in order to verify whether the perceptions of individuals who claim to trust certain companies may be more positive when related to previous product experiences, as well as to the influence of specialized professionals and regulatory bodies. Additionally, a more in-depth study of the AstraZeneca brand is suggested, since it appeared as a prominent brand in both the "trusted" and "untrusted" brand categories.

From the perspective of Purchase Intention, similarly to what was observed in the analysis of the concept of Reputation, the sample presents relevant behaviors in relation to the educational level variable of the participants. The results reveal that individuals with higher levels of education tend to show a stronger intention to consume brands they consider trustworthy. This allows us to conclude that, as the level of education increases, individuals demonstrate a lower intention to purchase brands they do not trust.

These results also suggest that the influence of specialized professionals and health institutions plays a more significant role among individuals with lower levels of education, as they show a high purchase intention when they receive a medical prescription or guidance from the government or the World Health Organization (WHO), even when the brands involved are those they personally consider untrustworthy.

Finally, regarding the correlation between the concepts of Reputation and Purchase Intention, this study was not able to confirm a direct influence between these two phenomena, since the results obtained are not statistically relevant in this respect.

In summary, although the conclusions presented here contribute to advancing the understanding of the pharmaceutical sector and consumer behavior, the study has some limitations. One of the main limitations is the small sample size, which is composed predominantly of young individuals under 30 years of age. A suggestion for future research is to conduct similar studies considering older age groups, in order to obtain conclusions based on the perceptions of older populations.

Furthermore, it is known that the pharmaceutical sector is influenced by the specific characteristics of healthcare systems in each country. The reputation of the sector is therefore strongly shaped by public policy management and the contextual environment in which it operates. In this sense, future research could replicate this study in different countries in order to conduct further analyses of the hypotheses tested in this research.

REFERENCES

Balmer, J. M., & Gray, E. (2000). Corporate identity and corporate communications: creating a competitive advantage. *Industrial and Commercial Training*, 256–261. 32.

Balmer, J. M. T., & Chen, W. (2017). Corporate heritage brands, augmented role identity and customer satisfaction.

Balmer, J. M. T., & Chen, W. (2017, September 12). Corporate heritage brands, augmented role identity and customer satisfaction. *European Journal of Marketing*, *51*(9/10), 1510–1521. DOI: 10.1108/EJM-07-2017-0449

Biloslavo, R., & Trnavčevič, A. (2009). Web sites as tools of communication of a "green" company. *Management Decision*, *47*(7), 1158–1173. DOI: 10.1108/00251740910978359

Busby, J. S. (2019). The co-evolution of competition and parasitism in the resource-based view: A risk model of product counterfeiting. *European Journal of Operational Research*, *276*(1), 300–313. DOI: 10.1016/j.ejor.2018.12.039

Caliber. (2023). *Global Pharma Study 2023*. https://www.groupcaliber.com/global-pharma-report-2023/

Cheah, E. T., Chan, W. L., & Chieng, C. L. L. (2007). The Corporate Social Responsibility of Pharmaceutical Product Recalls: An Empirical Examination of U.S. and U.K. Markets. *Journal of Business Ethics*, *76*(4), 427–449. DOI: 10.1007/s10551-006-9292-1

Kunsch, M. M. K. (2016). A comunicação nas organizações: dos fluxos lineares às dimensões humana e estratégica.

Lee, P. K. C., Lau, A. K. W., & Cheng, T. C. E. (2013). Employee rights protection and financial performance. *Journal of Business Research*, *66*(10), 1861–1869. DOI: 10.1016/j.jbusres.2013.02.007

Lippmann, W. (2010). Opinião Pública. *RP: Vozes*.

Mehrabian, A., & Russell, J. A. (1974). *An approach to environmental psychology*. The MIT Press.

Min, M., Desmoulins-Lebeault, F., & Esposito, M. (2017). Should pharmaceutical companies engage in corporate social responsibility? *Journal of Management Development*, *36*(1), 58–70. DOI: 10.1108/JMD-09-2014-0103

Oliver, R. L. (1980). A Cognitive Model of the Antecedents and Consequences of Satisfaction Decisions. *JMR, Journal of Marketing Research, 17*(4), 460–469. DOI: 10.1177/002224378001700405

Park, D.-H., Lee, J., & Han, I. (2007). The Effect of On-Line Consumer Reviews on Consumer Purchasing Intention: The Moderating Role of Involvement. *International Journal of Electronic Commerce, 11*(4), 125–148. DOI: 10.2753/JEC1086-4415110405

Iasbeck, L. C. (2007). Imagem e Reputação na Gestão da Identidade Organizacional. *Organicom*. 7.DOI: 10.1007/s10551-009-0259-x

Reis, M. do C. (2009). Comunicação Organizacional e Relações Públicas no Brasil são singulares? *Organicom*. 6.

Singh, V. (2007). Ethnic diversity on top corporate boards: A resource dependency perspective. *International Journal of Human Resource Management, 18*(12), 2128–2146. DOI: 10.1080/09585190701695275

Stevens, B. (2004). The Ethics of the US Business Executive: A Study of Perceptions. *Journal of Business Ethics, 54*(2), 163–171. DOI: 10.1007/s10551-004-9464-9

Swoboda, B., Huber, C., Schuster, T., & Hirschmann, J. (2017). Corporate Reputation Effects Across Nations: The Impact of Country Distances and Firm-Specific Resources. *MIR. Management International Review, 57*(5), 717–748. DOI: 10.1007/s11575-017-0313-3

Hemphill, T.A. (2010). Extraordinary Pricing of Orphan Drugs: Is it a Socially Responsible Strategy for the U.S. Pharmaceutical Industry?. J Bus Ethics 94, 225–242. https://doi.org/10.1007/s10551-009-0259-x

Van den Bogaert, S., Declercq, J., Christiaens, T., Jacobs, G., & Bracke, P. (2018). In the land of pharma: A qualitative analysis of the reputational discourse of the pharmaceutical industry. *Public Relations Inquiry, 7*(2), 127–147. DOI: 10.1177/2046147X18774588

van Riel, C. B. M. (1995). *Principles of Corporate Communication*. Prentice Hall.

Villena, V. H., & Gioia, D. A. (2018). On the riskiness of lower-tier suppliers: Managing sustainability in supply networks. *Journal of Operations Management, 64*(1), 65–87. DOI: 10.1016/j.jom.2018.09.004

Wu, P., Yeh, G., & Hsiao, C. (2011). The effect of store image and service quality on brand image and pur-chase intention for private label brands. *Australasian Marketing Journal*, *19*(1), 30–39. https://doi.org/10.%201016/j.ausmj.2010.11.001. DOI: 10.1016/j.ausmj.2010.11.001

Chapter 2
Digital Marketing Strategy in the Global HealthTech Ecosystem:
Aligning Innovation, Trust, and Value-Based Healthcare

Ricardo Marcao
http://orcid.org/0000-0003-3277-3078
NECE, University of Beira Interior, Portugal & ISLA Santarem, Portugal

Vasco Santos
Polytechnic University of Tomar, Portugal & NECE, University of Beira Interior, Portugal & GOVCOPP, Portugal & CiTUR, Portugal & ISLA Santarém, Portugal

Filipa Martinho
ISLA Santarém, Portugal

Filipe Peralta
ISLA Santarem, Portugal

Domingos Martinho
NECE, University of Beira Interior, Portugal & ISLA Santarem, Portugal

ABSTRACT

Digital transformation is reshaping healthcare through the rapid expansion of HealthTech solutions, including telemedicine, artificial intelligence, and data-driven diagnostics. In this context, digital marketing has evolved into a strategic function that supports user engagement, adoption, and value creation, while facing regulatory and ethical constraints. This paper examines how digital marketing strategies

DOI: 10.4018/979-8-3373-9410-7.ch002

can be integrated into strategic planning within the global HealthTech ecosystem. Using a qualitative approach that combines literature review and a case study of Knokcare, the study identifies key strategic dimensions for success. The findings highlight the importance of personalization, privacy-first communication, community engagement, localization, and value-based messaging. The study contributes by proposing an integrated framework that aligns digital marketing with the specific challenges of HealthTech.

1. INTRODUCTION

The global healthcare sector is undergoing a profound structural transformation driven by the convergence of digital technologies, data analytics, and medical innovation. This transformation, commonly referred to as HealthTech, encompasses a wide range of solutions, including telemedicine platforms, wearable devices, artificial intelligence (AI)-driven diagnostics, digital therapeutics, and electronic health records. These innovations are reshaping how healthcare is delivered, managed, and experienced, shifting from reactive and institution-centered models toward proactive, personalized, and patient-centered systems (Meskó et al., 2017; Topol, 2019).

The acceleration of digital transformation in healthcare has been further intensified by global events such as the COVID-19 pandemic, which exposed structural inefficiencies in traditional healthcare systems and accelerated the adoption of digital solutions at scale. Telehealth consultations, remote patient monitoring, and AI-assisted triage systems transitioned from optional innovations to essential components of healthcare delivery. As a result, healthcare organizations, technology providers, and policymakers have increasingly recognized digitalization as a strategic imperative rather than a technological upgrade (OECD, 2023).

Within this rapidly evolving environment, digital marketing has emerged as a critical strategic function. Traditionally perceived as a communication tool focused on promotion and brand visibility, digital marketing in HealthTech now plays a central role in shaping user engagement, facilitating adoption, and supporting long-term value creation. Through the use of data-driven insights, multichannel communication strategies, and real-time personalization, organizations are able to interact more effectively with diverse stakeholders, including patients, healthcare professionals, insurers, and regulators (Chaffey & Ellis-Chadwick, 2019; Kotler et al., 2021).

However, marketing in the HealthTech sector differs significantly from marketing in traditional industries. It operates within a highly regulated and ethically sensitive environment, where communication must balance innovation with clinical accuracy, transparency, and compliance. Regulatory frameworks such as the General Data Protection Regulation (GDPR) in the European Union and the Health Insurance

Portability and Accountability Act (HIPAA) in the United States impose strict requirements on data usage, consent, and communication practices. These constraints not only shape how marketing campaigns are designed but also influence the strategic positioning of HealthTech companies (Ventola, 2014; Abernethy et al., 2022).

In addition to regulatory complexity, HealthTech marketing must address a highly fragmented and multi-stakeholder ecosystem. Patients increasingly expect intuitive, personalized, and accessible digital experiences, while healthcare professionals prioritize clinical efficacy, reliability, and integration with existing workflows. At the same time, institutional stakeholders such as insurers and healthcare providers focus on cost-effectiveness, scalability, and measurable outcomes. This diversity of expectations requires organizations to develop differentiated and adaptive marketing strategies capable of addressing multiple audiences simultaneously.

Another defining characteristic of the HealthTech landscape is the central role of trust. Unlike other sectors, where marketing can rely heavily on emotional appeal or brand differentiation, HealthTech communication must be grounded in evidence, credibility, and ethical responsibility. The sensitive nature of health data, combined with the potential impact of digital solutions on patient outcomes, makes trust a fundamental determinant of adoption and long-term engagement (Topol, 2019).

Despite the growing importance of digital marketing in HealthTech, the academic literature remains fragmented. Existing studies often analyze digital marketing tools in isolation or focus primarily on technological innovation without fully integrating strategic, regulatory, and stakeholder perspectives. As a result, there is a need for a more comprehensive framework that connects digital marketing strategies with the broader dynamics of the HealthTech ecosystem.

This paper addresses this gap by examining how digital marketing strategies can be effectively integrated into strategic planning within the global HealthTech context. Specifically, it explores how organizations can leverage digital tools to enhance market penetration, foster stakeholder engagement, and support value-based healthcare outcomes. By combining theoretical insights with a real-world case study of Knokcare, this study contributes to the literature in three main ways. First, it provides an integrated perspective that links digital marketing with HealthTech-specific constraints and opportunities. Second, it highlights the role of trust, personalization, and regulatory compliance as key strategic pillars. Third, it proposes actionable recommendations for organizations seeking to scale digital health solutions in a global and heterogeneous environment.

2. THEORETICAL FRAMEWORK

2.1. Digital Marketing as a Strategic Capability

Digital marketing has evolved from a set of tactical communication tools into a core strategic capability that shapes how organizations create, deliver, and capture value. In contemporary business environments, particularly in technology-intensive sectors, digital marketing is no longer confined to promotion but is deeply embedded in strategic decision-making processes (Kotler et al., 2021).

At its core, digital marketing refers to the use of digital technologies, platforms, and data-driven approaches to achieve marketing objectives through personalized and interactive engagement (Chaffey & Ellis-Chadwick, 2019). Its evolution can be understood across three main phases. The first phase was characterized by static web presence, where organizations used digital platforms primarily as informational channels. The second phase, enabled by Web 2.0, introduced interactivity, social media, and user-generated content, allowing bidirectional communication between firms and stakeholders (Kaplan & Haenlein, 2010). The current phase, often associated with artificial intelligence and advanced analytics, is defined by hyper-personalization, automation, and predictive decision-making.

This transformation has significantly altered the role of marketing within organizations. Rather than acting as a downstream function, marketing now contributes to upstream strategic processes, including product development, customer experience design, and innovation management. In this sense, digital marketing can be conceptualized as a dynamic capability, enabling firms to sense market opportunities, seize them through targeted engagement strategies, and continuously reconfigure their resources in response to changing environments.

A key feature of digital marketing is its reliance on data. The ability to collect, process, and analyze user data allows organizations to understand behavior patterns, segment audiences, and optimize interactions in real time. Metrics such as customer lifetime value (CLV), cost per acquisition (CPA), and engagement rates are not merely performance indicators but strategic inputs that inform decision-making. As a result, digital marketing operates at the intersection of analytics, technology, and strategy, reinforcing its role as a critical driver of competitive advantage.

However, the increasing reliance on data also introduces new challenges, particularly in sectors where privacy and ethical considerations are paramount. In HealthTech, the use of sensitive health data requires a careful balance between personalization and data protection, making digital marketing strategies inherently constrained by regulatory and ethical frameworks.

2.2. Strategic Planning in Digital Environments

Strategic planning in digital contexts involves defining long-term objectives and aligning organizational resources to achieve sustainable competitive advantage in rapidly evolving environments. Traditional strategic frameworks remain relevant but must be adapted to account for the dynamics of digital ecosystems.

Porter's Five Forces model (Porter, 2008) continues to provide a valuable lens for analyzing competitive intensity, even in digital markets. However, the rise of platform-based business models and network effects has altered the structure of competition, requiring organizations to consider factors such as ecosystem participation, data ownership, and technological interoperability. In HealthTech, for instance, competitive advantage is not determined solely by product features but also by integration capabilities with existing healthcare systems and compliance with regulatory standards.

Similarly, the Ansoff Matrix (Ansoff, 1972) offers a framework for identifying growth strategies, including market penetration, product development, market development, and diversification. In digital environments, these strategies are often accelerated by technological innovation, allowing firms to scale rapidly across geographies and customer segments. However, this expansion also introduces complexity, particularly in sectors with heterogeneous regulatory environments.

The SOSTAC model (Smith & Zook, 2011) provides a structured approach to digital marketing planning, encompassing situation analysis, objective setting, strategy formulation, tactical execution, action planning, and control mechanisms. Its adaptability makes it particularly suitable for HealthTech, where organizations must continuously monitor performance and adjust strategies in response to regulatory changes and stakeholder feedback.

Performance measurement plays a central role in digital strategic planning. Unlike traditional marketing, digital environments allow for real-time tracking of user behavior, enabling organizations to refine their strategies dynamically. However, in HealthTech, performance metrics must extend beyond conventional indicators such as clicks or conversions. Increasingly, organizations are expected to demonstrate value in terms of health outcomes, patient satisfaction, and system efficiency, aligning marketing efforts with the principles of value-based healthcare (Porter & Teisberg, 2006).

2.3. HealthTech as a Complex and Regulated Ecosystem

The HealthTech sector is characterized by the coexistence of high innovation potential and stringent regulatory oversight. This duality creates a unique context in which digital marketing strategies must operate, requiring organizations to navigate complex institutional, ethical, and technological landscapes.

One of the defining characteristics of HealthTech is the centrality of trust. Unlike other industries, where consumer decisions may be driven by price or brand preference, healthcare decisions are closely linked to perceived reliability, safety, and clinical effectiveness. As a result, marketing communication must be grounded in evidence-based claims and transparent messaging (Topol, 2019).

Regulation plays a critical role in shaping the HealthTech environment. Frameworks such as the GDPR and HIPAA impose strict requirements on data collection, processing, and communication. These regulations not only limit the scope of marketing activities but also influence the design of digital platforms and user interfaces. For example, consent mechanisms, data anonymization, and secure data storage are not only technical requirements but also elements that must be communicated effectively to users as part of the value proposition.

Another key feature of the HealthTech ecosystem is its multi-stakeholder nature. Patients, healthcare professionals, providers, insurers, and regulators all play distinct roles, with different priorities and expectations. Patients often value accessibility, usability, and personalization, while healthcare professionals prioritize clinical validity and integration with existing workflows. Insurers and institutional stakeholders, in turn, focus on cost-effectiveness and measurable outcomes.

This complexity requires organizations to adopt a stakeholder-oriented approach to digital marketing. Rather than targeting a single audience, HealthTech firms must develop differentiated strategies that address the needs of multiple stakeholders simultaneously. This often involves combining B2B and B2C approaches within the same strategic framework, as well as adapting communication styles to different cultural and regulatory contexts.

Furthermore, the global nature of the HealthTech market introduces additional challenges. Variations in digital infrastructure, healthcare systems, and regulatory environments require organizations to localize their strategies while maintaining global consistency. This tension between standardization and adaptation is a defining feature of digital marketing in HealthTech.

2.4. Integrating Digital Marketing and Value-Based Healthcare

An emerging perspective in both healthcare and marketing literature is the alignment between digital strategies and value-based healthcare. Value-based healthcare emphasizes the delivery of improved patient outcomes relative to cost, shifting the focus from volume to value (Porter & Teisberg, 2006).

In this context, digital marketing is no longer limited to promoting products or services but becomes a mechanism for communicating value. HealthTech organizations must demonstrate how their solutions improve clinical outcomes, enhance patient experience, and reduce system inefficiencies. This requires integrating clinical evidence, user feedback, and performance data into marketing narratives.

Digital tools play a critical role in enabling this integration. Data analytics, for instance, allows organizations to track user behavior and measure the impact of digital interventions on health outcomes. Similarly, personalized communication strategies can support patient adherence to treatment plans, thereby contributing directly to value creation.

However, aligning marketing with value-based healthcare also introduces challenges. Measuring outcomes in healthcare is inherently complex, involving multiple variables and long time horizons. Moreover, communicating these outcomes in a clear and credible manner requires a high level of transparency and scientific rigor.

Despite these challenges, the integration of digital marketing and value-based healthcare represents a significant opportunity for HealthTech organizations. By aligning marketing strategies with clinical value and stakeholder expectations, firms can enhance trust, improve adoption, and achieve sustainable competitive advantage.

3. THE GLOBAL HEALTHTECH ECOSYSTEM

3.1. Global Market Dynamics and Digital Transformation

The global HealthTech ecosystem has experienced rapid expansion over the past decade, driven by the convergence of demographic pressures, technological innovation, and increasing demand for more accessible and efficient healthcare solutions. Aging populations, the rise of chronic diseases, and growing expectations for personalized care have created structural pressures on healthcare systems, accelerating the adoption of digital technologies.

The digital health market has demonstrated sustained growth, supported by advancements in artificial intelligence, telemedicine, wearable technologies, and remote patient monitoring. However, this growth is not uniform across regions. North America continues to lead in terms of investment and innovation, largely due to its mature venture capital ecosystem and strong presence of technology-driven healthcare companies. Europe, while more fragmented, benefits from regulatory harmonization efforts and public health initiatives that promote digital integration. Meanwhile, the Asia-Pacific region has emerged as a high-growth market, leveraging large populations, rapid digital adoption, and government-led digital health programs (OECD, 2023).

Despite this expansion, structural asymmetries persist. Differences in digital infrastructure, healthcare system maturity, and regulatory frameworks create uneven adoption patterns. Emerging markets often rely on mobile-based health solutions to overcome infrastructure limitations, while developed economies focus on advanced analytics and integrated care models. This heterogeneity introduces both opportunities and constraints for HealthTech companies operating globally.

From a strategic perspective, digital transformation in healthcare is not solely a technological shift but a systemic reconfiguration of how value is created and delivered. The increasing consumerization of healthcare – where patients expect seamless, on-demand digital experiences – has redefined competitive dynamics. HealthTech firms must therefore compete not only on clinical outcomes but also on user experience, accessibility, and service integration.

3.2. Stakeholder Interdependencies and Ecosystem Complexity

The HealthTech ecosystem is inherently multi-layered, comprising a diverse set of stakeholders whose interactions shape the adoption and scalability of digital health solutions. These stakeholders include patients, healthcare providers, technology developers, regulators, insurers, and intermediary organizations, each with distinct roles and incentives.

Patients have evolved from passive recipients of care to active participants in healthcare decision-making. Digital tools empower individuals to manage their health, access information, and engage with providers more directly. This shift has significant implications for marketing strategies, which must now prioritize transparency, usability, and personalized communication.

Healthcare providers, including hospitals and clinicians, act as critical gatekeepers within the ecosystem. Their acceptance of HealthTech solutions depends on factors such as clinical validity, workflow integration, and regulatory compliance. As a result, marketing efforts targeting this group must emphasize evidence-based outcomes and operational efficiency rather than promotional messaging.

Technology developers, particularly startups, serve as key innovation drivers. However, their success depends heavily on strategic partnerships with healthcare institutions, research organizations, and regulatory bodies. These interdependencies highlight the importance of ecosystem thinking, where value is co-created rather than delivered unilaterally.

Regulators and policymakers play a dual role as both enablers and constraints. While they ensure safety, efficacy, and data protection, they also influence the pace of innovation through approval processes and compliance requirements. Similarly, insurers and payers shape market adoption by determining reimbursement models and evaluating cost-effectiveness.

This complex network of interdependencies requires HealthTech firms to adopt a stakeholder-centric approach. Digital marketing strategies must be designed not only to attract users but also to align with the expectations and constraints of multiple actors simultaneously. This often involves balancing technical accuracy with accessibility, as well as aligning communication with regulatory and institutional frameworks.

3.3. Strategic Opportunities in the HealthTech Landscape

The HealthTech ecosystem offers significant strategic opportunities, particularly in areas where digital technologies can enhance efficiency, accessibility, and personalization of care.

Artificial intelligence represents one of the most transformative forces in healthcare, enabling predictive analytics, early disease detection, and decision support systems. These capabilities create opportunities for more targeted and effective marketing strategies, as organizations can leverage data insights to deliver personalized content and recommendations (Kietzmann et al., 2018).

Telemedicine and remote patient monitoring have also emerged as key growth areas, particularly following the COVID-19 pandemic. These technologies enable continuous patient engagement and expand access to care, especially in underserved regions. From a marketing perspective, they provide new touchpoints for interaction, allowing organizations to build long-term relationships with users.

Emerging technologies such as blockchain, augmented reality, and edge computing further expand the scope of innovation. Blockchain enhances data security and transparency, reinforcing trust—a critical factor in healthcare adoption. Augmented and virtual reality offer immersive experiences for training and product demonstration, particularly in B2B contexts.

Another important opportunity lies in the shift toward value-based healthcare. As healthcare systems increasingly prioritize outcomes over volume, HealthTech companies have the opportunity to position their solutions as drivers of measurable value. This requires integrating clinical data, user feedback, and performance metrics into marketing narratives, moving beyond traditional promotional approaches.

3.4. Structural Challenges and Strategic Constraints

Despite its potential, the HealthTech ecosystem is characterized by significant structural challenges that constrain innovation and market expansion.

Data privacy and security remain among the most critical concerns. The sensitive nature of health data makes it a prime target for breaches, requiring robust security measures and strict compliance with regulatory frameworks such as GDPR and HIPAA. These constraints limit the extent to which organizations can leverage data for marketing purposes, creating a tension between personalization and privacy (Abernethy et al., 2022).

Interoperability is another major challenge. Many healthcare systems rely on legacy infrastructure that is incompatible with modern digital solutions, leading to fragmented data and limited integration. This fragmentation not only affects operational efficiency but also restricts the effectiveness of digital marketing strategies, which depend on unified data ecosystems.

Regulatory fragmentation further complicates global expansion. HealthTech companies must navigate diverse regulatory environments, each with its own requirements for approval, data handling, and communication. This increases operational complexity and necessitates localized marketing strategies.

Financial and reimbursement uncertainties also pose barriers. In many cases, digital health solutions lack clear reimbursement pathways, limiting their adoption despite demonstrated value. This creates additional pressure on marketing strategies to communicate cost-effectiveness and long-term benefits.

Finally, the digital divide continues to limit equitable access to HealthTech solutions. Variations in digital literacy, infrastructure, and socioeconomic conditions create disparities in adoption, particularly in emerging markets. Addressing these challenges requires not only technological innovation but also inclusive and adaptive marketing approaches.

3.5. Implications for Digital Marketing Strategy

The complexity of the global HealthTech ecosystem has direct implications for digital marketing strategy. Unlike traditional sectors, where marketing can focus on a relatively homogeneous audience, HealthTech requires a multidimensional approach that accounts for regulatory constraints, stakeholder diversity, and global variability.

First, marketing strategies must be inherently adaptive, capable of responding to changing regulatory environments and evolving user expectations. Second, they must integrate both global consistency and local relevance, ensuring that communication resonates across different cultural and institutional contexts. Third, they must prioritize trust and credibility, leveraging evidence-based messaging and transparent communication practices.

Ultimately, effective digital marketing in HealthTech is not defined solely by technological sophistication but by its ability to align with the broader ecosystem in which it operates. Organizations that successfully navigate this complexity will be better positioned to achieve sustainable growth and meaningful impact in the global healthcare landscape.

4. DIGITAL MARKETING STRATEGIES IN THE HEALTHTECH SECTOR

4.1. B2B and B2C Strategic Approaches

Digital marketing strategies in the HealthTech sector must account for the dual nature of its market structure, which encompasses both business-to-business (B2B) and business-to-consumer (B2C) interactions. These two approaches differ significantly in terms of decision-making processes, communication styles, and value propositions, requiring organizations to develop differentiated yet integrated strategies (Chaffey & Ellis-Chadwick, 2019).

In B2B contexts, marketing efforts are primarily directed toward institutional stakeholders, including hospitals, insurers, and healthcare providers. These decision-making processes tend to be complex, involving multiple stakeholders, longer sales cycles, and a strong emphasis on clinical evidence, regulatory compliance, and return on investment. As a result, effective B2B strategies rely heavily on content-driven approaches such as white papers, case studies, webinars, and industry events. These formats enable organizations to demonstrate expertise, build credibility, and support evidence-based decision-making (Kotler et al., 2021).

Conversely, B2C strategies focus on engaging end users, typically patients or individual consumers. In this context, emotional resonance, trust, and ease of use become critical factors influencing adoption. Digital channels such as social media, mobile applications, and video content are commonly used to communicate value propositions in an accessible and relatable manner. Storytelling, testimonials, and educational content play a central role in building trust and encouraging user engagement (Desai, 2019).

Importantly, many HealthTech companies operate within hybrid models, combining B2B and B2C approaches. This requires a coordinated strategy that aligns institutional credibility with user-centric communication, ensuring consistency across all touchpoints.

4.2. User-Centered Digital Strategies

User-centered design has emerged as a fundamental principle in HealthTech marketing, reflecting the broader shift toward patient-centered care. This approach emphasizes the involvement of users throughout the product development and communication process, ensuring that solutions address real needs and expectations (Sanders & Stappers, 2014).

In digital marketing, user-centered strategies translate into personalized communication, intuitive user experiences, and continuous feedback mechanisms.

Organizations leverage data analytics to understand user behavior, preferences, and engagement patterns, enabling them to tailor content and interactions accordingly. This level of personalization enhances user satisfaction and increases the likelihood of adoption and retention (Kietzmann et al., 2018).

Moreover, the integration of user feedback into marketing narratives can strengthen credibility and authenticity. Sharing user experiences, satisfaction metrics, and real-world outcomes allows organizations to build trust and demonstrate value in a transparent manner. This is particularly important in healthcare, where perceived reliability is a key determinant of user behavior.

4.3. Leveraging Emerging Technologies in Marketing

Emerging technologies are redefining the scope and capabilities of digital marketing in the HealthTech sector. Artificial intelligence, in particular, has become a central enabler of advanced marketing strategies. Through machine learning algorithms and predictive analytics, organizations can segment audiences, personalize content, and optimize campaigns in real time (Kietzmann et al., 2018).

AI-driven tools also support automation, enabling organizations to scale their marketing efforts while maintaining personalization. Chatbots, recommendation systems, and automated content generation are increasingly used to enhance user interaction and streamline communication processes. These technologies not only improve efficiency but also contribute to a more responsive and engaging user experience.

In addition to AI, technologies such as augmented reality (AR) and virtual reality (VR) offer new opportunities for immersive communication. In B2B contexts, these tools can be used for product demonstrations, clinical simulations, and training environments, providing stakeholders with a deeper understanding of complex solutions (Pantelidis, 2009).

Blockchain technology also plays a role in strengthening trust within digital marketing ecosystems. By ensuring data integrity and transparency, blockchain can enhance user confidence in how their data is managed and used. This is particularly relevant in healthcare, where concerns about data privacy and security are prevalent (Agbo et al., 2019).

4.4. Social Media and Digital Communities

Social media platforms have become essential components of digital marketing strategies in HealthTech, enabling organizations to engage directly with diverse audiences. In B2B contexts, platforms such as LinkedIn are used to share thought leadership content, industry insights, and professional updates, helping organizations establish authority and build networks (Ventola, 2014).

In B2C contexts, social media serves as a channel for community building and user engagement. Digital communities centered around specific health conditions or shared experiences provide spaces for knowledge exchange, peer support, and validation of digital health solutions. These communities play a significant role in shaping user perceptions and influencing adoption decisions (Johansson et al., 2021).

The integration of digital communities into marketing strategies allows organizations to move beyond one-way communication toward participatory engagement. By involving users in content creation and feedback processes, companies can foster a sense of belonging and enhance brand loyalty.

4.5. Strategic Integration and Marketing Effectiveness

The effectiveness of digital marketing strategies in HealthTech depends on the integration of multiple elements, including technology, user experience, regulatory compliance, and stakeholder alignment. Isolated marketing efforts are unlikely to succeed in such a complex and highly regulated environment. Instead, organizations must adopt a holistic approach that aligns marketing activities with broader strategic objectives and ecosystem dynamics (Kotler et al., 2021; Porter, 2008).

This integration requires the establishment of continuous feedback loops, where data derived from marketing performance informs strategic decision-making and enables the ongoing refinement of communication strategies. Digital analytics tools allow organizations to monitor user behavior, engagement patterns, and conversion metrics in real time, transforming marketing into an adaptive and iterative process (Chaffey & Ellis-Chadwick, 2019).

At the same time, marketing messages must be aligned with clinical evidence and regulatory requirements. In the HealthTech sector, communication that lacks credibility or fails to comply with established standards can undermine trust and hinder adoption. Therefore, marketing effectiveness is closely linked to the ability to integrate persuasive communication with scientific rigor and transparency (Ventola, 2014; Topol, 2019).

Ultimately, digital marketing in HealthTech is most effective when it is positioned as a strategic function that contributes directly to value creation. By aligning marketing efforts with user needs, technological capabilities, and ecosystem constraints, organizations can enhance adoption, strengthen stakeholder relationships, and achieve sustainable competitive advantage (Porter & Teisberg, 2006).

5. CASE STUDY: KNOKCARE

The application of digital marketing strategies within the HealthTech sector can be more effectively understood through the analysis of real-world implementations. Knokcare, a Portuguese HealthTech company specializing in AI-powered telemedicine and hybrid care solutions, provides a relevant example of how digital marketing, strategic alignment, and ecosystem awareness can converge to support international growth and user adoption.

Founded in Porto in 2015, Knokcare initially emerged as a video consultation platform but has since evolved into a comprehensive hybrid care provider. Its offering integrates remote consultations, artificial intelligence-assisted triage, and in-person services, positioning the company at the intersection of digital innovation and patient-centered care (Meskó et al., 2017; Topol, 2019). Operating across multiple markets, including Portugal, Brazil, Angola, and the United Kingdom, Knokcare addresses diverse healthcare needs while navigating distinct regulatory and cultural environments.

From a strategic perspective, Knokcare adopts a hybrid B2B2C model, targeting both institutional clients—such as hospitals, insurers, and corporate partners—and end users. This dual approach reflects the broader complexity of the HealthTech ecosystem and requires a coordinated marketing strategy capable of addressing multiple stakeholder groups simultaneously (Friedman et al., 2010).

On the institutional side, the company emphasizes clinical credibility, operational efficiency, and cost-effectiveness, aligning its communication with the expectations of healthcare providers and payers. Content such as webinars, white papers, and participation in international conferences supports its positioning as a trusted and innovative partner (Kotler et al., 2021).

In parallel, Knokcare's engagement with end users is characterized by a strong focus on accessibility, trust, and user experience. Digital campaigns leverage storytelling, testimonials, and educational content to demystify telemedicine and promote adoption. Social media platforms and intuitive digital interfaces are used to create seamless user journeys, reinforcing engagement and satisfaction (Desai, 2019; Johansson et al., 2021).

A key strength of Knokcare's strategy lies in its alignment with the core characteristics of the HealthTech sector. The company operates under strict compliance with data protection regulations, particularly GDPR, and incorporates privacy and security considerations into both its technological infrastructure and communication strategies. This alignment is critical in building trust, especially in markets where digital health adoption is still evolving (Abernethy et al., 2022).

Furthermore, Knokcare demonstrates a strong commitment to user-centered design. By incorporating user feedback into product development and continuously refining its digital interfaces, the company ensures that its services remain aligned with user expectations. This approach enhances usability while strengthening marketing effectiveness, as communication reflects real user needs and experiences (Sanders & Stappers, 2014).

The company's growth trajectory provides further evidence of the effectiveness of its integrated strategy. With more than one million consultations conducted across multiple countries, Knokcare has achieved significant market penetration and user engagement. High levels of user satisfaction further indicate successful alignment between technological capabilities and marketing communication (OECD, 2023).

Despite these achievements, the case of Knokcare also highlights ongoing challenges. Expanding across multiple geographies requires continuous adaptation to local regulatory frameworks, cultural norms, and healthcare system structures. Maintaining brand consistency while localizing communication strategies remains a complex task, particularly in diverse and evolving markets (World Health Organization, 2019).

Overall, Knokcare illustrates how a HealthTech organization can leverage digital marketing as a strategic enabler of growth. Its ability to integrate technology, user experience, and regulatory compliance into a coherent strategy demonstrates the importance of aligning marketing with the broader dynamics of the HealthTech ecosystem.

6. STRATEGIC RECOMMENDATIONS FOR THE FUTURE

The evolution of the HealthTech sector requires organizations to rethink digital marketing as an integral component of strategic value creation. As the ecosystem becomes increasingly complex, successful organizations will be those capable of aligning technological innovation with user expectations, regulatory requirements, and measurable healthcare outcomes (Porter & Teisberg, 2006; OECD, 2023).

One of the most critical strategic directions is the expansion of personalization through artificial intelligence and advanced analytics. By leveraging predictive models and behavioral data, organizations can deliver highly tailored communication and anticipate user needs. This approach enhances engagement and supports adherence to digital health solutions, contributing to improved outcomes (Kietzmann et al., 2018; Topol, 2019).

Closely related to this is the adoption of privacy-first marketing strategies. In a sector where trust is paramount, compliance with regulatory frameworks such as GDPR and HIPAA is not sufficient on its own. Organizations must proactively communicate their data practices, emphasizing transparency, security, and user autonomy. Trust should be positioned as a central element of the value proposition (Abernethy et al., 2022).

Another important strategic dimension is the development of digital communities. HealthTech solutions often address conditions that require long-term engagement and behavioral change. By fostering communities where users can share experiences and support each other, organizations can enhance engagement and strengthen emotional connections with their services (Johansson et al., 2021).

Global expansion further requires a strong emphasis on localization. HealthTech organizations operate in diverse environments with varying cultural norms, regulatory frameworks, and levels of digital maturity. Effective marketing strategies must therefore adapt content, channels, and communication styles to local contexts, ensuring relevance and trust (World Health Organization, 2019).

Finally, digital marketing in HealthTech must align with the principles of value-based healthcare. This implies a shift from traditional performance metrics toward indicators that reflect real-world impact, including patient outcomes, satisfaction, and system efficiency. Communicating value in these terms strengthens relationships with both users and institutional stakeholders (Porter & Teisberg, 2006).

Taken together, these strategic directions highlight the need for an integrated approach to digital marketing – one that combines personalization, trust, community engagement, localization, and value-based communication.

7. CONCLUSION

The transformation of the global healthcare sector through digital technologies has fundamentally altered the role of marketing within HealthTech organizations. Digital marketing has evolved into a strategic function that supports user engagement, drives adoption, and contributes directly to value creation (Kotler et al., 2021).

This paper has demonstrated that effective digital marketing in HealthTech requires alignment between technological innovation, regulatory compliance, and stakeholder expectations. The sector's complexity demands a balance between personalization and privacy, innovation and credibility, and global scalability and local adaptation (Topol, 2019; OECD, 2023).

The case of Knokcare illustrates how these principles can be operationalized in practice. By integrating a hybrid B2B2C model with user-centered design and compliance with regulatory standards, the company has achieved significant growth and user adoption across multiple markets. At the same time, the challenges identified reinforce the need for continuous strategic adaptation (World Health Organization, 2019).

In conclusion, digital marketing in HealthTech should be understood not as a set of isolated tools, but as a dynamic strategic capability. Organizations that align their marketing efforts with value-based healthcare principles and ecosystem dynamics will be better positioned to achieve sustainable growth and contribute to more effective and inclusive healthcare systems (Porter & Teisberg, 2006).

REFERENCES

Abernethy, A. P., Adams, L., Barrett, M., Bechtel, C., Brennan, P., Butte, A., Faulkner, J., Fontaine, E., Friedhoff, S., Halamka, J., Howell, M., Johnson, K., Long, P., McGraw, D., Miller, R., Lee, P., Perlin, J., Rucker, D., Sandy, L., & Valdes, K. (2022). The promise of digital health: Then, now, and the future. *NAM Perspectives*, *6*(22). Advance online publication. DOI: 10.31478/202206e PMID: 36177208

Agbo, C. C., Mahmoud, Q. H., & Eklund, J. M. (2019). Blockchain technology in healthcare: A systematic review. *Health Care*, *7*(2), 56. DOI: 10.3390/healthcare7020056 PMID: 30987333

Ansoff, H. I. (1972). Strategies for diversification. *Long Range Planning*, *5*(2), 65–69. DOI: 10.1016/0024-6301(72)90048-9

Chaffey, D., & Ellis-Chadwick, F. (2019). *Digital marketing* (7th ed.). Pearson.

Desai, V. (2019). Digital marketing: A review. *International Journal of Trend in Scientific Research and Development*, (Special Issue), 196–200. DOI: 10.31142/ijtsrd23100

Friedman, C. P., Wong, A. K., & Blumenthal, D. (2010). Achieving a nationwide learning health system. *Science Translational Medicine*, *2*(57). Advance online publication. DOI: 10.1126/scitranslmed.3001456 PMID: 21068440

Johansson, V., Islind, A. S., Lindroth, T., Angenete, E., & Gellerstedt, M. (2021). Online communities as a driver for patient empowerment: Systematic review. *Journal of Medical Internet Research*, *23*(2), e19910. Advance online publication. DOI: 10.2196/19910 PMID: 33560233

Kaplan, A. M., & Haenlein, M. (2010). Users of the world, unite! The challenges and opportunities of social media. *Business Horizons*, *53*(1), 59–68. DOI: 10.1016/j.bushor.2009.09.003

Kietzmann, J., Paschen, J., & Treen, E. (2018). Artificial intelligence in advertising: How marketers can leverage artificial intelligence along the consumer journey. *Journal of Advertising Research*, *58*(3), 263–267. DOI: 10.2501/JAR-2018-035

Kotler, P., Kartajaya, H., & Setiawan, I. (2021). *Marketing 5.0: Technology for humanity*. Wiley.

Meskó, B., Drobni, Z., Bényei, É., Gergely, B., & Győrffy, Z. (2017). Digital health is a cultural transformation of traditional healthcare. *mHealth*, *3*, 38. DOI: 10.21037/mhealth.2017.08.07 PMID: 29184890

OECD. (2023). *Health at a glance 2023: OECD indicators*. OECD Publishing. DOI: 10.1787/7a7afb35-en

Pantelidis, V. S. (2009). Reasons to use virtual reality in education and training courses and a model to determine when to use virtual reality.

Porter, M. E. (2008). The five competitive forces that shape strategy. *Harvard Business Review*, *86*(1), 78–93. PMID: 18271320

Porter, M. E., & Teisberg, E. O. (2006). *Redefining health care: Creating value-based competition on results*. Harvard Business School Press.

Sanders, E. B. N., & Stappers, P. J. (2014). Probes, toolkits and prototypes: Three approaches to making in co-designing. *CoDesign*, *10*(1), 5–14. DOI: 10.1080/15710882.2014.888183

Smith, P. R., & Zook, Z. (2011). *Marketing communications: Integrating offline and online with social media*. Kogan Page.

Topol, E. (2019). *Deep medicine: How artificial intelligence can make healthcare human again*. Basic Books.

Ventola, C. L. (2014). Social media and health care professionals: Benefits, risks, and best practices. *P&T : a Peer-Reviewed Journal for Formulary Management*, *39*(7), 491–520. PMID: 25083128

World Health Organization. (2019). *WHO guideline: Recommendations on digital interventions for health system strengthening*. WHO. https://apps.who.int/iris/handle/10665/311980

Chapter 3
Executive Decision-Making in Regulated Innovation Environments

Deepak Gupta
http://orcid.org/0000-0003-3929-1362
Institute of Technology and Management, Gwalior, India

Ulugbek Vosikov
Kimyo International University in Tashkent, Uzbekistan

Ilyos Khursandov
Termez University of Economics and Service, Termez, Uzbekistan

Yulchiyev Asiljon Ortiqali ugli
Fergana State University, Fergana, Uzbekistan

Karimov Rashid Salayevich
Mamun University, Khiva, Uzbekistan

Begimov Uktam Ibrogimovich
Alfraganus University, Tashkent, Uzbekistan

Narimonov Sayfullakhon Sunnatilla Ugli
Tashkent State University of Economy, Uzbekistan

ABSTRACT

Executive decision-making in regulated innovation environments demands a nuanced convergence of strategic leadership, regulatory intelligence, and organisational adaptability. This chapter examines how pharmaceutical and medical device executives navigate complex regulatory frameworks—including FDA pathways, EU MDR, and evolving AI-specific guidelines—to drive sustainable innovation. Drawing on recent empirical and conceptual literature, the chapter presents a framework integrating top management team competencies, risk governance, and digital transformation imperatives. . Key themes include the role of regulatory affairs in shaping pipeline strategy, leadership capabilities required for Industry 4.0 adoption, and the organ-

DOI: 10.4018/979-8-3373-9410-7.ch003

isational enablers of innovation performance. The chapter contributes actionable insights for executives, policymakers, and scholars concerned with optimising the intersection of human capital, compliance, and value-creation in highly regulated industries.

1. INTRODUCTION

The pharmaceutical and medical device industries hold a distinctive place in the contemporary global economy. They are, at once, among the most innovation-driven sectors and among the most comprehensively regulated. This duality is not incidental—it is constitutive. The therapeutic promise of a novel molecule or a diagnostic platform is only realisable when the product clears an intricate sequence of regulatory hurdles: pre-clinical assessment, phased clinical trials, manufacturing compliance, marketing authorisation, and the ongoing obligations of post-market surveillance. Executives steering organisations through this sequence face decisions that are both scientifically demanding and institutionally complex, with consequences that can span a decade of commercial and clinical impact.

The difficulty is that these two imperatives—rapid innovation and rigorous compliance—generate real tension. Regulatory compliance was once conceived, in many organisations, as a downstream activity: a quality-assurance exercise that checked work already done. That model has broken down. As Nwoke (2024) argues, compliance and risk management are now organisational capabilities that shape competitive positioning from the earliest stages of development. When a top management team (TMT) misreads the regulatory landscape—underestimating approval timelines, misjudging the evidence threshold for a novel pathway, or failing to anticipate post-approval surveillance obligations—the consequences can be ruinous: delayed launches, forced re-submissions, product withdrawals, and investor confidence that erodes alongside the balance sheet.

The regulatory environment itself has not stood still. In medical devices, the European Union's shift from the Medical Device Directive (MDD) to the Medical Device Regulation (EU MDR 2017/745) imposed substantially elevated clinical evidence requirements and brought new post-market clinical follow-up obligations that disrupted the pipelines of manufacturers large and small (Beddoe-Rosendo et al., 2023; Maresova, 2023). In pharmaceuticals, the proliferation of adaptive trial designs, accelerated approval mechanisms, and AI-enabled drug discovery tools expanded the frontier of what is developmentally possible while generating fresh categories of regulatory uncertainty (Lenarczyk et al., 2025; Suriyaamporn et al., 2024). The appearance of software as a medical device (SaMD) and AI-enabled combination products has further complicated matters, pushing executives to navigate across historically separate regulatory frameworks that were not designed to accommodate hybrid products (Santra et al., 2024).

Against that backdrop, this chapter takes up a central question: how do executives in the pharmaceutical and medical device industries make high-stakes innovation strategy decisions within—and in response to—regulatory environments of growing complexity? The question is examined through three interlocking lenses. The first is structural: which regulatory frameworks and pathways shape the decision space currently available to executive teams, and in what directions are those frameworks moving? The second is human and organisational: which competencies, leadership orientations, and governance arrangements enable effective navigation, and which constrain it? The third is strategic: by what means can regulatory affairs be repositioned from a compliance overhead into a source of genuine competitive intelligence?

The chapter is organised as follows. Section 2 maps the regulatory architecture that executive teams in both industries currently confront. Section 3 develops a conceptual framework for decision-making in regulated innovation environments. Section 4 addresses the human capital and leadership competencies that underpin effective navigation. Section 5 examines digital transformation as both an enabler of innovation and a generator of new regulatory complexity. Section 6 considers risk governance and the management of regulatory uncertainty. Section 7 synthesises the analysis into strategic imperatives for practitioners and future directions for scholarship.

2. REGULATORY ARCHITECTURE: EVOLVING FRAMEWORKS AND EXECUTIVE IMPLICATIONS

2.1 Pharmaceutical Regulatory Pathways

Pharmaceutical regulation rests on a layered architecture. Foundational approval mechanisms—standard review, priority review, accelerated approval—are supplemented by designations that modify procedural requirements for therapies addressing unmet medical needs. In the United States, the FDA administers four principal expedited programmes: Breakthrough Therapy Designation, Fast Track, Accelerated Approval, and Priority Review. Each programme alters the timeline and evidence requirements in different ways, and executives who understand those differences can structure development programmes to take advantage of the most favourable applicable pathway. Gupte et al. (2025) provide a comparative analysis showing that while accelerated approval has expanded patient access to promising therapies, the attendant post-market confirmation trial obligations generate ongoing strategic commitments that portfolios must absorb—a fact that executive teams frequently underweight in early-stage planning.

The economics of pharmaceutical R&D are substantially shaped by pathway choices. Schuhmacher et al. (2024), studying the top twenty global pharmaceutical companies over the period 2014 to 2023, found that the group averaged 3.1 FDA approvals per year, with pronounced variation by therapeutic area and company scale. More troublingly, R&D productivity—measured as approvals relative to spending—declined across the period, which sharpens the strategic necessity of prioritising programmes with favourable risk-adjusted regulatory profiles. Schuhmacher (2024) frames this challenge through evolutionary economics: firms capable of learning adaptively within their regulatory engagement processes accumulate an efficiency advantage that compounds over multiple development cycles. In practical terms, this means that regulatory experience is not merely procedural memory; it is a form of competitive capital.

Innovation incentives interact with these pathways in ways that are often under-appreciated at the executive level. Rejon-Parrilla et al. (2022) identify three evaluative dimensions along which regulatory and health technology assessment bodies assess drug innovativeness: clinical added value over existing alternatives, the urgency of the unmet medical need, and technical novelty in the product's formulation or delivery mechanism. Executives who align their clinical development strategy with these dimensions—rather than treating efficacy data and regulatory data as separable concerns—increase the probability of favourable assessments from both regulators and payers. Sachs et al. (2023) extend this argument by showing that the incentive structures embedded in regulatory pathways and those embedded in reimbursement architectures can pull in different directions when policy is designed without cross-institutional coordination, a misalignment with direct consequences for executive portfolio decisions.

The Italian case documented by Jommi and Galeone (2023) is instructive in this regard. Their analysis of the Agenzia Italiana del Farmaco (AIFA) classification system for drug innovativeness found that the determinants of high innovativeness ratings clustered around strong clinical unmet need, robust and unambiguous clinical evidence, and genuine therapeutic novelty. Critically, the internal consistency of the evaluation—the degree to which comparable products received comparable ratings—depended heavily on procedural clarity and the training of evaluators. For executive teams, this observation highlights the value of investing in regulatory intelligence capabilities that track not just the letter of published guidelines but the evolving interpretive practice of regulatory bodies, which often diverges from formal guidance in ways that only sustained engagement can reveal.

Table 1. Strategic Regulatory Frameworks: Opportunities, Challenges, and Executive Implications

Regulatory Pathway / Framework	Strategic Opportunity	Key Challenge	Executive Decision Implication
FDA Accelerated Approval / Breakthrough Therapy	High investor interest; faster ROI timelines	Post-market commitment burden; surrogate endpoint risk	Strong executive appetite for pipeline acceleration
EU MDR / IVDR (2017/745)	Enhanced harmonisation; clearer clinical evidence standards	Longer approval cycles; SME resource strain	Strategic need for early regulatory engagement
EMA PRIME Designation	Early dialogue with regulators; rolling review advantage	Qualifying threshold ambiguity	Proactive portfolio strategy with unmet-need focus
ICH E8(R1) Clinical Design	Risk-proportionate trials; adaptive design legitimacy	Protocol complexity; statistical re-planning	Decision-analytical frameworks favoured
AI/Algorithm-based SaMD Regulation	Enables predictive diagnostics; digital health market entry	Predetermined change control plans still evolving	Investment in regulatory science capacity required

2.2 Medical Device Regulatory Challenges

Medical device regulation in Europe has undergone its most consequential structural change in a generation. The transition from the MDD to EU MDR 2017/745 has raised clinical evidence requirements substantially, introduced mandatory post-market clinical follow-up studies for higher-risk devices, and placed new demands on notified bodies whose capacity has not expanded proportionately to the volume of applications they must now review. Beddoe-Rosendo et al. (2023) document the consequences through interviews with device engineers and regulatory professionals, identifying three distinct mechanisms through which MDR constrains innovation: legacy portfolios rendered non-compliant by the elevated clinical evidence threshold; reduced notified body capacity creating backlogs; and interpretive uncertainty around general safety and performance requirements for device categories that MDR's drafters did not have in mind. The cumulative effect has been a measurable extension of time-to-market for devices that would have received clearance faster under the prior regime.

Han et al. (2024) add an important conceptual layer to this picture. Their qualitative research among regulatory affairs professionals resists the temptation to reduce MDR's complexity to bureaucratic excess. Instead, it uncovers a structured taxonomy of complexity types—technical, procedural, relational, and temporal—each of which demands a qualitatively different organisational response. The relational dimension deserves particular attention from executives. Relationships with notified bodies and regulatory agencies that are built over years—through consistent conduct, transparent disclosure, and professional engagement—constitute a form of organisational capital that measurably accelerates review processes. This capital cannot be manufactured on demand, which means it must be cultivated as a strategic investment well in advance of any particular submission.

Digital health solutions, IVDs, and digital therapeutics introduce a further layer of complexity through fragmented market access pathways. Mantovani et al. (2023) map the divergence in national reimbursement arrangements across EU member states, demonstrating that successful MDR conformity assessment provides market authorisation but does not guarantee market access. Coverage decisions vary substantially by member state, which means that executive teams must engage with health economics and outcomes evidence requirements that differ across jurisdictions and that are frequently not synchronised with the regulatory submission process. The implication is straightforward but often neglected in practice: regulatory strategy and market access strategy must be developed together, not sequentially.

The experience of medical device innovators in lower-resource settings adds further texture to this picture. Nakandi et al. (2023), drawing on fieldwork with device developers in Uganda, find that the challenges of regulatory navigation in resource-constrained environments—unclear timelines, limited regulatory agency capacity, and guidance documentation that lags behind the technologies being submitted—are qualitatively different from those encountered in mature regulatory systems. The core principles of regulatory intelligence and proactive engagement translate across settings, but the competencies required to operationalise them under resource constraints are distinctive. Executives managing global device portfolios must therefore develop regulatory leadership capabilities that are context-sensitive rather than generically portable.

3. A CONCEPTUAL FRAMEWORK FOR EXECUTIVE DECISION-MAKING IN REGULATED INNOVATION ENVIRONMENTS

3.1 Theoretical Foundations

The study of executive decision-making in regulated industries draws from several distinct but complementary theoretical traditions. Strategic leadership theory, as surveyed comprehensively by Singh et al. (2023), positions the TMT as the organisation's primary locus of strategic cognition, information processing, and consequential decision authority. Krause et al. (2022) offer a thoroughgoing conceptualisation and operationalisation of the TMT construct, identifying three analytically separable dimensions—composition, process, and structure—each of which influences strategic outcomes through different pathways. For regulated industries, these theoretical foundations must be extended to treat the regulatory environment not as an exogenous constraint acting on the firm from outside but as a strategic domain in which purposeful investment and skilled engagement can generate genuine competitive differentiation.

The resource-based view (RBV) provides an important complementary lens. Firms accumulate regulatory knowledge through repeated submission experience, post-market surveillance cycles, and sustained engagement with regulatory agencies. This accumulated knowledge—embedded in organisational routines, information systems, procedural templates, and the tacit expertise of regulatory professionals—satisfies the RBV conditions for sustained competitive advantage: it is valuable, heterogeneous across firms, imperfectly imitable, and not straightforwardly substitutable. Gupta et al. (2023) provide empirical support for this claim, showing in an Indian pharmaceutical context that intellectual capital—specifically, the combination of human capital, structural capital, and relational capital—significantly predicts financial performance, with innovation output acting as the mediating mechanism. The clear implication for executives is that investment in regulatory capability should be treated as capital formation, not as a discretionary overhead.

Decision analysis theory offers a third contribution. The pharmaceutical pipeline involves a succession of go/no-go decisions at escalating levels of investment, each made under conditions of genuine uncertainty about regulatory outcomes, clinical results, and commercial trajectories. Methling et al. (2022) demonstrate the practical value of structured decision-analytic tools—specifically multi-criteria decision analysis (MCDA)—in early-stage pharmaceutical portfolio management. Their work shows that MCDA improves portfolio decision quality by requiring explicit specification of the assumptions, probabilities, and value trade-offs underlying each programme, thereby disciplining what would otherwise be judgements vulnerable to cognitive biases and political dynamics within the TMT. For regulated environments, the additional value of decision-analytic frameworks lies in their capacity to incorporate regulatory risk as a quantified variable rather than a qualitative hedge.

3.2 The Integrated Decision-Making Framework

Drawing on the theoretical traditions outlined above and the empirical literature reviewed in Section 2, this chapter presents an integrated framework for executive decision-making in regulated innovation environments. The framework is organised around four interconnected strategic domains: Regulatory Intelligence, Strategic Positioning, Human Capital, and Governance Architecture. Each domain is analytically distinct but operationally interdependent; the failure of any one domain undermines the capacity of the others to generate value. Figure 1 represents the full framework, including the bidirectional linkages between domains and the feedback relationship with innovation performance outcomes.

The Regulatory Intelligence domain encompasses the organisational systems and processes through which executives gather, interpret, and act on information about the regulatory environment. Effective regulatory intelligence is neither passive monitoring nor reactive compliance tracking—it is active horizon scanning conducted with a strategic purpose: to identify, before competitors do, which regulatory pathways are opening, which are narrowing, and which novel guidance frameworks are in development. Chisholm and Critchley (2023) argue that the future of regulatory affairs will be defined by closer and more continuous collaboration between industry and regulatory agencies, enabled by digital platforms, standardised data architectures, and shared scientific frameworks. Khalil et al. (2023), documenting the FDA's and EMA's digitalisation of review processes, show that industry engagement with these digital infrastructure developments—early adoption of eCTD standards, participation in pilot submission programmes—translates into faster review cycles and fewer costly re-submissions.

The Strategic Positioning domain concerns the translation of regulatory intelligence into competitive strategy. This translation is where many organisations fall short. Regulatory knowledge that resides only in the regulatory affairs function, rather than flowing upward into portfolio investment decisions and outward into business development negotiations, generates only partial value. Executives who treat regulatory pathway options as strategic assets—making earlier investment decisions when pathways are favourable, structuring licensing agreements to leverage breakthrough designations, designing clinical programmes with HTA evidence requirements built in from the outset—generate a systematically different competitive posture from those who engage with regulators only when submission deadlines force the issue. Graham (2024) finds that pharmaceutical companies pursuing Industry 4.0 strategies consistently identify regulatory uncertainty as a primary obstacle to digital strategy execution, a finding that points to the regulatory intelligence domain as a prerequisite for the strategic positioning domain's effectiveness.

The Human Capital domain recognises that both the quality and the speed of executive decisions are ultimately constrained by the knowledge and capabilities of the people making them. Singh and Srivastava (2024), working in the Indian pharmaceutical context, identify systems thinking, multi-stakeholder management, and the capacity to translate regulatory signals into operational directives as the qualities most strongly associated with effective strategic leadership in the sector. Takawira et al. (2022, 2023) provide parallel evidence from South African pharmaceutical distribution, identifying visionary orientation, ethical grounding, and adaptive responsiveness to regulatory change as the competencies distinguishing sustainable from fragile business models in resource-constrained settings. Together, these bodies of evidence suggest that regulatory leadership capability is not a generic managerial attribute but a contextually specific competency cluster that organisations must deliberately cultivate.

The Governance Architecture domain encompasses the formal and informal structures through which strategic decisions are made, reviewed, and implemented. Handoyo et al. (2023) find that the moderating effect of market uncertainty on the strategy-performance relationship is strongest in firms with high operational efficiency, suggesting that lean, well-integrated operating models are more resilient in the face of regulatory turbulence. The chapter argues that governance architectures designed for regulated innovation must include at least three structural features: explicit mechanisms for escalating regulatory risk to the TMT level, cross-functional forums that integrate regulatory, clinical, commercial, and finance perspectives in portfolio decisions, and accountability frameworks that align executive performance metrics with long-term compliance outcomes rather than short-term approval rates alone.

Figure 1. Integrated Framework for Executive Decision-Making in Regulated Innovation Environments

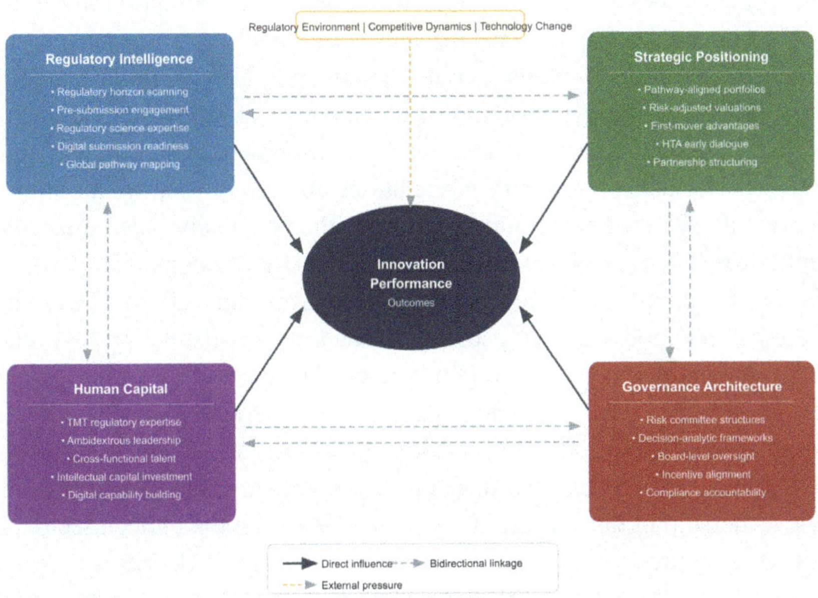

4. HUMAN CAPITAL AND LEADERSHIP COMPETENCIES

4.1 Top Management Team Composition and Regulatory Expertise

The composition of a pharmaceutical or medical device firm's TMT is a first-order determinant of that organisation's capacity to navigate the regulatory environment effectively. Krause et al. (2022) distinguish three analytically separable dimensions of TMT composition—demographic heterogeneity, functional background diversity, and cognitive style variation—each of which shapes decision outcomes through different mechanisms. For the purposes of regulated innovation, functional background diversity is particularly consequential. When regulatory affairs expertise is embedded within the TMT—whether through a dedicated Chief Regulatory Officer, a Chief Medical Officer with deep regulatory experience, or cross-trained executives who have rotated through regulatory functions—the quality and timeliness of portfolio-level regulatory judgements improve measurably. Firms that confine regulatory expertise to the middle-management level run the risk that regulatory considerations enter the strategic conversation too late, after commercial assumptions have already been locked in and development investments committed.

Evidence from diverse national contexts confirms this general principle. Hussain et al. (2024), studying pharmaceutical companies in Pakistan, find that talent acquisition, training, and performance management practices significantly predict innovation performance, and that this relationship is amplified by an innovative organisational climate. Their findings reinforce the conclusion that human capital investment in regulatory and scientific competencies is not a soft people-management concern but a hard performance driver. Specifically, organisations that create deliberate cross-functional career pathways—enabling regulatory professionals to acquire commercial experience and commercial managers to develop regulatory literacy—build TMTs with a richer integrative perspective than those that treat regulatory affairs as a technical specialism siloed from strategic management.

O'Neill et al. (2025) bring a different but complementary angle, examining strategic leadership in the context of outsourced teams in the biotech sector. Their analysis of outsourced regulatory and clinical operations identifies a structural tension that many biotech executives navigate poorly: the cost efficiency logic of outsourcing regulatory work pushes toward external service providers, while the strategic logic of maintaining regulatory intelligence at the decision-making core pushes in the opposite direction. The resolution, as O'Neill et al. propose, lies in a clear competency boundary—distinguishing the regulatory capabilities that constitute genuine core competencies to be retained and developed in-house from those that are procedural and replicable and can therefore be safely contracted out. Drawing that boundary well requires strategic clarity that many rapidly growing firms have not yet developed.

The governance dimension of TMT composition also merits attention. At the board level, the presence of non-executive directors with regulatory, scientific, or clinical backgrounds provides a form of oversight that generalist directors cannot easily replicate. Board members who understand the clinical evidence requirements for a Category III medical device, or the pharmacovigilance obligations attached to a Breakthrough Therapy Designation, are better positioned to scrutinise executive proposals that trade regulatory risk for speed, and to hold management accountable for the quality of regulatory engagement over time. As regulatory complexity increases—particularly with the overlay of AI-specific guidance frameworks on existing device and pharmaceutical regulation—the demand for board-level regulatory literacy will only intensify.

4.2 Leadership Styles and Regulatory Navigation

Singh et al. (2023), in a comprehensive review of the strategic leadership literature, identify three constructs as particularly important in contemporary organisations: transformational leadership, ambidextrous leadership, and strategic entrepreneurship. Each has distinctive application in regulated innovation contexts, and the most effective pharmaceutical and medical device executives tend to draw on all three, shifting emphasis as circumstances demand.

Transformational leadership—characterised by visionary communication, intellectual stimulation, and genuine concern for followers as individuals—is particularly valuable in mobilising organisational commitment to complex, long-horizon compliance programmes. Regulatory compliance involves disciplines that employees may experience as burdensome rather than meaningful: meticulous documentation, repetitive training requirements, pharmacovigilance reporting obligations that generate paperwork without visible clinical benefit. Transformational leaders reframe these obligations within a larger purpose narrative—patient safety, therapeutic integrity, the earned trust of regulators whose oversight ultimately enables market access—that converts procedural compliance into motivated professional practice. Without this reframing, regulatory compliance organisations frequently experience the burnout, turnover, and quality failures that attend any role whose purpose is not visible to those performing it.

Ambidextrous leadership—the sustained capacity to manage exploration and exploitation simultaneously—addresses a structural feature of pharmaceutical and device management that has no easy resolution. Executives must simultaneously manage the exploitation of approved portfolios, with their post-market surveillance obligations, lifecycle management requirements, and pricing and reimbursement renewals, and the exploration of development pipelines, with their early-stage regulatory uncertainties and their investment decisions made against incomplete evidence. Leaders who collapse this tension by prioritising one orientation over the other—becoming either purely compliance-oriented risk managers or purely entrepreneurial pipeline builders—generate characteristic failure modes. The former underinvests in innovation and loses competitive position; the latter accumulates regulatory risk that surfaces, often catastrophically, at the point of regulatory review.

Takawira et al. (2023) provide qualitative evidence from South African pharmaceutical distribution that corroborates this analysis. Their case study evidence identifies what the authors call 'regulatory strategic acumen'—an integrated competency that combines the ability to read regulatory signals early, translate those signals into operational responses without delay, and maintain organisational agility under regulatory change pressure—as the most differentiating capability in the sector. This competency, the evidence suggests, develops through a specific developmental trajectory: formal regulatory education provides the foundational knowledge; accumulated direct experience in regulatory interactions provides the situational judgement; and exposure to senior mentors who model constructive, trust-based engagement with regulatory bodies provides the relational and ethical orientation that sustains the capability over time.

4.3 Building Regulatory Capabilities as Organisational Assets

Individual competence matters, but regulatory capability at the organisational level is more than the sum of individual expertise. It is embedded in the routines, information systems, and institutional memory that persist across personnel changes and accumulate through repeated regulatory interactions. Gupta et al. (2023) demonstrate that intellectual capital—the combination of human capital, structural capital, and relational capital—predicts innovation performance in pharmaceutical firms over and above individual talent measures, suggesting that the organisational infrastructure through which individual regulatory expertise is captured and leveraged matters as much as the expertise itself.

In operational terms, this means that investments in regulatory information systems, lessons-learned processes that follow every major regulatory interaction (whether the outcome was favourable or not), and structured relationship management programmes with regulatory agencies and notified bodies should be treated as capital expenditure with an expected return, not as administrative overhead. The governance implication is equally direct: regulatory affairs budgeting decisions should be made at the TMT level, informed by a view of the cumulative capability that successive investment cycles are building, rather than delegated to functional managers who lack the portfolio-level vantage point needed to assess the strategic value of incremental capability investments.

A related challenge—and one that many organisations handle inconsistently—is the measurement of regulatory capability at the organisational level. Most pharmaceutical and medical device companies track regulatory outcome metrics: approval rates, complete response letter rates, review timelines, inspection outcomes, and corrective action completion rates. These are lagging indicators; they capture the results of capability investment decisions made years earlier. Forward-looking, capability-building indicators are rarer in practice: the proportion of submissions that benefit from prior pre-submission meeting dialogue with the relevant agency; the depth and recency of the firm's regulatory intelligence monitoring across its key therapeutic and technology areas; the degree of cross-functional integration between regulatory affairs, clinical development, and commercial functions in portfolio decision processes; and the pipeline of regulatory science expertise under development within the human resources system. Organisations that develop balanced scorecard approaches to regulatory affairs—incorporating both outcome metrics and capability-building metrics—create the measurement infrastructure that allows executives to manage regulatory performance proactively rather than discover its inadequacy retrospectively.

Figure 2. Leadership Competency Architecture for Regulated Innovation Environments

Source: Authors' synthesis drawing on Singh et al. (2023); Takawira et al. (2023); Hussain et al. (2024); O'Neill et al. (2025). 2025

Competency architecture applicable to pharmaceutical and medical device TMTs navigating complex regulatory environments.

5. DIGITAL TRANSFORMATION: INNOVATION ENABLER AND REGULATORY FRONTIER

5.1 Industry 4.0 Adoption in Pharma and Medical Devices

Few questions on the current strategic agenda of pharmaceutical and medical device executives are more consequential—or more contested—than how to manage the intersection of digital transformation and regulatory compliance. The technological opportunity is substantial. Industry 4.0 capabilities—process analytical technology, digital twins, AI-powered quality control, cloud-based clinical trial data platforms, real-world evidence generation systems—offer the prospect of substantially higher R&D productivity, more reliable manufacturing quality, and pharmacovigilance systems that detect safety signals earlier and with greater precision than conventional adverse event reporting allows. The regulatory challenge is that many of these same capabilities were not anticipated when the governance frameworks that govern their use were designed.

Graham (2024), in a study of generic pharmaceutical companies pursuing Industry 4.0 strategies, finds that regulatory uncertainty is one of the most consistently cited organisational barriers to digital strategy execution. Companies that have developed robust data governance frameworks, hired staff with hybrid regulatory and data science skills, and established working relationships with regulatory agency counterparts who understand digital process validation are better positioned to realise the productivity benefits of Industry 4.0 technologies without incurring the compliance costs that less prepared firms encounter. The implication is that digital transformation strategy and regulatory strategy must be co-designed: an Industry 4.0 roadmap developed without regulatory input will encounter friction at the implementation stage that erodes much of its anticipated value.

Miozza et al. (2024) offer a management studies perspective on pharmaceutical digital transformation that is particularly valuable for its emphasis on the governance dimensions of digital change. Their analysis identifies four domains of transformation—R&D processes, manufacturing and supply chain, commercial operations, and regulatory affairs—and argues that the governance challenges associated with cross-domain digital integration are among the least-studied but most consequential aspects of the transformation agenda. Their framework repositions digital transformation not as a technology investment programme but as a strategic leadership challenge in which executive teams must simultaneously manage internal resistance to change, capability gaps that open faster than training programmes can close them, and regulatory uncertainty about the acceptability of novel digital approaches.

Suriyaamporn et al. (2024) contribute a detailed review of AI applications across the pharmaceutical value chain. Their analysis documents real productivity gains in target identification and early-stage drug discovery—areas where AI systems have been applied longest and where regulatory acceptance of AI-generated evidence is most advanced. They also identify a recurring pattern of difficulty in the later stages of development: AI-generated evidence struggles to achieve regulatory acceptance when the explainability of model outputs is insufficient, when training data provenance cannot be adequately documented, or when the performance of AI systems under distribution shift—performance on data that differs from the training distribution—has not been characterised with sufficient rigour. These are not merely technical challenges; they are governance challenges that require executive ownership.

Figure 3. Regulatory Pathway Adoption and Executive Decision Priority Scores: Comparative Analysis Across Five Frameworks

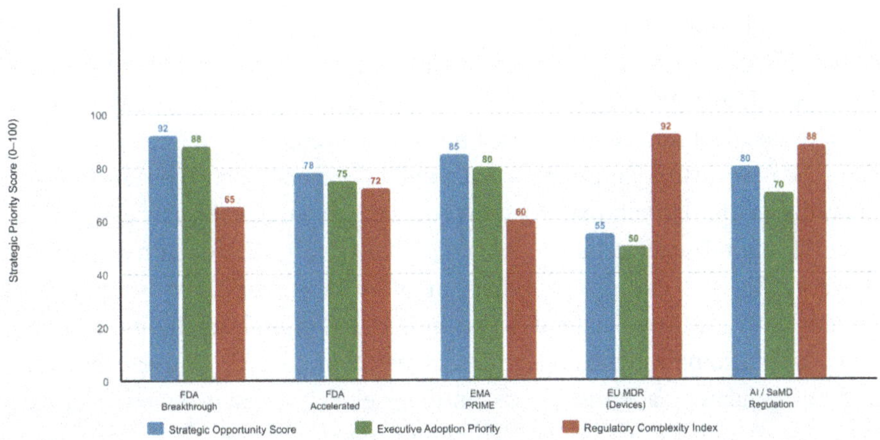

Source: Authors' synthesis from Gupte et al. (2025); Lenarczyk et al. (2025); Maresova (2023); Santra et al. (2024), Schuhmacher et al. (2024). Scores are indicative synthesis values (0–100 scale).

5.2 Regulatory Dimensions of AI and Digital Health

The regulatory treatment of AI in drug development and medical devices is among the most rapidly evolving areas of international regulatory policy. Lenarczyk et al. (2025) provide a systematic comparative analysis across the United States, European Union, and selected other jurisdictions, finding significant and—so far—growing divergence in how these systems classify, evaluate, and oversee AI-enabled tools. In the United States, the FDA has developed a risk-tiered framework for AI/ML-based SaMD that distinguishes between locked algorithms—those that do not change post-deployment—and continuously learning algorithms that adapt based on incoming data, and introduces the concept of predetermined change control plans (PCCPs) as the mechanism through which manufacturers seek advance regulatory acceptance for changes to continuously learning systems. The elegance of the PCCP concept as a regulatory solution is real, but so is the practical difficulty of drafting PCCPs comprehensive enough to satisfy regulatory expectations while remaining operationally meaningful.

The European Union's AI Act, adopted in 2024, establishes a horizontal risk classification framework that cuts across existing sectoral regulation, including MDR. For AI-enabled medical devices, the consequence is potential dual compliance obligations: the device must satisfy MDR's clinical evidence and safety requirements, and the AI components must satisfy the AI Act's requirements for high-risk AI systems—which most medical AI applications will be. Santra et al. (2024) examine the particular challenge of AI-enabled combination devices, products that integrate a pharmaceutical with an AI-driven diagnostic or dosing algorithm and that therefore cross the jurisdictional boundary between pharmaceutical and device regulation. Their analysis identifies the absence of a clear agreed regulatory pathway for such products as a significant and growing innovation barrier, and highlights the multi-stakeholder coordination challenge that resolving it requires.

The good news in this landscape is that regulatory agencies are themselves investing in the digital infrastructure needed to process and evaluate the new categories of evidence that digital health products generate. Khalil et al. (2023) document the FDA's and EMA's efforts to digitalise submission and review workflows—standardised eCTD formats, real-time data access for inspectors, digital labelling—and argue that industry participants who engage proactively with these initiatives, rather than waiting for mandatory adoption, position themselves for faster review cycles and better-quality regulatory interactions. The digital transformation of regulatory review is, in other words, an opportunity as well as a compliance obligation, and executive teams that recognise this duality are better positioned to exploit it.

6. RISK GOVERNANCE AND THE MANAGEMENT OF REGULATORY UNCERTAINTY

6.1 Conceptualising Regulatory Risk in Executive Decision-Making

Regulatory risk—the risk that regulatory decisions, changes, or uncertainties damage the commercial value of a firm's innovation pipeline—is a distinctive category of strategic risk. It is distinctive in several ways that have direct governance implications. The time horizons involved are often long: a regulatory decision on a novel therapy may remain formally open for years, during which time the firm has committed substantial capital but cannot predict the commercial outcome with confidence. The outcome structure is, in many cases, binary: approval or non-approval, with the commercial consequences of non-approval typically catastrophic relative to the cost of development. And the information asymmetry between firm and regulator—the regulator has access to all of the firm's submitted data, while the firm has only partial insight into the regulator's interpretive framework and current scientific views—creates decision uncertainty that cannot be fully resolved through additional internal analysis alone.

Nwoke (2024) provides a useful taxonomy of regulatory risk categories in the pharmaceutical and healthcare context, distinguishing compliance failure risk, regulatory change risk, and regulatory relationship risk. These categories demand different governance responses. Compliance failure risk—the risk of non-conformance with current requirements—is most amenable to internal control frameworks: quality management systems, audit programmes, and structured deviation management processes. Regulatory change risk—the risk that the framework itself shifts—requires horizon-scanning capabilities and strategic agility: the capacity to recognise early signals of regulatory change and to adjust development strategies before the change becomes binding. Regulatory relationship risk—the risk arising from a deteriorated relationship with the regulatory agency or notified body—is the most intangible of the three, and the most difficult to recover from once it has materialised. Its mitigation is primarily a function of conduct: consistent transparency, honest disclosure of unfavourable data, and engagement styles that build, rather than deplete, the trust that is regulatory review's lubricant.

6.2 Decision-Analytic Approaches to Regulatory Risk

Methling et al. (2022) provide a practically grounded analysis of how decision-analytic frameworks can improve regulatory risk management in the early stages of pharmaceutical development. Their MCDA-based portfolio prioritisation method structures the go/no-go decision by requiring the TMT to specify, explicitly and prior to full investment commitment, the probability of regulatory approval under different development scenarios, the timeline distributions associated with different pathway options, and the post-market requirement obligations that approval under each scenario would entail. By surfacing these assumptions before they are embedded in committed expenditure, the framework forces a quality of regulatory thinking that is often absent from early-stage portfolio discussions, where enthusiasm for pharmacological novelty routinely outpaces analysis of regulatory feasibility.

The practical benefits documented by Methling et al. (2022) include a systematic shift in portfolio composition away from programmes with attractive pharmacological profiles but unclear regulatory pathways toward programmes with more tractable regulatory risk profiles—not because pharmacological novelty is undervalued, but because the framework makes visible the cost of regulatory risk that was previously invisible. Firms that institutionalise decision-analytic approaches to regulatory risk management also develop a collateral capability: because they have systematically documented their regulatory assumptions at each stage of development, they accumulate a longitudinal record of regulatory prediction quality that enables continuous improvement in the accuracy of future predictions. This learning loop is one of the mechanisms through which regulatory capability, as an organisational asset, compounds over time.

6.3 Governance Structures for Regulatory Risk

Structural governance mechanisms for regulatory risk management should be calibrated to the size, complexity, and development stage of the organisation. For larger pharmaceutical and device companies with multiple products in active development, a dedicated Regulatory Risk Committee—comprising regulatory affairs, legal, clinical, commercial, and finance leadership—provides the cross-functional forum needed to identify, assess, and actively manage regulatory risks across the portfolio. This is distinct from the regulatory affairs management committee that handles submission planning and compliance tracking; its remit is explicitly strategic, concerned with portfolio-level regulatory positioning and the governance of regulatory uncertainty rather than submission logistics.

Handoyo et al. (2023) find that the relationship between business strategy and manufacturing performance is more resilient to market uncertainty when operational efficiency is high, a finding with direct governance implications. Firms whose operating models are lean and well-integrated are better positioned to absorb regulatory turbulence—a sudden MDR interpretation change, an unexpected FDA complete response letter, a post-market safety signal requiring rapid regulatory action—without cascading performance disruption. This suggests that the governance architecture for regulatory risk management should not be a structural overlay imposed on an otherwise inefficient operating model, but an embedded feature of a disciplined, process-capable organisation.

Mantovani et al. (2023) raise an important governance challenge that frequently falls between the standard accountability frameworks of regulatory affairs and market access functions: the risk that a product achieves regulatory approval but fails to achieve meaningful market access due to divergent national reimbursement decisions. For digital health solutions, IVDs, and ATMPs—product categories whose commercial models depend on sustained reimbursement rather than one-time adoption—this risk is particularly material. Governing it requires direct executive engagement with HTA bodies, reimbursement agencies, and patient advocacy communities, beginning substantially earlier in the development process than most organisations currently initiate such engagement.

Smaller and mid-size biotech and device companies face particular challenges in designing governance structures adequate to regulatory complexity. With leaner corporate functions, narrower financial headroom for delayed approvals, and fewer past interactions to draw on in building regulatory agency relationships, these organisations are disproportionately vulnerable to the regulatory risk categories that Nwoke (2024) identifies. For such firms, two governance responses deserve particular attention. The first is the use of regulatory advisory boards—external panels of regulatory scientists, former agency staff, and clinical development experts whose accumulated knowledge supplements the firm's internal capability on a flexible-cost basis. The second is participation in industry consortia and regulatory science initiatives—bodies such as TransCelerate Biopharma, the Critical Path Institute, and their device sector equivalents—that pool the regulatory learning of multiple firms and create pre-competitive platforms for building shared regulatory capability. Neither of these mechanisms substitutes for in-house regulatory expertise at the executive level, but both extend the effective regulatory intelligence resources available to organisations that cannot afford to internalise the full scope of regulatory capability that their portfolios require.

7. STRATEGIC IMPERATIVES AND FUTURE DIRECTIONS

7.1 From Compliance to Competitive Advantage

The core strategic argument of this chapter is that pharmaceutical and medical device executives who continue to treat regulatory compliance as a cost centre and constraint—rather than as a capability with competitive value—are operating with an increasingly deficient mental model of their industry. Regulatory frameworks are not merely guardrails; they are structures that reshape competitive dynamics, reward firms that engage with them intelligently, and punish those that engage with them belatedly or inadequately. The FDA's Breakthrough Therapy Designation creates first-mover advantages that extend well beyond the approval date; EMA PRIME eligibility shapes the dialogue with regulators in ways that improve evidence quality and reduce re-submission risk; and participation in the FDA's digital health pilot programmes generates institutional knowledge about the acceptable use of real-world evidence that competitors who sit on the sidelines do not accumulate.

Schuhmacher et al. (2025), benchmarking R&D success rates of leading pharmaceutical companies across the period 2006 to 2022, find persistent and substantial differences in FDA approval rates that cannot be explained by therapeutic area composition or molecular type alone. The residual variation points to organisational factors—regulatory strategy quality, clinical development rigour, and portfolio management discipline—that compound over multiple development cycles. This is strong empirical support for the proposition that regulatory capability, conceived as an organisational asset, generates measurable returns in the currency that ultimately matters: approved products that reach patients and generate sustainable commercial returns.

7.2 Synthesising Key Strategic Imperatives

Synthesising the evidence reviewed in this chapter, five strategic imperatives emerge for pharmaceutical and medical device executives navigating regulated innovation environments.

The first imperative is to elevate regulatory intelligence to a TMT-level strategic function. Regulatory knowledge that sits only in the regulatory affairs department, filtered upward only when submissions are pending, contributes a fraction of its potential value. The organisations that generate the most consistent regulatory performance—as measured by approval rates, review timelines, and post-market compliance records—are those in which regulatory intelligence flows continuously into portfolio investment decisions, partnership negotiations, and business development strategy.

The second imperative concerns human capital. The convergence of AI, digital health, and advanced therapy development with increasingly complex regulatory frameworks creates demand for professionals who can think across the science, technology, regulatory, and business strategy domains simultaneously. This profile does not emerge from standard regulatory affairs or R&D career paths; it must be deliberately cultivated through structured cross-functional experience, mentoring relationships, and investment in regulatory science education that goes beyond certification programmes. Executives who treat this talent strategy as a strategic priority—and who create the organisational conditions that retain this scarce capability once developed—build an advantage that competitors cannot quickly replicate.

The third imperative is to institutionalise decision-analytic frameworks in portfolio management. The evidence from Methling et al. (2022) is clear: structured regulatory risk analysis at the portfolio level improves decision quality and generates a learning record that continuously improves future analytical accuracy. Executives who champion these tools—and who invest in the scenario modelling and probabilistic valuation capabilities needed to operationalise them—create a durable advantage in the consistency and quality of strategic decision-making.

The fourth imperative is to design digital transformation strategies with regulatory compliance as an architectural requirement, not a retrofit. Every major pharmaceutical and device firm that has underestimated this imperative has paid a price: delayed deployment of manufacturing automation, remediation costs for AI systems that could not clear validation, and re-work on regulatory submissions that used data generated by processes whose validation status was uncertain. The organisational habit of involving regulatory affairs in the design stage of digital transformation initiatives—not the validation stage—is one that executive leadership must drive, because functional silos will not create it voluntarily.

The fifth imperative is to extend the regulatory engagement framework beyond the approval environment into the access and reimbursement environment. For an expanding range of product categories—digital therapeutics, combination devices, cell and gene therapies, AI-enabled diagnostics—regulatory approval is a necessary but insufficient condition for commercial success. Executives who develop engagement strategies with HTA bodies, payers, and patient communities in parallel with regulatory submission strategies will achieve more predictable, more rapid, and more durable market access outcomes than those who treat reimbursement as a post-approval problem.

7.3 Directions for Future Research

Several research directions would materially advance understanding of executive decision-making in regulated innovation environments. Longitudinal empirical studies tracking regulatory decision processes across complete product development cycles—from early-stage portfolio selection through post-market surveillance—would provide the causal evidence base that cross-sectional research cannot supply. Such studies would allow stronger tests of the relationships posited in the integrated framework presented here and would enable researchers to distinguish the TMT characteristics and governance structures that predict regulatory performance from those that merely correlate with it.

Comparative research across regulatory jurisdictions would illuminate which executive capabilities and governance structures are genuinely portable across regulatory contexts and which require context-specific adaptation. The contrast between mature regulatory systems—the FDA and EMA, with their sophisticated guidance frameworks and high-capacity review infrastructure—and the resource-constrained regulatory environments documented by Nakandi et al. (2023) suggests substantial contextual variation in the regulatory competencies that effective executives must deploy. A more nuanced, context-sensitive model of regulatory leadership capability is needed.

The governance implications of AI adoption for regulatory decision-making deserve dedicated empirical investigation. As AI tools become embedded in clinical trial design, pharmacovigilance workflows, and regulatory submission processes, the question of how TMTs govern the introduction of these tools—and how they manage the novel regulatory risks that embedded AI generates—becomes pressing. Research should examine not only the technical governance mechanisms involved but the executive competencies and board-level oversight capabilities needed to discharge these responsibilities adequately.

Finally, the political economy of regulatory framework development—the processes by which industry leaders engage with policymakers and regulatory agencies to shape the evolution of the frameworks within which they operate—warrants scholarly attention. Firms with proactive regulatory engagement strategies achieve better outcomes not only in individual submissions but in the design of the frameworks within which they submit. Future research should examine the mechanisms and ethics of this engagement, with sustained attention to the boundary between legitimate knowledge-sharing—which improves regulatory quality—and regulatory capture, which undermines it.

8. CONCLUSION

This chapter has examined executive decision-making in regulated innovation environments, drawing on recent empirical and conceptual scholarship across the pharmaceutical and medical device industries. Three principal conclusions emerge from this analysis. The first is that the regulatory environment is a strategic variable, not merely a constraint. It shapes competitive dynamics, creates first-mover advantages for firms that engage with it intelligently, and exacts substantial penalties on organisations that engage with it reactively or inadequately. Regulatory compliance is not opposed to competitive advantage; done well, it is a source of it.

The second conclusion concerns human capital. The competencies required to navigate regulated innovation environments effectively—regulatory science literacy, systems thinking across clinical and commercial domains, the capacity to build productive relationships with regulatory agencies over time, and the executive judgment to govern digital transformation without accumulating regulatory liability—are not generically available in management labour markets. They are built through deliberate investment in talent strategy, cross-functional career architecture, mentoring relationships, and organisational learning systems that capture and distribute regulatory experience across the firm. Executives who treat this investment as discretionary will find their regulatory performance constrained by the resulting talent gaps at precisely the moments of highest strategic consequence.

The third conclusion concerns governance. The structural mechanisms through which regulatory intelligence flows into strategic decisions, through which regulatory risk is identified and managed at the portfolio level, and through which digital transformation is executed within regulatory guardrails, are not natural products of standard corporate governance arrangements. They must be deliberately designed, adequately resourced, and actively maintained by senior leaders who understand their strategic value. The integrated framework proposed in this chapter—Regulatory Intelligence, Strategic Positioning, Human Capital, and Governance Architecture—provides both a conceptual map for scholars and a practical diagnostic for executive teams examining where their organisations are strong and where they are exposed.

The patients who depend on innovative pharmaceuticals and medical devices have a direct and substantial stake in the quality of these executive decisions. The regulatory frameworks that govern product development exist because safety and efficacy matter, and because the consequences of failure are borne by patients who had no role in the development decisions that produced the failure. Executives, governance bodies, and regulators who navigate these decisions together carry a responsibility that extends beyond shareholder value to encompass social welfare in its most concrete form. A deeper understanding of how these decisions are made—and how they can be made better—is, accordingly, a contribution not only to management scholarship but to public health.

REFERENCES

Beddoe-Rosendo, J., Heaysman, C. L., Hajnal, J. V., Ourselin, S., & Vanhoestenberghe, A. (2023). Medical device regulatory challenges in the UK are affecting innovation and its potential benefits. *Proceedings of the Institution of Mechanical Engineers. Part H, Journal of Engineering in Medicine*, *237*(12), 1349–1358. DOI: 10.1177/09544119231203776 PMID: 37840272

Chisholm, O., & Critchley, H. (2023). Future directions in regulatory affairs. *Frontiers in Medicine*, *9*, 1082384. DOI: 10.3389/fmed.2022.1082384 PMID: 36698838

Graham, J. (2024). Factors influencing the creation of an Industry 4.0 strategy in the generic pharmaceutical industry. *Journal of Generic Medicines*, *58*(3), 485–497. DOI: 10.1177/17411343241238178

Gupta, J., Rathore, P., & Kashiramka, S. (2023). Impact of intellectual capital on the financial performance of innovation-driven pharmaceutical firms: Empirical evidence from India. *Journal of the Knowledge Economy*, *14*(2), 1052–1076. DOI: 10.1007/s13132-022-00927-w

Gupte, T., Nitave, T., & Gobburu, J. (2025). Regulatory landscape of accelerated approval pathways for medical devices in the United States and the European Union. *Frontiers in Medical Technology*, *7*, 1586070. DOI: 10.3389/fmedt.2025.1586070 PMID: 40444060

Han, Y., Ceross, A., & Bergmann, J. (2024). More than red tape: Exploring complexity in medical device regulatory affairs. *Frontiers in Medicine*, *11*, 1415319. DOI: 10.3389/fmed.2024.1415319 PMID: 39144660

Handoyo, S., Suharman, H., Ghani, E. K., & Soedarsono, S. (2023). A business strategy, operational efficiency, ownership structure, and manufacturing performance: The moderating role of market uncertainty and competition intensity and its implication on open innovation. *Journal of Open Innovation*, *9*(2), 100039. DOI: 10.1016/j.joitmc.2023.100039

Hussain, S., Waheed, A., Waheed, S., & Majeed, A. (2024). The HR revolution: Redefining performance paradigms in Pakistan's pharma landscape through the moderating role of innovative climate. *PLoS One*, *19*(5), e0301777. DOI: 10.1371/journal.pone.0301777 PMID: 38820526

Jommi, C., & Galeone, C. (2023). The evaluation of drug innovativeness in Italy: Key determinants and internal consistency. *PharmacoEconomics Open*, *7*(3), 373–381. DOI: 10.1007/s41669-023-00393-3 PMID: 36763319

Khalil, R., Macdonald, J. C., Gustafson, A., Aljuburi, L., Bisordi, F., & Beakes-Read, G. (2023). Walking the talk in the digital transformation of regulatory review. *Frontiers in Medicine*, *10*, 1233142. DOI: 10.3389/fmed.2023.1233142 PMID: 37564043

Krause, R., Roh, J., & Whitler, K. A. (2022). The top management team: Conceptualization, operationalization, and a roadmap for scholarship. *Journal of Management*, *48*(6), 1496–1529. DOI: 10.1177/01492063211072459

Lenarczyk, G., Minssen, T., Nicholson, P., & Rai, A. (2025). The future of AI regulation in drug development: A comparative analysis. *Journal of Law and the Biosciences*, *12*(2), lsaf028. Advance online publication. DOI: 10.1093/jlb/lsaf028 PMID: 41221487

Mantovani, A., Leopaldi, C., Nighswander, C. M., & Di Bidino, R. (2023). Access and reimbursement pathways for digital health solutions and in vitro diagnostic devices: Current scenario and challenges. *Frontiers in Medical Technology*, *5*, 1101476. DOI: 10.3389/fmedt.2023.1101476 PMID: 36891483

Maresova, P. (2023). Impact of regulatory changes on innovations in the medical device industry. *International Journal of Health Policy and Management*, *12*, 7262. DOI: 10.34172/ijhpm.2022.7262 PMID: 35942961

Methling, F., Borden, S. A., Veeraraghavan, D., Sommer, I., Siebert, J. U., von Nitzsch, R., & Seidler, M. (2022). Supporting innovation in early-stage pharmaceutical development decisions. *Decision Analysis*, *19*(4), 337–353. DOI: 10.1287/deca.2022.0452

Miozza, M., Brunetta, F., & Appio, P. F. (2024). Digital transformation of the pharmaceutical industry: A future research agenda for management studies. *Technological Forecasting and Social Change*, *207*, 123580. DOI: 10.1016/j.techfore.2024.123580

Nakandi, B. T., Muhimbise, O., Djuhadi, A., Mulerwa, M., McGrath, J., Makobore, P. N., Rollins, A. M., & Ssekitoleko, R. T. (2023). Experiences of medical device innovators as they navigate the regulatory system in Uganda. *Frontiers in Medical Technology*, *5*, 1162174. DOI: 10.3389/fmedt.2023.1162174 PMID: 37181098

Nwoke, J. (2024). Regulatory compliance and risk management in pharmaceuticals and healthcare. *International Journal of Health Sciences*, *7*(6), 60–88. DOI: 10.47941/ijhs.2223

O'Neill, A., Vaz, R., Marques, M., & Piedade, L. (2025). Strategic leadership of outsourced teams in the biotech sector: Unlocking value chain efficiency. *Journal of Law and Sustainable Development*, *13*(7), 1–20. DOI: 10.55908/sdgs.v13i7.4493

Rejon-Parrilla, J. C., Espin, J., & Epstein, D. (2022). How innovation can be defined, evaluated, and rewarded in health technology assessment. *Health Economics Review*, *12*(1), 1. DOI: 10.1186/s13561-021-00342-y PMID: 34981266

Sachs, R., Adler, L., & Frank, R. (2023). A holistic view of innovation incentives and pharmaceutical policy reform. *Health Affairs Scholar*, *1*(1), qxad004. Advance online publication. DOI: 10.1093/haschl/qxad004 PMID: 38756835

Santra, S., Kukreja, P., Saxena, K., Gandhi, S., & Singh, O. V. (2024). Navigating regulatory and policy challenges for AI-enabled combination devices. *Frontiers in Medical Technology*, *6*, 1473350. DOI: 10.3389/fmedt.2024.1473350 PMID: 39669903

Schuhmacher, A. (2024). Pharma innovation: How evolutionary economics is shaping the future of pharma R&D. *Drug Discovery Today*, *29*(12), 104222. DOI: 10.1016/j.drudis.2024.104222 PMID: 39510495

Schuhmacher, A., Brief, E., Gassmann, O., Hartl, D., & Hinder, M. (2025). Benchmarking R&D success rates of leading pharmaceutical companies: An empirical analysis of FDA approvals (2006–2022). *Drug Discovery Today*, *30*(2), 104291. DOI: 10.1016/j.drudis.2025.104291 PMID: 39805539

Schuhmacher, A., Gassmann, O., Hinder, M., & Hartl, D. (2024). Comparative analysis of FDA approvals by top 20 pharma companies (2014–2023). *Drug Discovery Today*, *29*(9), 104128. DOI: 10.1016/j.drudis.2024.104128 PMID: 39097219

Singh, A., Lim, W. M., Jha, S., Kumar, S., & Ciasullo, M. V. (2023). The state of the art of strategic leadership. *Journal of Business Research*, *158*, 113676. DOI: 10.1016/j.jbusres.2023.113676

Singh, V. K., & Srivastava, V. (2024). A statistical analysis of strategic leadership qualities in the pharmaceutical sector of India's National Capital Region. International Journal of Experimental Research and Review, 41(Spl Vol), 259–279. DOI: 10.52756/ijerr.2024.v41spl.022

Suriyaamporn, P., Pamornpathomkul, B., Patrojanasophon, P., Ngawhirunpat, T., Rojanarata, T., & Opanasopit, P. (2024). The artificial intelligence-powered new era in pharmaceutical research and development: A review. *AAPS PharmSciTech*, *25*(6), 188. DOI: 10.1208/s12249-024-02901-y PMID: 39147952

Takawira, B., Kanyangale, M., & Mutambra, E. (2022). An exploratory study towards business sustainability through strategic leadership in emerging pharmaceutical business of South Africa: A case of Alpha distribution. *International Journal of Research in Business and Social Science*, *11*(7), 109–120. DOI: 10.20525/ijrbs.v11i7.2077

Takawira, B., Kanyangale, M., & Mutambra, E. (2023). Competencies of strategic leadership towards business sustainability in emerging pharmaceutical business of South Africa: A case of Alpha distribution. *Cogent Social Sciences*, *9*(2), 2275443. DOI: 10.1080/23311886.2023.2275443

KEY TERMS AND DEFINITIONS

Executive Decision-Making: At the senior level, decision-making is rarely straightforward. Leaders must weigh incomplete information, navigate internal politics, and act within tight timeframes. Good judgment here draws on experience, a clear sense of organizational priorities, and the ability to accept accountability when outcomes are uncertain.

Medical Device Regulation: Before a device can be used on a patient, it must demonstrate that it works as claimed and does not pose unacceptable risks. Regulators set the standards for how that evidence is gathered, reviewed, and maintained over a product's lifetime — from initial approval through years of post-market monitoring.

Pharmaceutical Innovation: Bringing a new medicine to patients is a long, expensive, and high-risk endeavor. It begins with a scientific hypothesis and moves through years of laboratory work, clinical trials, and regulatory review before anything reaches a pharmacy shelf. Success depends as much on strategic execution as on the underlying science.

Regulatory Compliance: Running a compliant organization means more than checking boxes. It requires building a culture where teams understand why rules exist and take ownership of following them. That means staying current with evolving requirements, catching gaps before regulators do, and treating compliance as an ongoing discipline rather than a one-time exercise.

Strategic Leadership: Good strategic leaders do not simply plan — they shape how an organization thinks about its future. They make deliberate choices about where to compete, how to build capability, and how to bring people along through change. Their influence is felt not just in the decisions they make, but in the direction and confidence they give to others.

Chapter 4
Human Resources Strategies to Support the Development of Medical Devices

Afonso Sansana
http://orcid.org/0009-0004-4780-0352
ISLA Santarém, Portugal

Rui Martins
http://orcid.org/0000-0001-5002-8907
ISLA Santarém, Portugal

Isabel Reis
http://orcid.org/0000-0002-2008-9124
ISLA Santarém, Portugal

Filipa Martinho
ISLA Santarém, Portugal

ABSTRACT

This chapter per the authors examines the critical role of Human Resources in the development of medical devices, a sector characterized by high technical complexity, stringent regulatory requirements, and rapidly evolving healthcare needs. The purpose is to analyze how HR practices contribute to organizational success in this environment. The content discusses how multidisciplinary collaboration, deep technical and regulatory expertise, and ethical awareness are essential for effective product development. It further highlights HR as a strategic partner beyond administrative functions, focusing on recruitment, continuous professional development,

DOI: 10.4018/979-8-3373-9410-7.ch004

and talent retention to ensure highly skilled and adaptable teams. The chapter also explores knowledge management as a key mechanism for preserving institutional expertise, fostering collaboration, and supporting innovation. Finally, it emphasizes aligning HR strategies with industry-specific demands to enhance quality, safety, and competitiveness.

1. INTRODUCTION

The medical device industry operates at the intersection of technological innovation, clinical need, and stringent regulatory oversight. Developing new devices is not only a scientific and engineering challenge but also an organizational one, requiring coordinated efforts across multiple domains of expertise, including engineering, life sciences, quality management, regulatory affairs, clinical research, and market access. Unlike many other technology-driven sectors, progress in medical devices is constrained and guided by strict safety, efficacy, and compliance requirements, while simultaneously being pushed forward by rapid advances in digitalization, data science, materials engineering, and biomedical knowledge (Wizemann, 2010).

This dual pressure, to innovate quickly while ensuring uncompromising quality and patient safety, creates a uniquely demanding environment for organizations. Success depends not only on access to cutting-edge technologies but, fundamentally, on the quality, adaptability, and coordination of human capital (Shipton et al., 2005). Highly skilled professionals must be able to work across disciplinary boundaries, interpret evolving regulatory frameworks, translate clinical needs into technical specifications, and continuously update their competencies as standards and technologies change (Anwar, G. & Abdullah, N., 2021).

In this context, Human Resources (HR) management moves beyond its traditional administrative and operational role and becomes a strategic function (Zhang & Griffith, 2023). Rather than focusing solely on recruitment and routine people management, HR must actively shape the organization's capability to innovate, comply, and grow internationally. This involves attracting scarce and specialized talent, designing continuous learning systems, fostering collaboration and knowledge sharing, and aligning organizational culture with both innovation goals and ethical and regulatory imperatives.

The strategic relevance of HR is particularly evident in sectors characterized by high knowledge intensity and rapid change. In medical devices, competitive advantage increasingly derives from the ability to integrate diverse expertise, learn faster than competitors, and reliably translate new ideas into safe and approved products. These capabilities are rooted in people and in the organizational practices that develop, connect, and retain them (Sheehan et al., 2023; Al Marzooqi, 2024).

Consequently, HR policies and practices can be understood as key enablers of innovation, effective collaboration networks, successful internationalization, and sustainable market expansion.

Despite this, discussions of competitiveness and innovation in the medical device sector often emphasize technology, funding, or regulation, while underestimating the role of human capital and HR strategy. This chapter argues that HR should be seen as a central actor in executive decision-making in medical device companies. By intentionally aligning talent management, learning, collaboration, and mobility practices with the specific demands of the sector, organizations can enhance their capacity to innovate, navigate regulatory complexity, and enter new markets more effectively.

To explore this argument, the chapter is structured around four strategic pillars for sustainable development in the medical device industry: innovation, collaboration networks, internationalization, and market expansion. Across these pillars, a cross-cutting theme of knowledge management and organizational learning is highlighted as a critical mechanism for maintaining quality, compliance, and innovative performance over time.

Empirically, the chapter draws on a qualitative case study of a medical device company (Organization Alpha), based on a semi-structured interview with its HR Director. This case provides practical insight into how HR strategies are designed and implemented to support innovation, multidisciplinary collaboration, global growth, and adaptation to diverse regulatory and cultural contexts.

By combining conceptual discussion with empirical evidence, the chapter aims to demonstrate how strategically oriented HR management can act as a dynamic capability in medical device organizations (Sheehan et al., 2023; Tsugita et al., 2023). In doing so, it offers both analytical insight for scholars of human capital and practical guidance for executives seeking to strengthen their organizations' innovative and competitive performance in a highly regulated and rapidly evolving global industry.

2. HUMAN CAPITAL AND INNOVATION IN MEDICAL DEVICES

Innovation in the medical device sector is characterized by a continuous interplay between technological advancement, clinical validation, and regulatory approval (Wizemann, 2010; Dutta & Rao, 2024). Unlike purely digital industries, where iteration cycles can be extremely fast and market entry barriers relatively low, medical device innovation requires structured development processes, extensive testing, and formal certification (Wizemann, 2010). As a result, innovation is not only about generating novel ideas but about reliably transforming those ideas into safe, effective, and compliant products (Wizemann, 2010).

This transformation is fundamentally dependent on human capital (Qian, 2017). Engineers, clinicians, regulatory specialists, quality managers, software developers, and data scientists must work in an integrated manner throughout the product lifecycle (Ryu et al., 2021). The growing convergence of technologies, such as artificial intelligence, connected devices, advanced materials, and robotics, further increases the breadth of expertise required within development teams (Hu & Yao, 2021). Consequently, competitive advantage increasingly stems from the organization's ability to attract, develop, and retain highly specialized and continuously learning professionals (Qian, 2017; Hu & Yao, 2021).

From an HR perspective, fostering innovation means going beyond static job descriptions and investing in dynamic capability building (Qian, 2017). Continuous upskilling is essential to keep pace with evolving standards (e.g., cybersecurity requirements, usability engineering, post-market surveillance obligations) and emerging technologies (Hu et al., 2021; Aon, 2024). Structured learning pathways, technical academies, and partnerships with external training providers and universities can ensure that employees regularly update their competencies (Qian, 2017; Aon, 2024).

Equally important is the organizational culture in which these professionals operate (Ryu et al., 2021). Innovation in regulated environments requires what can be described as "controlled experimentation": encouraging new ideas and problem-solving while maintaining rigorous documentation, traceability, and risk management (Ryu et al., 2021). HR plays a critical role in embedding this balance through performance management systems that reward learning, collaboration, and improvement, not only short-term output (Ryu et al., 2021).

Talent management practices such as targeted recruitment of niche profiles (e.g., regulatory data analysts, clinical evidence specialists), dual technical and managerial career paths, and project-based team structures further support innovation (Aon, 2024). By aligning recruitment, development, and evaluation criteria with innovation and compliance goals, HR policies become a direct enabler of technological progress that is both creative and safe (Aon, 2024; Qian, 2017).

In this sense, innovation capacity in medical devices can be understood as an organizational outcome of deliberate human capital strategies rather than a purely R&D-driven phenomenon (Qian, 2017; Ryu et al., 2021).

3. COLLABORATION NETWORKS AND MULTIDISCIPLINARY WORK

Medical device development is inherently multidisciplinary (Wizemann, 2010). A single product may require expertise in mechanical and electrical engineering, software, biology, clinical workflows, human factors, manufacturing, and regulatory affairs (Edmondson & Harvey, 2018). No individual or isolated department can master this full spectrum. Effective innovation therefore depends on collaboration networks that integrate diverse knowledge domains (Powell, Koput & Smith-Doerr, 1996).

These networks operate at two levels. Internally, organizations must connect traditionally separate functions such as R&D, quality, regulatory, manufacturing, marketing, and post-market surveillance (Song, Thieme & Xie, 1998). Externally, collaboration with universities, hospitals, research institutes, suppliers, start-ups, and even competitors in pre-competitive spaces is increasingly common (Pisano, 2006).

HR has a strategic role in enabling both levels of collaboration. Internally, HR can design structures that reduce silos, for example through multidisciplinary project teams, rotational assignments, and internal mobility programs (Boxall & Purcell, 2022). Such practices expose employees to different perspectives and create shared languages across functions, which is essential for translating clinical needs into technical and regulatory solutions (Edmondson & Harvey, 2018).

Externally, HR can support collaboration by facilitating joint appointments, visiting researcher programs, and participation in innovation ecosystems and clusters (Powell et al., 1996). Recruitment strategies that value hybrid profiles (e.g., engineer with clinical experience, scientist with regulatory knowledge) also act as bridges between domains (Aon, 2024).

Beyond structures and recruitment, collaboration requires specific skills and behaviors: communication across disciplines, conflict management, and collective problem-solving (Edmondson & Harvey, 2018). Training in teamwork, design thinking, and agile project methods helps teams work productively despite different professional cultures and vocabularies (Brown & Katz, 2019).

By institutionalizing collaboration rather than leaving it to chance, HR turns networks into a repeatable organizational capability (Boxall & Purcell, 2022). This capability accelerates learning, reduces development errors, and increases the likelihood that innovations are technically sound, clinically relevant, and regulatorily acceptable (Wizemann, 2010).

4. INTERNATIONALIZATION AND GLOBAL TALENT MANAGEMENT

For many medical device companies, growth depends on entering and operating in multiple geographic markets (Keller & Chinta, 2013). However, internationalization in this sector is particularly complex due to heterogeneous regulatory systems, reimbursement models, clinical practices, and cultural expectations (Gulati et al., 2004).

Success therefore requires global talent strategies (Tarique, Schuler & Gong, 2006). Organizations must combine centralized expertise with strong local knowledge. Regulatory specialists need to understand both global standards and country-specific requirements; commercial teams must adapt value propositions to local healthcare systems; and R&D may need to consider regional clinical practices during design (Keller & Chinta, 2013).

HR contributes by building globally competent workforces. Recruitment of professionals with international experience, multilingual capabilities, and cross-border regulatory knowledge is a first step (Scullion & Collings, 2011). Equally important is the development of intercultural competence among existing employees through targeted training and international project exposure (Stahl et al., 2010).

Mobility programs such as short-term assignments, expatriation, and intercompany exchanges create global mindsets and transfer tacit knowledge between sites (Scullion & Collings, 2011). These experiences develop leaders who can operate across contexts and make informed strategic decisions about localization versus standardization (Tarique et al., 2006).

At the same time, maintaining a coherent organizational culture is essential to ensure consistent quality and compliance worldwide (Ghemawat, 2007). HR must therefore balance global HR frameworks (values, competency models, leadership principles) with local adaptation of policies and practices to respect legal and cultural specificities (Stahl et al., 2010).

Effective global talent management allows companies to coordinate innovation, quality, and commercialization across borders, turning geographic diversity into a source of resilience and opportunity rather than fragmentation (Tarique et al., 2006).

5. MARKET EXPANSION, DIVERSITY AND LOCAL EMBEDDEDNESS

Entering new markets is not only a regulatory or commercial exercise; it is also a human and organizational one (Meyer, Mudambi & Narula, 2011). Understanding local clinical needs, user behaviors, and institutional structures requires people who are embedded in those contexts (Andersson, Forsgren & Holm, 2002).

Workforce diversity becomes a strategic asset in this process (Richard, Murthi & Ismail, 2007). Teams composed of individuals with different cultural, professional, and experiential backgrounds are better equipped to interpret varied market signals and avoid one-size-fits-all solutions (Stahl et al., 2010). From an HR standpoint, diversity and inclusion policies are therefore directly linked to competitive positioning (Richard et al., 2007).

Local recruitment is often crucial for regulatory navigation, stakeholder engagement, and trust building with healthcare professionals and authorities (Meyer et al., 2011). At the same time, connections to the global organization must be preserved to ensure transfer of best practices and technical knowledge. HR can support this balance through mentoring links between headquarters and local teams, shared training platforms, and global communities of practice (Andersson et al., 2002).

Partnerships with local universities, hospitals, and industry associations further strengthen local embeddedness and access to talent (Meyer et al., 2011). HR-led internship and graduate programs tied to these institutions can create sustainable talent pipelines aligned with regional needs (Stahl et al., 2010).

By integrating diversity, local knowledge, and global coordination, organizations can adapt devices and go-to-market strategies more rapidly and responsibly, improving both adoption and compliance in new regions (Meyer et al., 2011).

6. KNOWLEDGE MANAGEMENT AND ORGANIZATIONAL LEARNING

In highly regulated industries, knowledge is not only a source of innovation but also a safeguard against risk (Nonaka & Takeuchi, 1995). Design rationales, test results, regulatory interpretations, and lessons from post-market surveillance must be captured, shared, and reused (Argote & Ingram, 2000). Loss of critical knowledge through employee turnover or poor documentation can lead to delays, non-conformities, or even safety issues (Nonaka & Takeuchi, 1995).

Organizational learning therefore becomes a central pillar of sustainable performance (Argyris & Schön, 1978). This includes formal mechanisms such as document management systems, design history files, and standard operating procedures, but also informal mechanisms such as mentoring, peer review, and communities of practice (Crossan, Lane & White, 1999).

HR plays a pivotal coordinating role in these processes. Structured onboarding programs accelerate the transfer of tacit knowledge to new hires (Nonaka & Takeuchi, 1995). Succession planning and overlap periods reduce the risk of knowledge gaps in key roles (Argote & Ingram, 2000). Continuous professional development ensures that existing knowledge is regularly updated rather than becoming obsolete (Crossan et al., 1999).

Learning loops between projects are particularly important. Post-project reviews, failure analyses, and cross-project forums allow insights from one device generation to inform the next (Schindler & Eppler, 2003). Embedding time and recognition for such activities into performance systems signals that learning is a valued output, not an optional extra (Argyris & Schön, 1997).

In this way, knowledge management links directly to both innovation and compliance: organizations that learn systematically can innovate faster while avoiding repeated mistakes and regulatory setbacks (Nonaka & Takeuchi, 1995; Argote & Ingram, 2000).

7. METHODOLOGY

In order to explore how HR strategies support innovation, collaboration, internationalization, and market expansion in the medical device sector, a qualitative research design was adopted. Qualitative approaches are particularly suitable for understanding complex organizational phenomena and the underlying "how" and "why" of strategic practices.

A single in-depth case study was chosen to allow detailed examination of HR processes within their real organizational context. Case study methodology provides flexibility in data collection and enables rich, contextualized insights that may be difficult to capture through large-scale quantitative surveys.

Data was collected through a semi-structured interview – the most common primary data source in case study research. This format was able to ensure comparability across topics while allowing the interviewer to probe emerging themes and obtain concrete examples.

The interview guide was structured around the chapter's four strategic pillars: innovation, collaboration networks, internationalization and market expansion; and the cross-cutting theme of knowledge management. The questions explored topics such as recruitment, training, organizational culture, mobility, partnerships, and how the organization adapts to regulatory and cultural differences.

The interview was recorded, transcribed, and analyzed through a thematic approach with eachstatement being coded according to the strategic pillars and then compared with the concepts identified in the literature, allowing us to identify both points of convergence and distinctive organizational practices.

8. CASE STUDY: ORGANIZATION ALPHA

Aiming to preserve confidentiality, the company examined in this study is referred to as *Organization Alpha*. Alpha is a large, nationally based medical device manufacturer with international commercial activities and a strong focus on technology-intensive products. Its operations require close coordination among R&D, regulatory affairs, quality, and commercial functions.

Data was gathered through an in-person semi-structured interview conducted in December 2024 with the company's HR Director. The interviewee was selected based on their comprehensive oversight of Alpha's people and talent management practices across the organization.

Innovation and skills development: According to the HR Director, one of Alpha's main challenges resides in recruiting professionals who possess both deep technical expertise and a solid understanding of regulatory requirements. To address rapid sectoral change, the organization invests heavily in continuous training, including workshops on emerging technologies and AI applications. In addition to formal training, the company promotes a culture where employees are encouraged to propose and test ideas within controlled quality frameworks. This approach reflects an intentional HR strategy aimed at integrating creativity with regulatory compliance.

Collaboration and multidisciplinary integration: Alpha promotes collaboration through cross-functional project teams that bring together engineering, regulatory, and commercial expertise from early development stages. The company also encourages internal mobility, allowing employees to rotate across departments and gain exposure to different functional persperctives. This practice strengthens mutual understanding whilst reducing handover frictions. These practices were able to increase problem-solving speed and reduce late-stage redesigns as explained by the HR Director.

Internationalization and global readiness: As Alpha moves into new international markets, it prioritizes the recruitment of professionals with experience in those regions and on preparing its current employees through intercultural training. Futhermore, the offered international mobility policies also allow the staff to spend time abroad and to build a stronger global mindset, creating globally aware leaders. Finally, Alpha works closely with local institutions and industry associates to navigate regulations and make market entry smoother.

Market expansion and local adaptation: Entering new regions required adapting to local regulations and cultural expectations. Alpha addressed this by combining local hires with experienced internal staff seconded from headquarters. This dual structure enabled both local embeddedness and transfer of organizational know-how. Diversity within teams was viewed as a practical advantage for understanding varied customer and clinical needs.

Knowledge sharing and retention: To avoid knowledge loss, Alpha emphasizes documentation, mentoring, and structured handovers between projects. Lessons learned from audits, validations, and post-market feedback are systematically shared across teams. HR supports these processes through onboarding programs and career paths that retain critical expertise.

Overall, the case of Organization Alpha illustrates how deliberately designed HR practices can translate strategic intentions into operational capabilities. Recruitment, continuous learning, collaboration structures, mobility, and knowledge management jointly support innovation, regulatory compliance, and international growth, reinforcing the view of HR as a strategic partner in executive decision-making within the medical device industry.

9. DISCUSSION

The analysis of Organization Alpha illustrates in practical terms how HR strategies can function as enabling mechanisms for innovation, compliance, and international growth in the medical device industry. When contrasted with the conceptual arguments presented earlier, several reinforcing patterns emerge.

First, innovation in this context is not solely the outcome of R&D investment or technological capability, but of structured and continuous human capital development. Alpha's emphasis on ongoing technical and regulatory training, combined with a culture that legitimizes experimentation within quality constraints, demonstrates how HR practices translate abstract innovation goals into daily behaviors. This supports the view that innovation capability is embedded in organizational routines and skills, not only in breakthrough ideas.

Second, collaboration networks are shown to be actively constructed rather than naturally occurring. Cross-functional teams, internal mobility, and hybrid talent profiles reduce functional silos and create shared understanding between engineering, regulatory, and commercial domains. This confirms that multidisciplinary work requires intentional organizational and HR design. Without such mechanisms, knowledge remains fragmented and development cycles become longer and riskier.

Third, internationalization appears as a talent challenge as much as a market or regulatory one. Alpha's combination of intercultural training, targeted international recruitment, and mobility programs builds a workforce able to interpret and respond to heterogeneous global requirements. Rather than treating international expansion as a purely commercial activity, the case highlights the need for globally competent human capital as a prerequisite for sustainable growth.

Fourth, diversity and local embeddedness emerge as operational necessities. Local hires supported by strong links to headquarters allow simultaneous adaptation and standardization. This balance is essential in regulated industries, where excessive localization can threaten compliance consistency while excessive centralization can hinder market fit. HR acts as the broker of this balance through staffing models, mentoring links, and shared learning platforms.

Finally, the case underscores knowledge management as a connective tissue across all pillars. Systematic documentation, mentoring, and transfer of lessons learned reduce the risk of repeating errors and accelerate subsequent innovation cycles. In regulated environments, this is not only an efficiency issue but also a compliance and safety imperative.

Taken together, these observations suggest that HR in medical device firms operates as a dynamic capability: it continually reconfigures skills, relationships, and knowledge flows to match evolving technological, regulatory, and market conditions. Executive decision-making that neglects this dimension risks underestimating the organizational foundations of innovation and growth.

10. AN INTEGRATIVE HR FRAMEWORK FOR MEDTECH INNOVATION AND GROWTH

Building on the conceptual discussion and the empirical insights from Organization Alpha, an integrative framework can be proposed to guide executive and HR decision-making in medical device organizations.

The framework links three layers:

HR Practices

- Targeted recruitment of scarce and hybrid profiles
- Continuous technical and regulatory upskilling
- Multidisciplinary team design and internal mobility
- International mobility and intercultural development
- Diversity and inclusion with strong local hiring
- Structured knowledge management (documentation, mentoring, lessons learned)

Human Capital Capabilities

- Cross-disciplinary problem solving
- Regulatory and quality-aware innovation
- Global and intercultural competence
- Rapid organizational learning and knowledge reuse
- Strong internal and external collaboration networks

Strategic Outcomes

- Faster and safer innovation cycles
- Reduced regulatory risk and rework
- Effective entry and adaptation to new markets
- Scalable international operations
- Sustainable competitive advantage

The key insight of the framework is that HR practices do not directly produce market or innovation success; they first build organizational capabilities, which in turn enable strategic outcomes. This highlights the need for alignment and coherence among HR initiatives rather than isolated actions.

For executives, the framework offers a decision tool:

- When innovation slows, the question is not only "Do we need more R&D funding?" but also "Do our learning and collaboration systems enable rapid capability renewal?"
- When international expansion struggles, the issue may be less about market strategy and more about the availability of globally competent and locally embedded talent.
- When compliance issues arise, the root cause may lie in knowledge transfer and onboarding rather than in formal procedures alone.

By viewing HR as an architect of capabilities rather than a support function, leaders can make more informed and systemic strategic choices.

11. LIMITATIONS AND FUTURE RESEARCH

This chapter is based on a single qualitative case study and one in-depth interview with an HR executive. While this approach provides rich, contextualized insight, it limits generalizability. Different organizations, sizes, and regulatory or geographic contexts may exhibit alternative HR configurations and challenges.

The perspective captured is primarily that of HR leadership. Including viewpoints from R&D, regulatory, and executive management could provide a more multi-voiced understanding of how HR practices are perceived and experienced across the organization.

Future research could extend this work in several directions:

- Comparative case studies across multiple medical device firms to identify common patterns and contingencies.
- Longitudinal studies examining how HR strategies evolve alongside regulatory and technological change.
- Quantitative analyses linking specific HR practices to measurable innovation and compliance outcomes (e.g., time-to-market, audit findings, post-market incident rates).
- Cross-industry comparisons with pharmaceuticals or digital health to understand which insights are sector-specific and which are more general.

Such research would strengthen the evidence base for positioning HR as a central lever of strategic performance in regulated innovation sectors.

12. CONCLUSION

Medical device development is shaped by constant technological change, strict regulation, and diverse global markets. In this environment, sustainable success depends not only on superior technologies but on the organization's ability to continuously build, connect, and renew its human capital.

This chapter has argued and illustrated that HR plays a strategic role in this process. Through targeted recruitment, continuous learning, multidisciplinary collaboration, global talent management, diversity and local embeddedness, and systematic knowledge management, HR practices create the capabilities that underpin safe innovation and effective growth.

The case of Organization Alpha demonstrates that when these practices are deliberately aligned with sector-specific demands, they enhance both innovative performance and regulatory robustness. HR thus acts as a dynamic capability that enables organizations to adapt to evolving scientific, regulatory, and market conditions.

For executives in the medical device industry, the implication is clear: decisions about talent, learning, and organizational design are not peripheral administrative matters but core strategic choices. Investing in integrated and forward-looking HR strategies strengthens the foundations on which innovation, internationalization, and competitive advantage are built.

In highly regulated and knowledge-intensive industries, the path to better devices and better health outcomes runs through better management of people and knowledge.

REFERENCES

Andersson, U., Forsgren, M., & Holm, U. (2002). The strategic impact of external networks: Subsidiary performance and competence development in the multinational corporation. *Strategic Management Journal, 23*(11), 979–996. DOI: 10.1002/smj.267

Anwar, G., & Abdullah, N. N. (2021). Inspiring future entrepreneurs: The effect of experiential learning on the entrepreneurial intention at higher education. *International Journal of English Literature and Social Sciences, 6.*

Aon. (2024). Managing human capital to drive innovation in life sciences. https://www.aon.com/en/insights/articles/managing-human-capital-to-drive-innovation-in-life-sciences

Argote, L., & Ingram, P. (2000). Knowledge transfer: A basis for competitive advantage in firms. *Organizational Behavior and Human Decision Processes, 82*(1), 150–169. DOI: 10.1006/obhd.2000.2893

Argyris, C., & Schön, D. A. (1997). Organizational learning: A theory of action perspective. *Revista Española de Investigaciones Sociológicas*, (77/78), 345–348. DOI: 10.2307/40183951

Boxall, P., & Purcell, J. (2022). *Strategy and human resource management.* Bloomsbury Publishing.

Brown, T., & Katz, B. (2019). *Change by design: How design thinking transforms organizations and inspires innovation* (Vol. 20091). HarperBusiness.

Crossan, M. M., Lane, H. W., & White, R. E. (1999). An organizational learning framework: From intuition to institution. *Academy of Management Review, 24*(3), 522–537. DOI: 10.2307/259140

Dutta, B., & Rao, V. (2024). *Human capital and innovation capability in organizations. Heliyon.* https://www.sciencedirect.com/science/article/pii/S2405872624000443

Edmondson, A. C., & Harvey, J. F. (2018). Cross-boundary teaming for innovation: Integrating research on teams and knowledge in organizations. *Human Resource Management Review, 28*(4), 347–360. DOI: 10.1016/j.hrmr.2017.03.002

Ghemawat, P. (2007). *Redefining global strategy: Crossing borders in a world where differences still matter.* Harvard Business Press.

Gulati, R., Freeman, K. W., & Nolen, G. (2004). How CEOs Manage Growth Agendas. *Harvard Business Review, 82*(7-8), 124–132. PMID: 15241959

Hu, G.-G., & Yao, L.-P. (2021). Do Human Capital Investment and Technological Innovation Have a Permanent Effect on Population Health? An Asymmetric Analysis of BRICS Economies. *Frontiers in Public Health, 9*, 723557. DOI: 10.3389/fpubh.2021.723557 PMID: 34368074

Meyer, K. E., Mudambi, R., & Narula, R. (2011). Multinational Enterprises and Local Contexts: The Opportunities and Challenges of Multiple Embeddedness. *Journal of Management Studies*, *48*(2), 235–252. DOI: 10.1111/j.1467-6486.2010.00968.x

Nonaka, I., & Takeuchi, H. (1995). *The knowledge-creating company: How Japanese companies create the dynamics of innovation*. Oxford University Press. DOI: 10.1093/oso/9780195092691.001.0001

Pisano, G. P. (2006). *Science Business: The Promise, the Reality, and the Future of Biotech*. Harvard Business School Press.

Powell, W. W., Koput, K. W., & Smith-Doerr, L. (1996). Interorganizational collaboration and the locus of innovation: Networks of Learning in Biotechnology. *Administrative Science Quarterly*, *41*(1), 116. DOI: 10.2307/2393988

Richard, O. C., Murthi, B. S., & Ismail, K. (2007). The impact of racial diversity on intermediate and long-term performance: The moderating role of environmental context. *Strategic Management Journal*, *28*(12), 1213–1233. DOI: 10.1002/smj.633

Ryu, J. M., Park, S., Park, Y., Park, J., & Lee, M. (2021). Innovative Culture and Firm Performance of Medical Device Companies: Mediating Effects of Investment in Education and Training. *International Journal of Environmental Research and Public Health*, *18*(17), 8926. DOI: 10.3390/ijerph18178926 PMID: 34501515

Schindler, M., & Eppler, M. J. (2003). Harvesting project knowledge: A review of project learning methods and success factors. *International Journal of Project Management*, *21*(3), 219–228. DOI: 10.1016/S0263-7863(02)00096-0

Scullion, H., & Collings, D. G. (2011). Global talent management: Introduction. In *Global talent management* (pp. 19–32). Routledge. DOI: 10.4324/9780203865682

Sheehan, M., Garavan, T. N., & Morley, M. J. (2023). The Microfoundations of Dynamic Capabilities for Incremental and Radical Innovation in Knowledge-Intensive Businesses. *British Journal of Management*, *34*(1), 220–240. DOI: 10.1111/1467-8551.12582

Shipton, H., Fay, D., West, M., Patterson, M., & Birdi, K. (2005). Managing people to promote innovation. *Creativity and Innovation Management*, *14*(2), 118–128. DOI: 10.1111/j.1467-8691.2005.00332.x

Song, X. M., Thieme, R. J., & Xie, J. (1998). The impact of cross-functional joint involvement across product development stages: An exploratory study. *Journal of Product Innovation Management, 15*(4), 289–303. DOI: 10.1111/1540-5885.1540289

Stahl, G. K., Maznevski, M. L., Voigt, A., & Jonsen, K. (2010). Unraveling the effects of cultural diversity in teams: A meta-analysis of research on multicultural work groups. *Journal of International Business Studies, 41*(4), 690–709. DOI: 10.1057/jibs.2009.85

Tarique, I., Schuler, R., & Gong, Y. (2006). A model of multinational enterprise subsidiary staffing composition. *International Journal of Human Resource Management, 17*(2), 207–224. DOI: 10.1080/09585190500404424

Tsugita, Y., Ushimaru, Y., Kato, T., Sasaki, M., Hata, T., Hosaka, M., Eguchi, H., Doki, Y., & Nakajima, K. (2023). Efficacy of human resource development program for young industry personnel who will be involved in future medical device development. *Surgical Endoscopy, 37*(12), 9633–9642. DOI: 10.1007/s00464-023-10474-3 PMID: 37891373

Wizemann, T. (2010). Public Health Effectiveness of the FDA 510(k) Clearance Process: Balancing Patient Safety and Innovation: Workshop Report. Washington (DC): National Academies Press (US). 4, The Medical Device Industry Innovation Ecosystem. Available from: https://www.ncbi.nlm.nih.gov/books/NBK209786/

Zhang, Y., & Griffith, M. D. (2023). Human Resource Management Systems and Firm Innovation: A MetaAnalytic Study. Economic and Business Review, 25(4), 202-215. https://doi.org/DOI: 10.15458/2335-4216.1327

Chapter 5

Impact of Strategic Leadership on Human Capital Management:
Mediating Role of Organizational Culture in Ethiopia's Healthcare Sector

Shashi Kant
http://orcid.org/0000-0003-4722-5736
St. Joseph University in Tanzania, Tanzania

Wako Jio
http://orcid.org/0009-0003-6192-459X
Bule Hora University, Ethiopia

Shashank Mittal
http://orcid.org/0009-0007-8643-4350
O.P. Jindal Global University, India

Thompson Xavier Ananth
St. Joseph University in Tanzania, Tanzania

ABSTRACT

This chapter attempts to discuss the role of strategic leadership on human capital management by focusing on the mediating effect of organisational culture in the context of the healthcare sector in Ethiopia. As the sector of healthcare organisations becomes more challenged, insight into the dynamics between the leadership structure and human capital becomes imperative. A sample size of 394 healthcare

DOI: 10.4018/979-8-3373-9410-7.ch005

professionals was used in this study to collect data using structured questionnaires. The findings show that strategic leadership has an important influence on human capital management, where organisational culture plays its part as a key mediator in this relationship. This mediating effect adheres to the significance of encouraging a cultural game plan to attain the most out of strategic leadership initiatives. The chapter concludes with practical implications to healthcare management in Ethiopia, such as the need for focused leadership development programmes and culture improvement through human capital management initiatives for a better use of human capital.

INTRODUCTION

The global scenario of healthcare is continuously changing that depends on various factors such as technological changes, demographic changes, and increasing expectations of patients (Kwiliński et al., 2024). As healthcare systems work to achieve better performance and patient outcomes, strategic leadership's role in ensuring effective human capital management becomes a critical factor in ensuring performance. Strategic leadership, which includes the skills of influencing and leading an organization toward the accomplishment of long-term directions, has demonstrated very profound implications for human capital management, namely of improving the capabilities of the workforce in the healthcare industry (Ninassi & Burrell, 2023).

The origin of the concept can be tracked from the theories of management strategies centered on the dynamic between leadership behavior and the outcomes in the organization. As defined in various empirical studies, effective leadership does not just improve the performance of employees, but it produces a culture that gives birth to talent and innovation. However, although many studies have found links between leadership styles and organizational effectiveness, the lack of knowledge about the mediating role played by organizational culture, especially in developing countries such as Ethiopia, is significant (Abawari et al., 2024).

Empirical literature reported the possibility of organizational culture to act as a catalyst in human capital management practices. Yet, practical obstacles remain, including so poor leadership training programs, resistance to cultural changes and so misalignment of strategic objectives with human resource policies. These challenges make the successful implementation of strategic leadership in healthcare systems, especially in resource-limited settings especially problematic.

This chapter aims to address these gaps in research attempts by outlining a dense analysis of the impact of strategic leadership in human capital management and its mediate role of organizational culture in healthcare sector in Ethiopia. By zeroing in on this particular situation, the research will help identify subtle information that can inform future researchers and policymakers in the development of leadership development initiatives and improvements in organizational culture.

The issue addressed in this research study is to find out: How does strategic leadership affect human capital management in the healthcare sector? in Ethiopia, and what is the role of organizational culture in the relationship between strategic leadership and human capital management? Addressing this question is essential to a better understanding of the complexities at play and for offering recommendations to address them that can be implemented as actionable steps to improve healthcare services and workforce management in Ethiopia and similar contexts.

BACKGROUND OF STUDY

The healthcare sector in Ethiopia has undergone immense changes in the past two decades, with commitments to provide better health and quality access (Tarekegn et al., 2025). However, this progress is challenged by problems that are grounded in complex relationships between strategic leadership, human capital management and organizational culture. Despite increased government investment and donor funding, the performance of healthcare delivery is still hampered by poor human resource practice, leadership training, and lack of cordination between healthcare policies and organizational culture (Chelagat et al., 2021).

A good example in practice that illustrates these challenges is the implementation of the Health Sector Transformation Plan (HSTP) in Ethiopia. The HSTP's goals were to improve service delivery by strategic leadership activities targeting capacity-building and workforce management. However, a lack of well-defined organizational culture that supports the leadership directives, among other things, became a problem for many healthcare facilities in actualizing these goals. For example, in a regional hospital in the Amhara region, strategic leaders took the lead to organize training programs to build the competencies of staff. However, the efforts could not be translated into better performance as the current culture had not encouraged continuous learning and integration of feedback by healthcare workers. As a result, staff remained disengaged and their turnover rates were high, along with poor patient care (Chessell et al. 2022).

Another pertinent case is the experience of a health center in Addis Ababa which was included in a pilot program to improve management competencies among health center managers. While some indication was found in the early testing about enhanced comprehension of the principles of strategy, lack of any supporting organizational culture prevented the implementation of these concepts. Staff resistance and the lack of staff collaboration was pervasive, providing evidence to support the pervasive practices of traditional hierarchies and ineffective communication practices obstructing the strategic initiatives (Kaapanda, 2023).

Such case studies highlight the urgent need to learn the role of strategic leadership on human capital management in certain cultural settings of Ethiopian healthcare. They highlight the role of strategic leadership in creating organizational change and underscore how strategic leadership is greatly diminished in its ability to effect change unless an organization possesses an aligned and supportive organizational culture. Improving these dynamics is an important chance for advancing the capacity and efficiency of Ethiopia's healthcare system in a way that promotes an environment where strategic initiatives can thrive and make real improvements in health outcomes.

STATEMENT OF PROBLEM

Strategic leadership has been acknowledged as a key factor of effectively managing human capital in healthcare organizations, still there is a severe divergence between the ideal situation in the theory, compared to the actual scenario in real practice, especially in the Ethiopian healthcare sector. Ideally, strategic leadership should also work hand in hand with human capital practices to foster an empowered workforce and enhance the overall healthcare delivery (Gile et al., 2022). However, there are pieces of evidence in the existing literature that are contradictory to the effect of strategic leadership on human capital outcomes. While some studies represent positive correlation, and others show a neutral or negative impact, it means there is a huge gap in understanding the contextual and cultural factors that mediate these relations (Takawira & Mutambara, 2023).

Empirical studies in different settings have come out inconclusive on the effectiveness of strategic leadership initiatives. For example, while leadership training programs promise to boost the managerial capabilities of leaders, their benefits do not often translate in the context of the organization being operated within and dealing with organizational cultures that have matured around a resistance to change. Theoretical gaps exist in the models that are used in analyzing these relationships with many models being developed in western contexts and thus do not find relevance in unique Ethiopian cultural and organizational settings (Duressa & Kidane, 2024).

Along with, there is currently some level of significant knowledge gap regarding the specific mediating role of organizational culture in the interplay between strategic leadership and human capital management. Existing research tends to think of culture as a backdrop rather than a dynamic factor in how well a leader is being effective. Contextual gaps in the way Ethiopian healthcare organizations uniquely represent cultural characteristics, further make it difficult for global strategic leadership theories to be applied.

Practical challenges also prevent strategic leadership from being effective in healthcare settings. Some of the issues including a lack of resources for developing leaders and a lack of alignment between strategic objectives and human resource practices, and the resistance from employees to new forms of leadership, highlight the complexities involved in implementing strategic initiatives (Woolley & Currie, 2023).

This research aims to address these gaps that exist through offering a nuanced examination of the impact of strategic leadership on human capital management in the Ethiopian healthcare sector with a focal emphasis on the mediating role of organizational culture. Through substantive examinations, using empirical data, this work will be of service to other scholars and policy makers in the future by emphasizing the need for culturally relevant frameworks and practical implementations. Ultimately, results will help us develop focused leadership training initiatives and organizational culture interventions, and to inform such strategies, and to promote stronger levels of engagement among their employees and patient-related outcomes in healthcare in Ethiopia and other contexts.

RELATED THEORIES

Transformational Leadership Theory: It is based on the idea that leaders have the ability to inspire and motivate followers to go beyond their own personal self-interests for the benefit of the organization. This theory emphasizes the importance of vision, inspiration, and the stimulation of intellectual work in the creation of a motivational work environment. Transformational leaders encourage supportive relationships, create a shared vision, and stimulate innovation-all important factors in the successful management of human capital. In the context of Ethiopian healthcare system, this theory emphasizes the need for leaders who are able to both lead and ensure the culture of ongoing improvement and engagement of staff (Demeke et al., 2025).

Human Capital Theory: It argues that people's skills, knowledge, and experience are their economic value, and their productivity in an organization. Within the field of healthcare, the use of Human Capital Theory stresses the importance of strategic leadership in order to focus on the development of its workforce in order to enhance service provision and patient outcomes. This perspective is particularly relevant in Ethiopia, where the use of human capital management can help reduce the substantial healthcare gap in the country (Gile et al., 2022).

Organizational Culture Theory: It is the concern of the group of shared values, beliefs, and norms that influence the manner in which groups of an organization interact and work together. Rooted in the anthropological study of organisations and enriched by such scholars as Edgar Schein, this theory emphasises the significant influence of organisational culture on behaviour; performance and efficacy of leadership initiatives. In Ethiopia, particularly in the healthcare sector, an understanding of the prevailing organizational culture is critical for analyzing the reason behind the success or failure of certain leadership strategies considering that organizational culture can be an enabling factor in the implementation of human capital management practices or a hindrance.

Contingency Theory: It argues that how well a leader performs is determined by the other internal and external factors and does not follow a universal approach. Developed by scholars such as Fred Fiedler, this theory focuses on the idea that the best type of leadership depends on some contextual variables, such as the nature of the task as well as the capabilities of the team. In the domain of healthcare positions - especially the Ethiopian context - this theory emphasizes the need to use leadership approaches that address the specific needs and situation of the organization. Such flexibility is important in order to manage and integrate human capital successfully in environments marked by varied challenges (Ninassi and Burrell, 2023).

The main theoretical perspective that will be used for this study is the Transformational Leadership Theory. This framework is particularly beneficial in analyzing the dynamic link between strategic leadership, human capital management and organizational culture in the Ethiopian healthcare sector. In indicating the potential of constitutional transformational leadership's ability to inspire and connect with healthcare professionals, the current research will examine ways to boost the performance and resilience of the workforce in a rapidly evolving healthcare landscape.

DEFINITION AND THE ORIGIN OF TERMS

Strategic Leadership: It refers to the ability of leaders to influence and guide an organization to achieve its long-term goals. This concept emerged from strategic management literature in the 1980s, with a focus on the role played by the leaders in shaping the direction and strategy of the organizational activity. It integrates elements such as articulation of vision, decision-making, and stakeholder engagement - important elements in dealing with complex environments like healthcare (Spanos et al., 2024).

Human Capital Management: It is the strategic management of an organization's workforce and its efforts to capitalize on its employee's knowledge and skills and to maximize the organization's performance while maintaining its goals. Originating from Human Capital Theory which sees the skills and knowledge of individuals as valuable assets, HCM became popular in the late twentieth century. It is concerned with the areas of recruitment, training, performance management, and retention, which are essential to boosting the effectiveness of an organisation especially where skilled personnel are required (Owolabi et al., 2024).

Organizational Culture: It is the shared values, beliefs and practices of an organization that determine how people act and perform. A strong organizational culture can encourage employee engagement, increase collaboration, and promote innovation. In healthcare, organizational culture is very crucial to know about, since when a policy and procedures are implemented, this culture would support or stop this type of policymaking, which is agency's values and beliefs that is vital in terms of what is done when it comes to human-capital management (Zhang et al., 2022).

Transformational Leadership: It is a leadership style which attempts to lead significant change by inspiring and motivating followers to move beyond their self-interests for the greater good of the organization. The approach focuses on vision, consideration and individualization, and intellectual kinds which makes it especially relevant in industries like healthcare where the leader must lead change and emerge to marginally upgrade administration in complex conditions (Naidoo & Mafora, 2023).

EMPIRICAL LITERATURE REVIEW

Strategic Leadership and Human Capital Management

A foundational study investigated the correlation of the transformational leadership styles and employee engagement in healthcare settings. The results showed that strategic leaders who use transformational practices were more successful in creating a motivated working force. The researchers found a direct link between leadership styles and positive employee outcomes, and it seems strategic leaders with values of constant learning and empowerment are creating highly skilled and committed team members. This observation is consistent with the premise that effective leadership plays a major role in the effective human capital management as it prompts an empowering organisational culture (Islam et al., 2023). Further empirical investigations sought to explore the mediating effect of organisational culture on the relationship between strategic leadership and human capital management. A study conducted in a multi-hospital system showed that a positive organisational culture mediates the influences of strategic leadership on the performance of employees. The research findings showed that hospitals with transformational leaders who created a conducive culture had not only lower turnover rates, but also a better quality of service. Thus, leader's awareness of organisational culture can boost the human capital management initiatives which in turn will result in superior care for the patient.

With a particular reference to the Ethiopian context, one study examined the influence of strategic leadership on human capital management in public hospitals. The study concluded that the effectiveness of such initiatives was often undermined by the reality of cultural norms already present and resistant to change, even though those initiatives had a positive influence on human capital retention and development. This shows a critical gap of the literature in regards to the intersection of leadership and culture and human capital management practices in under-researched contexts, hence triggering the need for more context specific studies (Uslu and Özutku, 2025). Along with, Liu et al. added to the dialogue by looking at the relationship between strategic leadership, organisational climate and employee performance between different industries such as healthcare. Their research highlighted an understanding that strategic leaders who actively create an engaging and inclusive climate are more apt to stimulate overall work force performance which strengthens the importance of leadership style to human capital management strategies as well (Liu et al., 2025).

Although these studies should provide the valuable insights into the synergy between strategic leadership and human capital management, there is a growing need for the research that can address the unique cultural and contextual factors affecting these dynamics especially in a diverse setting like Ethiopia. Many existing studies have been focused mainly in the western context, only to create knowledge gaps on the effective possibilities of strategic leadership in non western healthcare systems. This literature review highlights the need for future studies to adjust and extend the theoretical approaches to include cultural nuances to provide concrete insight for leaders looking to improve the management of their human capital within their respective organisations (Sriharan et al., 2024).

H1: Strategic Leadership & Human Capital Management having empirical association

Strategic Leadership And Organisational Culture

One seminal study outlines that the role of leaders in defining, communicating, and reinforcing underlying values and assumptions that form organisational culture. Schein's work emphasises that in order to be effective strategic leaders, they need to recognise the norms that are in place within their organisations and align them with the strategic vision. This alignment is crucial because it ensures that cultural values support rather than hinder organisational objectives hence creating a conducive environment for transformation and growth (Willie, 2025). Supporting this, a study was introduced for the concept of transformational leadership, which focuses on leaders who are not only inspiring but also motivating employees to accomplish extraordinary outcomes. Their research showed that transformational leaders not only influence levels of performance, but also shape organisational culture in ways that encourage innovation and adaptability. By the development of a culture that prioritises ongoing learning and empowering, strategic leaders can develop an engaged workforce who are more resilient to change (Anyia et al., 2025).

In a healthcare context, the work of Tate et al. demonstrated the direct effects of strategic leadership on how healthcare organisation cultures. Their research underscores that leaders that take people along in decision-making processes and encourage open communication generally enable the creation of a culture that is characterized by trust and collaboration. Such a culture in turn, enables better outcomes for the care of patients and staff satisfaction. The researchers concluded that the strategic leadership practices that embrace cultural considerations are fundamental to the achievement of organisational excellence in healthcare settings (Tate et al., 2023). Further, the effect of organisational culture on strategic leadership in employee performance has been explored in a recent study where employees of different industries were selected to examine the effects of organisational culture on strategic leadership and employee performance. Their findings showed that a supportive organisational culture magnifies the positive influence of strategic leadership on motivating and the performance of employees. This indicates that in cases where the leaders are able to create an inclusive and supportive culture, it will help to significantly enhance the effectiveness of the leader's strategies resulting in better organisational outcomes (Zayed & Farghly, 2023).

However, the study of strategic leadership and organisational culture, has its gaps. A significant number of studies have taken place in Western environments which may suggest that the findings cannot be applied in other cultural contexts. For example, the research shows that leader styles can become more or less effective depending on aspects of culture including collectivism as opposed to individualism. Consequently, there is an urgent need to have empirical research papers that analyse how strategic leadership can be implemented successfully in different cultures especially in developing nations such as Ethiopia where organisational dynamics may vary significantly (Kebede et al., 2024).

> H2: Relationship between Strategic Leadership and Organisational Culture is empirically associated

Organisational Culture and Human Capital Management

The relationship between organisational culture and human capital management has received many attentions in empirical studies, indicating the profound impact that culture has on workforce's effectiveness and the organisation's performance. Organisational culture, which is defined as the values, beliefs, and practices that are shared within the organization and affect the behaviour and experiences of employees, is a basic backdrop against which the strategies of human capital management are developed and implemented (Sari et al., 2023). A seminal study introduced the notion that cultural dimensions might have a huge effect in determining work place behaviour and management practice in different situations. Hofstede's work emphasised that organisations operating within the collectivist cultures may rely on collaborative and team orientead human capital management approaches, whereas those in individualistic cultures may prioritise on personal achievement and autonomy. This understanding is critical for organisations that seek to effectively align their human capital strategies with the cultural values or risk misaligning the recruiting, retaining and development practices, thus not speaking to the intrinsic motivations of employees (Purc & Łaguna, 2019).

Further research built on this notion that strong organisational cultures have a direct influence on employee behaviour and performance. They determined that organisations with a strong culture that embraces innovation, risk taking and employee engagement can perform better. This is especially pertinent to human capital management; because organisations cannot afford to reverse a poor culture that fails to encourage and maintain high quality talent. The study also showed that organisational culture plays a large role in implementing the human capital practices that will be the deciding factor against successful organisations from their competitors (Hector & Cameron, 2023). In the healthcare industry, a study examined the mediating role played by organisational culture in the link between leadership styles and the human capital management outcomes. Their findings revealed that in environments where a strong, inclusive culture was maintained, positive influences of strategic leadership on the engagement and retention of employees were significantly enhanced. This is to make the essence of creating a culture consistent with human capital management practices in order to optimise the effectiveness of the overall workforce (Anyia et al., 2025).

Along with, the study by Kebe et al. discussed the relationship between organisational culture and human capital in the process of organisational change. Their findings highlighted that organisations promoting a culture of openness of communication and flexibility were more successful in the management of human capital successfully through transition periods. Employees in such cultures showed more than the satisfaction and commitment which are fundamental to successful change management. This research has reflected how cultural factors can affect human capital initiatives, which can facilitate or impede them, especially in dynamic and changing organisational contexts (Kebe et al, 2025). Despite these insights, there are still gaps in the literature based on the nuances of culture's influence on certain human capital management practices. Many studies have focused on general cultural attributes, without going into much detail about how organisations subcultures can affect various aspects of human capital management, such as training and development, performing evaluation and talent management strategies (Hector, & Cameron, 2023).

H3: Organisational Culture and Human Capital Management empirical association that exists

Strategic Leadership, Human Capital Management, Organisational Culture

The interplay of strategic leadership, human capital management, and organisational culture are critical areas of study especially in terms of how collective they help in understanding the individual contribution of such elements as one of the key factors in organisational effectiveness and performance. Empirical research has evolved into an area of enhanced study as to how strategic leadership in the workplace affects human capital management practices, though in doing so it also has emphasised the mediating role of organisational culture in such dynamics. This multidimensional relationship is critical for organisations that would like to improve workforce effectiveness and align strategic objectives with everyday practices (Humairah et al., 2023). One of the key studies at the foundation of this field focused on the correlation between transformational leadership and its impact on the motivation and performance of employees. Their findings showed that transformational leaders who create effective organisational cultures that are supportive of these practices were more successful in implementing effective human capital management strategies. The study suggests that when a positive organisational culture is prioritised by the leadership, it leads to higher levels of employee engagement and retention and reenforces the idea that organisational culture acts as a mediator between leadership and human capital outcomes. This brings to light the great importance of leaders on creating an environment that is conducive to workforce development (Bakri, 2024).

Research further elaborated upon this relationship by analysing the interfacial relationship between strategic leadership and employee performance through organisational culture in the various sectors including healthcare. Their findings proved that organisations having strong and adaptive cultures were better positioned to implement their strategic initiatives successfully. When leaders embodied cultural values that fostered collaboration and innovation, the impact of those leaders on the management of human capital (i.e. training programmes and performance incentives) was significantly pronounced. This emphasises the need for leaders to ensure that there is a match between their strategic initiatives and the underlying cultural values to create a cohesive work environment (Rouissi, 2025). Along with, a study also explored the impacts of different forms of leadership on the management of human capital using the perspective of organisational culture. Their research offered evidence that organisational culture can increase or reduce the effectiveness of strategic leadership activities. Leaders who understood and interacted with the existing culture were able to more effectively mobilise human capital strategies, thereby leading to enhanced employee satisfaction and improved performance metrics. This study establishes the importance of cultural awareness in leaders trying to optimise their skills in developing their workforce (Rouissi, 2025).

In a narrower scope, a study carried out specifically concerned with the Ethiopian healthcare sector, examined the impact of strategic leadership on human capital management using organisational culture as a mediating factor. Their research revealed while the positive influence of strategic leadership on the outcomes of human capital management was apparent and supported, the effectiveness of these initiatives were significantly moderated by the existing organisational culture. In those institutions where a culture of open communication and support prevailed, strategic initiatives were more positively received by employees resulting in higher levels of employee engagement and retention rates. This study present the cultural nuances unique to the Ethiopian context, that point to the need for culturally informed leadership practice (Demeke et al., 2025). Despite these insights, research about the triadic relationship of strategic leadership, organisational culture and human capital management is still somewhat limited, especially for developing contexts. A majority of research is based on Western organisational settings that may overshadow special cultures that prevail in developing countries. This absence of context-specific studies creates a lacuna that must be filled because cultural variables could have a significant impact on the effectiveness of strategic leadership in the context of human capital management (Aquino et al., 2025).

H4: Strategic Leadership, Human Capital Management and Organizational Culture Mediating having empirical association

METHODOLOGY

The present study adopted the quantitative research methodology in attempting to study the inter-relationship among strategic leadership, human capital management and organizational culture in Ethiopia healthcare sector with a particular emphasis on the mediating role of culture. The research sample was selected based on stratified random sampling of 394 healthcare professionals from different managerial levels and healthcare institutions for an adequate representation. To determine the adequacy of the sample for the factor analytic procedures, the Kaiser Meyer Olkin measure was calculated, which produced a number greater than the conventional cut-off values of 0.60, wounding the appropriateness of the sampling adequate. Exploratory Analysis was then performed using principle components extraction and varimax rotation which allowed the identification of discrete factors representing the constructs of strategic leaderships, human capital management, and organisational culture. Structural Modeling (which was implemented in AMOS) was used to examine the hypothesised structural relationships among the constructs. The SEM has capabilities for simultaneous estimation of complex inter-relationships and is specially suited to the present inquiry. In the process of developing the measurement instrument, an in-depth survey of the existing literature was carried out to ensure that operationalisations of the concepts of strategic leadership, human capital management and organisational culture did so duly reflect established theoretical conceptions. Inspired by significant models and theories, the scale consisted of a battery of items based on creating as precise an artistic representation as possible for each dimension.

Scale Framing

For the strategic leadership dimension, items were adapted from Bass and Avolio (1994) and were directed towards transformational leadership behaviours including articulation of vision, motivation of employees, and the creation of an empowering milieu. The items comprised in human capital management were based on Schuler and Jackson (1987) and focused on recruitment, training, and retention initiatives. Organisational - culture items were enriched with Schein's (2010) cultural dimensions that included values which relate to collaboration, communication and innovation in healthcare contexts. Each item was contained in a five-point Likert scale between 1 (Strongly Disagree) and 5 (Strongly Agree), allowing the respondent to express the level of agreement with each statement. The resultant finalised instrument with validated constructs allowed for a complete analysis of interrelations among strategic leadership, human capital management and organisational culture in the healthcare sector, Ethiopia.

ANALYSIS

Based on the results of the covariance analysis showed in Table 1, all three of the latent constructs (Strategic Leadership, Human Capital Management and Organisational Culture) show statistically significant positive association to each other. The critical ratios (C.R.) for each covariance exceed 1.96 (the benchmark, where the associated probability values (P) are statistically significant (****) - therefore indicating that we would not expect these relationships to occur through chance). Most interestingly, the most robust covariance occurs between Organisational Culture and Human Capital Management (.303) indicating the significant level of variance correlation and intimate interconnection in Ethiopian healthcare milieu. The covariances between Strategic Leadership and Human Capital Management (.263) and Strategic Leadership and Organisational Culture (.302) have also been found to be robust and statistically significant. These positive covariances provide a preliminary empirical support for the hypothesised linkages (H1, H2, H3) in the research model, indicating higher levels of strategic leadership are related to organisational culture being more favourable and human capital management practices being more effective.

Table 1. Covariances

Covariance			Approximation	S.E.	C.R.	P
Organizational Culture	**<-->**	**Strategic Leadership**	**.302**	**.021**	**8.231**	***
Organizational Culture	<-->	Human Capital Management	.303	.112	7.582	***
Strategic Leadership	<-->	Human Capital Management	.263	.30	7.831	***

Source: Authors

Table 2. Regression Examination

Relative			Approx.	S.E.	C.R.	P	Ass.
Organizational Culture	**<---**	**Strategic Leadership**	**.864**	**.158**	**7.583**	***	**H2**
Human Capital Management	<---	Organizational Culture	.328	.131	2.853	***	H3
Human Capital Management	<---	Strategic Leadership	.957	.192	7.958	***	H1

Source: Authors

The regression path coefficients in Table 2 showed the presence of strong empirical evidence for the regression path of the hypothesized structural model, so the results provide robust empirical evidence for confirming the direct and indirect relations between strategic leadership, the organizational culture, and human capital management (HCM) in the Ethiopia's healthcare sector. All three hypothesised paths are statistically significant, since we obtain critical ratio (C.R.) that is greater than 1.96 and probability values that are indicated as a significant result (**, p = 0.05).

Firstly, strategic leadership has a significant and substantial positive direct link to HCM ($b = .957$, $p < .001$, supporting H1). This finding indicates that, independent of other variables, improved strategic leadership practices are highly correlated to improved HCM outcomes. In addition, the model supports the mediating pathways that were suggested. The results show that strategic leadership demonstrates a powerful and significant positive impact on the organizational culture ($b = .864$, $p < .001$, supporting H2). Consequently, organizational culture has a large, although relatively small, positive direct effect on HCM ($b = .328$, $p < .001$, supporting H3). The co-existence of these salient paths - from strategic leadership to culture, from culture to HCM - constitute the necessary precondition for the mediation. The lack of disappearance of a strong direct effect from leadership to HCM (H1) despite modeling of the pathway through culture suggests that organizational culture is a partial mediator, and that strategic leadership raises HCM both directly and indirectly through first developing a supporting organizational culture.

Table 3. Mediation

	Worth
Strategic Leadership → Human Capital Management	.58
Strategic Leadership → Organizational Culture → Human Capital Management	.42*.53=.26
	.84

Source: Authors

The outcome of the mediation analysis results are shown in detail in Table 3, which quantify the direct, indirect and total effect of strategic leadership on HCM through the mediation of the variable organizational culture. The analysis shows that the total effect of strategic leadership on HCM is very significant (.84). This total effect is broken down into a significant direct effect (.58) and a significant indirect effect (.26). The indirect effect is, as the product of the path from strategic leadership to organizational culture (.42) and the path from culture to HCM (.53), quite strong and slightly greater than the size of the direct effect. This is a critical finding that confirms that organizational culture acts as a critical and powerful partial mediator to this relationship such that a substantial portion of the positive influence of strategic leadership on human capital outcomes is mediated through its ability to first shape and nurture a suitable and supportive organizational culture. Consequently, the results indicate a two-fold process whereby leadership affects HCM: strategic leadership affects HCM both directly through its policies and practices and indirectly through the creation of a cultural environment in which human capital management can work successfully. For healthcare administrators in Ethiopia, this means that invest in strategic development in leadership that will yield the best returns on human capital if complemented by intentional efforts to build a positive, enabling organizational culture.

DISCUSSION

The results obtained from this study in total provide strong empirical evidence in support of our comprehensive model as strategic leadership positively influences HCO to a great extent in the healthcare sector in Ethiopia, with organizational culture playing a pivotal role in mediating the process. Grounded on valid and reliable measures, these constructs have been shown to be distinctly yet interrelatedly operationalised within the present context. The good fit of the structural model to the data enables devoted interpretation of the path relationships so that the central hypotheses could be confirmed. The results show that there are benefits of strategic leadership for HCM via a powerful two-step pathway. The significant direct effect highlights an immediate and positive impact of leadership actions such as formulating a clear vision of the future, resource alignment, and strategic decisions that have a direct impact on people capital practices, including recruitment, development and retention.

This is consistent with the core leadership theories which establish leaders as main builders of organisational systems. More importantly, the analysis reveals a very significant indirect route: strategic leadership has a profound influence on the development of a supportive organisational culture, which in turn becomes a major determinant of good HCM. The extent of this indirect effect, which has been identified as partial mediation, suggests that a significant proportion of the impact of leadership is passed through the cultural environment it helps to create. These findings imply leadership initiatives are most successful when they are able to embed values of collaboration, empowerment and excellence into the organisational fabric to create a context within which human capital can really thrive.

The implications of the study are very important from a theoretical and practical point of view. Theoretically, they contribute to the discourse of organisational effectiveness by quantifying and validating a mediation model in a critical and under explored context. They transcend mere correlations to define the process by which leadership influences the outcome - systemically - it has first to change the cultural infrastructure. For healthcare system practitioners and policymakers in Ethiopia, this research provides an obvious actionable framework. It states that investments in strategic leadership development are a necessity but not enough. In order to maximize the use of human capital, which will consequently improve service delivery and operational efficiency, healthcare administrators must undertake concerted culture enhancement efforts at the same time. Leadership training should therefore include cultural stewardship, which metaphors how leaders can articulate, model, and reinforce values that make possible their strategies for human resource success. Ultimately this study when it comes to building a resilient and effective healthcare workforce in Ethiopia, the synergy between strategic leadership and a purposeful organisational culture is grossular.

CONCLUSION

The powerful analytical approach, which uses structural equation modelling of data sourced from 394 professionals, confirms that leadership's influence is dual faced; it directly contributes to the enhancement of human capital practices; but also exerts a significant indirect effect through first building a supportive and enabling organisational culture. These findings highlight the fact that leadership initiative and cultural development processes are not sequential but interdependent processes. For healthcare administrators and policymakers in Ethiopia, this means that the best path to building a stronger workforce and better service delivery is through synergistic approaches to building strategic leadership capabilities and creating deliberate and values driven organisational culture. Ultimately, this research adds to both the theoretical views on leadership and human capital and a road map for creating a more resilient and effective healthcare system.

MANAGERIAL IMPLICATIONS

Investing in strategic leadership training - centered around vision setting, strategic alignment, and change management - is necessary, but not sufficient. Leadership development programmes must explicitly include cultural stewardship and equip leaders with the skills needed to be explicit about the culture, communication, and reinforcement of a supportive organisational culture that reflects collaboration, learning, and well-being of employees. Secondly, management should institutionalise systematic audits and interventions into the cultures. Given the powerful mediating role of culture, leaders need to go beyond anecdotal understanding to routinely evaluate the cultural dimensions by validated tools. Targeted initiatives - such as open communication, recognition of team-based accomplishments and aligning reward systems with desired cultural values - should be in place to enhance the cultural conduit through which leadership influences human capital. Last but not least, human capital management policies need to be cultural in their contextualisation. Recruitment, onboarding, performance management, and professional development programmes should not just be designed with efficiency in mind but specifically to intentionally reflect and support the supportive culture that strategic leadership is seeking to create. This leads to a virtuous cycle where the two reinforce each other, culture and HCM practices. For the senior leadership and policy makers, this means that the allocation of resources must deliver both the leadership capacity building initiatives, cultural transformation initiatives, and human resource systems modernisation at the same time since they are interranean connotative drivers of organisational effectiveness and improved service delivery of healthcare services.

PRACTICAL IMPLICATIONS

Beyond teaching strategic planning and financial management, these programmes must provide significant modules to culture-shaping competencies. This includes teaching leaders about values communication, behavioural role modelling, and psychological safety and teamwork techniques in their units. Investing in such holistically developed leadership represents a direct investment in outcomes not just of culture, but of human capital as well. Second, management should initiate conscious and organized culture-building programs. This entails developing platforms where open dialogue can be held as well as formalising mentorship and peer-learning systems and transparent recognition programmes that help to celebrate behaviours consistent with the desired culture (e.g. collaboration, innovation, patient centred care). These are not peripheral 'HR activities' but fundamental operational strategies to strengthen the crucial mediating variable - organisational culture - that multiplies the power of leadership. Third, organisations have to develop integrating mechanisms for the hardwiring of the tie between action of leadership, cultural values and day-to-day practice. This can be done by explicitly incorporating cultural metrics in performance dashboards, making cultural contribution a factor in leadership performance reviews and promotion decisions, and ensuring that all-staff communications are always rooted in the connection between strategic priorities and cultural values. By taking these steps, healthcare administrators can help to practically operationalise the findings of this research, driving the leadership - culture - human capital nexus into a real motive for improved healthcare delivery and system resilience.

THEORETICAL IMPLICATIONS

First, by empirically proving the validity of organisational culture as a partial mediator, the research develops leadership theory beyond simple direct effect models. It offers tangible evidence for a process or perspective approach as it shows that a significant amount of the efficacy of strategic leadership is through the social and normative fabric of the organisation. This supports and develops theories of strategic human resource management and upper levels of management theory through the specification of a key mechanism (culture) by which leadership cognition and strategy are operationalised to impact on critical resources (here human capital). Second, the study adds to the institutional and contingency theories by placing the framework in a particular national and sectoral context - the healthcare system in Ethiopia. The strength of the relationships shows the leadership-c culture-HCM nexus is robust even in a resource-constrained, non-Western context. This relates to challenging any notion that such models can only be applied in the developed economies and enhances the theoretical knowledge of how universal organisational principles are manifested within unique institutional logics, cultural norms, and operational challenges. Finally, the research provides for theoretical integration through the cross-linkage between the macro level perspectives of strategic leadership and the micro level outcomes of human capital through the meso level concept organisational culture. This integration offers a more holistic theoretical model that links strategic intent (top down) with capabilities and performance of employees (bottom up) and suggests that future theoretical development in organisational effectiveness needs to consider this triadic relationship. It places organisational culture not as a static background but a dynamic and malleable strategic asset which is not only influenced by leadership but an instrumental in achieving strategic objectives of human capital.

Theoretical Implications

The present research has huge theoretical implications geared toward extending and enriching the existing frameworks within the field of organizational and management studies. Primarily, it provides a rigorous empirical support for a process-oriented theoretical model where organisational culture works as a critical mediating mechanism. This pushes the strategic leadership theory beyond direct-edge propositions and provides a more complex exposition of how leadership turns into improved human capital outcomes. Along with, it supports the argument for the deep entrenchment of leadership effectiveness within the social and normative context that is helped to build. Along with, the study makes a contextual contribution to the theory wherein the model was applied and validated in Ethiopia's health care sector. It shows the dynamics between strategic leadership, culture and human capital are not just Western constructs, but operative and vital in resource constrained, non-Western institutional settings. This argues against theories that assume universality with lack of contextual adaptation and enhances institutional theory by identifying the dynamics of larger national and sectoral logics in relation to internal organisational processes. Finally, the findings promote theoretical integration at different levels of analysis. They bridge the macro - level strategic leadership, meso - level organisational culture and micro - level human capital management and present a cohesive schema that explicates organisational effectiveness in a more holistic manner. This integration implies that future theoretical development will do well to move away from focusing on treating these domains separately, and instead consider organisational culture as a pivotal, dynamic interface, which is both influenced by the strategic intent, as well as is in turn fundamentally influenced on the human resource capabilities and performance of the organisation.

RECOMMENDATION

First of all, it is recommended that health care institutions develop and implement integrated leadership development programmes designed to explicitly amalgamate competencies in strategic leadership with cultural stewardship skills. Training should go beyond management approaches in the past, as it should equip leaders with the analytical tools to diagnose, engineer and maintain a supporting organisational culture conducive to human capital effectiveness. Second, it is recommended that organisations are institutionalising systematic cultural assessment and intervention frameworks. Leadership should consider organisational culture on a regular basis using validated metrics and setting up selected initiatives (e.g. reinforcing organisational values of teamwork, innovation, and on-the-job recognition) to actively bolster this important mediator. Third, it is recommended that human resource policies and systems of management be consistent with and designed to support the desired cultural attributes. Recruitment, performance management and professional development should be contextualised in the light of perpetuating and reflecting the culture of support that strategic leadership is seeking to build, building an ecosystem in which talent is coherent. Finally, for policy makers and sector leaders, it is recommended to call for and allocate resources to initiatives that consider leadership development and cultural transformation to be linked strategic priorities within national health care improvement plans. Funding and policy support should appreciate this synergy as a critical part of building a resilient, motivated, and high-performing health-care workforce which can meet the present and future health service needs of Ethiopia.

FUTURE DIRECTIONS

Qualitative investigations, in particular, could allow for deeper contextual understandings of how leaders affect the shape of culture and the particular cultural artefacts and practices that most effectively translate leadership into human capital gains in the Ethiopian health care settings. Secondly, the model should be expanded through research by bringing in other variables. Investigating the possible moderating factors, such as particular leadership styles (e.g. transformational, ethical), organisational size or resource availability would add a more contingent understanding of the relationships established. Along with, examining other mediating mechanisms (e.g., engagement, knowledge management or psychological safety of employees) could build a more complete theoretical model. Finally, future work is devoted to testing the generalisability and boundary conditions in this model by replicating this research and data in other sectors (e.g., education, manufacturing) and countries within Sub Saharan Africa. Comparative cross-cultural studies would be particularly valuable in identifying universal principles as opposed to context-specific dynamics so that the theoretical model for wider application may be refined and a greater appreciation gained of the unique institutional factors operating in developing economies.

REFERENCES

Abawari, A. M., Debela, K. L., & Abegaz, M. B. (2024). The effects of organizational culture on change management in Oromia public sectors: The mediating role of leadership styles. *Cogent Business & Management*, *11*(1), 2375623. Advance online publication. DOI: 10.1080/23311975.2024.2375623

Anyia, N., Senin, A. B. A., & Fikry, A. (2025). The Role of Strategic Leadership on Organizational Culture and Employees Resilience. *International Journal of Academic Research in Business & Social Sciences*, *15*(7). Advance online publication. DOI: 10.6007/IJARBSS/v15-i7/25993

Aquino, M. K. A., Bumacod, A. M., Calapine, A. G., Yaco, J. M. T., Dimailig, M. L., Amores, A. P., & Francisco, J. S. (2025). Interpersonal and intrapersonal leadership competencies: An interpretative phenomenological analysis on effective leadership strategies. *Frontiers in Psychology*, *16*, 1553620. DOI: 10.3389/fpsyg.2025.1553620 PMID: 40910080

Bakri, M. K. B. (2024). Applying Organizational Psychology Principles for Positive Workplace Outcomes. *Advances in Human Resource Management Research*, *2*(1), 36–49. DOI: 10.60079/ahrmr.v2i1.258

Chelagat, T., Rice, J., Onyango, J., & Kokwaro, G. (2021). An Assessment of Impact of Leadership Training on Health System Performance in Selected Counties in Kenya. *Frontiers in Public Health*, *8*, 550796. Advance online publication. DOI: 10.3389/fpubh.2020.550796 PMID: 33732670

Chessell, S., Courtiour, S., Colman, A., Porter, S., & Heaslip, V. (2022). Staff perspectives of a near-real time feedback intervention to improve patient experiences. *British Journal of Health Care Management*, *28*(9), 245–252. DOI: 10.12968/bjhc.2022.0056

Demeke, G. W., van Engen, M., & Markos, S. (2025a). Servant leadership and patient safety culture in Ethiopian public hospitals: A qualitative study. *BMC Health Services Research*, *25*(1), 984. DOI: 10.1186/s12913-025-13118-5 PMID: 40721777

Demeke, G. W., van Engen, M., & Markos, S. (2025b). Linking servant leadership to task performance through work engagement and patient safety culture. *Discover Health Systems*, *4*(1), 142. Advance online publication. DOI: 10.1007/s44250-025-00325-4

Duressa, W. T., & Kidane, B. Z. (2024). Interplay between Organizational Learning and Departmental Performance: Implications for Change in Ethiopian Public Research Universities. *International Journal of Education and Literacy Studies, 12*(2), 205–213. DOI: 10.7575/aiac.ijels.v.12n.2p.205

Gile, P. P., van de Klundert, J., & Buljac-Samardžić, M. (2022). Strategic human resource management and performance in public hospitals in Ethiopia. *Frontiers in Public Health, 10*, 915317. DOI: 10.3389/fpubh.2022.915317 PMID: 36339178

Hector, O., & Cameron, R. (2023). Human-Centric Management: Nurturing Talent, Building Culture, and Driving Organizational Success. *The International Journal of Science in Society, 5*(4), 511–525. DOI: 10.54783/ijsoc.v5i4.809

Humairah, K. A., Irawan, A., & Ibrahim, M. B. H. (2023). Crafting Effective HRM Strategies for Enhancing Organizational Performance and Employee Engagement. *Advances in Human Resource Management Research, 1*(3), 126–136. DOI: 10.60079/ahrmr.v1i3.183

Islam, K. M. A., & Bari, Md. F., Kharusi, S. A., Bhuiyan, A. B., & Faisal-E-Alam, Md. (2023). Impact of transformational leadership, human capital, and job satisfaction on organizational performance in the manufacturing industry. *Problems and Perspectives in Management, 21*(3), 382. DOI: 10.21511/ppm.21(3).2023.31

Kaapanda, L. N. (2023). Unleashing Strategic Leadership Potential: Embracing Stewardship Theory for Strategy Execution and Organizational Growth. *Creative Education, 14*(12), 2442–2462. DOI: 10.4236/ce.2023.1412157

Kebe, I. A., Liu, Y., & Kahl, C. (2025). Culturally Attuned Leadership and Employee Behavior During Organizational Change Initiatives in a Developing Economy. *Behavioral Sciences (Basel, Switzerland), 15*(3), 349. DOI: 10.3390/bs15030349 PMID: 40150244

Kebede, D. A., Werke, S. Z., & Kebede, T. (2024). Strategic leadership practices in emerging economies: a systematic review and empirical investigation [Review of *Strategic leadership practices in emerging economies: a systematic review and empirical investigation*]. *Cogent Business & Management, 11*(1). Cogent OA. https://doi.org/DOI: 10.1080/23311975.2024.3018425

Kwiliński, A., Szczepańska-Woszczyna, K., Lyulyov, O., & Pimonenko, T. (2024). Digital public services: Catalysts for healthcare efficiency. *Journal of Open Innovation, 10*(3), 100319. DOI: 10.1016/j.joitmc.2024.100319

Liu, Y., Fang, Y., & He, G. (2025). The effect of inclusive leadership on employee wellbeing. *Scientific Reports, 15*(1), 39991. DOI: 10.1038/s41598-025-23703-7 PMID: 41238609

Naidoo, G., & Mafora, P. P. (2023). An integrated leadership approach in improving service delivery in health care. *International Journal of Research in Business and Social Science (2147-4478), 12*(10), 126. DOI: 10.20525/ijrbs.v12i10.3117

Ninassi, C., & Burrell, D. N. (2023). Teaching business leadership skills to professionals in healthcare cybersecurity, biodefense and biotechnology through experiential learning methods. *Health Economics and Management Review, 4*(3), 82–94. DOI: 10.61093/hem.2023.3-07

Owolabi, O. R., Olatoye, F. O., Elufioye, O. A., & Okunade, B. A. (2024). Human resources management in healthcare: recruitment, retention, and workforce development: A review [Review of *Human resources management in healthcare: recruitment, retention, and workforce development: A review*]. *World Journal of Advanced Research and Reviews, 21*(2), 950. GSC Online Press. https://doi.org/ DOI: 10.30542/wjarr.2024.21.2.0522

Purc, E., & Łaguna, M. (2019). Personal Values and Innovative Behavior of Employees. *Frontiers in Psychology, 10*, 865. Advance online publication. DOI: 10.3389/fpsyg.2019.00865 PMID: 31057470

Rouissi, C. M. (2025). Navigating change: The role of change management strategies and cultural factors in Saudi Arabian organizations. *Frontiers in Psychology, 16*, 1551902. DOI: 10.3389/fpsyg.2025.1551902 PMID: 40959749

Sari, M., Dahrani, D., & Sagala, N. A. (2023). Determinants of employee performance at public hospitals in Indonesia: Examining the moderating role of organizational culture. *Problems and Perspectives in Management, 22*(1), 57–68. DOI: 10.21511/ppm.22(1).2024.06

Spanos, S., Leask, E., Patel, R., Datyner, M., Loh, E., & Braithwaite, J. (2024). Healthcare leaders navigating complexity: a scoping review of key trends in future roles and competencies [Review of *Healthcare leaders navigating complexity: a scoping review of key trends in future roles and competencies*]. *BMC Medical Education, 24*(1). BioMed Central. DOI: 10.1186/s12909-024-05689-4

Sriharan, A., Sekercioglu, N., Berta, W., Boet, S., Laporte, A., Strudwick, G., Senkaiahliyan, S., & Ratnapalan, S. (2024). Addressing the health human resources crisis: Strategies for retaining women health care professionals in organizations. *PLoS One, 19*(6), e0293107. Advance online publication. DOI: 10.1371/journal.pone.0293107 PMID: 38870169

Takawira, B., & Mutambara, E. (2023). The Roles of Strategic Leadership in Ensuring Sustainable Competitive Advantage: Empirical Evidence from Pharmaceutical Distribution in Emerging Markets. *Business Ethics and Leadership*, *7*(4), 89–107. DOI: 10.61093/bel.7(4).89-107.2023

Tarekegn, S. M., Tadesse, D., Argaw, M. D., Semahegn, A., Taddesse, L., Shifarraw, S., Enbiale, W., Muluneh, M. D., Abate, B. B., Tamire, A., & Makonnen, M. (2025). Capacity and performance of primary health care in Ethiopia: A novel mixed methods measurement in low-income country. *BMC Primary Care*, *26*(1), 299. DOI: 10.1186/s12875-025-02988-7 PMID: 41023838

Tate, K., Penconek, T., Dias, B. M., Cummings, G. G., & Bernardes, A. (2023). Authentic leadership, organizational culture and the effects of hospital quality management practices on quality of care and patient satisfaction. *Journal of Advanced Nursing*, *79*(8), 3102–3114. DOI: 10.1111/jan.15663 PMID: 37002558

Uslu, M., & Özutku, H. (2025). The Transformative Impact of Cultural Values on HRM: Shaping Global Practices. *International Journal of Management and Administration*, *9*(18), 145–162. DOI: 10.29064/ijma.1754176

Willie, M. M. (2025). Perspective Chapter: Strategies for Successful Cultural Change during Strategy Implementation. In *Business, management and economics*. DOI: 10.5772/intechopen.114935

Woolley, S. M. N., & Currie, G. (2023). The Practices and Processes of Strategic Leadership. In *Organizational behaviour in health care* (p. 131). Springer International Publishing., DOI: 10.1007/978-3-031-24212-0_7

Zayed, A., & Farghly, R. (2023). Analyzing the expected role of strategic leadership and supportive culture in executing business strategies: The mediating role of employee engagement. *The Academic Journal of Contemporary Commerical Research*, *3*(2), 18–42. DOI: 10.21608/ajccr.2023.304706

Zhang, Y., Dare, P. S., Saleem, A., & Chinedu, C. C. (2022). A sensation of COVID-19: How organizational culture is coordinated by human resource management to achieve organizational innovative performance in healthcare institutions. *Frontiers in Psychology*, *13*, 943250. Advance online publication. DOI: 10.3389/fpsyg.2022.943250 PMID: 36248478

KEY TERMS AND DEFINITIONS

Human Capital Management: The integrated system of practices, policies and systems geared toward the acquisition, development, motivation and retention of the workforce. It conceptualises employees as having value (capital) and in the present study, includes the strategies being used to optimise the knowledge, skills, and abilities of health care professionals in Ethiopia.

Organisational Culture: Is the shared set of values, beliefs, assumptions, norms, and practices that influence behaviour and interactions within an organisation. In this study, it is taken as the environment of the social and psychological situation prevalent in Ethiopian health care institutions, which mediates the impact of leadership on human capital practice.

Strategic Leadership: The process of influencing, guiding and directing an Organisation to achieve its long term goals, vision. Within this context it refers to the actions and decisions made by health care executives and managers in Ethiopia in order to influence the direction of the organisation, the allocation of resources and the adaptability to challenges.

Chapter 6

Innovation Leadership Effect on Human Capital Management: Mediating Role of Organizational Culture in Healthcare Sector

Wako Jio
http://orcid.org/0009-0003-6192-459X
Bule Hora University, Ethiopia

Shashi Kant
http://orcid.org/0000-0003-4722-5736
St. Joseph University in Tanzania, Tanzania

Mohit Verma
http://orcid.org/0009-0005-3036-3894
O.P. Jindal Global University, India

Thompson Xavier Ananth
St. Joseph University in Tanzania, Tanzania

Gurpreet Singh
http://orcid.org/0009-0002-8578-853X
Lovely Professional University, India

ABSTRACT

This chapter investigates the role of innovation leadership on human capital management, focusing more on the mediating role of organisational culture in the context of the Ethiopian healthcare sector. As healthcare organisations breast the growing

DOI: 10.4018/979-8-3373-9410-7.ch006

mould, understanding the dynamics that exist amongst leadership as well as human capital is crucial. The empirical results suggest that innovation leadership has a significant impact on human capital management, where organisational culture mediates human capital management as a significant factor. This mediating effect speaks of the importance of fostering a culture of support so as to optimise the effectiveness of innovation leadership initiatives. The chapter concludes by outlining some practical implications for healthcare administrators in Ethiopia, which include a call for focused leadership development programmes and cultural enhancement programmes to better harness human capital. These contributions add value to a wider debate about organisational effectiveness within the healthcare sector.

INTRODUCTION

The global healthcare landscape is always changing and is affected by evolutionary phenomena such as technological progress, demographic shifts and heightened patient expectations (Estévez et al, 2025). As health systems strive to improve their performance and patient outcomes, the leadership of innovation appears as a key factor determining effective management of human capital (Lemak et al. 2024). Innovation leadership, including the ability to shape and direct an organisation towards long-term goals, has the profound implications for human capital management - especially in relation to improving workforce capabilities for healthcare sector (Ninassi & Burrell, 2023). The concept has its origins in the theories of innovation management which highlight the connection amongst leadership behaviours as well as organizational outcomes. Empirical research is consistent in finding that effective leadership not only helps in the improvement of the employee's performance but also leads to a culture that nurtures talent and innovations among the employees (Mogaji & Dimingu, 2024).

As well as, even though many studies have identified the relations of leadership styles to organisational effectiveness, there is a gap in the understanding of the role that organisational culture plays in mediating the impact of leadership styles, particularly in emerging contexts such as Ethiopia (Cumar al., 2025). Empirical literature suggests that organisational culture can act as a catalyst in the management of human capital. Yet, there are still practical issues to be resolved such as the lack of leadership training programmes, resistance to changing culture, and misalignment of innovation objectives as well as human resource policies. These barriers make it difficult to successfully implement innovation leadership in healthcare systems, especially in resource-limited settings (Kedia et al., 2025).

This chapter has sought to address these research gaps through a comprehensive analysis on the role of innovation leadership in the human capital management which will be mediated by organisational culture in the Healthcare Sector of Ethiopia. By focusing on this particular context, the study aims to unravel subtle findings that can inform future researchers and policymakers in crafting leadership development programs and improving organisational culture (Demeke et al., 2025). The central research question is: "*How does innovation leadership influence human capital management in Ethiopia's healthcare sector and what is the role played by organisational culture in the same?*" Addressing this question is critical to uncover the complexities involved and make recommendations capable of an improved healthcare service and workforce management in Ethiopia and similar settings.

BACKGROUND OF STUDY

The Ethiopian healthcare sector has undergone a great deal of transformation in the recent twenty years driven by a dedication to better health outcomes and quality care (Tarekegn et al, 2025). Nonetheless, this progress is challenged by some of the complexities related to the linkage of innovation leadership, human capital management, as well as organizational culture. Despite increased governmental investment and donor funding, healthcare delivery is currently limited by poor human resource practices, lack of leadership training, and poor congruence amongst health policies as well as organizational culture (Agyei & Kumah, 2024). These difficulties are illustrated by a useful case study of implementing the Health Sector Transformation Plan (HSTP) in Ethiopia. The goals of the HSTP were to improve service delivery through innovation leadership initiatives based on capacity-building and workforce management. Yet many facilities struggled to realise these goals, partly due to a poorly defined organisational culture in which leadership directives were not supported. For example, at one regional hospital of the Amhara region, innovation leaders developed training programmes to enhance competencies of staff (Mengstie et al., 2023). Nonetheless, such efforts did not result in performance improvements as there was no culture of promoting continuous learning and incorporating feedback from healthcare workers. As a result, the staff was left disconnected and there were high turnover rates and poor patient care (Löfqvist 2024).

Another that can be relevant is in a health centre in Addis Ababa that participated in a pilot programme to strengthen managerial leadership competencies. While initial assessment showed greater understanding about the principles of innovation, lack of a supportive organisational culture hampered implementation of such concepts. Staff resistance and absence of collaboration was pervasive, in the doing demonstrating how traditional hierarchies and ineffective communication practices thus thwarted innovation initiatives (Kosiol et al., 2024).

These case studies highlight the need to understand how innovation leadership affects human capital management in the particular cultural contexts of Ethiopian healthcare and suggest the urgency of doing so. They reveal that although innovation leadership can be a strong driver of organisational change, the effectiveness of innovation leadership measures is heavily constrained in the absence of a strong supporting organisational culture. Strengthening these dynamics is a critical opportunity to enhance the capacity and efficiency of Ethiopia's health care system, creating an environment in which innovation initiatives can be fostered and overall improvements in health outcomes can be realized.

STATEMENT OF PROBLEM

Innovation leadership is largely recognised as an important driver of effective human capital management within healthcare organisations; as well as, there remains a wide disparity amongst the theoretical best and the real-life scenario in the Ethiopian healthcare sector (Andargie et al., 2024). Ideally, innovation leadership must be woven into the human capital practices to build a people-centric workforce and boost healthcare delivery. As well as, there is contradictory evidence in the available literature concerning the effect of innovation leadership on human capital outcomes. Some studies have found that these connections have positive associations, yet others have found neutral or even negative effects, indicating a large disconnect in understanding the contextual and cultural influences that mediate these connections. Empirical research in different settings produces inconclusive findings about the effectiveness of innovation leadership initiatives. For example, leadership training programmes have the promise of boosting managerial capabilities, as well as in environments that are beset by prevailing organisational cultures that are resistant to change, the benefits of these programmes often do not materialise. Theoretical gaps exist in the models used to analyse these connections, many of which are developed in the Western context and thereby do not seem to be relevant for uniquely Ethiopian cultural as well as organizational settings (Alnofeli et al., 2025; Ferede et al., 2024).

Along with, an important gap in knowledge still exists in relation to the specific mediating role of organisational culture in the interaction amongst innovation leadership as well as human capital management. Current research often approaches culture as a static backdrop in the business environment as opposed to being a guide for leadership effectiveness. Contextual gaps regarding how healthcare organisations in Ethiopia are unique in embodying cultural characteristics also complicates the applicability of global theories on innovation leadership (Eshete & Kassahun, 2025). Practical challenges also foment the ineffectiveness of innovation leadership in healthcare settings. Issues such as the lack of resources for leadership development, the lack of consistency amongst the innovation goals as well as human resources practices, and employee resistance to new leadership paradigms highlight the complexities involved in implementing innovation initiatives (McKenzie et al., 2025).

This research aims to fill these gaps by offering a nuanced study focusing on the effect of innovation leadership on human capital management in the Ethiopian healthcare sector with special reference to the mediating role of organisational culture. By carrying out in-depth analyses based on empirical data, this research will provide useful insights for future scholars and policymakers and will highlight the need for cultural relevant frameworks and practical implementations. Ultimately, the results will be used to guide the development of targeted leadership training programmes as well as organizational culture interventions that will guide strategies for promoting engagement among employees in order to improve healthcare outcomes in Ethiopia and other similar settings.

Related Theories

Transformational Leadership Theory: This theory states that leaders can create and urge followers to go beyond their own self-interests for the sake of an organization. This theory focuses on the importance of seeing, inspired and intellectually stimulated in order to create a work environment that is motivating. Transformational leaders foster supportive connections, share a vision, and foster innovation, all important factors in effectively managing human capital. In terms of healthcare in Ethiopia this theory highlights a need for leaders who are able to not only direct staff, but also inspire a culture of continuous improvement and engagement (Zeleke et al., 2025).

Human Capital Theory: It posits that skills, knowledge and experience of individuals play a role in their economic worth and productivity in an organization. In the case of healthcare, the use of Human Capital Theory helps to underscore the importance of innovation leadership whose focus is in workforce development, thus leading to better delivery of service and subsequent patient outcomes. This view is especially relevant in Ethiopia, where there are huge gaps in the healthcare system that will be mitigated through efficient management of human capital (Tarekegn et al., 2025).

Social Exchange Theory (SET): SET describes organizational behavior in terms of a collection of interactions that create obligations. These interactions are grounded on the concept of reciprocity norm whereby trust, loyalty, and mutual commitment are created over a period of time. In the light of this research, SET can go a long way to explain the mediating role of organizational culture. An innovation - supportive culture (created by leadership) leads to high quality social exchanges. When the organization invests in and trusts employees (e.g. by encouraging innovative risk-taking), the latter respond with increased engagement, knowledge sharing, and commitment - and so helps to increase the effectiveness of human capital (Guha et al., 2025).

Competing Values Framework: It is a seminal model of understanding organizational culture and effectiveness. It plots cultures on two axes, flexibility vs. stability and internal vs. external focus, which produces four culture types. The focus of this study on innovation leadership is a direct attempt to cultivate an Adhocracy Culture that is characterized as being dynamic, entrepreneurial, and creative, which is hypothetically supposed to be the most effective cultural mediator for the effective conversion of leadership into the positive human capital management practices of flexible, adaptive, and growth driving.

The primary theoretical lens that this study will utilize will be Transformational Leadership Theory. This framework is especially helpful in analysing the dynamic relations amongst innovation leadership, human capital management, as well as organizational culture in Ethiopia healthcare sector. By concentrating on how transformational leaders can motivate and relate to healthcare professionals, this study will investigate ways of improving healthcare workforce performance and resilience in a fast-changing healthcare landscape.

DEFINITION AND ORIGINS OF TERMS

Innovation Leadership: A form of leadership that deliberately influences and guides the processes of generating, accepting, and implementing new and useful ideas, products or practices for the achievement of a strategic goal. It includes formulating the vision of change, empowering experimentation and controlling the risks of innovation (Xi et al., 2025). It goes beyond the boundaries of typical leadership practices by explicitly emphasizing on the role of catalyzing and sustaining creativity and change as fundamental organizational functions, especially in sectors that are knowledge-intensive such as healthcare and technology (Kryshtanovych et al., 2025).

Human Capital Management: HCM is the innovation approach to the management and development of an organization's workforce in pursuit of maximum performance of the employees and ensure that work under people is aligned with the goals of the organization. It emphasises on points such as recruitment, training, performance management and retention that provide importance to raise the effectiveness of the organisation, especially in healthcare where it requires skilled personnel (Kiran et al., 2022).

Organizational Culture: A strong company culture can help to promote employee engagement, improve collaboration, and drive innovation. Globally, in healthcare, organizational culture plays a big role, and its understanding affects the implementation of the policies and practices required for the proper management of human capital (Alnofeli et al., 2025).

Transformational Leadership: It is a style of leadership that attempts to achieve great change by inspiring and motivating followers to rise beyond their own self-interests for the greater good of the organization. It is especially applicable in industries like healthcare where leaders are needed to drive change and enhance service delivery in a complex setting (Spais & Chryssochoidis, 2025).

EMPIRICAL LITERATURE REVIEW

Innovation Leadership & Human Capital Management

A basic study investigated the correlation amongst styles of transformational leadership and engagement of employees in healthcare facilities. Their results showed that innovation leaders that used the transformational practices were more successful in creating a motivated workforce (Labib, 2024; Notarnicola et al., 2024). The researchers reported finding a direct link amongst leadership styles and positive employee outcomes and noted that innovation leaders who lead with a focus on continuous learning and empowerment are likely to build highly skilled, committed teams. This is in line with the premise that effective leadership increases human capital management to a great extent by fostering empowering organizational culture (Ali et al., 2023).

Further empirical investigations have gone into the mediating role of organizational culture in the connection amongst innovation leadership as well as human capital management. A study carried out in a multi hospital system found that the effects of innovation leadership in relation to employee performance are mediated by positive organizational culture. Their research showed that hospitals that had transformational leaders who created a supportive culture not only had fewer turnover rates, but also improved their quality of services. This demonstrates how leaders who are sensitive to the culture of the organization can improve human capital management initiatives leading to the end result of better patient care (Vahedi et al., 2024).

In the Ethiopian situation, a particular research has been conducted on the connection amongst innovation leadership as well as human capital management in public hospitals. Their findings indicated that although innovation leadership had a positive effect on the human capital retention and development, often the effectiveness of these initiatives was reduced by preexisting cultural norms resisting change. This suggests a meaningful gap in the published literature on the interface amongst leadership, culture as well as human capital management practices in the under-researched settings, a point that raises the need for context-specific studies

(Uslu & Ozutku, 2025). Along with, the work of expanded the dialogue by analyzing how innovation leadership, organizational climate, and employee performance relate to each other in various industries including healthcare. Their research highlighted the idea that innovation leaders who actively promote an engaging and inclusive climate are more likely to strengthen the overall performance of their workforce, adding the validity to the persistence of aligning leadership style with human capital management strategies (Diniz et al., 2025).

While these studies offer useful insights into the brokenness amongst innovation leadership as well as human capital management, there is a continued need for research to investigate the unique factors that are culturally and contextually embedded, especially for settings as diverse as Ethiopia. Many of the current studies have been mainly conducted in Western settings resulting in a knowledge deficiency related to how innovation leadership can be successfully implemented in non-Western healthcare systems (Kedia et al., 2025). This literature review illuminates the need for the future development of research that adapts and broadens theoretical frameworks to incorporate cultural nuances that will make actionable information for leaders who strive to achieve greater human capital management within their organizations.

> H1: Innovation Leadership as well as human Capital management have empirical association.

Innovation Leadership as Well as Organizational Culture

The interplay amongst innovation leadership along with organizational culture has received much empirical attention, underlining the important role of leadership in setting and maintaining the cultural atmosphere of an organization. A base notion is that innovation leadership does not only shape organizational path and direction but also creates a culture that is in line with long-term objectives and values. One seminal study put it that leaders play an indispensable role in defining, communicating, and reinforcing the underlying values and assumptions that constitute organizational culture. Schein's scholarship emphasises that effective innovation leaders need to be sensitive to the cultural norms of their existing organisations and try to accommodate these with the innovation vision. This alignment is very important because it ensures that culture values are in support of rather than against organizational objectives, thus providing a conducive environment for transformation and growth (Grecu & Denes, 2024).

Supporting this proposition, a study introduced the construct of transformational leadership that is characterized by leaders who inspire and motivate employees to achieve extraordinary results. Their research showed that transformational leaders did not only affect performance results but also influenced the culture of the organization in such a way that encouraged innovation and flexibility. Innovation leaders can develop an engaged workforce by cultivating a culture that prioritizes continuous learning and empowerment, learning how to be resilient against change (Kupa et al., 2024). In a healthcare context, the work described how the leadership of innovation directly insinuates in the culture of healthcare organizations. Their research emphasised that leaders that involve staff in decision-making processes and encourage open communication are likely to create a culture that is characterised by trust and collaboration. Such a culture, in turn, enables better outcomes in patient care and also staff satisfaction. The researchers concluded that innovation leadership practices that have a cultural focus are central to achieving organisational excellence in healthcare settings (Estevez et al., 2025).

Along with, a recent study discussed moderating impacts of organisational culture on the-related association of innovation leadership and work performance in different industries. Their findings showed that a supportive organisational culture increases the positive effects of innovation leadership on employee motivation and performance. This can be interpreted as leaders who create an inclusive and supportive culture see their strategies much more effective, in the sense that they generate better organisational results (Estevez et al., 2025). As well as, in terms of research on innovation leadership as well as organizational culture, there are some gaps. A substantial proportion of studies have been conducted in Western contexts and this could potentially constrain the generalisability of findings to diverse cultural contexts. For example, studies have shown that the effectiveness of leadership styles can depend on such cultural factors as collectivism versus individualism. Consequently, there is a great need for empirical studies that address how innovation leadership could be successfully implemented in different cultural contexts especially in developing countries such as Ethiopia where organisational dynamics might be markedly different (Emiru & Berhanu, 2025).

Along with, a lot of he literature already out there particularly concerns the direct effects of leadership on culture and fails to sufficiently discuss feedback loops - how culture, in turn, affects leadership effectiveness. Future studies could explore this two-way connection, providing a more extensive knowledge of how innovation leaders are able to adapt their behaviour depending on the organisational culture they foster (Diniz et al., 2025).

H2: Innovation Leadership as well as organizational Culture are Empirically Associated.

Organisational Culture & Human Capital management

The connection amongst the organisational culture and human capital management has been widely studied by scholars and there is a great deal of attention that culture has on the effectiveness of the workforce and the performance of the organisational entity. Organisational culture, which is defined as the shared values, beliefs and practices that influence employee behavior and experience, is a basic environment against which human capital management strategies are developed and implemented (Sari et al. 2023). A seminal study introduced the concept that cultural dimensions can play a major role in the dynamics of workplace behaviour and management practices in a variety of situations. Hofstede's research focused on the concept that organisations in collectivist cultures might rely on collaborative and team-orientated human capital management strategies whereas organisations in individualistic cultures might prefer to prioritise personal achievement and levels of autonomy. This understanding is critical for those organisations looking to match their human capital strategies to the current cultural values, to ensure that recruitment, retention and development strategies are valued by the intrinsic motivations of employees (Aldjic & Farrell, 2022).

Further research built on this idea and it was strongly believed that strong organisational cultures have a direct effect on employee behaviour and performance. They found that organisations that have a strong culture that encourages innovation, risk-taking, and engagement of employees, perform better. This is especially relevant when it comes to human capital management, as organisations with a culture of support are better able to attract and retain high-quality talent. The study also showed that organisational culture has a significant effect on the employment of human capital practices, possibly acting as a crucial determinant in distinguishing amongst successful organisations and their competitors (Hector & Limoges, 2022). In healthcare sector, a study examined the mediating effect of organisational culture on the link amongst leadership styles and human capital management outcomes. Their findings showed that in communities where they were able to maintain a strong, inclusive culture, positive impacts of innovation leadership on engagement and retention rates were enhanced by a lot. This shows that there is a need to promote a culture consistent with the human capital management practices that will help improve the effectiveness of the workforce as a whole (Diniz et al., 2025).

Along with, research that was done looked at organisational culture and human capital interaction during organisational change. Their findings brought out significant points on the successful ability of the organisations to effectively manage human capital through transitional periods by absence of any lacuna of communication and adaptability in the culture of the various organisations. Employees in such cultures showed higher levels of satisfaction and commitment that are basic requirements of change management. The current cultural research demonstrates the beneficial or detrimental role that cultural factors play in human capital initiatives, especially in dynamic and evolving organisational perspectives (Kebe et al., 2025). Despite all these insights, there are still gaps, especially at the level of the nuances amongst the roles culture plays in the specific practices of human capital management. Many studies have focused on general cultural attributes at face value without going deep into how subcultures within organisations can affect discrete aspects of human capital management, such as training and development, performance evaluation and talent management strategies (Hector & Cameron, 2023).

One other gap is marked in understanding how organisations can effectively bridge amongst the existing and desired cultures in terms of desired human capital outcomes. For example, while a culture may be characterised by collaboration, individual performance metrics may be emphasised within practices of human capital management, contradictory employee experiences may follow. Research investigating adaptation mechanisms to match organisational culture with human capital practices in different contexts is imperative to design strong frameworks that will, ultimately, lead to higher organisational effectiveness (Estevez et al., 2025).

H3: Organisational Culture and Human Capital Management have an empirical association.

Innovation Leadership, Human Capital Management, Organisational Culture

The interactions amongst innovation leadership, human capital management as well as organizational culture comprise an important area of research, especially when exploring their connections in terms of the contribution they make to organisational effectiveness and performance. Empirical research is becoming increasingly concerned with how innovation leadership affects human capital management practices, but emphasises the mediating role of organisational culture in this dynamic. This multidimensional connection is vital for organisations aiming to improve efficiency of workforce and match the goals of innovation with the daily practices (Diniz et al., 2025). One basic study examined the linkage amongst transformational leadership and its impact on motivation and performance of employees. Their findings showed that successful transformational leaders who stimulate supportive organisational cultures are more successful in implementing effective human capital management strategies. The study says, when leadership is concerned with a positive organisational culture, it boosts engagement and retention of employees and this reinforces the idea that culture mediates the connection amongst the leadership and human capital outcomes. This emphasises the importance of leaders in creating an environment that supports the development of the workforce (Bulan et al. 2025).

This connection has been further elaborated in research that examines the mediating effect of organisational culture amongst innovation leadership and employee performance in a range of sectors including healthcare. The good news that their findings brought to light is that organisations with strong, adaptive cultures are more equipped to successfully implement innovation initiatives. When leaders shared cultural values that fostered collaboration and innovation, their impacts on human capital management via, for instance, training programmes and performance incentives were significantly pronounced. This underlines the necessity for leaders to participate binding their innovation initiatives with underlying cultural values to create an united work environment (Figueroa & Abellana, 2025). Along with, a study has been done about the impact of different leadership styles on human capital management through the view of organisational culture. Their research presented evidence that organisational culture can make innovation leadership initiatives more or less effective. Leaders who understood and engaged with the prevalent culture were able to mobilise human capital strategies to a far greater extent, resulting in greater employee satisfaction and better performance metrics. This study makes a compelling case for the need for cultural awareness for leaders wishing to maximise their influence on workforce development initiatives (Diniz et al., 2025).

In a more specific context, a study was conducted specifically on the Ethiopian healthcare sector where it investigated the impact of innovation leadership on human capital management using organisational culture as a mediating factor. Their research showed that although innovation leadership was found to have positive effects on the outcome of human capital management efforts, the success of such initiatives was substantially moderated by the existing organisational culture. In institutions where a culture of open communication and support prevailed, innovation initiatives were more positively received by employees, which led to higher levels of employee engagement and retention rates. This study made a point of the culture specific to the Ethiopian context and acknowledged the need for culturally informed leadership practices (Manzoor et al., 2025). Despite these insights, studies on the triadic connection amongst innovation leadership, organisational culture and human capital management are still few, more so in the developing contexts. A majority of the studies are based on Western organisational settings and this may tend to overlook unique cultural dynamics that prevail in the developing world. This absence of context-specific examination creates a potential gap that should be addressed since cultural factors could have a substantial impact on the impact of innovation leadership on the management of human capital (Waheed et al., 2024).

Along with, the feedback loop amongst these elements is often poorly studied in the empirical literature. While the role of innovation leadership in the management of culture and human capital is well documented, knowledge of how human capital outcomes in turn impact the culture and leadership practices of organisations is just as important. This two-way interaction offers rich possibilities for further research and practical application (Diniz et al., polarity of interactions amongst children and digital technology and the impact on surreal well-being and personal growth).

> H4: Innovation Leadership, Human capital management as well as organizational culture mediating showing empirical association.

METHODOLOGY

Present chapter explores the link amongst innovation leadership, human capital along with organizational culture using quantitative research methodology in order to examine about the interlinkage amongst innovation leadership and human capital management, as well as organizational culture in terms of Ethiopian healthcare sector in relation to mediator's role of organizational culture. The sample consisted of 394 healthcare professionals selected using random sampling techniques with stratification random sampling to ensure that the representatives came from different levels of management and various healthcare institutions. o assess whether the sample was suitable for factor analysis, the kaiser-olkin (KMO) criterion was used and the resulting coefficient was greater than the acceptable value of 0.540, thus indicating that the sample was adequate for the statistical analysis. An exploratory analysis (EFA) was then conducted to reveal the underlying dimensional structure of the variables under consideration. Principal components analysis using varimax rotation was used and helped in the determination of clear factors related to innovation leadership, human capital management along with organizational culture. Structural modeling (SEM) was subsequently used in order to test the hypothesized theoretical connections among constructs. The advantage of SEM is the estimation of complex interconnections amongst multiple variables at the same time.

Scale

The development of the measurement scale included a thorough review of the literature to avoid incorrect representation of the constructs relating to innovation leadership, human capital management, along with organizational culture. Leveraging existing models and theoretical frameworks, the scale included several items that were meant to effectively operationalize each dimension. Items for innovation leadership were adapted from the seminal work of Bass and Avolio and focused on transformational leadership behaviors such as vision articulation, the motive of employees, and the creation of an empowering milieu. The human capital management scale was based on the framework of Schuler and Jackson by focusing on recruitment, training and retention activities. Organisational culture items were based on Schein's cultural dimensions and included values associated with collaboration because of the need for communication and innovation in healthcare settings. All the items were in five-point Likert scale form ranging from 1 (Strongly Disagree) through 5 (Strongly Agree), thereby enabling the respondent to express their level of agreement. Pretesting with a small cohort allowed for modification of items based on feedback regarding item clarity and relevance of items. The finalized instrument that includes validated constructs that are theoretically based on literature was used to investigate the connection of innovation leadership, human capital management, along with organizational culture comprehensively in the healthcare sector of Ethiopia.

Data Analysis

Table 1. Adequacy of Data Test

Sampling Measure Adequacy.		**.906**
Bartlett's Test of Sphericity	Chi-Square	2095.96
	Df	126
	Sig.	.000

Source: Authors

Sampling Adequacy giving excellent value of .906 in Table number 1. This figure, which is significantly above the recommended threshold of .80 and in the "marvelous" range (above .90), shows that the patterns of correlation amongst the variables (items) are compact and distinct. A high KMO value (.906) indicates that the sample of 394 healthcare professionals exhibits sufficient and reliable variance to provide from which robust underlying factors can be extracted with minimal dispersion that may be attributed to random error.

Table 2. Total Variance

C	Initial Eigenvalues			Extraction Sums of Squared Loadings			Rotation Sums		
	Total	% of Variance	Cumulative %	Total	% of Variance	Cumulative %	Total	% of Variance	Cumulative %
1	4.09	32.5	32.5	4.09	32.5	32.5	3.0	30.09	30.09
2	1.548	9.548	42.18	1.548	9.548	42.18	2.54	15.09	36.18
3	1.548	9.548	64.0	1.548	9.548	64.0	1.8	14.8	64.0

Source: Authors

As also is shown in Table 1, the Test of Sphericity is statistically significant (Chi - Square = 2095.96, p = .000). This result provides that one could reject the null hypothesis that correlation matrix equals an identity matrix (where variables are unrelated). The significant chi ^ statistic indicates that there are appreciably substantial correlations amongst the variables in a population from which the sample is drawn in order to justify the use of data reduction procedures like factor analysis. The analysis in Table 2 was able to find three distinct components or factors with initial Eigen values of greater than 1, which is the standard criterion for factor retention. These three factors explain a cumulative amount of 64.0% of the total variance of the data set after extraction. The in starting solution reveals that the in starting factor is the most significant accounting for 32.5% of the variance. Along with, the application of rotation (in this case, the application of Varimax rotation indicated by the "Rotation Sums of Squared Loadings") redistributed this explained variance in an equitable way across the three retained components. After rotation, variance explained is distributed as follows: Factor 1 variance explained = 30.09%, Factor 2 variance explained = 15.09% and Factor 3 variance explained = 14.8%. This redistribution is methodologically correct, as rotation improves interpretability of the factors, by ensuring high loadings and weak loadings, to ensure clarity as to which items of the survey relate to which underlying construct. The cumulative explained variance 64.0% can be regarded as acceptable in social science, as well as organizational research, especially in complex areas such as healthcare, where human and systemic variables are likely to account for significant percentage of unique variance in the data. This outcome appears to provide strong evidence that the items that are measured for Innovation Leadership, Organizational Culture and Human Capital Management converge into three coherent and theoretically justifiable latent constructs. The clear emergence of three factors enables strong empirical support of the discriminant validity of the fundamental variables of the study.

Table 3. Mediation

	worth
Innovation Leadership → Human Capital Management	.44
Innovation Leadership → Organizational Culture → Human Capital Management	.5483*.548=.49
	.94

Source: Authors

The analysis presented in Table 3 shows a strong total effect of .94 which confirms that Innovation Leadership is a great driver of HCM results in the healthcare sector in Ethiopia. This total effect is significantly decomposed into two pathways. The direct effect (.44) shows that a significant portion of the impact of leadership is independent, and has an influence on HCM through formal policies, strategic decisions and direct managerial interventions. More importantly, the indirect effect (.49), which is the product of the path from Innovation Leadership to Organizational Culture (.5483) and from Culture to HCM (.548) is slightly larger than the direct effect. This highlights the fact that the main mechanism through which the leadership's impact is delivered is through its initial creation of a supportive and innovating organizational culture and this turns into the instrumental force that boosts the practices of human capital. The fact that the direct path, as well as the indirect path, are significant and substantial leads to the conclusion of partial mediation. This result fulfils a deadly important theoretical and practical weight. Theoretically, it confirms that organizational culture is not just a background context, but a dynamic generative mechanism for transmitting and amplifying the vision of leadership into tangible outcomes in human capital. Practically, for health care administrators in Ethiopia, it highlights a dual imperative: on one hand, investing in innovation-grounded leadership development and purposefully engineering an organization-wide culture that deems learning, psychological safety and collaboration worth their meet is a powerful middle-range meta-analytic vision; it is syngetic and non imperative to achieve a resilient, adaptive and high performing occupational force capable of meeting complex health care challenge.

DISCUSSION

The results of this study all together together yield very strong empirical evidence for a comprehensive model whereby Innovation Leadership has a significant positive effect on Human Capital Management (HCM) in the context of the healthcare sector in Ethiopia with organizational culture playing a very important mediating role. The analysis based on necessary and reliable measures shows that these constructs are clearly but interrelatedly operationalized in this context. The good fit of the structural model to the data is possible to confidently interpret the path connections and these verify the central hypotheses. The findings show that Innovation Leadership has a powerful two-pronged way to improving HCM. The significant direct effect underscores the importance of how the actions of leaders in places such as setting a clear vision, aligning resources, and making Innovation decisions have immediate and positive impacts on human capital practices including recruitment and development, as well as retention. This is consistent with the basic theories of leadership, which have depicted leaders as the primary system-architects of organizations. More importantly, the analysis uncovers a powerful indirect pathway: Innovation Leadership influences a supportive organizational culture in a powerful way, which in turn becomes a powerful driver of effective HCM. The strength of this indirect effect, which turned out to be a partial mediation, means that a considerable portion of the effect of leadership is channelled through the cultural environment which it fosters. This points to the fact that leadership initiatives are most effective when they succeed in raming values of collaboration, empowerment and excellence into the fabric of the organization, thereby providing a context in which human capital can truly flourish.

These results have important implications for theory and practice. Theoretically speaking, they move the discourse about organizational effectiveness forward by quantifying and validating a mediation model in a critical and understudied context. They go beyond establishing simple correlations to outline the process by which leadership affects the outcomes - i.e. by in starting changing the cultural infrastructure. For persons who work in the healthcare field and make policy decisions in the Ethiopian healthcare system, this research presents a clear, actionable framework. It makes a strong case for why investments in Innovation Leadership development are needed, but they are not in themselves enough. To maximize the benefits of human capital and thereby boost service delivery and operational effectiveness, healthcare administrators must simultaneously introduce conscious initiatives to enhance and improve cultural options. Leadership training should thus include cultural stewardship, meaning how leadership should communicate and demonstrate the values that make their human resource strategies work. Ultimately, this study proposes the synergy amongst Innovation Leadership together with a purposeful organizational culture to be the cornerstone in building up a resilient and effective healthcare workforce in Ethiopia.

CONCLUSION

In conclusion, the current study provides a reliable framework that proves that Innovation Leadership is a critical determinant of successful Human Capital

Management in Ethiopia's healthcare sector while organizational culture acts as a significant and strong partial mediator. The powerful analytical approach using Structural Equation Modeling on data from 394 professionals confirms how the influence of leadership is dual-faced: directly facilitating human capital practices while exerting a huge indirect impact by in starting fostering a conducive inculcating organisational culture. These findings highlight the fact that leadership initiatives and cultural development are not sequential, regardless of a process that is interdependent. For healthcare administrators and policymakers in Ethiopia, that means that the best path to addressing the need to strengthen the workforce and enhance service delivery is through the synergistic growth of Innovation Leadership capabilities and a carefully considered, values-driven organizational culture. Ultimately, this research offers both a theoretical contribution to the discourse on leadership as well as human capital and a practical road of how to build up a more resilient and effective healthcare system.

MANAGERIAL IMPLICATIONS

The results of this research have salient managerial implications for both the healthcare administrators and policymakers of Ethiopia. Primarily, they should take a holistic strategy that will meld leadership growth with developing the culture. While investment in innovation-focused leadership training (including a focus on setting the vision, alignment of vision with innovation, and management of change) is essential, this is not enough. Leadership development initiatives need to have an explicit focus on cultural stewardship, and therefore equip leaders with the competent necessary to consciously influence, communicate, and sustain a supportive organisational culture characterised by collaboration, continuous learning and employee well-being. After firstly, management should institutionalise the mechanisms of a systematic cultural auditor and intervention. Recognising the powerful mediating role of culture, leaders will go beyond anecdotal understandings and regularly assess the cultural factors using validated measuring instruments. Targeted interventions - like fostering open communication, recognising team-based achievements and aligning reward systems with sought-after cultural values - should be used to strengthen the cultural transmission line amongst leadership and human capital.

At the end, human capital management (HCM) policies need to be culturalised. Recruitment, onboarding, performance management, and professional development programmes must be designed less as a way to make processes and systems more efficient and more as a way to actively reflect and perpetuate the supporting culture that innovation leadership seeks to create. This creates an upward spiral whereby culture and HCM practices support each other. Consequently, it means senior leadership and policymakers will have to dedicate resources simultaneously towards leadership capacity building, cultural transformation initiatives, and human resource systems modernisation because both interdependent factors are equally important when it comes to creating organisational effectiveness and improving healthcare services delivery.

PRACTICAL IMPLICATIONS

The practical implications of this study proved clear-cut and easy-to-understand actions that can be taken by healthcare institutions in Ethiopia. In starting, leadership development programmes need to be radically re-designed. Beyond the teaching of innovation planning and financial management, these programmes need to spend significant amounts of time teaching competencies that determine culture. This involves training the leadership in value communications, behavioural role-modeling, and methods for building psychological safety and teamwork in their units. Investing in such holistic leadership training is a direct investment in culture, as well as outcomes measured in terms of human capital. After first, management should launch deliberate and structured culture building efforts. This includes developing mechanisms for open conversations, designing formal mentorship and peer learning systems, and implementing transparent recognition programmes that reward behaviours that are consistent with the culture that is being sought (e.g. collaboration, innovation, patient centred care). These are not supplementary human resource activities and the core operational strategies that strengthen the critical mediating variable i.e. organisational culture which enhances the impact of leadership.

After second, organisations need to develop integrating mechanisms intended to hard-wire the connection amongst leadership action, cultural values and day-to-day practice. This can be achieved by explicitly incorporating cultural measures into performance dashboards, making the contribution of culture to performance a criterion in leadership performance reviews and promotion decisions, and ensuring that all - staff communications are consistently linked to innovation priorities in connection with cultural values. By taking these steps, healthcare administrators can operationalise the research findings to turn the leadership-curriculum-culture paradigms and human capital nexus into an operational measurement of change to how healthcare is delivered and how healthcare systems become more resilient to a potentially devastating and persistently devastating series of events.

THEORETICAL IMPLICATIONS

The outcomes of this study offer important implied theoretical perspectives for elaborating on the discourse on innovation leadership, human capital management (HCM) and organisational culture. In starting, by demonstrating the empirical validity of organisational culture as a partial mediator, the research goes beyond leadership theories that assume direct and straightforward impacts to explain leadership. It provides concrete evidence to support a process-oriented view that shows that a significant amount of the efficacy of innovation leadership is carried over in the social and normative fabric of the organization. This strengthens and refines theories of innovation human resources management and upper echelons theory by defining culture as a central mechanism whereby leadership cognition and strategy work to operate their effects upon critical resources such as human capital.

After first, the study contributes to the institutional and contingency theories by putting the framework into the context of a specific national and sectoral context - the Ethiopian healthcare system. The strength of the connections implies that the leadership-culture-HCM nexus is strong, even in a non-Western resource-constrained context. Such findings challenge assumptions of these models being constrained to developed economies and adds to the theoretical understandings of how universal organisational principles take form in institutional logics, cultural norms and operational challenges that are unique. At the end, the research provides theoretical integration, addressing macro and micro level of innovation-leadership viewpoints and human capital outcomes via the meso-level organisational culture. This integration, taken together, provides a more holistic theoretical model of how top-down innovation intent can be integrated with the bottom-up employee capabilities and performance. It implies that future theoretical development regarding organisational effectiveness needs to take consideration of this triadic connection, as the role of organisational culture cannot just be to sit within the context, but to be a partaking, malleable innovation asset which is both shaped by leadership and instrumental in actualising innovation-human-capital objectives.

MANAGERIAL IMPLICATIONS

The results of this study have serious theoretical implications that extend the discourse on innovation leadership, HCM and organisational culture. In starting, the empirical validation of organisational culture as a partial mediator extends the theory of leadership beyond simple, direct-effect versions and provides a process-oriented approach to leadership theory, which explains that a significant part of the impact of innovation leadership is mediated by the social and normative fabric of the organization: This advancement supports and refines theories of innovation human resource management and upper echelon theory by emphasises the culture as a critical mechanism through which leadership cognition and strategy influence human capital outcomes. After first, the study puts the characterisation of the model into context within Ethiopia's healthcare system and therefore demonstrates the robustness of the leadership - culture - HCM nexus in a resource constrained, non Western setting. These findings challenge the idea that such frameworks are confined to the developed economy sphere and contribute to institutional theory by showing how universal organizational principles take shape in the context of specific institutional logic, cultural norms and operation constraints that are predominant in emerging contexts.

At the end, the research advocates for the unifying framework of linking macro-level innovation leadership, meso-level organisational culture, and micro-level human capital management. By so doing, it provides a comprehensive model that takes account of the dynamic interplay amongst top-down innovation intent, middle-level cultural processes, and bottom-up human capital performance and encourages future theoretical work to take a triadic perspective in explaining organisational effectiveness.

RECOMMENDATION

In starting, it is recommended that healthcare institutions design and implement integrated leadership development programmes that explicitly combine innovation-leadership related competencies with cultural stewardship skills. Training should go beyond traditional management and provide the leader with the tools to diagnose, create, and maintain a supportive organisational culture that encourages the effectiveness of human capital. After first, it is recommended that organisations work to institutionalise systematic frameworks of cultural assessment and intervention. Leadership should also regularly assess organisational culture using validated measurement and take specific initiative, such as reinforcing values of teamwork, innovation and employee recognition, to specifically enhance this important mediator.

After second, it is recommended that organization human-resource policies and management systems be aligned with, and which reinforce, the existence of desired cultural attributes. Recruitment, performance management and professional development need to be contextualised to reflect and perpetuate the supportive culture that innovation leadership aims to create, and in so doing, create a coherent ecosystem for talent. At the end, for policy makers and sector leaders, it is recommended that they advocate for and obtain resources for initiatives that ensure that leadership development and cultural transformation are linked innovation priorities in the national healthcare improvement plans. Funding and policy support should recognize this synergy in terms of how we learn to build a resilient, motivated and high performing healthcare workforce able to meet the present and future health service needs of Ethiopia.

FUTURE DIRECTIONS

Based on the findings of and limitations inherent in the present study, a number of promising avenues for future research are raised. In starting, future studies should use longitudinal or mixed methods study designs to capture the dynamic, causal evolution of the linkages amongst innovation leadership, culture and human capital over time. Qualitative inquiries in particular could offer more contextual clues to how leaders created culture and the specific cultural artifacts and practices that most effectively turned leadership into human capital gains in the Ethiopian healthcare settings. After first, research should make the model more complex by including more variables. Investigating potential moderating factors (e.g. specific leadership styles interplaying with other factors such as transformational, ethical; organisational size; resource availability, etc.) would give a more contingent understanding of the established connections. Along with, further investigating mediating mechanisms such as employee engagement, knowledge management or psychological safety might develop a more comprehensive theoretical framework. At the end, future work should cover the generalisability and boundary conditions of this model by duplicating in different sectors (i.e. education, manufacturing) and other Sub-Sahara African nations. Comparative cross-curtain studies would be of particular value in identifying universal principles vis-a-vis context-based dynamics, to refine the theoretical model for wider application while enhancing understanding of the special institutional factors involved in developing economies.

REFERENCES

Agyei, E., & Kumah, E. (2024). Navigating the complex terrain of healthcare systems in Sub-Saharan Africa: Challenges and opportunities for progress. *Discover Health Systems*, *3*(1), 39. Advance online publication. DOI: 10.1007/s44250-024-00108-3

Aldjic, K., & Farrell, W. (2022). Work and Espoused National Cultural Values of Generation Z in Austria. *European Journal of Management Issues*, *30*(2), 100–115. DOI: 10.15421/192210

Ali, M. I. A., Khassawneh, O., Haak-Saheem, W., Zeng, J., & Darwish, T. K. (2023). Unveiling Dubai's knowledge economy: A journey toward enhancing knowledge exchange as well as human capital. *Global Knowledge, Memory and Communication*. Advance online publication. DOI: 10.09108/gkmc-06-2023-0214

Alnofeli, K. K., Akter, S., & Yanamandram, V. (2025). Unlocking the power of AI in CRM: A comprehensive multidimensional exploration. *Journal of Innovation & Knowledge*, *10*(3), 100731. DOI: 10.1016/j.jik.2025.100731

Andargie, E. M., Negash, W. D., Geto, A. K., & Atnafu, A. (2024). Healthcare leadership practice and associated factors among primary healthcare managers in East Gojam Zone, Northwest Ethiopia: A mixed method study. *BMC Health Services Research*, *24*(1), 1247. DOI: 10.1186/s12913-024-11712-7 PMID: 39420335

Bulan, T. R. N., Muhar, A. M., & Junita, A. (2025). The role of talent management in mediating the effect of workforce engagement as well as organizational culture on workforce agility in educational foundations. *Problems and Perspectives in Management*, *23*(3), 567–580. DOI: 10.21511/ppm.23(3).2025.41

Cumar, M. A., Kidane, B. Z., Golga, D. N., & Dinsa, F. (2025). Leadership as cultural architect: A path-goal theory analysis of leadership styles as well as organizational culture in Somaliland higher education. *Discover Education*, *4*(1), 448. Advance online publication. DOI: 10.1007/s44217-025-00887-8

Demeke, G. W., van Engen, M., & Markos, S. (2025). Linking servant leadership to task performance through work engagement and patient safety culture. *Discover Health Systems*, *4*(1), 142. Advance online publication. DOI: 10.1007/s44250-025-00325-4

Diniz, P. V. L., Marques, I. C. P., & Pereira, Â. M. (2025). Leadership, Human-Centered Management as well as organizational Culture: Pathways to Well-Being and Innovative Work Based on a Systematic Review. *Sustainability (Basel)*, *17*(24), 11181. DOI: 10.3390/su172411181

Emiru, E. K., & Berhanu, K. Z. (2025). Distributed Leadership and Student Engagement in Ethiopia: The mediating role of Teacher Self Efficacy. *Research in Educational Administration & Leadership*, *10*(3), 672–721. DOI: 10.30828/real.1618955

Eshete, B. M., & Kassahun, T. (2025). Adaptive leadership, organizational culture and patient-perceived service quality in private healthcare: Evidence from Addis Ababa. *International Journal of Health Care Quality Assurance*, *1*. Advance online publication. DOI: 10.09108/ijhcqa-09-2025-0136

Estévez, M., Ballestar, M. T., & Sáinz, J. (2025). Market research and knowledge using Generative AI: The power of Large Language Models. *Journal of Innovation & Knowledge*, *10*(5), 100796. DOI: 10.1016/j.jik.2025.100796

Ferede, W. L., Endawoke, Y., & Tessema, G. (2024). Change management through strategic leadership: The mediating effect of knowledge management in public organizations, Ethiopia. *Future Business Journal*, *10*(1), 93. Advance online publication. DOI: 10.1186/s43093-024-00363-z

Figueroa, K. M., & Abellana, A. L. (2025). Organizational Culture and Strategic Leadership on Teachers' Innovative Work Behavior. *International Journal of Research and Innovation in Social Science*, *23*(VI), 23–35. Advance online publication. DOI: 10.47772/IJRISS.2025.90600003

Grecu, V., & Dene , C. (2024). The Role of Organizational Culture in Driving Innovation: A Study of Contemporary Business Practice. *Acta Universitatis Cibiniensis Technical Series*, *76*(1), 46–54. DOI: 10.2478/aucts-2024-0007

Guha, S., Rabby, S. K. M. A. H. R., Chowdhury, S. R., & Julee, S. A. (2025). Enhancing employee innovation capabilities through high-involvement HRM: Mediating role of knowledge sharing and transformational leadership. *Future Business Journal*, *11*(1), 59. Advance online publication. DOI: 10.1186/s43093-025-00482-1

Hector, O., & Cameron, R. (2023). Human-Centric Management: Nurturing Talent, Building Culture, and Driving Organizational Success. *The International Journal of Science in Society*, *5*(4), 641. DOI: 10.54783/ijsoc.v5i4.809

Kebe, I. A., Liu, Y., & Kahl, C. (2025). Culturally Attuned Leadership and Employee Behavior During Organizational Change Initiatives in a Developing Economy. *Behavioral Sciences (Basel, Switzerland)*, *15*(3), 349. DOI: 10.3390/bs15030349 PMID: 40150244

Kedia, S., Kiwuwa-Muyingo, S., Uppal, R., Sindi, J. K., & Gitau, E. (2025). Leadership and culture change to advance innovation in women's health. *BMJ (Clinical Research Ed.), 391*, e085994. Advance online publication. DOI: 10.1136/bmj-2025-085994 PMID: 41073075

Kiran, V. S., Shanmugam, V., Raju, R. K., & Kanagasabapathy, J. R. (2022). Impact of Human Capital Management on Organizational Performance With the Mediation Effect of Human Resource Analytics. *International Journal of Professional Business Review*, *7*(3), e0667. Advance online publication. DOI: 10.26668/businessreview/2022.v7i3.0667

Kosiol, J., Silvester, T., Cooper, H., Alford, S., & Fraser, L. (2024). Revolutionising health and social care: innovative solutions for a brighter tomorrow – a systematic review of the literature [Review of *Revolutionising health and social care: innovative solutions for a brighter tomorrow – a systematic review of the literature*]. *BMC Health Services Research, 24*(1). BioMed Central. https://doi.org/DOI: 10.09186/s12913-024-11099-5

Kryshtanovych, M., Bekh, Y., Zhyzhko, T., Povstyn, O., & Molnar, O. (2025). The role of creative leadership in change management. *Creativity Studies*, *18*(2), 506–522. DOI: 10.3846/cs.2025.22189

Kupa, E., Adanma, U. M., Ogunbiyi, E. O., & Solomon, N. O. (2024). Cultivating a culture of safety and innovation in the FMCG sector through leadership as well as organizational change. *International Journal of Management & Entrepreneurship Research*, *6*(6), 1787–1803. DOI: 10.51594/ijmer.v6i6.1165

Labib, E. (2024). Artificial intelligence in marketing: Exploring current and future trends. *Cogent Business & Management*, *11*(1), 2348728. Advance online publication. DOI: 10.1080/23311975.2024.2348728

Lemak, C. H., Pena, D., Jones, D. A., Kim, D. H., & Guptill, J. (2024). Leadership to Accelerate Healthcare's Digital Transformation: Evidence From 33 Health Systems. *Journal of Healthcare Management / American College of Healthcare Executives*, *69*(4), 267–279. DOI: 10.1097/JHM-D-23-00210 PMID: 38976787

Löfqvist, N. (2024). Enhancing capability for continuous organisational improvement and learning in healthcare organisations: a systematic review of the literature 2013–2022 [Review of *Enhancing capability for continuous organisational improvement and learning in healthcare organisations: a systematic review of the literature 2013–2022*]. *BMJ Open Quality*, *13*(2). *BMJ (Clinical Research Ed.)*. Advance online publication. DOI: 10.09136/bmjoq-2023-002566

Manzoor, S., Dhand, S., & Pandey, A. (2025). The Role of Innovation Culture in Enhancing Employee Engagement: Evidence from Selected IT Firms. *Journal of Neonatal Surgery*, *14*(5S), 676–684. DOI: 10.52783/jns.v14.2117

McKenzie, F., Hewitt, C., Holmes, H., Johnson, M. L., & Clarke, T. (2025). Facilitating innovation in healthcare: Insights from the frontline of adoption. *BMJ Innovations*, *11*(3), 126–132. DOI: 10.1136/bmjinnov-2025-001407

Mengstie, M. M., Biks, G. A., Cherlin, E., & Curry, L. (2023). Organizational culture and barriers to change in University of Gondar Comprehensive Specialized Hospital Cardiac Unit. *BMC Health Services Research*, *23*(1), 296. Advance online publication. DOI: 10.1186/s12913-023-09278-x PMID: 36978055

Mogaji, I. M., & Dimingu, H. (2024). A Conceptual Exploration of the Impact of Leadership Styles on the Innovative Culture of Organizations. *Open Journal of Leadership*, *13*(2), 136–153. DOI: 10.4236/ojl.2024.132009

Ninassi, C., & Burrell, D. N. (2023). Teaching business leadership skills to professionals in healthcare cybersecurity, biodefense and biotechnology through experiential learning methods. *Health Economics and Management Review*, *4*(3), 82–94. DOI: 10.61093/hem.2023.3-07

Notarnicola, I., Duka, B., Lommi, M., Grosha, E., Maria, M. D., Iacorossi, L., Mastroianni, C., Ivziku, D., Rocco, G., & Stievano, A. (2024). Transformational Leadership and Its Impact on Job Satisfaction and Personal Mastery for Nursing Leaders in Healthcare Organizations. *Nursing Reports*, *14*(4), 3561–3574. DOI: 10.3390/nursrep14040260 PMID: 39585151

Sari, M., Dahrani, D., & Sagala, N. A. (2023). Determinants of employee performance at public hospitals in Indonesia: Examining the moderating role of organizational culture. *Problems and Perspectives in Management*, *22*(1), 57–68. DOI: 10.21511/ppm.22(1).2024.06

Spais, G. S., & Chryssochoidis, G. (2025). Trends and future of artificial intelligence (AI), machine learning (ML) algorithms, and data analytics and their applications and implications for digital marketing and digital promotions. *Journal of Marketing Analytics*. https://doi.org/DOI: 10.09057/s41270-025-00406-6

Tarekegn, S. M., Tadesse, D., Argaw, M. D., Semahegn, A., Taddesse, L., Shifarraw, S., Enbiale, W., Muluneh, M. D., Abate, B. B., Tamire, A., & Makonnen, M. (2025). Capacity and performance of primary health care in Ethiopia: A novel mixed methods measurement in low-income country. *BMC Primary Care*, *26*(1), 299. DOI: 10.1186/s12875-025-02988-7 PMID: 41023838

Uslu, M., & Özutku, H. (2025). The Transformative Impact of Cultural Values on HRM: Shaping Global Practices. *International Journal of Management and Administration, 9*(18), 145–162. DOI: 10.29064/ijma.1754176

Vahedi, H., Shivyari, S. R., Soltanmohamadi, S., & Babakhanian, F. (2024). The Role of Leadership Competence as well as organizational Culture in Enhancing Healthcare Service Quality. *Journal of Archives in Military Medicine, 12*(3). Advance online publication. DOI: 10.5812/jamm-156498

Waheed, A., Waheed, S., Hussain, S., & Majeed, A. (2024). The HR revolution: Redefining performance paradigms in Pakistan's pharma landscape through moderating role of innovative climate. *PLoS One, 19*(5), e0301777. Advance online publication. DOI: 10.1371/journal.pone.0301777 PMID: 38820526

Xi, Y., Zhou, L., & Wang, H. (2025). Ambidextrous leadership and innovation: A process perspective and an experimental approach. *Humanities & Social Sciences Communications, 12*(1), 612. Advance online publication. DOI: 10.1057/s41599-025-04922-9

Zeleke, L. W., Guyo, W., & Moronge, M. (2025). Adaptive Leadership Styles as well as organizational Performance: Evidence from Local NGOs in Ethiopia. *Innovation Journal of Social Sciences and Economic Review., 59*(2), 68–75. Advance online publication. DOI: 10.36923/ijsser.v7i2.323

KEY TERMS AND DEFINITIONS

Human Capital Management: The systematic strategy of policies, practices, and systems to acquire and develop the workforce, to motivate it, and to sustain and retain it. It treats the employees as valuable assets (capital), and within the framework of this study, it covers the strategies for optimising the knowledge, skills and abilities of the healthcare professionals in Ethiopia.

Innovation Leadership: This is a strategic leadership style that is all about initiating, enabling, and sustaining organisational innovation. It means inspiring creativity, calculated risk-taking and putting into action new ideas, in order to improve processes, services and performance. In this particular study, it refers to the behaviours and vision of the healthcare leaders in Ethiopia that provide an environment for novel solutions to flourish and adaptive change to take place.

Organisational Culture:: What is seen as shared values, beliefs, assumptions, norms, and how the behaviour and organisational interactions are produced. In this study, it means social and psychological environment in the Ethiopian healthcare institutions, which mediates the effect of leadership on human capital practices.

Chapter 7
Leadership, Organizational Culture, and Innovation Governance in Pharmaceutical and Medical Device Firms

Maria Shafaqat
http://orcid.org/0009-0008-7399-2529
School of Natural Sciences, University of Kent, UK

Abu Sulman
http://orcid.org/0009-0008-7194-5219
University of Agriculture, Faisalabad, Pakistan

Adnan Afzal
http://orcid.org/0009-0001-4359-5695
Government College University, Faisalabad, Pakistan

Muhammad Saad Naeem
University of Agriculture, Faisalabad, Pakistan

Adeeba Riaz
http://orcid.org/0009-0009-6093-9777
Department of Biotechnology, University of Okara, Pakistan

Aleeha Afzal
University of Agriculture, Faisalabad, Pakistan

Hina Nawab
http://orcid.org/0009-0002-8250-5856
Institute of Physiology and Pharmacology, University of Agriculture, Faisalabad, Pakistan

Hafiz Aamir Ali Kharl
http://orcid.org/0000-0002-7365-2937
Narcotics Forensic Laboratory, Anti-Narcotics Force, Ministry of Interior and Narcotics Control, Islamabad, Pakistan

DOI: 10.4018/979-8-3373-9410-7.ch007

Maham Shehzadi
Cholistan University of Veterinary and Animal Sciences, Bahawalpur, Pakistan

Fahad Ahmad
University of Agriculture, Faisalabad, Pakistan

ABSTRACT

This chapter examines the interrelationship between leadership, organizational culture, and innovation governance in pharmaceutical and medical device firms. Operating within highly regulated and research-intensive environments, these organizations require strategic leadership that balances scientific creativity with regulatory compliance and ethical responsibility. The chapter explores how leadership styles influence R&D effectiveness, how organizational culture shapes innovation performance, and how governance frameworks ensure accountability and risk management. By integrating ethical values, structured decision-making processes, and adaptive strategic oversight, firms can sustain innovation while safeguarding patient safety and public trust in an evolving global healthcare landscape.

INTRODUCTION TO INNOVATION LEADERSHIP IN HEALTHCARE INDUSTRIES

Innovation in healthcare industries particularly within pharmaceutical and medical device firms exists at the intersection of science, regulation, ethics, and market demand (Javanmardi et al., 2024). Unlike many other sectors, innovation in these industries directly affects human life, public health outcomes, and societal trust. As a result, leadership within these domains carries a responsibility that extends beyond profitability and competitive advantage. It must balance scientific advancement, patient safety, regulatory compliance, and sustainable growth. Understanding innovation leadership in healthcare therefore requires an appreciation of the unique institutional, technological, and ethical complexities that shape the sector. Pharmaceutical and medical device industries operate in environments characterized by high research and development (R&D) intensity, long product development cycles, and substantial financial risk. The journey from laboratory discovery to market approval can span over a decade, involving clinical trials, regulatory scrutiny, and post-market surveillance. During this process, leadership plays a critical role in aligning scientific exploration with strategic objectives (Kipasika, 2024). Effective leaders must foster a vision that encourages discovery while maintaining disciplined governance structures capable of navigating regulatory frameworks and market pressures. Innovation leadership in healthcare is not limited to directing R&D departments. It encompasses strategic foresight, organizational culture shaping, stakeholder engagement, and ethical stewardship. Leaders must anticipate emerging trends such as digital health integration, personalized medicine, artificial intelligence-driven diagnostics, and advanced biomaterials. At the same time, they must manage uncertainties related to regulatory shifts, intellectual property protection, and global supply chain disruptions. This dual responsibility—driving innovation while managing risk—defines the distinctive leadership paradigm of healthcare industries. A defining feature of pharmaceutical and medical device innovation is its dependency on cross-functional collaboration. Scientists, clinicians, regulatory specialists, manufacturing experts, marketing teams, and compliance officers must work in concert to transform ideas into viable products (Lee et al., 2019). Leadership in this context requires the ability to integrate diverse expertise and create shared objectives across functional boundaries. Transformational leadership approaches, which emphasize inspiration, empowerment, and long-term vision, are particularly relevant (Chitiga, 2018). However, transactional and compliance-oriented leadership elements are equally necessary due to the strict regulatory requirements governing healthcare products.

Regulatory oversight significantly influences innovation leadership strategies. Agencies such as the U.S. Food and Drug Administration (FDA), the European Medicines Agency (EMA), and other national regulatory authorities impose rigorous standards for safety, efficacy, and quality. Leaders must therefore cultivate governance systems that ensure adherence to regulatory expectations without stifling creativity. This involves establishing transparent decision-making processes, maintaining robust documentation practices, and embedding compliance awareness within the organizational culture. Innovation cannot thrive in an environment of regulatory negligence; conversely, excessive bureaucratic rigidity can suppress creative thinking. Effective leadership seeks equilibrium between these forces. Ethics constitutes another foundational pillar of innovation leadership in healthcare industries (Abdulai et al., 2025). Pharmaceutical and medical device firms operate under intense public scrutiny, particularly regarding clinical trial transparency, pricing strategies, and patient data management. Leaders must uphold ethical principles while pursuing innovation goals. Ethical leadership strengthens stakeholder trust, enhances corporate reputation, and mitigates legal risks. Moreover, ethical considerations often influence innovation priorities, encouraging firms to address unmet medical needs, rare diseases, and equitable healthcare access. Technological advancement further reshapes innovation leadership dynamics. The convergence of biotechnology, nanotechnology, data analytics, and digital health platforms has transformed the innovation landscape (Tanvir et al., 2020). Leaders must demonstrate technological literacy and adaptability to harness these advancements effectively. Strategic investments in research partnerships, academic collaborations, and open innovation ecosystems are increasingly vital. Healthcare innovation rarely occurs in isolation; it is embedded within networks of universities, research institutions, startups, and global supply chains. Leaders must therefore function as boundary spanners, facilitating knowledge exchange and collaborative ventures. Organizational learning is another critical dimension of innovation leadership. Pharmaceutical and medical device firms frequently encounter project failures, clinical trial setbacks, and regulatory rejections (Krieger, 2021). Rather than perceiving failure solely as a loss, effective leaders treat it as an opportunity for institutional learning. Building a resilient organization that can absorb setbacks and refine strategies is essential for long-term innovation sustainability. Learning-oriented leadership fosters experimentation while maintaining structured evaluation mechanisms to assess performance and risk. Globalization also influences leadership approaches in healthcare innovation (Weintraub & McKee, 2018). Firms operate across multiple jurisdictions, each with distinct regulatory regimes, cultural expectations, and healthcare infrastructures. Leaders must navigate these differences while maintaining coherent global strategies. This requires cultural intelligence, strategic alignment across subsidiaries, and adaptive governance frameworks capable of responding to diverse market conditions.

Figure 1. Innovation Leadership in Healthcare Industries

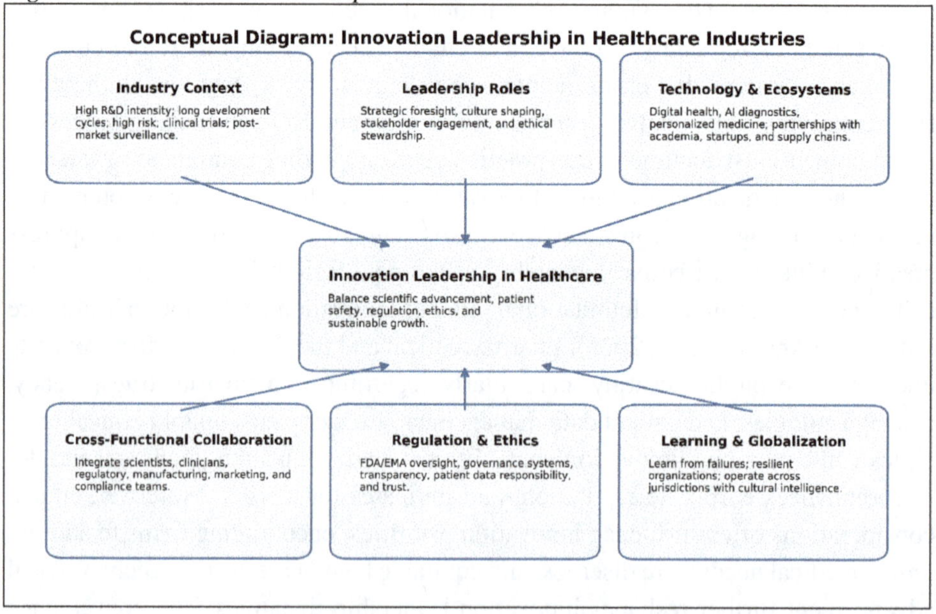

THE STRATEGIC ROLE OF LEADERSHIP IN PHARMACEUTICAL AND MEDICAL DEVICE FIRMS

Leadership within pharmaceutical and medical device firms extends far beyond operational management; it serves as the central driver of strategic direction, competitive positioning, and long-term sustainability. In industries defined by high uncertainty, scientific complexity, and regulatory rigor, leadership becomes a critical determinant of whether innovation efforts translate into commercial success and societal impact (Gao & McDonald, 2022). The strategic role of leadership in these sectors is therefore multidimensional, encompassing vision formulation, resource allocation, risk governance, stakeholder alignment, and global competitiveness. At the core of strategic leadership lies the articulation of a clear and compelling vision. Pharmaceutical and medical device organizations must continuously identify emerging therapeutic areas, unmet clinical needs, and technological disruptions (Scavone et al., 2019). Leaders are responsible for scanning the external environment, interpreting scientific trends, and translating them into actionable strategic priorities. Whether investing in oncology pipelines, digital health technologies, biologics, or minimally invasive surgical devices, leadership decisions determine the organization's future innovation trajectory. Strategic foresight enables firms to anticipate shifts in patient demographics, disease patterns, and regulatory frameworks, thereby positioning themselves proactively rather than reactively. Resource allocation represents another fundamental strategic function of leadership. Research and development in these industries demands substantial financial investment, often with uncertain outcomes (Ross et al., 2018). Leaders must make calculated decisions regarding portfolio management, balancing high-risk breakthrough projects with incremental innovation initiatives. Effective portfolio diversification reduces dependency on a single product or therapeutic area and spreads risk across multiple development streams. Strategic leaders evaluate scientific feasibility, market potential, regulatory complexity, and competitive dynamics before committing resources. These decisions influence not only profitability but also the firm's innovation reputation and long-term resilience. Risk governance is intrinsically tied to strategic leadership in pharmaceutical and medical device firms (Chatterji et al., 2019). The stakes associated with product failure, regulatory non-compliance, or safety concerns are exceptionally high. Leaders must develop comprehensive risk management frameworks that address clinical, operational, financial, and reputational risks. This includes establishing internal review boards, compliance committees, and robust quality assurance systems. Strategic leadership ensures that risk-taking in innovation is disciplined and informed rather than speculative. By embedding risk assessment mechanisms into decision-making processes, leaders create an environment where innovation is encouraged but responsibly governed (Florin, 2022).

Stakeholder engagement further defines the strategic role of leadership in healthcare industries. Unlike many other sectors, pharmaceutical and medical device firms operate within a complex ecosystem that includes patients, healthcare providers, regulators, investors, insurers, research institutions, and advocacy groups. Strategic leaders must align organizational goals with stakeholder expectations to maintain trust and legitimacy. Transparent communication, ethical conduct, and collaborative partnerships strengthen stakeholder relationships (Chukwurah et al., 2024). For example, engaging clinicians during product development enhances clinical relevance, while collaboration with regulatory authorities facilitates smoother approval processes. Leadership thus becomes a bridging force between the organization and its broader healthcare ecosystem. Another strategic dimension involves fostering competitive advantage through innovation differentiation. In markets characterized by rapid technological advancement and intense rivalry, leadership must cultivate unique value propositions (Schoemaker et al., 2018). This may involve investing in proprietary technologies, securing strong intellectual property protections, or leveraging advanced manufacturing capabilities. Leaders who prioritize strategic alliances and acquisitions can accelerate innovation pipelines and access complementary expertise. Strategic mergers, licensing agreements, and joint ventures are often leadership-driven initiatives designed to expand capabilities and market reach.

Global expansion strategies also fall within the purview of strategic leadership. Pharmaceutical and medical device firms increasingly operate across international markets, each presenting diverse regulatory requirements and healthcare infrastructures (Amaral et al., 2024). Leaders must determine entry strategies, pricing models, and distribution networks that align with local conditions while preserving global brand consistency. Strategic leadership in a global context requires balancing standardization with localization, ensuring compliance across jurisdictions, and managing geopolitical risks. The ability to integrate global operations while maintaining strategic coherence distinguishes high-performing firms from their competitors (Collings et al., 2019). Organizational capability development constitutes another essential strategic responsibility. Leaders must invest in human capital, technological infrastructure, and knowledge management systems that sustain innovation capacity. Recruiting scientific talent, promoting interdisciplinary collaboration, and supporting continuous professional development enhance organizational competence. Moreover, digital transformation initiatives—such as implementing data analytics platforms or artificial intelligence tools—require strategic oversight to ensure alignment with corporate objectives. Leadership determines whether technological adoption becomes a source of competitive strength or operational inefficiency. Strategic leadership also shapes corporate culture in ways that influence innovation outcomes. By promoting accountability, transparency, and performance measurement, leaders ensure that strategic objectives are consistently pursued (Akhigbe et al., 2025). Incentive structures, performance evaluation systems, and recognition mechanisms reflect leadership priorities and reinforce strategic alignment across departments. When leaders communicate a coherent strategy and model commitment to innovation, employees are more likely to engage meaningfully in achieving organizational goals. Ultimately, the strategic role of leadership in pharmaceutical and medical device firms integrates vision, governance, stakeholder management, and capability development into a cohesive framework. Leaders are not merely administrators of existing processes; they are architects of future growth and innovation sustainability. Through informed decision-making, disciplined risk management, and strategic alignment, leadership determines whether scientific discoveries evolve into transformative healthcare solutions (Tessema, 2025). In industries where innovation directly influences human well-being, strategic leadership carries both economic and societal significance, underscoring its indispensable role in shaping the future of healthcare.

Table 1. Strategic Dimensions of Leadership in Pharmaceutical and Medical Device Firms

Strategic Dimension	Leadership Role	Key Activities	Impact on Organization	Supporting References
Vision Formulation	Define long-term innovation direction	Identify therapeutic areas, interpret scientific trends, set strategic priorities	Drives future innovation trajectory and competitiveness	Gao & McDonald (2022); Scavone et al. (2019)
Resource Allocation	Manage R&D investments strategically	Portfolio diversification, funding allocation, project evaluation	Enhances resilience and balances risk vs. return	Ross et al. (2018)
Risk Governance	Ensure responsible innovation	Compliance systems, QA frameworks, risk assessments	Reduces regulatory and reputational risks	Chatterji et al. (2019); Florin (2022)
Stakeholder Alignment	Maintain trust within healthcare ecosystem	Collaboration with regulators, clinicians, investors, advocacy groups	Improves legitimacy and smoother approvals	Chukwurah et al. (2024)
Competitive Differentiation	Build strategic advantage	IP protection, alliances, acquisitions, technology investment	Strengthens market position and innovation capacity	Schoemaker et al. (2018)
Global Strategy	Guide international expansion	Market entry, localization, pricing, regulatory adaptation	Expands market reach while maintaining coherence	Amaral et al. (2024); Collings et al. (2019)
Capability & Culture Development	Develop internal strengths	Talent management, digital transformation, performance systems	Sustains long-term innovation and organizational alignment	Akhigbe et al. (2025); Tessema (2025)

ORGANIZATIONAL CULTURE AND ITS IMPACT ON INNOVATION PERFORMANCE

Organizational culture plays a foundational role in shaping innovation performance within pharmaceutical and medical device firms (Park et al., 2023). While leadership provides strategic direction and governance structures establish formal controls, culture determines how employees think, behave, collaborate, and respond to uncertainty. In highly regulated and research-intensive industries, the internal cultural environment can either accelerate innovation or significantly hinder it. Therefore, understanding the relationship between organizational culture and innovation performance is essential for sustaining long-term competitiveness in healthcare sectors. Organizational culture refers to the shared values, beliefs, norms, and practices that guide behaviour within an organization. In pharmaceutical and medical device firms, culture influences how scientific inquiry is conducted, how risk is perceived, how failures are interpreted, and how cross-functional collaboration occurs (Shah, 2024). Because innovation in these industries requires creativity alongside compliance, the cultural balance between flexibility and control becomes particularly significant. A rigid, overly bureaucratic culture may suppress experimentation, whereas an excessively informal culture may undermine regulatory discipline. High-performing organizations cultivate a culture that integrates innovation with accountability (Riza et al., 2025). One of the most critical cultural elements influencing innovation is openness to experimentation. Pharmaceutical and medical device development involves trial-and-error processes, iterative testing, and frequent setbacks. A culture that penalizes failure harshly discourages scientists and engineers from exploring novel ideas. Conversely, a learning-oriented culture treats setbacks as opportunities for knowledge acquisition and refinement. When employees feel psychologically safe to propose unconventional solutions, question assumptions, and share concerns, innovation performance improves. Psychological safety, therefore, becomes a key cultural driver of creative output and scientific advancement (Edmondson, 2018). Collaboration culture also significantly affects innovation outcomes. The development of drugs and medical devices requires multidisciplinary teamwork among researchers, clinicians, regulatory experts, manufacturing specialists, and marketing professionals. Silos between departments can delay projects, increase misunderstandings, and reduce efficiency. An organizational culture that promotes knowledge sharing, transparency, and mutual respect enhances integration across functional boundaries. Cross-functional communication accelerates problem-solving and ensures that innovations are not only scientifically sound but also commercially viable and compliant with regulatory standards (Attah et al., 2024).

Figure 2. Organizational Culture and Its Impact on Innovation Performance

Ethical culture further influences innovation performance in healthcare industries. Given the direct impact of products on patient safety and public health, ethical lapses can result in severe legal and reputational consequences. An ethical organizational culture emphasizes integrity, transparency in clinical trials, accurate reporting of data, and responsible marketing practices. Such a culture not only ensures compliance but also strengthens stakeholder trust. When ethical standards are deeply embedded in daily practices, innovation processes become more credible and sustainable. Ethical culture thus supports long-term innovation performance by reducing risk and enhancing legitimacy.

Another cultural dimension relevant to innovation is adaptability. The healthcare landscape is rapidly evolving due to technological advancements, digital transformation, personalized medicine, and global health challenges (Matcha, 2023). Organizations that resist change may struggle to integrate new technologies or adjust to regulatory reforms. An adaptive culture encourages continuous learning, skill development, and responsiveness to environmental changes. Employees in such environments are more likely to embrace digital tools, adopt new research methodologies, and explore emerging therapeutic areas. Adaptability enhances organizational agility, allowing firms to respond effectively to market and technological disruptions (Penchev & Kenarova-Pencheva, 2025). Leadership behaviour strongly shapes organizational culture. Leaders who model transparency, encourage dialogue, and reward innovative contributions set the tone for cultural norms. Symbolic actions such as recognizing research achievements, supporting diversity in scientific teams, and investing in professional development reinforce cultural priorities. When leadership consistently aligns words with actions, cultural values become institutionalized rather than merely aspirational statements. This alignment is particularly important in pharmaceutical and medical device firms, where regulatory scrutiny demands consistency between declared values and operational conduct. Performance measurement systems also interact with organizational culture. If evaluation metrics focus solely on short-term financial returns, employees may deprioritize long-term research initiatives (Grishunin et al., 2022). Conversely, balanced performance indicators that include innovation milestones, quality standards, and collaborative contributions encourage behaviours aligned with sustainable innovation. Culture is reinforced through incentives; therefore, innovation-oriented cultures often integrate recognition systems that reward creativity, teamwork, and compliance excellence simultaneously. Diversity and inclusion further enrich organizational culture and innovation performance. Pharmaceutical and medical device innovation benefits from diverse scientific perspectives, cultural insights, and problem-solving approaches. Diverse teams are more likely to generate novel solutions and address complex healthcare challenges comprehensively (Zajac et al., 2021). Inclusive cultures ensure that diverse voices are heard and valued, enhancing collective intelligence and decision-making quality. In global healthcare markets, cultural diversity within organizations also strengthens responsiveness to varied patient populations and regulatory contexts. Ultimately, organizational culture serves as the invisible infrastructure supporting innovation in pharmaceutical and medical device firms. It shapes how individuals interpret goals, manage uncertainty, collaborate across disciplines, and uphold ethical standards. A culture that balances creativity with compliance, encourages learning from failure, and promotes collaboration enhances innovation performance and strategic resilience. As competition intensifies and technological disruption accelerates, cultivating a strong innovation-oriented culture becomes not merely desirable but essential for sustained success in healthcare industries.

GOVERNANCE STRUCTURES AND REGULATORY COMPLIANCE IN HEALTHCARE INNOVATION

Governance structures and regulatory compliance form the backbone of innovation management in pharmaceutical and medical device firms (Ramesh, 2023).

Unlike many industries where innovation is primarily market-driven, healthcare innovation operates within a tightly regulated environment designed to protect patient safety, ensure product efficacy, and maintain public trust. As a result, governance systems in these sectors must be robust, transparent, and strategically aligned with innovation objectives. Effective governance does not merely enforce rules; it creates a structured environment where innovation can flourish responsibly and sustainably. Governance structures refer to the formal frameworks, policies, oversight mechanisms, and decision-making processes that guide organizational activities. In pharmaceutical and medical device firms, governance encompasses board oversight, executive leadership committees, compliance departments, research ethics boards, and quality assurance systems (Kabir et al., 2024). These structures ensure accountability across all stages of product development—from early research and clinical trials to manufacturing, marketing, and post-market surveillance. Clear governance frameworks reduce ambiguity in roles and responsibilities, enabling coordinated action in complex innovation processes. Regulatory compliance is a central component of healthcare governance. Pharmaceutical and medical device firms must adhere to strict national and international regulations governing product safety, quality standards, and clinical evaluation. Compliance requirements influence nearly every stage of innovation. During preclinical research, companies must follow Good Laboratory Practices (GLP). In clinical development, Good Clinical Practices (GCP) guide trial design, data collection, and participant protection (Bolon et al., 2018). Manufacturing operations must comply with Good Manufacturing Practices (GMP) to ensure consistent product quality. Governance systems integrate these standards into daily operations to prevent regulatory violations and safeguard patient welfare. Effective governance structures facilitate strategic decision-making in innovation portfolios. Given the high costs and risks associated with healthcare R&D, organizations must evaluate projects rigorously before committing resources. Governance committees often review scientific feasibility, ethical implications, financial projections, and regulatory pathways before approving advancement to the next development phase. Stage-gate processes are commonly employed to monitor progress and ensure that projects meet predefined criteria. This structured evaluation helps prevent resource misallocation and strengthens organizational discipline. Transparency is another critical element of governance in healthcare innovation (Reich, 2018). Pharmaceutical and medical device firms are subject to scrutiny from regulators, investors, healthcare professionals, and the public. Transparent reporting of clinical trial results, adverse events, and research findings reinforces credibility. Governance frameworks that prioritize accurate documentation, internal audits, and open communication channels contribute to accountability. Transparency not only ensures compliance but also enhances stakeholder trust, which is essential for long-term innovation sustainability.

Table 2. Governance Structures and Regulatory Compliance in Healthcare Innovation

Governance Dimension	Core Function	Key Mechanisms / Practices	Impact on Innovation Management	Supporting References
Governance Frameworks	Provide organizational oversight and accountability	Board supervision, executive committees, compliance units, ethics boards, QA systems	Ensures coordinated decision-making and structured innovation processes	Ramesh (2023); Kabir et al. (2024)
Regulatory Compliance	Align innovation with legal and safety standards	GLP, GCP, GMP implementation across development stages	Protects patient safety and ensures regulatory approval readiness	Bolon et al. (2018)
Strategic Portfolio Governance	Guide innovation investment decisions	Stage-gate reviews, scientific and ethical evaluations, feasibility assessments	Reduces resource misallocation and improves R&D discipline	Kabir et al. (2024)
Transparency & Accountability	Maintain stakeholder trust and credibility	Clinical reporting, audits, documentation integrity, open communication	Strengthens legitimacy and long-term innovation sustainability	Reich (2018)
Risk Governance	Manage uncertainty and protect organizational stability	Risk assessments, monitoring boards, compliance audits, mitigation strategies	Balances innovation ambition with patient safety	Schweizer & Renn (2019)
Ethical Oversight	Ensure responsible research conduct	Institutional review boards, informed consent procedures, confidentiality safeguards	Reduces legal risk and supports ethical innovation	Bolon et al. (2018)
Global & Digital Governance	Manage international and technology-driven regulatory complexity	Regulatory harmonization, localized compliance expertise, data privacy and cybersecurity policies	Enables global innovation while addressing digital-era risks	Cosens et al. (2021); Raut et al. (2023); Ogbodo et al. (2025)

Risk management is deeply embedded within governance structures. Healthcare innovation carries clinical, financial, operational, and reputational risks. Governance systems identify potential risks early and implement mitigation strategies (Schweizer & Renn, 2019). For example, clinical trial monitoring boards assess safety data to protect participants, while internal compliance audits identify deviations from regulatory standards. By integrating risk assessment into governance processes, firms maintain a balance between innovation ambition and patient safety. This proactive risk governance supports responsible innovation rather than reactive crisis management. Ethical oversight further strengthens governance frameworks. Research involving human participants demands strict adherence to ethical principles such as informed consent, confidentiality, and equitable participant selection. Institutional review boards and ethics committees evaluate study protocols to ensure alignment with ethical standards. Governance mechanisms that prioritize ethics protect organizations from misconduct allegations and legal liabilities. More importantly, they uphold the moral responsibility inherent in developing products that directly impact human health. Globalization adds complexity to governance and compliance systems (Cosens et al., 2021). Pharmaceutical and medical device firms often conduct clinical trials across multiple countries and distribute products internationally. Each jurisdiction may have distinct regulatory requirements, documentation standards, and approval processes. Governance structures must therefore coordinate compliance efforts across diverse regulatory landscapes. Centralized oversight combined with localized regulatory expertise enables organizations to navigate these complexities effectively. Harmonization initiatives, such as international regulatory collaborations, further influence governance practices (Raut et al., 2023). Digital transformation is also reshaping governance models in healthcare innovation. The integration of artificial intelligence, big data analytics, and digital health technologies introduces new regulatory challenges, particularly concerning data privacy and cybersecurity. Governance frameworks must evolve to address these emerging risks. Policies regarding data protection, electronic record management, and digital system validation are increasingly essential (Ogbodo et al., 2025). Leaders must ensure that technological innovation aligns with regulatory expectations and ethical considerations. Importantly, governance should not be perceived as a constraint on innovation. When properly designed, governance structures provide clarity, stability, and strategic focus. They enable organizations to pursue ambitious research initiatives within well-defined ethical and regulatory boundaries. By embedding compliance into organizational culture rather than treating it as an external imposition, firms can create an environment where innovation and regulation coexist productively.

LEADERSHIP STYLES AND THEIR INFLUENCE ON R&D EFFECTIVENESS

Leadership style significantly influences research and development (R&D) effectiveness in pharmaceutical and medical device firms. Given the high complexity, uncertainty, and long development cycles associated with healthcare innovation, the way leaders guide, motivate, and structure R&D teams directly affects scientific productivity, regulatory success, and overall innovation performance. Different leadership styles shape team dynamics, risk-taking behaviour, collaboration patterns, and decision-making processes, thereby determining whether R&D initiatives achieve strategic objectives (Essandoh et al., 2023). Transformational leadership is often considered highly effective in R&D-intensive environments. This leadership style emphasizes vision, inspiration, intellectual stimulation, and individualized support. In pharmaceutical and medical device firms, transformational leaders articulate a compelling long-term vision—such as addressing unmet medical needs or pioneering breakthrough therapies—that motivates scientists and engineers to pursue ambitious goals. By encouraging creative thinking and challenging existing assumptions, transformational leaders stimulate innovation. They foster an environment where researchers feel empowered to explore novel hypotheses and pursue cutting-edge technologies. Such inspiration is particularly valuable in R&D contexts characterized by uncertainty and potential failure. Transactional leadership, while sometimes viewed as less innovation-oriented, also plays an important role in R&D effectiveness (Hansen & Pihl-Thingvad, 2019). This style focuses on structured goals, performance monitoring, and reward-based incentives. In healthcare industries where regulatory compliance and quality standards are critical, transactional leadership ensures discipline and accountability (Abou Abbas, 2025). R&D projects must adhere to strict timelines, documentation requirements, and procedural protocols. Leaders who establish clear expectations and performance benchmarks help maintain project momentum and regulatory readiness. Therefore, a balanced integration of transformational and transactional approaches often yields optimal outcomes in healthcare R&D. Participative or democratic leadership further enhances R&D performance by promoting collaboration and shared decision-making. Pharmaceutical and medical device innovation requires multidisciplinary expertise, including biology, chemistry, engineering, clinical medicine, and regulatory science (Morrison et al., 2018). Participative leaders encourage input from diverse team members, facilitating knowledge integration. By valuing different perspectives, they enhance problem-solving capacity and reduce the likelihood of oversight errors. Inclusive decision-making processes also increase team commitment and ownership, which can improve productivity and morale within R&D departments. Servant leadership, characterized by prioritizing employee development and well-being, can also positively influence R&D effectiveness.

Figure 3. Leadership Styles and Their Influence on R&D Effectiveness

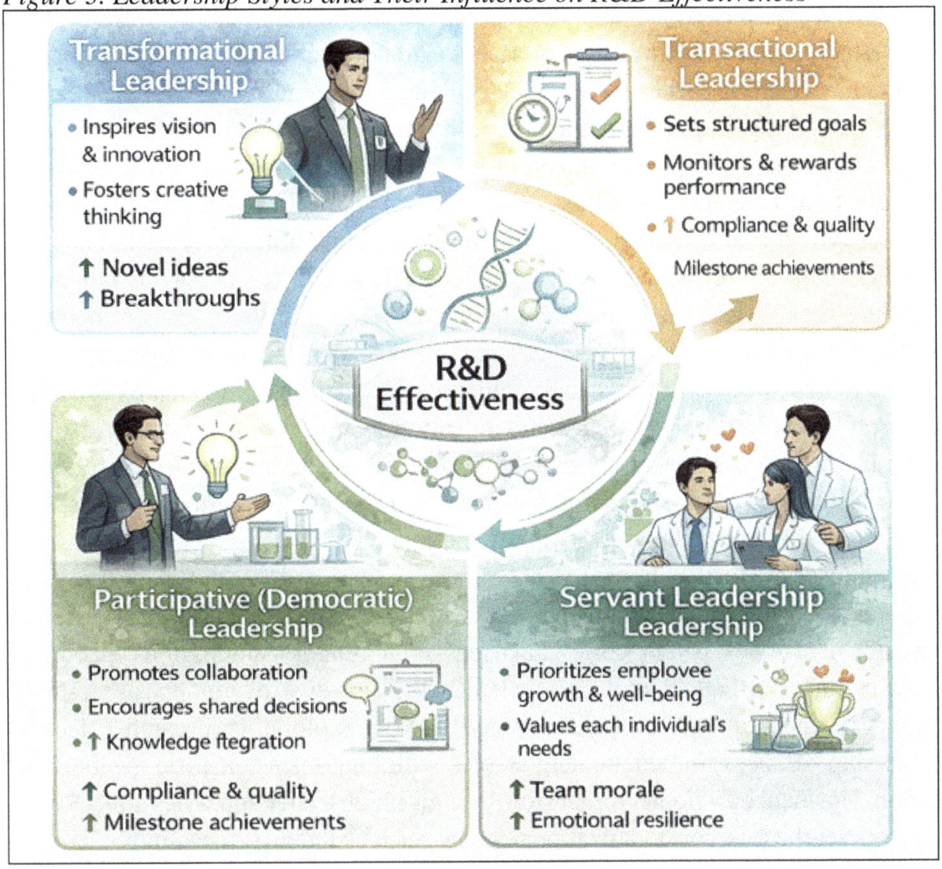

In high-pressure environments where project setbacks and regulatory delays are common, emotional resilience and team cohesion are essential. Leaders who support professional growth, provide mentorship, and address individual concerns foster a supportive research climate. Such environments promote psychological safety, enabling researchers to communicate challenges openly without fear of blame. This openness accelerates issue resolution and enhances overall project quality. Autocratic leadership, in contrast, may have mixed effects on R&D performance. In crisis situations—such as urgent regulatory responses or critical safety concerns—decisive and directive leadership can be beneficial (Post et al., 2022). Clear, centralized decision-making ensures rapid action and minimizes confusion. However, prolonged autocratic leadership may suppress creativity and discourage independent thinking. Overly rigid control can stifle innovative ideas and reduce intrinsic motivation among researchers. Therefore, while directive leadership may be necessary in specific circumstances, it is generally less conducive to sustained innovation. Leadership adaptability is particularly important in R&D settings. The lifecycle of pharmaceutical and medical device development includes exploratory research, preclinical testing, clinical trials, regulatory submission, and post-market evaluation. Each stage presents distinct challenges and requires different leadership behaviours. Early-stage research may benefit from visionary and exploratory leadership, whereas later stages demand precision, compliance oversight, and operational coordination. Leaders who adjust their style according to project phase enhance efficiency and effectiveness across the development continuum. Communication practices also reflect leadership style and significantly influence R&D outcomes (Alblooshi et al., 2021). Transparent communication ensures alignment between scientific teams and executive management. When leaders clearly articulate strategic priorities, resource constraints, and regulatory expectations, R&D teams can align their efforts accordingly. Open communication channels reduce misunderstandings, facilitate cross-functional collaboration, and accelerate problem resolution. Conversely, poor communication may lead to duplication of efforts, delays, and regulatory non-compliance. Motivation and incentive systems, shaped by leadership philosophy, further impact R&D effectiveness. Leaders who recognize both individual and team achievements reinforce innovative behaviour. Incentives tied to research milestones, patent filings, or successful regulatory submissions encourage sustained effort (Bhattacharya & Packalen, 2020). However, overemphasis on short-term performance metrics may discourage long-term exploratory research. Effective leadership balances immediate deliverables with long-term scientific exploration. Cultural influence is another dimension through which leadership styles affect R&D. Leaders set the tone for organizational values such as integrity, accountability, and collaboration. In healthcare industries, ethical considerations and patient safety must remain central. Leadership styles that model ethical conduct and scientific rigor create a culture of responsibility within R&D teams. This alignment strengthens compliance, enhances data reliability, and builds stakeholder trust.

BUILDING A CULTURE OF ETHICAL INNOVATION AND RISK MANAGEMENT

Building a culture of ethical innovation and risk management is essential in pharmaceutical and medical device firms, where innovation directly impacts human lives and public health systems. Unlike many other industries, healthcare innovation operates under intense ethical scrutiny and regulatory oversight. The development of drugs, biologics, diagnostic tools, and medical devices involves clinical experimentation, patient data handling, and long-term safety monitoring (Opderbeck, 2019). Therefore, innovation must be guided not only by scientific ambition and commercial objectives but also by ethical responsibility and structured risk governance. Establishing a culture that integrates ethical values with proactive risk management strengthens organizational credibility, regulatory compliance, and sustainable innovation performance. An ethical innovation culture begins with clearly defined organizational values. Ethical principles such as integrity, transparency, accountability, and patient-centricity must be embedded into the mission and vision of the firm. When leadership consistently reinforces these values, they become institutional norms rather than symbolic statements. In healthcare industries, ethical commitment influences decisions regarding clinical trial design, informed consent processes, data reporting accuracy, pricing strategies, and marketing practices (Suhag, 2024). A culture that prioritizes patient welfare over short-term profit fosters long-term trust among regulators, healthcare professionals, and the public. Leadership plays a pivotal role in cultivating ethical innovation. Ethical leadership involves modelling responsible behaviour, maintaining transparency in decision-making, and holding individuals accountable for misconduct. When leaders demonstrate zero tolerance for data manipulation, regulatory shortcuts, or misleading promotional practices, employees internalize these expectations. Ethical role modelling at senior levels creates a trickle-down effect throughout the organization. Conversely, inconsistency between stated values and executive actions can erode cultural integrity and increase reputational risk (Olawale et al., 2024). Risk management is intrinsically connected to ethical innovation. Pharmaceutical and medical device development carries multiple categories of risk, including clinical risks, operational risks, financial risks, technological risks, and reputational risks. A strong risk management culture does not eliminate risk but ensures that risks are identified, assessed, mitigated, and monitored systematically. Structured risk assessment tools—such as risk matrices, failure mode analysis, and internal audits—support informed decision-making. By proactively addressing uncertainties, organizations protect patient safety and maintain regulatory compliance. Ethical innovation also requires transparency in research and development processes. Clinical trials must be designed to protect participants, ensure data integrity, and provide accurate reporting of outcomes—whether positive or negative. Suppressing unfavourable results or exaggerating efficacy undermines both ethics and long-term innovation sustainability. Transparent communication with regulatory authorities and healthcare professionals reinforces trust and supports evidence-based practice (Fasasi). A culture that values honesty over competitive pressure strengthens organizational resilience. Employee empowerment contributes significantly to ethical risk management. When employees feel psychologically safe to report concerns, potential compliance violations can be identified early. Whistleblower protection policies, confidential reporting channels, and open-door leadership practices encourage transparency. In highly regulated industries, early detection of deviations from protocols can prevent costly recalls, litigation, and reputational damage. Thus, ethical culture and risk management systems function collaboratively to safeguard both patients and organizational stability. Training and continuous education further reinforce ethical innovation culture. Pharmaceutical and medical device firms must regularly train employees on regulatory requirements, clinical ethics, data protection standards, and quality management systems (Mehrotra, 2024). Continuous learning ensures that staff remain aware of evolving regulations and emerging ethical challenges, such as those related to digital health technologies and artificial intelligence applications. Ethical awareness becomes embedded in daily operations rather than treated as a one-time compliance requirement. Balancing innovation ambition with patient safety represents a central challenge in building this culture. Rapid technological advancement can create pressure to accelerate product development timelines (Morgan & Liker, 2020). However, cutting corners in safety evaluation or regulatory documentation can have severe consequences. A mature ethical innovation culture recognizes that sustainable success depends on maintaining rigorous standards even under competitive pressure. Long-term credibility outweighs short-term market advantage.

Table 3. Building a Culture of Ethical Innovation and Risk Management in Healthcare Firms

Key Dimension	Core Concept	Main Practices / Mechanisms	Impact on Organization	Supporting References
Ethical Innovation Culture	Embedding ethical values into innovation processes	Integrity, transparency, accountability, patient-centricity in decision-making	Strengthens trust, credibility, and sustainable innovation	Opderbeck (2019); Suhag (2024)
Ethical Leadership	Leadership as a driver of ethical behaviour	Role modeling, accountability enforcement, transparent decision-making	Reduces misconduct risk and reinforces organizational values	Olawale et al. (2024)
Risk Management Integration	Systematic identification and control of risks	Risk matrices, failure mode analysis, audits, monitoring systems	Improves patient safety and regulatory compliance	Morgan & Liker (2020)
Transparency in R&D	Honest and accurate research practices	Ethical clinical trial design, data integrity, open reporting	Supports evidence-based practice and stakeholder confidence	Fasasi

continued on following page

Table 3. Continued

Key Dimension	Core Concept	Main Practices / Mechanisms	Impact on Organization	Supporting References
Employee Empowerment & Reporting	Encouraging ethical voice and early issue detection	Whistleblower protection, confidential reporting, open communication	Prevents compliance failures and reputational damage	Mehrotra (2024)
Training & Ethical Awareness	Continuous development of ethical competencies	Regulatory training, ethics education, data protection learning	Embeds ethics into everyday operations	Mehrotra (2024)
Incentives & Global Ethical Governance	Aligning rewards and global compliance consistency	Quality-based performance metrics, standardized frameworks with local oversight	Promotes responsible innovation across jurisdictions	Brandhorst & Kluge (2022); Ughulu (2024)

Organizational incentives must also align with ethical objectives. Performance evaluation systems that reward only speed and profitability may inadvertently encourage risky behaviour (Brandhorst & Kluge, 2022). Conversely, incorporating quality metrics, compliance adherence, and collaborative behaviour into evaluation frameworks promotes responsible innovation. When ethical conduct is visibly recognized and rewarded, employees are more likely to internalize these priorities. Global operations introduce additional complexity to ethical risk management. Different countries may have varying regulatory standards, cultural expectations, and healthcare infrastructures. Firms must ensure that ethical principles are applied consistently across jurisdictions, avoiding the exploitation of regulatory gaps. Standardized global compliance frameworks combined with localized oversight enhance governance integrity.

INNOVATION GOVERNANCE FRAMEWORKS IN PHARMACEUTICAL AND MEDICAL DEVICE ORGANIZATIONS

Innovation governance frameworks provide the structural and strategic foundation through which pharmaceutical and medical device firms manage the complex process of transforming scientific ideas into safe, effective, and commercially viable healthcare solutions. In highly regulated and research-intensive industries, innovation cannot rely solely on creativity or market opportunity. It must operate within clearly defined governance mechanisms that ensure accountability, transparency, risk control, and alignment with organizational objectives. Effective innovation governance frameworks integrate strategic oversight, regulatory compliance, ethical standards, and performance management into a cohesive system that supports sustainable innovation (Ciasullo et al., 2020). At its core, innovation governance refers to the policies, processes, committees, and decision-making structures that oversee innovation activities across the organization. These frameworks establish clear roles and responsibilities for boards of directors, executive leadership teams, R&D heads, compliance officers, and quality assurance units. In pharmaceutical and medical device firms, governance mechanisms are particularly important because product development cycles are long, resource-intensive, and subject to regulatory scrutiny. Without structured oversight, projects may suffer from scope creep, misaligned priorities, or compliance failures. One commonly used innovation governance model in healthcare industries is the stage-gate framework (Nunes et al., 2023). This structured process divides product development into sequential stages—such as discovery, preclinical testing, clinical trials, regulatory submission, and commercialization. At each gate, cross-functional committees evaluate predefined criteria, including scientific validity, financial feasibility, regulatory readiness, and strategic alignment. Only projects that meet established benchmarks proceed to the next phase. This disciplined evaluation ensures that resources are allocated efficiently and that weak projects are discontinued before incurring excessive costs. Stage-gate governance enhances transparency and strengthens decision accountability (Puttaraju, 2024). Strategic alignment is a critical function of innovation governance frameworks. Pharmaceutical and medical device firms often manage multiple R&D projects simultaneously, each targeting different therapeutic areas or technological platforms. Governance systems ensure that innovation portfolios align with corporate strategy, market positioning, and long-term growth objectives. Portfolio review committees assess whether projects support priority disease areas, emerging technologies, or geographic expansion strategies. This alignment prevents fragmentation of innovation efforts and promotes coherent organizational direction. Regulatory integration is another defining element of innovation governance in healthcare sectors (Wagner & Fain, 2018). Governance frameworks must incorporate regulatory compliance checkpoints throughout the development lifecycle. Regulatory affairs teams play a central role in advising R&D leaders on evolving guidelines, documentation standards, and approval pathways. Early integration of regulatory considerations reduces the likelihood of delays or rejections during submission. By embedding compliance expertise into governance structures, firms minimize regulatory risk while maintaining innovation momentum. Risk oversight mechanisms further strengthen governance frameworks. Pharmaceutical and medical device innovation involves clinical, operational, technological, and reputational risks (Shivakumar, 2025). Governance committees conduct periodic risk assessments to identify vulnerabilities and implement mitigation strategies. For instance, safety monitoring boards oversee clinical trial data to detect adverse events promptly.

Internal audit functions evaluate adherence to quality standards and operational protocols. Structured risk governance enhances organizational resilience and protects both patients and corporate reputation.

CONCLUSION

Leadership, organizational culture, and innovation governance collectively determine the sustainability and effectiveness of innovation in pharmaceutical and medical device firms. In industries characterized by high uncertainty, strict regulatory oversight, and profound societal impact, innovation cannot thrive without structured guidance and ethical responsibility. Strategic leadership provides direction, allocates resources, and ensures alignment between long-term vision and operational execution. Leadership styles that integrate inspiration with accountability enhance R&D productivity while maintaining regulatory discipline. Organizational culture serves as the internal environment that either accelerates or constrains innovation performance. A culture that promotes collaboration, psychological safety, ethical integrity, and adaptability strengthens cross-functional coordination and supports scientific exploration. When employees feel empowered to share ideas and address challenges transparently, innovation processes become more resilient and efficient. Innovation governance frameworks provide the formal mechanisms necessary to oversee complex development lifecycles. Stage-gate systems, risk assessment protocols, compliance checkpoints, and transparent reporting structures ensure that innovation remains aligned with strategic objectives and regulatory standards. Governance does not restrict creativity; rather, it channels it within responsible and sustainable boundaries. Ultimately, the integration of visionary leadership, supportive culture, and robust governance enables pharmaceutical and medical device organizations to deliver safe, effective, and transformative healthcare solutions. As technological advancements and global health challenges continue to evolve, firms that strengthen these interconnected dimensions will be better positioned to maintain competitive advantage, regulatory trust, and long-term societal impact.

REFERENCES

Abdulai, A.-M., Iddrisu, O. A., Osman, A., & Iddrisu, A. B. (2025). Leadership Integrity: A Strategic Pillar for Ethical Decision Making and Organizational Excellence. *Advances in Research*, *26*(1), 65–73. DOI: 10.9734/air/2025/v26i11233

Abou Abbas, A. (2025). Transformational Leadership and Regulatory Compliance: Strategies for Safer Healthcare Delivery. *J Glob Health Soci Med*, *1*(1), 1–8. DOI: 10.61440/JGHSM.2025.v1.06

Akhigbe, R., Falemi, A., & Akin-Oluyomi, O. T. (2025). An Advanced Governance Model for Improving Transparency Accountability and Strategic Execution in Complex Enterprises. *Article, Dec.*

Alblooshi, M., Shamsuzzaman, M., & Haridy, S. (2021). The relationship between leadership styles and organisational innovation: A systematic literature review and narrative synthesis. *European Journal of Innovation Management*, *24*(2), 338–370. DOI: 10.1108/EJIM-11-2019-0339

Amaral, C., Paiva, M., Rodrigues, A. R., Veiga, F., & Bell, V. (2024). Global regulatory challenges for medical devices: Impact on innovation and market access. *Applied Sciences (Basel, Switzerland)*, *14*(20), 9304. DOI: 10.3390/app14209304

Attah, R. U., Garba, B. M. P., Gil-Ozoudeh, I., & Iwuanyanwu, O. (2024). Cross-functional team dynamics in technology management: A comprehensive review of efficiency and innovation enhancement. *Eng Sci Technol J*, *5*(12), 3248–3265. DOI: 10.51594/estj.v5i12.1756

Bhattacharya, J., & Packalen, M. (2020). *Stagnation and scientific incentives.*

Bolon, B., Baze, W., Shilling, C. J., Keatley, K. L., Patrick, D. J., & Schafer, K. A. (2018). Good laboratory practice in the academic setting: Fundamental principles for nonclinical safety assessment and GLP-compliant pathology support when developing innovative biomedical products. *ILAR Journal*, *59*(1), 18–28. DOI: 10.1093/ilar/ily008 PMID: 30566589

Brandhorst, S., & Kluge, A. (2022). Incentive schemes increase risky behavior in a safety-critical working task: An experimental comparison in a simulated high-reliability organization. *Safety (Basel, Switzerland)*, *8*(1), 17. DOI: 10.3390/safety8010017

Chatterji, A. K., Cunningham, C. M., & Joseph, J. E. (2019). The limits of relational governance: Sales force strategies in the US medical device industry. *Strategic Management Journal*, *40*(1), 55–78. DOI: 10.1002/smj.2964

Chitiga, M. (2018). An exploration of the implications of transformational leadership behaviors on empowering employees and transforming organisations. *African Journal of Public Affairs, 10*(1), 60–82.

Chukwurah, N., Ige, A. B., Idemudia, C., & Adebayo, V. I. (2024). Strategies for engaging stakeholders in data governance: Building effective communication and collaboration. *Open Access Res J Multidiscip Stud, 8*(1), 57–67. DOI: 10.53022/oarjms.2024.8.1.0045

Ciasullo, M. V., Troisi, O., Grimaldi, M., & Leone, D. (2020). Multi-level governance for sustainable innovation in smart communities: An ecosystems approach. *The International Entrepreneurship and Management Journal, 16*(4), 1167–1195. DOI: 10.1007/s11365-020-00641-6

Collings, D. G., Mellahi, K., & Cascio, W. F. (2019). Global talent management and performance in multinational enterprises: A multilevel perspective. *Journal of Management, 45*(2), 540–566. DOI: 10.1177/0149206318757018

Cosens, B., Ruhl, J., Soininen, N., Gunderson, L., Belinskij, A., Blenckner, T., Camacho, A. E., Chaffin, B. C., Craig, R. K., Doremus, H., Glicksman, R., Heiskanen, A.-S., Larson, R., & Similä, J. (2021). Governing complexity: Integrating science, governance, and law to manage accelerating change in the globalized commons. *Proceedings of the National Academy of Sciences of the United States of America, 118*(36), e2102798118. DOI: 10.1073/pnas.2102798118 PMID: 34475210

Edmondson, A. C. (2018). *The fearless organization: Creating psychological safety in the workplace for learning, innovation, and growth.* John Wiley & Sons.

Essandoh, S., Sakyi, J. K., Ibrahim, A. K., Okafor, C. M., Wedraogo, L., Ogunwale, O. B., Babalola, A. S., & Adenuga, M. A. (2023). *Analyzing the Effects of Leadership Styles on Team Dynamics and Project Outcomes. Journal not specified. Fasasi.* G. O. Digital Communication Policy Framework Enhancing Transparency and Accountability in Health-Social Service Collaboration.

Florin, M.-V. (2022). Risk governance and'responsible research and innovation'can be mutually supportive. *Journal of Risk Research, 25*(8), 976–990. DOI: 10.1080/13669877.2019.1646311

Gao, C., & McDonald, R. (2022). Shaping nascent industries: Innovation strategy and regulatory uncertainty in personal genomics. *Administrative Science Quarterly, 67*(4), 915–967. DOI: 10.1177/00018392221112641

Grishunin, S., Suloeva, S., & Burova, E. (2022). Development of risk management mechanism and the system of risk metrics to evaluate and enhance the long-term orientation of the strategies of non-financial companies. *Risks*, *10*(9), 182. DOI: 10.3390/risks10090182

Hansen, J. A., & Pihl-Thingvad, S. (2019). Managing employee innovative behaviour through transformational and transactional leadership styles. *Public Management Review*, *21*(6), 918–944. DOI: 10.1080/14719037.2018.1544272

Javanmardi, E., Maresova, P., Xie, N., & Mierzwiak, R. (2024). Exploring business models for managing uncertainty in healthcare, medical devices, and biotechnology industries. *Heliyon*, *10*(4), e25962. DOI: 10.1016/j.heliyon.2024.e25962 PMID: 38370194

Kabir, M., Rana, M. R. H., & Debnath, A. (2024). The role of quality assurance in accelerating pharmaceutical research and development: Strategies for ensuring regulatory compliance and product integrity. *Journal of Angiotherapy*, *8*(12), 1–11.

Kipasika, H. J. (2024). Expression of leadership mission, vision, values, and strategic objectives in academic institution development practices. *Journal of Research Innovation and Implications in Education*, *8*(1), 393–402.

Krieger, J. L. (2021). Trials and terminations: Learning from competitors' R&D failures. *Management Science*, *67*(9), 5525–5548. DOI: 10.1287/mnsc.2020.3775

Lee, M., Ly, H., Möller, C. C., & Ringel, M. S. (2019). Innovation in regulatory science is meeting evolution of clinical evidence generation. *Clinical Pharmacology and Therapeutics*, *105*(4), 886–898. DOI: 10.1002/cpt.1354 PMID: 30636288

Matcha, A. (2023). Innovations in healthcare: Transforming patient care through technology, personalized medicine, and global health crises. [IJSR]. *International Journal of Science and Research (Raipur, India)*, *12*(12), 1668–1672. DOI: 10.21275/SR231222082955

Mehrotra, A. (2024). The Strategic Imperative of Quality Management in Pharmaceuticals and Biotechnology. *International Animal Health Journal, 11*(4).

Morgan, J., & Liker, J. K. (2020). *The Toyota product development system: integrating people, process, and technology*. Productivity press.

Morrison, T. M., Pathmanathan, P., Adwan, M., & Margerrison, E. (2018). Advancing regulatory science with computational modeling for medical devices at the FDA's Office of Science and Engineering Laboratories. *Frontiers in Medicine*, *5*, 241. DOI: 10.3389/fmed.2018.00241 PMID: 30356350

Nunes, M., Bagnjuk, J., Abreu, A., Cardoso, E., Smith, J., & Saraiva, C. (2023). Managing collaborative risks of integrated open-innovation and hybrid stage-gate model by applying social network analysis—A case study. *Sustainability (Basel), 15*(6), 5474. DOI: 10.3390/su15065474

Ogbodo, D. C., Awan, I.-U., Cullen, A., & Zahrah, F. (2025). From regulation to reality: A framework to bridge the gap in digital health data protection. *Electronics (Basel), 14*(13), 2629. DOI: 10.3390/electronics14132629

Olawale, H. O., Isibor, N. J., & Fiemotongha, J. E.Habeeb Olatunji OlawaleNgozi Joan IsiborJoyce Efekpogua Fiemotongha. (2024). A cultural conduct risk assessment model for embedding ethical governance in financial and insurance sales practices. *International Journal of Scientific Research in Science and Technology, 11*(2), 1033–1045. DOI: 10.32628/IJSRST251222712

Opderbeck, D. W. (2019). Artificial intelligence in pharmaceuticals, biologics, and medical devices: Present and future regulatory models. *Fordham Law Review, 88*, 553.

Park, S., Kim, H.-K., Lee, H.-J., Choi, M., Lee, M., & Jakovljevic, M. (2023). Strategic management and organizational culture of medical device companies in relation to corporate performance. *Journal of Medical Economics, 26*(1), 781–792. DOI: 10.1080/13696998.2023.2224168 PMID: 37300440

Penchev, P., & Kenarova-Pencheva, I. (2025). Agility, Flexibility, Responsiveness and Competitiveness–the Challenge to Define the Difference. Proceedings of the International Conference on Business Excellence, Post, C., De Smet, H., Uitdewilligen, S., Schreurs, B., & Leysen, J. (2022). Participative or directive leadership behaviors for decision-making in crisis management teams? *Small Group Research, 53*(5), 692–724.

Puttaraju, K. H. (2024). Accelerating Innovation Through Data-Enabled Agile Stage-Gate Processes: Implications For Business Strategy And Execution. *International Journal of Core Engineering & Management, 7*(11), 204–216.

Ramesh, H. (2023). A framework for corporate innovation management and managerial innovation in medical devices industry.

Raut, N., Bajaj, K., Matte, P., Vhora, M., Kale, V., Umekar, M., & Harane, S. (2023). Building bridges: Harmonization efforts for enhanced collaboration between developed and developing countries. *Int J Drug Regul Aff, 11*(3), 68–79. DOI: 10.22270/ijdra.v11i3.622

Reich, M. R. (2018). The core roles of transparency and accountability in the governance of global health public–private partnerships. *Health Systems and Reform*, *4*(3), 239–248. DOI: 10.1080/23288604.2018.1465880 PMID: 30207904

Riza, M. F., Hutahayan, B., & Chong, H. Y. (2025). Fostering high-performing organizations in higher education: The effect of participative leadership, organizational culture, and innovation on organizational performance and commitment. *Cogent Education*, *12*(1), 2448884. DOI: 10.1080/2331186X.2024.2448884

Ross, J. M., Fisch, J. H., & Varga, E. (2018). Unlocking the value of real options: How firm-specific learning conditions affect R&D investments under uncertainty. *Strategic Entrepreneurship Journal*, *12*(3), 335–353. DOI: 10.1002/sej.1275

Scavone, C., Di Mauro, G., Mascolo, A., Berrino, L., Rossi, F., & Capuano, A. (2019). The new paradigms in clinical research: From early access programs to the novel therapeutic approaches for unmet medical needs. *Frontiers in Pharmacology*, *10*, 111. DOI: 10.3389/fphar.2019.00111 PMID: 30814951

Schoemaker, P. J., Heaton, S., & Teece, D. (2018). Innovation, dynamic capabilities, and leadership. *California Management Review*, *61*(1), 15–42. DOI: 10.1177/0008125618790246

Schweizer, P.-J., & Renn, O. (2019). Governance of systemic risks for disaster prevention and mitigation. *Disaster prevention and management: an international journal, 28*(6), 862-874.

Shah, N. P.Nirali P Shah. (2024). Navigating challenges in new product development: Strategies for reducing failure rates in the medical device industry. *World Journal of Advanced Research and Reviews*, *22*(03), 786–795. DOI: 10.30574/wjarr.2024.22.3.1740

Shivakumar, P. (2025). *The role of open innovation in medical device development: challenges of navigating the European regulatory landscape* Kauno technologijos universitetas.].

Suhag, D. (2024). Regulatory and ethical considerations. In *Handbook of Biomaterials for Medical Applications, Volume 2: Applications* (pp. 355-372). Springer. DOI: 10.1007/978-981-97-5906-4_11

Tanvir, A., Juie, B. J. A., Tisha, N. T., & Rahman, M. M. (2020). Synergizing big data and biotechnology for innovation in healthcare, pharmaceutical development, and fungal research. *International Journal of Biological. Physical and Chemical Studies*, *2*(2), 23–32.

Tessema, D. B. (2025). Pillars of organizational transformation and sustainability: Leadership, learning, culture, and knowledge management as key success factors in environmental public health. *Health Economics and Management Review*, *6*(1), 1–21. DOI: 10.61093/hem.2025.1-01

Wagner, B., & Fain, N. (2018). Regulatory influences on innovation in the public sector: The role of regulatory regimes. *Public Management Review*, *20*(8), 1205–1227. DOI: 10.1080/14719037.2017.1350282

Weintraub, P., & McKee, M. (2018). Leadership for innovation in healthcare: An exploration. *International Journal of Health Policy and Management*, *8*(3), 138–144. DOI: 10.15171/ijhpm.2018.122 PMID: 30980629

Zajac, S., Woods, A., Tannenbaum, S., Salas, E., & Holladay, C. L. (2021). Overcoming challenges to teamwork in healthcare: A team effectiveness framework and evidence-based guidance. *Frontiers in Communication*, *6*, 606445. DOI: 10.3389/fcomm.2021.606445

Chapter 8
Leading Digital Transformation in Healthcare:
Ethical Responsibility, Innovation, and Executive Accountability

Jyoti Kumari
http://orcid.org/0000-0001-9648-2494
G.D. Goenka University, India

ABSTRACT

With fast-paced digitalization, including the advent of artificial intelligence, cloud computing, genomics, and patient-oriented innovations, in the healthcare industry, there are many opportunities and challenges for healthcare leaders. This chapter addresses the issues associated with leading healthcare organizations in the process of digitalization in terms of ethics, governance, and innovation. The analysis of current research (from 2015 to 2026) along with a regulatory framework and case study analysis allows developing a conceptual framework about the connection between leadership skills and innovation performance, based on ethics and governance. It turns out that for the efficient digital transformation, three main components are necessary: ethics in leadership, governance, and patient-centeredness in innovation.

1. INTRODUCTION

This sector has seen the most transformative period in terms of technology ever since the inception of evidence-based medicine. Technology has ceased to be an optional supplement of healthcare activities and has become a major determinant

DOI: 10.4018/979-8-3373-9410-7.ch008

of patient safety, operational effectiveness, work sustainability, and competitive advantage. According to the WHO's global strategy on digital health (2020-2025), digital transformation represents one of the foundations of universal health coverage, stressing that it is essential for members states and health organizations to integrate digital innovations in their healthcare strategies (World Health Organization, 2021). At the same time, due to the outbreak of the COVID-19 pandemic, processes of digitalization took up to a year-and-a-half, when, in fact, it could have been accomplished in the next ten years (Keesara et al., 2020).

However, the rapid pace of change in this process has increased both the opportunities and risks inherent in the process. Health systems that have made large investments in EHR systems must now contend with physician burnout due to burdensome documentation processes (Sinsky et al., 2016). AI algorithms designed to enhance diagnostic precision have revealed demographic biases that can jeopardize equality in care provision (Obermeyer et al., 2019). Healthcare cybersecurity breaches, which today represent the most expensive form of data breach across all industries, pose threats to patient privacy and critical service disruption (Siwicki, 2022). This underscores the notion that digital transformation within healthcare presents more than just a problem for technological management.

The leaders of healthcare organizations – chief executive officers (CEOs), chief medical officers (CMOs), chief information officers (CIOs) and their colleagues – are in a position where the opportunities offered by technology and the obligations arising from their financial responsibility collide. The choices made by these leaders regarding what types of technology are used, who is served by the resulting innovations, and the way in which clinicians are assisted in using these new technologies have direct human impact. In this chapter, we assert that digital leadership in the healthcare sector requires the combination of three overlapping capabilities – ethical stewardship, innovation governance, and executive accountability. The structure of this chapter is as follows: Section 2 sets the scene in relation to the concepts surrounding healthcare digital transformation; Section 3 deals with ethical considerations; Section 4 focuses on innovation and emerging technologies; Section 5 discusses executive accountability; Section 6 proposes an integrated framework for governance; Section 7 covers practical implications; and Section 8 summarizes.

2. CONCEPTUAL LANDSCAPE OF HEALTHCARE DIGITAL TRANSFORMATION

2.1 Defining Digital Transformation in Healthcare

The concept of digital transformation has come under debate since it has been vaguely used in various sectors. According to Topol (2019), when the discussion revolves around digital transformation in healthcare, it refers to a complete change of the way health services are perceived, provided, and experienced via digital technology integration in the key processes of health service delivery such as clinical care, health management, and organizational management. Importantly, it can be contrasted with the concepts of digitization (transfer of paper documents into digital form) and digitalization (improvement of processes using digital technology). Digital transformation is more related to changes in organizational logic, value creation, and power relations rather than improving current practices (Vial, 2019).

As Kane et al. (2019) note, transformation can be effective only if there is a strategy in place, if organizational culture is ready for change, and there is a focus on people. When organizations make technology the key focus in their transformations, they tend to fail as technology alone cannot create a true transformation. For healthcare organizations, this becomes even more significant because there is a lot of human involvement due to clinical work, regulation, and a clash between standardization and personalized patient care (Bates et al., 2021).

2.2 Drivers and Inhibitors of Healthcare Digital Transformation

There are several converging factors contributing to the rapid adoption of digital transformations in healthcare organizations around the world. First, consumer demand has been shaped by their experience in using digital services in commerce, finance, entertainment, and now they expect the same ease of service delivery from healthcare organizations (Kruse et al., 2016). Second, the amount of health data that is being produced is expected to grow at an annual rate of 36%, which is faster than any other industry (Mathews et al., 2022).

Regulatory frameworks are another critical catalyst. In the US, the 21st Century Cures Act of 2016 called for interoperability and no information blocking, thus forcing health organizations to make their data ecosystems interoperable and promote data portability of patients' data (Office of the National Coordinator for Health Information Technology, 2020). In the EU, the EHDS regulation strives to achieve comparable goals in a GDPR privacy ecosystem (European Commission, 2022). It demonstrates a growing consensus on the political stage that data mobility is crucial for unleashing digital health's full potential.

Yet, there exist several formidable challenges. Many of the health-care systems suffer from considerable technical debt due to legacy IT systems (Vest & Gamm, 2017). Resistance to technology use in many health-care facilities is often misinterpreted as fear of change, yet it is actually associated with reasonable objections concerning overload, loss of professional discretion, and potential harm to patients (Mennemeyer et al., 2016). Budget limitations prevent health-care facilities from investing in necessary technological innovations, especially those related to safety net hospitals and rural settings. Cybersecurity threats have become a real problem for health-care systems owing to their increased use of connected devices and remote working (Jalali & Kaiser, 2018).

2.3 Maturity Models and Transformation Trajectories

Healthcare organizations vary widely in their digital maturity levels. HIMSS' Electronic Medical Record Adoption Model (EMRAM) is a well-known eight-stage classification framework, spanning from Stage 0 (no EMR use) to Stage 7 (completely digitalized, paperless environment with analytics). According to HIMSS (2023), only less than 10 percent of U.S. hospitals reached HIMSS Stage 7 by 2023, illustrating that there is still much work to be done for transformation in the industry (HIMSS, 2023). In addition to EHR maturity, other aspects of digital maturity include data analytics maturity, artificial intelligence readiness, cybersecurity preparedness, and digital engagement, all of which require separate focus and justification from leaders.

Table 1 synthesizes the five foundational pillars of healthcare digital transformation, providing executives with a structured map of the domains their organizations must develop concurrently to achieve sustainable transformation outcomes.

Table 1. Five Foundational Pillars of Healthcare Digital Transformation

Pillar	Core Components	Healthcare Applications
Technology Infrastructure	Cloud computing, IoT, AI/ML, big data analytics	Electronic health records (EHR), telemedicine platforms, remote patient monitoring
Data & Analytics	Predictive modeling, real-time dashboards, interoperability standards	Clinical decision support, population health management, readmission risk scoring
Process Redesign	Workflow automation, lean management, patient journey mapping	Automated prior authorizations, digital care pathways, discharge planning optimization

continued on following page

Table 1. Continued

Pillar	Core Components	Healthcare Applications
Cultural Change	Change management, digital literacy training, innovation culture	Clinician adoption programs, leadership rounding, digital champions networks
Patient Engagement	Omnichannel communication, shared decision-making tools, portal adoption	Patient portals, mobile health apps, digital consent management

Note. Each pillar requires dedicated executive sponsorship, resource allocation, and performance measurement. Adapted from Kane et al. (2019), Topol (2019), and Vial (2019).

3. ETHICAL DIMENSIONS OF DIGITAL HEALTHCARE LEADERSHIP

3.1 Bioethical Principles in the Digital Era

Beauchamp and Childress' (2019) principles approach, including autonomy, beneficence, non-maleficence, and justice, retains its fundamental importance in the realm of digital health, although it must be profoundly reinterpreted in relation to algorithms, data environments, and technology-driven care dynamics. The patient's right to informed consent with respect to clinical interventions has been redefined as the patient's right to know and control his or her data collection, analysis, use, and dissemination in decision making pertaining to care (Mittelstadt et al., 2016). While the attainment of patient data autonomy may seem straightforward at face value, it is a highly daunting challenge within the complex landscape of digital health, where data circulates across many different vendors, systems, and jurisdictions.

The two principles of beneficence and non-maleficence, in other words, doing good and avoiding harm, take on new meaning in relation to AI systems intervening in clinical decision-making processes. Systems programmed on the basis of past data could reinforce and exacerbate the existing inequality in the delivery of health services. According to Obermeyer et al. (2019), a commercially available algorithm being used to distribute health care funds had a tendency to under-prioritize the health needs of Black individuals compared to those of White individuals, thus revealing the power of digital tools to entrench prejudice on a systematic level.

3.2 Data Privacy, Security, and Trust

Data on patients represent the essential foundation of digital health transformation, while the handling of such data constitutes one of the most important ethical responsibilities of healthcare leaders. While the introduction of the Health Insurance

Portability and Accountability Act (HIPAA) served to outline the minimum legal standards for protected health information in the US, new technologies, especially those relating to cloud-based services, mobile health, and secondary data analysis, have generated considerable gaps between existing regulations and the realities of contemporary data management practices (Cohen & Mello, 2018). In this context, the availability of consumer health apps, wearables, and third-party data collectors implies an exchange of data beyond the reach of HIPAA, resulting in very little transparency in how patient data is used for commercial purposes (Price & Cohen, 2019).

The European Union's General Data Protection Regulation (GDPR), which came into effect in 2018, established a more rights-oriented approach to data protection based on data minimization, purpose limitation, and right to explanation of automated decisions—tenets which directly pertain to the regulation of AI in healthcare (Voigt & Von dem Bussche, 2017). Yet, adherence to GDPR or other similar regulatory regimes involves more than just the legal understanding of the law; it requires an organizational structure capable of conducting data mapping, consent management, privacy by design, and appointment of privacy officers such as the DPO and CPO.

Failing in the area of healthcare cybersecurity is a highly egregious act of ethical misconduct. From the years 2015 to 2023 alone, there have been over 5,000 major cyber attacks that resulted in the compromise of patient information involving more than 400 million health records, making it a problem that has evolved from being an IT issue to one that affects boardroom decisions in organizations today (HHS Office for Civil Rights, 2023). The 2020 cyberattack conducted through ransomware against Universal Health Services involved simultaneous attacks at 400 locations at once; this incident showcased the impact such a security threat can have on the health and wellbeing of patients as the operations in multiple emergency departments across several states were impacted (Collier, 2020).

3.3 Algorithmic Ethics and AI Governance

The use of AI in clinical contexts for tasks such as image analysis, risk assessment, clinical decision-making, and operational efficiencies presents an entirely new ethical challenge for health care administrators. In contrast to other medical technologies, AI is frequently characterized by opacity in its reasoning process, referred to as the 'black box', is adaptive as it learns from experience, and does not consistently perform across different populations or contexts (Char et al., 2018).

AI governance in healthcare should include pre-implementation validation procedures aimed at evaluating the accuracy, fairness, and clinical usefulness of AI technology among all pertinent demographic groups, a system for detecting performance drift and harmful consequences after implementation, and accountability procedures for identifying those responsible for harm caused by AI technologies.

Although the FDA's SaMD framework sets out the regulations for AI tools in terms of clinical decision support, the evidentiary requirements for AI governance still fall short of those associated with drug or device interventions (FDA, 2021).

Table 2 maps the five core bioethical principles to both traditional healthcare contexts and their digital transformation equivalents, identifying the executive accountability mechanisms appropriate to each domain.

Table 2. Ethical Principles Mapped to Digital Healthcare Transformation Contexts

Ethical Principle	Traditional Healthcare Context	Digital Transformation Context	Executive Accountability Mechanism
Autonomy	Informed consent for procedures	Consent for data sharing, algorithmic decision participation	Transparent consent policies, opt-out frameworks
Beneficence	Acting in the patient's best interest	Ensuring AI tools improve care quality and outcomes	Outcome-based KPIs, clinical validation of algorithms
Non-maleficence	Avoiding harm from treatments	Preventing algorithmic bias, system downtime, data breaches	Bias audits, cybersecurity governance, redundancy systems
Justice	Equitable access to care	Reducing digital divide, ensuring AI equity across demographics	Equity dashboards, community access programs
Privacy	Confidentiality of patient information	Data minimization, de-identification, HIPAA/GDPR compliance	Chief Privacy Officer role, regular data audits

Note. Adapted from Beauchamp and Childress (2019), Mittelstadt et al. (2016), and Obermeyer et al. (2019). HIPAA = Health Insurance Portability and Accountability Act; GDPR = General Data Protection Regulation.

4. THE INNOVATION IMPERATIVE: EMERGING TECHNOLOGIES AND STRATEGIC ADOPTION

4.1 Artificial Intelligence and Machine Learning

AI and machine learning are revolutionizing clinical practice through developments that outpace current frameworks for regulation, organization, and professional standards. In diagnostic imaging, deep learning methods have been shown to perform on par with—and in certain specialized niches even outperform—human experts in identifying diabetic retinopathy, pulmonary nodules, and skin cancers (Rajpurkar et al., 2022). In pathology, automated AI analysis of histological slides has the potential not only to increase throughput but also to enhance the sensitivity of early cancer detection (Esteva et al., 2021). In natural language processing, language models are emerging as a tool for clinical documentation, physician-patient communication, and literature review, although issues of accuracy, hallucination, and reasoning in complex clinical scenarios still pose serious challenges (Thirunavukarasu et al., 2023).

For decision-makers, the question is no longer whether to implement AI but rather how to do so appropriately and in a timely manner. Evidence-based implementation entails that decision-makers must subject AI tools to stringent standards such as: clinical validity (accuracy of tool in target clinical setting), algorithmic fairness (consistent performance among diverse population groups), implementation viability (incorporation into workflows), regulatory standing, and cost-effectiveness (training, monitoring, and governance costs) (Bates et al., 2021). Organizations seeking to obtain an edge over competitors through the use of AI run the risk of implementing technologies that may actually hurt patients and incur substantial legal and reputational liabilities.

4.2 Telehealth and Virtual Care Models

The quick growth in the use of telehealth services during the coronavirus pandemic provided a kind of natural experiment regarding telehealth provision on a large scale. Research done to investigate the impacts of this growth indicated that there were both positive and negative effects. Telehealth proved beneficial in improving access to healthcare among patients with transportation difficulties, managing chronic conditions among residents living in remote areas, and providing behavioral healthcare services. However, it was noted that the use of telehealth services was not even among elderly people, individuals from poor socioeconomic backgrounds, and those whose primary language is not English (Keesara et al., 2020; Shi et al., 2021).

Strategically sustainable virtual care programs demand a shift by organizational leaders from reacting in emergencies to strategically integrating virtual and in-person care modalities into care models. Hybrid care models, which can be referred to as bricks and clicks, have proven successful in the areas of primary care, oncology follow-ups, post-operative care, and behavioral medicine, allowing organizations to effectively allocate in-person care time to higher complexity situations while utilizing virtual care models for lower acuity consultations and education (Vogel et al., 2021).

4.3 Interoperability and Health Information Exchange

Interoperability, or the capacity of different digital technologies to communicate and utilize medical data, is an essential factor in making the maximum possible benefit from digital transformation initiatives. Even though billions have been invested in the development of electronic health records, fragmented digital environments are still a major issue in most healthcare markets. The average large health organization in the United States has 785+ different software products in its environment, which shows how fragmented the digital transformation efforts of the past two decades have been and presents many obstacles to healthcare delivery (Gettinger & Frisse, 2018).

While the implementation of HL7 FHIR, which is required to be used as the API standard for the mandate under the 21st Century Cures Act Interoperability and Patient Access Rule, is making progress on data portability, it has been unable to solve basic issues such as data standards, semantics, and identity matching between systems (Mandl et al., 2020). Interoperability governance frameworks that need to be put in place include policies, vendor contracts, and participation in regional health information exchange initiatives.

4.4 Precision Medicine and Genomics

The use of genomic data in clinical practice is one example of digital transformation and its tremendous impact on the individual prevention, diagnosis, and treatment of diseases. Genomic tools used to identify genetic markers that predict the reaction of patients to certain drugs have been shown clinically useful in cancer therapy, cardiology, and psychiatry, and research suggests genomically informed prescribing decreases adverse drug reactions and increases therapeutic efficiency (Relling & Evans, 2015). The falling prices on whole genome sequencing technology (dropping from approximately $100 million per genome in 2001 to less than $1,000 now) makes it easier to incorporate genomic data into clinical practice (National Human Genome Research Institute, 2023).

However, the organizational, ethical, and technical challenges associated with implementing genomics medicine are considerable. Healthcare organizations need to build capacity in the collection, analysis, and management of genomic data; prepare clinicians to interpret and explain genetic risks probabilistically; grapple with difficult issues of consent and feedback; and confront major health equity issues because the vast majority of genomic reference populations continue to consist of people of European heritage (Hindorff et al., 2018). All of which will require executive leaders who are fluent in both the science and ethics of genomic medicine.

5. EXECUTIVE ACCOUNTABILITY IN DIGITAL HEALTHCARE TRANSFORMATION

5.1 Redefining Executive Roles in the Digital Era

Digital transformation requires a profound realignment of the responsibilities of senior executives in healthcare organizations. The role of the CIO, which used to focus solely on ensuring technological stability and reducing IT expenditure, has significantly broadened to include strategic technology management, innovation portfolio management, data strategy management, AI governance, and cybersecurity within enterprises (Gartner, 2022). At the same time, the introduction of the Chief Digital Officer and the Chief Data Officer is an acknowledgment by organizations that digital and data strategy demand specialized senior management.

The responsibilities of CMOs have been undergoing transformations as well. Digital health, clinical informatics, artificial intelligence management, and digital health equity are currently key responsibilities of a CMO within advanced healthcare systems, rather than being delegated to IT employees (Simpao & Rehman, 2020). The importance of being digitally fluent is becoming increasingly critical for CEOs as they should not only support digital strategy but develop it actively, comprehend the ethical considerations underlying such developments, and monitor all the processes from the board level. According to Dery et al. (2017), firms where the CEO participated in the digital strategy formulation process performed better than companies where the same CEO supported the idea passively.

5.2 Building a Culture of Accountable Innovation

Innovations in healthcare have specific accountability considerations due to the potential for the negative outcomes of failure to materialize as physical harm to patients. Creating an environment of accountability for innovation, where failure is allowed but only within a safe space where learning can occur, is a critical leadership function. The application of Edmondson's (2018) concept of psychological safety in healthcare innovation settings implies that leaders need to create environments in which front-line healthcare practitioners are willing to report near-misses, question algorithmic outputs, and bring up issues with digital systems.

Innovation culture that encourages accountability goes beyond the realm of a soft-management principle. There needs to be an institutional process for clinicians to provide feedback in regard to technology assessment and design, avenues to escalate safety issues related to use of digital technologies, and review procedures post-implementation to ensure lessons learned are incorporated. According to the Agency for Healthcare Research and Quality (AHRQ), organizational safety culture marked by free-flowing communication, non-punitive approaches to error reporting, and executive walks have been linked with higher levels of patient safety outcomes. Furthermore, preliminary findings suggest such organizational safety culture features facilitate safe AI/IT implementation (Weaver et al., 2013).

5.3 Governing the Digital Portfolio

In the pursuit of digital transformation for healthcare organizations, managing an increasingly complex portfolio of technology projects such as EHR optimization, AI adoption, telehealth growth, cybersecurity improvement, interoperability advancement, and consumer digitalization is crucial, often concurrently with limited funding and staffing. Portfolio management entails utilizing criteria for decision-making that transcend the mere financial metric of return on investment, encompassing clinical relevance, equity implications, operational viability, and strategic coherence (Kaplan & Harris-Salamone, 2009).

One of the typical challenges in transforming healthcare with digital technologies is the concept of "initiative sprawl" described by Johnson et al. (2021). It refers to an abundance of digital initiatives that lack integration into enterprise architecture due to the nature of their origin – being advocated and funded by departments or external vendors. It is essential that executives create a governance structure that would have the necessary power and representation to review the current portfolio of initiatives, reduce redundancies, and focus efforts on the most innovative ideas. Such an approach would require not only organizational courage but also discipline.

5.4 Measuring Executive Accountability: KPIs and Reporting

Without measurement, accountability is simply wishful thinking. Healthcare administrators who seek to implement digital transformation in their organizations need to set up an appropriate measurement system that measures success on various levels: patient safety effects, efficiency improvements, financial benefits, employee experiences, and equity results. The Balanced Scorecard method can be applied to digital health by modifying it in a way suggested by various scholars (Kaplan & Norton, 2015).

It is important that any framework for measuring impact must be capable of including intended effects as well as any unintended effects. An example where an effort to enhance benefits and incur unintended negative impacts is seen is in EHR implementations. If such implementation increases billings but takes up much documentation time of physicians to lead to burnout, this can be regarded as either a partially successful strategy or even harmful. Executives that focus on financial benefits from such initiatives will inadvertently encourage dysfunctional behavior.

Table 3 presents a proposed set of executive-level key performance indicators (KPIs) for healthcare digital transformation accountability, organized by category, with measurement methods, target benchmarks, and executive ownership designations.

Table 3. Executive-Level KPIs for Healthcare Digital Transformation Accountability

KPI Category	Specific Metric	Measurement Method	Target Benchmark	Executive Owner
Patient Safety	AI alert override rate	EHR workflow analytics	<15%	CMO/CMIO
Data Security	Mean time to detect breach	SIEM monitoring logs	<24 hours	CISO
Digital Equity	Telehealth adoption by demographic	Patient demographic surveys	>80% parity	CDO/CEO
Operational Efficiency	EHR documentation time per encounter	Time-motion studies	Reduction >20%	COO/CMIO
Innovation ROI	Cost savings from digital initiatives	Financial reporting dashboard	>3:1 ratio	CFO/CIO
Clinician Well-being	EHR-related burnout score	Annual validated survey (MBI)	Score <25	CHRO/CMO

Note. KPIs should be customized to organizational context and strategic priorities. CMO = Chief Medical Officer; CMIO = Chief Medical Information Officer; CISO = Chief Information Security Officer; CDO = Chief Digital/Data Officer; COO = Chief Operating Officer; CFO = Chief Financial Officer; CIO = Chief Information Officer; CHRO = Chief Human Resources Officer; MBI = Maslach Burnout Inventory.

6. AN INTEGRATED GOVERNANCE MODEL FOR DIGITAL HEALTHCARE LEADERSHIP

6.1 Governance Architecture

All this evidence comes together to lead to a specific finding: in order for the digital transformation of healthcare to be sustainable, it needs to have a governance framework that is strategic, ethical, clinical, and agile at the same time, that is to say one that can align digital decisions with organizational missions, be guided by ethical standards, facilitate excellent clinical practices, and adapt to new technological environments.

Incorporating the models for governance proposed by Weill & Ross (2004) but tailored to the healthcare sector by Shortliffe & Cimino (2021), the following model proposes five interconnected levels of governance, each assigned with unique duties, responsible parties, and reporting processes. It is important to note that these levels do not exist in isolation but rather are integrated parts of a larger governance process.

Table 4 summarizes the proposed governance framework, mapping each layer to responsible organizational bodies, core responsibilities, and reporting mechanisms.

Table 4. Integrated Digital Transformation Governance Framework for Healthcare Organizations

Governance Layer	Responsible Body	Core Responsibilities	Reporting Mechanism
Strategic	Board of Directors / Executive Committee	Approve digital strategy, oversee ethical compliance, allocate capital	Quarterly board reports, annual digital maturity scorecard
Tactical	Digital Transformation Steering Committee	Coordinate cross-functional initiatives, manage program portfolio, resolve escalations	Monthly steering reports, OKR tracking dashboards
Clinical	Clinical Informatics Council / CMO Office	Validate clinical algorithms, oversee EHR adoption, manage workflow redesign	Bi-weekly clinical outcomes metrics, peer review of AI tools
Data & Privacy	Chief Data Officer / Privacy Office	Data governance policy, consent framework, regulatory compliance (HIPAA, GDPR)	Real-time data quality dashboards, annual compliance audit
Security	CISO / Cybersecurity Committee	Threat monitoring, incident response, vendor risk management	Monthly security posture reports, tabletop exercises

Note. OKR = Objectives and Key Results; SIEM = Security Information and Event Management. Adapted from Weill and Ross (2004) and Shortliffe and Cimino (2021).

6.2 Ethical Stewardship as a Governance Core

The unique characteristic of the suggested governance structure lies in the embedding of the principle of ethical stewardship not as a discrete compliance process, but rather as the common denominator within all layers of governance. This is based on the belief that ethical issues surrounding digital health technologies cannot be addressed solely through compliance, but rather demand active organizational values-based leadership (Mittelstadt et al., 2016; Vayena et al., 2018).

Ethical stewardship operationalization demands from executives a certain degree of structural action, including the formation of an independent Ethics Advisory Committee consisting of experts in bioethics, patient advocacy, health equity, and technology; performing ethical impact assessments for all important digital transformation projects before approving them; including stakeholder representation in the governing structure of digital projects that will have an effect on delivery of care; and ensuring a safe way for clinicians, patients, and staff to report any ethical issues they may observe in digital systems. As Vayena et al. (2018) argue, the last of these measures is particularly important due to the power inequality between healthcare institutions and their patients.

6.3 The Role of the Board in Digital Governance

The boards that govern healthcare organizations are ultimately responsible for the organization's ethics and legal obligations. However, it is clear that boards overseeing hospitals and health systems do not have the digital skills or governance frameworks to provide proper oversight of digital transformation efforts. In a survey conducted in 2020 among healthcare board directors, less than 40% said that they had enough digital skill sets represented in their boardroom, and less than 30% stated that cybersecurity is a regular topic of discussion at board meetings (Kaufman Hall, 2020).

Overcoming the board's deficiency in digital literacy will involve executives allocating resources for the development of knowledge among the board members regarding digital strategy, artificial intelligence ethics, cybersecurity, and digital equity, which should go beyond just orientation sessions but rather should include workshops for the board members, visits to the digital innovation lab, and discussions about case studies involving success and failure stories related to digital transformation. It is important to note that the inclusion of digital specialists within the board membership can be considered a strategic step, as some of the health systems' boards have already done (Dery et al., 2017).

6.4 Workforce Development and Digital Leadership Pipeline

For any governance strategy to work, it requires the right human resources behind it. In terms of digital transformation of the healthcare industry, it is all about people. It means that in addition to acquiring technologies, healthcare executives should focus on investing in their workforce just as much as in technologies. It involves educating their clinical frontline staff on digital transformation, change management, as well as responsible usage of AI solutions. It means hiring clinical informaticians, health data scientists, and experts in digital transformation (Topol Review, 2019).

According to the Topol Review (2019), sponsored by Health Education England, around 90% of healthcare jobs in the United Kingdom will need some level of digital literacy in the next ten years. The American Medical Informatics Association (AMIA) in the US is calling for an increase in the number of workers in the field of clinical informatics by ten times to address the need for specialists who can act as intermediaries between the fields of technology and clinical practice (AMIA, 2016). Such projections regarding the healthcare workforce have important implications on talent management strategy and partnership between academics and healthcare systems.

7. IMPLICATIONS FOR PRACTICE AND POLICY

7.1 For Healthcare Executives

There are numerous implications that the evidence and discussion provided in this chapter have on the role of executives within the healthcare industry. Most importantly, the concept of transformational leadership within the realm of digital transformation has become a mandatory component of the professional skillset of any executive; this skill cannot be delegated as a technological process. Active involvement in digital health executive education programs, participation in the relevant peer communities, and participation in technology governance are not additional features of the executive role but rather mandatory components of it.

Second, leaders need to avoid the seduction of thinking about digital transformation in terms of cost savings. Digital technologies offer enormous potential for efficiency gains; however, when transformation is considered only from the cost perspective, organizations end up cultivating a culture where the needs of patients, the quality of care, and employee well-being become secondary considerations in technology-related decisions. When viewed as a value creation problem, digital investments become an entirely different proposition.

Third, leaders should take active measures to promote health equity as an absolute requirement for any digital transformation efforts. Each time a company decides to make a new investment in technology, whether it's through EHR integration, AI application, or telemedicine use, it should evaluate the effect this innovation will have on health equity and measure it in the same manner as the organization evaluates its financial performance.

7.2 For Healthcare Boards and Governance Bodies

It is critical that healthcare governance bodies immediately make digital transformation, cybersecurity, and AI ethics key aspects of corporate governance. This will entail not only restructuring (formation of Digital/Technology Committees at the board level) but also a behavior shift, which means incorporating digital transformation status reports, ethical challenges, and workforce effects into their standard reporting procedures. Those governance bodies that fail to comprehend the strategy their organization follows in regard to its digital transformation will not be able to provide proper oversight.

7.3 For Policymakers and Regulators

Policy makers and regulators have to contend with creating governance regimes that encourage innovation and at the same time prevent potential harm. This issue is compounded by the speed of technological development, the complex nature of AI technology, and the globalized market of digital health technologies. Several policy considerations can be gleaned from the evidence presented in this chapter. The most pressing need is the need for robust federal-level privacy protections that would include consumer health apps and data brokers, as existing frameworks are inadequate and leave patients vulnerable to exploitation of their health data by businesses (Price & Cohen, 2019). There is a need for mandatory standards for algorithmic fairness in AI technologies used in clinical decision-making, as this would help to establish uniform accountability standards and encourage manufacturers to make investments in detecting and mitigating AI biases (FDA, 2021).

7.4 For Researchers and Educators

Although there has been rapid growth in the scholarly literature concerning the digital transformation of healthcare, the current state of affairs is one of fragmentation along disciplinary lines. Contributions from experts in fields such as health informatics, organizational behavior, bioethics, health economics, and public health have all been fruitful in their own ways, but an integrated approach to translating this diverse body of knowledge into executive action has thus far been lacking. Interdisciplinary collaboration between scholars who specialize in each field, in order to address important and practical research questions such as those regarding the design of effective AI governance frameworks, the development of predictive competencies for digital transformations, and the appropriate use of automation in care, would benefit practitioners greatly.

The inclusion of digital health skills should become part of all medical, nursing, pharmacology, public health, and health administration courses in higher education training, and not just part of elective informatics courses. Future leaders of the health profession will require graduating with at least minimum digital literacy, the ability to reason ethically concerning the governance of AI, and skills to manage organizational change.

8. CONCLUSION

The digital transformation of healthcare is taking place with such speed and impact that it calls for a corresponding change in the field of healthcare leadership.

Based on the findings of the reviewed literature, it is evident that the organizations that succeed in implementing sustainable, justifiable, and clinically meaningful digital transformation are those that do not differentiate themselves mainly due to technological advancements but rather because of strong governance and ethics.

The integrated approach outlined above – which integrates ethical stewardship, innovation governance, executive accountability, and talent management within a unified governance hierarchy – provides a guiding principle for health system leaders as they steer this transition. Essentially, it is based on a deep-rooted belief that within the healthcare industry, digital transformation is not an ultimate goal but rather a tool for achieving the unchanging mission of every healthcare provider, which is to take care of the ill, prevent diseases, foster health, and help people with kindness.

Those who continue to keep such a vision in the core of their digital transformation leadership—not only asking themselves about what technologies can do but also what they should be doing, who for, and under which circumstances—are most likely to achieve successful transformations in favor of improving the patient life, enhancing the capacity of the clinical workforce, and responding to the immense trust of the community in the institutions working for the well-being of the patients. The responsibility, opportunity, and accountability associated with digital transformation leadership in healthcare come together with unprecedented stakes for leaders, but, above all, they represent great opportunities and privileges.

REFERENCES

Agency for Healthcare Research and Quality. (2023). Digital health equity and access. AHRQ Digital Health Reports. https://www.ahrq.gov/digital-health

American Medical Informatics Association. (2016). AMIA 25x5 task force on reducing documentation burden on U.S. clinicians by 75% by 2025. https://amia.org/resources/25x5-task-force

Bates, D. W., Auerbach, A., Schulam, P., Wright, A., & Saria, S. (2021). Reporting recommendations for clinical use of AI-based prediction models. *Journal of the American Medical Association, 325*(19), 1951–1952. DOI: 10.1001/jama.2021.3782

Beauchamp, T. L., & Childress, J. F. (2019). *Principles of biomedical ethics* (8th ed.). Oxford University Press.

Char, D. S., Shah, N. H., & Magnus, D. (2018). Implementing machine learning in health care—Addressing ethical challenges. *The New England Journal of Medicine, 378*(11), 981–983. DOI: 10.1056/NEJMp1714229 PMID: 29539284

Cohen, I. G., & Mello, M. M. (2018). HIPAA and protecting health information in the 21st century. *Journal of the American Medical Association, 320*(3), 231–232. DOI: 10.1001/jama.2018.5630 PMID: 29800120

Collier, R. (2020). Hospitals shut down by ransomware attacks. *Canadian Medical Association Journal, 192*(46), E1427–E1428. DOI: 10.1503/cmaj.1095929

Dery, K., Sebastian, I. M., & van der Meulen, N. (2017). The digital workplace is key to digital innovation. *MIS Quarterly Executive, 16*(2), 135–152.

Edmondson, A. C. (2018). *The fearless organization: Creating psychological safety in the workplace for learning, innovation, and growth.* Wiley.

Esteva, A., Chou, K., Yeung, S., Naik, N., Madani, A., Mottaghi, A., Liu, Y., Topol, E., Dean, J., & Socher, R. (2021). Deep learning-enabled medical computer vision. *NPJ Digital Medicine, 4*(1), 5. DOI: 10.1038/s41746-020-00376-2 PMID: 33420381

European Commission. (2022). European Health Data Space. Directorate-General for Health and Food Safety. https://health.ec.europa.eu/ehealth-digital-health-and-care/european-health-data-space_en

Food and Drug Administration. (2021). Artificial intelligence/machine learning (AI/ML)-based software as a medical device (SaMD) action plan. U.S. Department of Health and Human Services. https://www.fda.gov/media/145022/download

Gartner. (2022). Gartner CIO and technology executive survey 2022: Healthcare insights. Gartner Research.

Gettinger, A., & Frisse, M. E. (2018). *Health information technology: Getting the governance right*. Health Affairs Blog., DOI: 10.1377/hblog20180124.985437

Healthcare Information and Management Systems Society. (2023). *HIMSS EMRAM worldwide survey results 2023*. HIMSS Analytics.

HHS Office for Civil Rights. (2023). HIPAA enforcement highlights 2023. U.S. Department of Health and Human Services. https://www.hhs.gov/hipaa/for-professionals/compliance-enforcement/data/enforcement-highlights

Hindorff, L. A., Bonham, V. L., Brody, L. C., Ginoza, M. E. C., Hutter, C. M., Manolio, T. A., & Green, E. D. (2018). Prioritizing diversity in human genomics research. *Nature Reviews. Genetics*, *19*(3), 175–185. DOI: 10.1038/nrg.2017.89 PMID: 29151588

Jalali, M. S., & Kaiser, J. P. (2018). Cybersecurity in hospitals: A systematic, organizational perspective. *Journal of Medical Internet Research*, *20*(5), e10059. DOI: 10.2196/10059 PMID: 29807882

Johnson, K. B., Wei, W., Weeraratne, D., Frisse, M. E., Misulis, K., Rhee, K., Zhao, J., & Snowdon, J. L. (2021). Precision medicine, AI, and the future of personalized health care. *Clinical and Translational Science*, *14*(1), 86–93. DOI: 10.1111/cts.12884 PMID: 32961010

Kane, G. C., Phillips, A. N., Copulsky, J., & Andrus, G. (2019). *The technology fallacy: How people are the real key to digital transformation*. MIT Press. DOI: 10.7551/mitpress/11661.001.0001

Kaplan, R. S., & Harris-Salamone, K. D. (2009). Health care IT project implementation success and failure. *Journal of Healthcare Information Management*, *23*(2), 20–27.

Kaplan, R. S., & Norton, D. P. (2015). *Balanced scorecard success: The Kaplan-Norton collection*. Harvard Business Review Press.

Kaufman Hall. (2020). *2020 State of healthcare performance improvement: Digital transformation in turbulent times*. Kaufman Hall & Associates.

Keesara, S., Jonas, A., & Schulman, K. (2020). Covid-19 and health care's digital revolution. *The New England Journal of Medicine*, *382*(23), e82. DOI: 10.1056/NEJMp2005835 PMID: 32240581

Kruse, C. S., Kothman, K., Anerobi, K., & Abanaka, L. (2016). Adoption factors of the electronic health record: A systematic review. *JMIR Medical Informatics*, *4*(2), e19. DOI: 10.2196/medinform.5525 PMID: 27251559

Mandl, K. D., Kreda, D. A., Kohane, I. S., Ramoni, R. B., & Haselkorn, J. K. (2020). SMART on FHIR: A standards-based, interoperable apps platform for electronic health records. *Journal of the American Medical Informatics Association : JAMIA*, *23*(5), 899–908. DOI: 10.1093/jamia/ocv189 PMID: 26911829

Mathews, S. C., McShea, M. J., Hanley, C. L., Ravitz, A., Labrique, A. B., & Cohen, A. B. (2022). Digital health: A path to validation. *NPJ Digital Medicine*, *2*(1), 38. DOI: 10.1038/s41746-019-0111-3 PMID: 31304384

Mennemeyer, S. T., Menachemi, N., Rahurkar, S., & Ford, E. W. (2016). Impact of the HITECH Act on physicians' adoption of electronic health records. *Journal of the American Medical Informatics Association : JAMIA*, *23*(2), 375–379. DOI: 10.1093/jamia/ocv103 PMID: 26228764

Mittelstadt, B. D., Allo, P., Taddeo, M., Wachter, S., & Floridi, L. (2016). The ethics of algorithms: Mapping the debate. *Big Data & Society*, *3*(2), 2053951716679679. DOI: 10.1177/2053951716679679

National Human Genome Research Institute. (2023). The cost of sequencing a human genome. National Institutes of Health. https://www.genome.gov/about-genomics/fact-sheets/Sequencing-Human-Genome-cost

Obermeyer, Z., Powers, B., Vogeli, C., & Mullainathan, S. (2019). Dissecting racial bias in an algorithm used to manage the health of populations. *Science*, *366*(6464), 447–453. DOI: 10.1126/science.aax2342 PMID: 31649194

Office of the National Coordinator for Health Information Technology. (2020). 21st Century Cures Act: Interoperability, information blocking, and the ONC health IT certification program. *Federal Register*, *85*(25), 25642–25961.

Price, W. N.II, & Cohen, I. G. (2019). Privacy in the age of medical big data. *Nature Medicine*, *25*(1), 37–43. DOI: 10.1038/s41591-018-0272-7 PMID: 30617331

Rajpurkar, P., Chen, E., Banerjee, O., & Topol, E. J. (2022). AI in health and medicine. *Nature Medicine*, *28*(1), 31–38. DOI: 10.1038/s41591-021-01614-0 PMID: 35058619

Relling, M. V., & Evans, W. E. (2015). Pharmacogenomics in the clinic. *Nature*, *526*(7573), 343–350. DOI: 10.1038/nature15817 PMID: 26469045

Shi, C. R., Anadkat, M. J., Mamo, A., & Ortiz, A. E. (2021). Disparities in telehealth access among minority and underserved patient populations in ambulatory dermatology. *Journal of the American Academy of Dermatology*, *85*(6), 1640–1642. DOI: 10.1016/j.jaad.2021.06.011 PMID: 33421478

Shortliffe, E. H., & Cimino, J. J. (Eds.). (2021). *Biomedical informatics: Computer applications in health care and biomedicine* (5th ed.). Springer. DOI: 10.1007/978-3-030-58721-5

Simpao, A. F., & Rehman, M. A. (2020). Telehealth, artificial intelligence, and the coronavirus disease 2019 pandemic: A perfect storm. *Anesthesia and Analgesia*, *131*(5), 1249–1251. DOI: 10.1213/ANE.0000000000005027

Sinsky, C., Colligan, L., Li, L., Prgomet, M., Reynolds, S., Goeders, L., Westbrook, J., Tutty, M., & Blike, G. (2016). Allocation of physician time in ambulatory practice: A time and motion study in 4 specialties. *Annals of Internal Medicine*, *165*(11), 753–760. DOI: 10.7326/M16-0961 PMID: 27595430

Siwicki, B. (2022). Healthcare data breach costs hit all-time high for 12th year in a row, IBM report finds. Healthcare IT News. https://www.healthcareitnews.com/news/healthcare-data-breach-costs-hit-all-time-high-12th-year-row-ibm-report-finds

Thirunavukarasu, A. J., Ting, D. S. J., Elangovan, K., Gutierrez, L., Tan, T. F., & Ting, D. S. W. (2023). Large language models in medicine. *Nature Medicine*, *29*(8), 1930–1940. DOI: 10.1038/s41591-023-02448-8 PMID: 37460753

Topol, E. J. (2019). *Deep medicine: How artificial intelligence can make healthcare human again*. Basic Books.

Topol Review. (2019). Preparing the healthcare workforce to deliver the digital future. Health Education England. https://topol.hee.nhs.uk

Vayena, E., Blasimme, A., & Cohen, I. G. (2018). Machine learning in medicine: Addressing ethical challenges. *PLoS Medicine*, *15*(11), e1002689. DOI: 10.1371/journal.pmed.1002689 PMID: 30399149

Vest, J. R., & Gamm, L. D. (2017). Health information exchange: Persistent challenges and new strategies. *Journal of the American Medical Informatics Association : JAMIA*, *17*(3), 288–294. DOI: 10.1136/jamia.2010.003673 PMID: 20442146

Vial, G. (2019). Understanding digital transformation: A review and a research agenda. *The Journal of Strategic Information Systems*, *28*(2), 118–144. DOI: 10.1016/j.jsis.2019.01.003

Vogel, L. (2021). How COVID-19 normalized virtual care. *Canadian Medical Association Journal, 193*(7), E247–E248. DOI: 10.1503/cmaj.1095946

Voigt, P., & Von dem Bussche, A. (2017). *The EU General Data Protection Regulation (GDPR): A practical guide*. Springer. DOI: 10.1007/978-3-319-57959-7

Weaver, S. J., Lubomksi, L. H., Wilson, R. F., Pfoh, E. R., Martinez, K. A., & Dy, S. M. (2013). Promoting a culture of safety as a patient safety strategy: A systematic review. *Annals of Internal Medicine, 158*(5 Pt 2), 369–374. DOI: 10.7326/0003-4819-158-5-201303051-00002 PMID: 23460092

Weill, P., & Ross, J. W. (2004). *IT governance: How top performers manage IT decision rights for superior results*. Harvard Business School Press.

World Health Organization. (2021). Global strategy on digital health 2020–2025. WHO Press. https://www.who.int/docs/default-source/documents/gs4dhdaa2a9f352b0445bafbc79ca799dce4d.pdf

KEY TERMS AND DEFINITIONS

Algorithmic Bias: Systematic and unfair discrimination in AI-generated outputs attributable to flawed assumptions, unrepresentative training data, or design decisions that produce disparate outcomes across demographic groups.

Clinical Decision Support (CDS): Digital tools that provide clinicians, staff, patients, and other individuals with knowledge and person-specific information, intelligently filtered or presented at appropriate times, to enhance health and health care.

Digital Health Equity: The principle and practice of ensuring that digital health technologies and services are accessible, appropriate, and beneficial for all individuals and communities, regardless of race, ethnicity, income, geography, age, or disability status.

Digital Transformation: The profound and fundamental change in organizational logic, value creation, and service delivery enabled by the integration of digital technologies into core processes and strategies.

Electronic Health Record (EHR): A digital version of a patient's medical chart, maintained in real time and accessible to authorized users, encompassing the full range of clinical, administrative, and financial data generated in the course of care.

Health Information Exchange (HIE): The electronic mobilization of health care information across organizations within a region, community, or hospital system.

Interoperability: The ability of different information systems, devices, and applications to access, exchange, integrate, and cooperatively use data in a coordinated manner.

Telehealth: The use of electronic information and telecommunications technologies to support and promote long-distance clinical health care, patient and professional health-related education, and public health and health administration.

Chapter 9
Marketing Strategy in Cross-National Pharmaceutical Campaigns: Ethics, Regulation, and Digital Transformation

Ricardo Marcao
http://orcid.org/0000-0003-3277-3078
NECE, University of Beira Interior, Portugal & ISLA Santarem, Portugal

Stephanie Monteiro
Institute for Systems and Robotics, Portugal

Filipa Martinho
ISLA Santarem, Portugal

Bablu Kumar Dhar
http://orcid.org/0000-0001-8768-8634
Mahidol University, Thailand

Maria Estrada
ISLA Santarem, Portugal

ABSTRACT

The pharmaceutical industry is highly complex and regulated, requiring adaptive and ethically grounded marketing strategies, particularly in cross-national contexts.

DOI: 10.4018/979-8-3373-9410-7.ch009

This study develops a conceptual literature review on transnational pharmaceutical marketing, focusing on regulation, ethics, cultural adaptation, and digital transformation. Drawing on multidisciplinary sources, it highlights the role of data-driven and personalized strategies. Findings suggest that effective campaigns balance global alignment with local adaptation, supported by ethical governance and technological capabilities, offering relevant managerial implications.

1. INTRODUCTION

The pharmaceutical industry operates at the intersection of healthcare, economics, and regulation, making it one of the most strategically sensitive and institutionally constrained sectors in the global economy. Unlike traditional consumer markets, where purchasing decisions are primarily driven by preferences and price considerations, pharmaceutical products have direct and often immediate implications for patient safety, treatment outcomes, and public health systems. This intrinsic connection to human well-being significantly elevates the level of ethical and regulatory scrutiny applied to marketing practices, requiring companies to operate within a framework that prioritizes accuracy, transparency, and accountability (Francer et al., 2014). As a result, pharmaceutical marketing is not merely a commercial function but a critical component of a broader healthcare ecosystem, where decisions must balance economic objectives with societal responsibilities.

Over recent decades, two major forces—globalization and digital transformation—have fundamentally reshaped the strategic landscape in which pharmaceutical companies operate. Globalization has expanded the geographic scope of pharmaceutical markets, increasing the need for cross-national marketing strategies capable of addressing diverse regulatory environments, cultural contexts, and healthcare infrastructures. Organizations are no longer confined to single-market operations but must design campaigns that can be implemented across multiple jurisdictions, each with its own legal requirements and institutional dynamics (Applbaum, 2006). This expansion has introduced new layers of complexity, as companies must reconcile global strategic objectives with local operational realities, often under conditions of significant uncertainty and variability.

Simultaneously, the rapid evolution of digital technologies has transformed how pharmaceutical companies engage with their stakeholders. Advances in data analytics, artificial intelligence, and digital communication platforms have enabled more targeted, interactive, and measurable forms of engagement, shifting the focus from broad, undifferentiated communication to highly personalized and data-driven strategies (Tsenov, 2022). These technologies have redefined the nature of interactions between pharmaceutical companies, healthcare professionals, and patients, facilitating real-time communication and continuous feedback loops. As a consequence, marketing strategies have become more dynamic and adaptive, capable of responding to changing conditions and stakeholder needs with greater precision.

Despite the increasing relevance of these developments, the existing body of literature remains fragmented, often addressing regulatory, ethical, and digital dimensions as separate domains of analysis. While valuable insights have been generated within each of these areas, there is a notable lack of integrative frameworks that capture how these dimensions interact and collectively shape pharmaceutical marketing strategies in cross-national contexts. This fragmentation limits the ability of both scholars and practitioners to fully understand the complexities of the field and to develop coherent and effective approaches to strategy design and implementation.

In response to this gap, the present study develops a conceptual synthesis of pharmaceutical marketing strategies in transnational environments, with a particular emphasis on the interdependencies between regulatory constraints, ethical considerations, cultural adaptation, and digital transformation. Rather than examining these elements in isolation, the analysis seeks to articulate how they converge within a unified strategic framework, influencing both the opportunities and limitations faced by pharmaceutical organizations. This integrative perspective is especially relevant in a context where regulatory requirements shape the boundaries of communication, ethical considerations define acceptable practices, cultural factors influence stakeholder engagement, and digital technologies enable new forms of interaction and value creation.

By bringing these dimensions together, the study contributes to the advancement of the literature in two key ways. First, it provides a structured and comprehensive understanding of cross-national pharmaceutical marketing as a multidimensional and interdependent system, rather than a collection of isolated practices. Second, it offers actionable insights that support managerial decision-making, particularly in the design of marketing strategies that are not only effective in achieving commercial objectives but also aligned with regulatory standards and ethical expectations. In doing so, the paper positions pharmaceutical marketing as a strategic function that must continuously adapt to a rapidly evolving global environment while maintaining its commitment to public health and societal trust.

2. THEORETICAL BACKGROUND ON PHARMACEUTICAL MARKETING

Marketing, as defined by Philip Kotler, involves identifying and satisfying customer needs more effectively than competitors. While this definition provides a solid foundation for understanding value creation and exchange in most industries, its application within the pharmaceutical sector requires a significant conceptual expansion. In this context, marketing cannot be understood solely as a mechanism for influencing demand or optimizing competitive positioning; it must also incorporate ethical responsibility, regulatory compliance, and clinical relevance as central components of strategic decision-making. The nature of pharmaceutical products, which directly affect human health and well-being, fundamentally alters the scope and implications of marketing activities, elevating them from purely commercial practices to socially consequential actions.

Pharmaceutical marketing differs from traditional marketing in several critical dimensions, each of which contributes to the complexity of the strategic environment. One of the most distinctive features is the structure of decision-making. Unlike conventional consumer markets, where purchasing decisions are typically made by end users, pharmaceutical consumption often involves multiple intermediaries. Physicians, pharmacists, and regulatory authorities play a decisive role in determining which medicines are prescribed, dispensed, and ultimately consumed. Patients, although increasingly empowered, are not always the primary decision-makers, and their choices are frequently mediated by professional judgment and institutional constraints (Smith, 2002). This multi-layered decision-making process requires pharmaceutical marketing strategies to address a broader set of actors, each with different informational needs, expectations, and levels of influence.

Another defining characteristic of pharmaceutical marketing is the inherent complexity of the product itself. Medicines are not standard consumer goods; they are scientifically developed interventions that require rigorous testing, regulatory approval, and continuous monitoring. Communicating the value of such products demands a high level of technical accuracy and evidence-based substantiation. Marketing messages must convey complex clinical information, including mechanisms of action, efficacy data, safety profiles, and comparative advantages, often to highly specialized audiences such as healthcare professionals. This requirement for precision and credibility imposes constraints on the form and content of communication, limiting the use of persuasive techniques that may be common in other industries but inappropriate in a clinical context.

Regulatory intensity further differentiates pharmaceutical marketing from its traditional counterparts. The promotion of medicines is subject to strict oversight by national and international regulatory bodies, which define what can be communicated, to whom, and through which channels. These regulations are designed to protect public health by ensuring that information is accurate, balanced, and not misleading (Francer et al., 2014). As a result, pharmaceutical companies must operate within a tightly controlled environment, where non-compliance can lead to severe legal and reputational consequences. The need to navigate diverse and evolving regulatory frameworks across different jurisdictions adds an additional layer of complexity, particularly in the context of cross-national campaigns.

Taken together, these characteristics give rise to a multi-stakeholder marketing environment in which strategies must be carefully designed to address the needs and expectations of a diverse set of actors. Healthcare professionals require detailed and scientifically robust information to support clinical decision-making. Patients seek accessible and trustworthy content that enables them to understand their conditions and treatment options. Regulators demand strict adherence to legal standards and ethical principles, ensuring that marketing practices do not compromise patient safety or public trust. Institutional actors, including hospitals, insurers, and governmental bodies, influence access, pricing, and reimbursement, further shaping the market dynamics.

In this complex ecosystem, effective pharmaceutical marketing requires a high degree of coordination and integration across multiple dimensions. Strategies must be capable of delivering differentiated value propositions to each stakeholder group while maintaining consistency, accuracy, and compliance. This necessitates a shift from traditional, product-centric approaches toward more holistic and system-oriented models, where marketing is embedded within broader organizational processes and aligned with clinical, regulatory, and societal objectives. Ultimately, the distinct characteristics of pharmaceutical marketing redefine the role of marketing itself, transforming it into a strategic function that not only drives commercial success but also contributes to the responsible delivery of healthcare solutions.

3. ETHICS AND REGULATORY COMPLEXITY IN CROSS-NATIONAL CAMPAIGNS

Ethics and regulation constitute foundational pillars of pharmaceutical marketing, shaping not only the boundaries within which companies operate but also the legitimacy of their communication strategies in the eyes of stakeholders. The promotion of medicines is subject to strict legal frameworks that vary significantly across countries, reflecting differences in public health policies, legal traditions, and societal expectations regarding the role of pharmaceutical companies. These regulatory constraints are particularly stringent when compared to other industries, given the direct impact that medicines have on patient safety and clinical outcomes.

A clear illustration of this divergence can be observed in the contrast between the United States and most European markets. In the United States, the Food and Drug Administration permits direct-to-consumer (DTC) advertising of prescription medicines under specific conditions, allowing pharmaceutical companies to communicate directly with patients through mass media channels. This regulatory environment has encouraged the development of consumer-oriented marketing strategies that emphasize awareness, education, and patient engagement. In contrast, most European countries impose strict limitations on such practices, restricting the promotion of prescription medicines exclusively to healthcare professionals. This distinction reflects a more conservative regulatory philosophy, prioritizing the role of medical expertise in prescribing decisions and seeking to minimize the risk of inappropriate self-medication or demand-driven prescribing behavior.

This divergence in regulatory frameworks creates a complex operational landscape for pharmaceutical companies engaged in cross-national marketing. Organizations must develop highly adaptable strategies that can be calibrated to comply with local legal requirements while maintaining a coherent global positioning. Achieving this balance requires not only technical knowledge of regulatory standards but also the capacity to design modular communication strategies, where core messages remain consistent but executional elements—such as channels, tone, and level of detail—are adjusted according to the specific constraints of each market (Cohen, 1988). Failure to adequately manage these differences can result in regulatory sanctions, reputational damage, and disruption of market access.

Beyond legal compliance, ethical considerations play an equally critical role in guiding pharmaceutical marketing practices. Regulatory frameworks establish minimum standards of conduct, but ethical responsibility extends further, encompassing the broader obligation to ensure that communication is truthful, balanced, and aligned with the interests of patients and society. The World Health Organization has emphasized the importance of transparent, accurate, and non-misleading information in the promotion of medicines, highlighting that marketing activities should contribute to informed decision-making rather than manipulate perceptions or exaggerate benefits. In this sense, ethical marketing is not merely a matter of compliance but a strategic imperative that underpins trust in both individual companies and the pharmaceutical industry as a whole.

The consequences of failing to uphold ethical standards can be severe and far-reaching, as illustrated by the widely documented case of OxyContin. The aggressive and misleading promotion of this opioid analgesic, particularly the downplaying of its addictive potential, contributed significantly to a large-scale public health crisis (Kolodny et al., 2015). This case demonstrates how marketing practices that prioritize short-term commercial gains over patient safety can generate long-term societal harm, legal liabilities, and irreversible reputational damage. It also underscores the limitations of relying solely on regulatory compliance, as formally permissible actions may still be ethically problematic if they distort scientific evidence or exploit informational asymmetries.

In light of these considerations, cross-national pharmaceutical marketing requires a multidimensional approach that integrates legal alignment, ethical integrity, and social responsibility into a coherent strategic framework. Legal alignment ensures that marketing activities conform to the regulatory requirements of each jurisdiction, reducing the risk of sanctions and enabling sustainable market participation. Ethical integrity provides the normative foundation for responsible communication, guiding organizations in situations where legal standards may be insufficient or ambiguous. Social responsibility extends this perspective further, recognizing the broader role of pharmaceutical companies in contributing to public health, supporting informed patient behavior, and fostering trust in healthcare systems.

Ultimately, the effective integration of these dimensions is essential for navigating the complexities of the global pharmaceutical landscape. Organizations that are able to align compliance, ethics, and societal expectations within their marketing strategies will be better positioned to achieve not only commercial success but also long-term legitimacy and positive impact in the markets in which they operate.

4. DIGITAL TRANSFORMATION IN PHARMACEUTICAL MARKETING

Digital transformation has emerged as a defining force in pharmaceutical marketing, fundamentally reshaping how organizations design, implement, and evaluate their communication strategies. The widespread adoption of digital tools has enabled pharmaceutical companies to engage with stakeholders in more efficient, scalable, and personalized ways, moving beyond traditional, predominantly face-to-face interaction models toward more dynamic and data-driven approaches. This transformation is not merely technological in nature; it reflects a broader shift in the structure of relationships between pharmaceutical companies, healthcare professionals, patients, and institutional actors, characterized by increased connectivity, immediacy, and access to information.

One of the most significant developments in this context is the rise of e-detailing as a central mechanism of digital engagement. E-detailing allows pharmaceutical representatives to deliver tailored, on-demand content to healthcare professionals through digital platforms, including tablets, web-based interfaces, and virtual meeting tools. Unlike traditional detailing, which is constrained by time, geography, and scheduling limitations, e-detailing offers greater flexibility and accessibility, enabling physicians to access relevant information at their convenience. This approach not only enhances the efficiency of communication but also allows for a higher degree of personalization, as content can be adapted to the specific clinical interests and needs of individual practitioners (Koyuncuoğlu, 2022). Furthermore, the integration of multimedia elements, interactive features, and real-time feedback mechanisms contributes to a more engaging and informative experience, strengthening the effectiveness of promotional and educational activities.

Closely related to the expansion of e-detailing is the growing importance of data-driven marketing and Customer Relationship Management (CRM) systems in the pharmaceutical industry. These systems play a critical role in collecting, organizing, and analyzing large volumes of data related to healthcare professionals, patients, and market dynamics. By leveraging this information, pharmaceutical companies can develop more precise segmentation strategies, identify high-value stakeholders, and design targeted communication initiatives that are more likely to generate meaningful engagement. CRM platforms also enable the tracking of interactions across multiple channels, providing a comprehensive view of stakeholder behavior and preferences. This, in turn, supports the development of more coherent and integrated marketing strategies, where decisions are increasingly guided by empirical evidence rather than intuition (Yadav et al., 2012). However, the effective use of these systems requires robust data governance frameworks, particularly in light of stringent data protection regulations and the ethical considerations associated with handling sensitive health-related information.

Another critical dimension of digital transformation in pharmaceutical marketing is the proliferation of mobile health applications, which have become increasingly embedded in both clinical practice and patient self-management. These applications provide healthcare professionals and patients with real-time access to a wide range of resources, including clinical guidelines, drug information, diagnostic tools, and treatment monitoring functionalities. For healthcare professionals, mobile applications facilitate more informed and efficient decision-making, supporting clinical workflows and enhancing the quality of care. For patients, these tools contribute to improved treatment adherence, greater awareness of health conditions, and more active participation in healthcare processes (Visser et al., 2013). From a marketing perspective, mobile applications represent a powerful channel for ongoing engagement, enabling pharmaceutical companies to maintain continuous interaction with stakeholders beyond traditional promotional contexts.

Taken together, these developments illustrate how digital transformation is redefining the strategic landscape of pharmaceutical marketing. The integration of e-detailing, data-driven marketing systems, and mobile health applications reflects a broader movement toward more connected, personalized, and responsive forms of engagement. At the same time, these advancements introduce new challenges related to data privacy, regulatory compliance, and the ethical use of technology, requiring organizations to adopt a balanced approach that combines innovation with responsibility. As digital capabilities continue to evolve, their effective integration into pharmaceutical marketing strategies will be essential for achieving both commercial objectives and positive health outcomes.

4.4 Artificial Intelligence and Predictive Analytics

AI-driven analytics have become a central capability in contemporary pharmaceutical marketing, enabling organizations to move beyond reactive decision-making toward more predictive and adaptive strategic models. By leveraging large volumes of structured and unstructured data, pharmaceutical companies are increasingly able to anticipate demand patterns, tailoring production, distribution, and communication strategies in a more proactive manner. This predictive capacity is particularly valuable in a sector characterized by fluctuating epidemiological trends and complex supply chains, where the ability to forecast demand can significantly enhance both operational efficiency and patient access to treatment.

In parallel, the integration of advanced analytics and machine learning techniques supports a higher degree of content personalization, allowing companies to design communication strategies that are more closely aligned with the specific needs, preferences, and behaviors of different stakeholder groups. Healthcare professionals, for instance, can receive targeted information based on their specialty, prescribing history, and clinical interests, while patients may be engaged through personalized educational content and adherence support tools. This level of customization not only improves the relevance and effectiveness of marketing initiatives but also contributes to a more meaningful and value-driven interaction between pharmaceutical companies and their audiences.

Moreover, AI-driven analytics play a critical role in optimizing campaign performance by enabling real-time monitoring and continuous refinement of marketing activities. Through the analysis of engagement metrics, behavioral data, and outcome indicators, organizations can rapidly identify which strategies are delivering the desired results and adjust their approaches accordingly. This iterative process enhances the efficiency of resource allocation and supports more evidence-based decision-making, reinforcing the strategic importance of data analytics in pharmaceutical marketing (Mikalef et al., 2019).

The COVID-19 pandemic acted as a powerful catalyst for the adoption of these digital and data-driven strategies, accelerating a transformation that was already underway but had not yet reached full maturity. Restrictions on physical interactions, including limited access to healthcare facilities and the suspension of in-person meetings, forced pharmaceutical companies to rapidly shift toward digital channels for communication and engagement. Virtual platforms, remote detailing, and digital educational tools became essential components of marketing strategies, fundamentally altering how organizations interact with healthcare professionals, patients, and institutional stakeholders.

This transition represents more than a temporary adaptation to exceptional circumstances; it marks a structural shift in the pharmaceutical marketing landscape.

The widespread acceptance of digital engagement models has reshaped expectations among stakeholders, who now demand more flexible, accessible, and personalized forms of interaction. As a result, pharmaceutical companies are likely to continue investing in digital capabilities and AI-driven analytics, embedding these technologies into their core strategic frameworks. In this evolving context, the ability to effectively integrate data, technology, and human-centered communication will be a key determinant of competitive advantage and long-term success.

5. CROSS-NATIONAL STRATEGY AND CULTURAL ADAPTATION

Effective transnational pharmaceutical campaigns require a carefully managed balance between global strategic consistency and local adaptation, a duality that lies at the core of international marketing in highly regulated industries. On the one hand, global consistency is essential to ensure a coherent brand identity, maintain scientific integrity, and optimize operational efficiency across multiple markets. On the other hand, local adaptation is critical to ensure that marketing strategies remain relevant, compliant, and culturally appropriate within diverse national contexts. The challenge for pharmaceutical organizations is not simply to choose between these two dimensions, but rather to integrate them in a way that maximizes both strategic alignment and contextual responsiveness.

Cultural, linguistic, and institutional differences play a decisive role in shaping how pharmaceutical marketing messages are perceived, interpreted, and acted upon. Health-related communication is particularly sensitive to these factors, as it is deeply embedded in local beliefs, values, and practices. For instance, attitudes toward medicine, trust in healthcare professionals, and expectations regarding treatment outcomes vary significantly across regions, influencing both the reception of marketing messages and the decision-making processes of patients and healthcare providers. As a result, standardized global campaigns often require substantial adaptation to ensure that their content resonates with local audiences and aligns with prevailing social norms.

In addition to cultural considerations, structural characteristics of healthcare systems represent a critical determinant of marketing strategy design. Differences in healthcare delivery models, reimbursement mechanisms, and access to medical services influence not only the positioning of pharmaceutical products but also the channels through which they are promoted. In markets with predominantly public healthcare systems, communication strategies may need to emphasize clinical effectiveness and cost-efficiency, whereas in more market-driven systems, branding and patient engagement may play a more prominent role. These structural variations require pharmaceutical companies to tailor their approaches in ways that reflect the specific dynamics of each healthcare environment.

Regulatory requirements further complicate the process of cross-national adaptation. Pharmaceutical marketing is subject to strict legal controls that vary widely between jurisdictions, particularly with regard to the promotion of prescription medicines and the use of direct-to-consumer communication. Compliance with these regulations is non-negotiable and often necessitates significant modifications to campaign content, format, and delivery channels. Moreover, regulatory frameworks are continuously evolving, especially in response to the rapid expansion of digital marketing practices, requiring organizations to maintain a high degree of agility and vigilance in their strategic planning.

Another important factor influencing adaptation is the level of health literacy within target populations. The ability of patients to understand medical information, assess risks and benefits, and make informed decisions varies considerably across countries and demographic groups. This variability has direct implications for the design of marketing messages, which must be calibrated to ensure clarity, accessibility, and accuracy without oversimplifying complex clinical information. In this context, effective communication is not merely a matter of translation but involves the careful adaptation of content to different levels of knowledge and cognitive engagement.

The interplay of these factors creates an inherent strategic tension between efficiency and effectiveness. Standardization offers clear advantages in terms of cost reduction, scalability, and brand consistency, enabling pharmaceutical companies to leverage economies of scale and streamline global operations. However, excessive reliance on standardized approaches may result in messages that are misaligned with local realities, reducing their impact and potentially leading to regulatory or reputational risks. Conversely, extensive localization enhances relevance and responsiveness but may increase complexity, costs, and the risk of fragmentation in brand positioning.

Managing this tension requires a sophisticated strategic approach that combines centralized coordination with decentralized flexibility. Organizations must establish global frameworks that define core brand values, scientific messaging, and ethical standards, while empowering local teams to adapt executional elements in accordance with specific market conditions. This hybrid approach allows companies to preserve strategic coherence while ensuring that campaigns remain contextually appropriate and effective. Ultimately, the success of cross-national pharmaceutical marketing depends on the ability to navigate this balance, integrating global vision with local insight in a manner that supports both organizational objectives and public health outcomes.

6. CASE-BASED INSIGHTS IN CROSS-NATIONAL PHARMACEUTICAL MARKETING

The analysis of real-world pharmaceutical campaigns provides valuable insights into how strategic principles are translated into practice within complex and highly regulated cross-national environments. These cases illustrate not only best practices in global marketing execution but also the risks associated with ethical misalignment and regulatory failure. By examining campaigns from leading pharmaceutical companies, it becomes possible to better understand how transparency, scientific credibility, cultural adaptation, and patient-centricity interact as critical determinants of marketing effectiveness and long-term organizational legitimacy.

The global vaccination campaign developed by Pfizer in collaboration with BioNTech during the COVID-19 pandemic stands as one of the most significant examples of pharmaceutical communication under conditions of extreme uncertainty and global scrutiny. Unlike traditional campaigns centered on competitive differentiation and brand positioning, Pfizer adopted an approach grounded in transparency and scientific credibility. The company emphasized the dissemination of clinical trial data, regulatory approvals, and real-world effectiveness evidence, ensuring that its communication remained closely aligned with scientific validation and institutional endorsement (Semeraro et al., 2022). This strategy was reinforced through collaboration with public health authorities and international organizations, which contributed to enhancing trust among both healthcare professionals and the general population. In a context characterized by widespread misinformation and vaccine hesitancy, the emphasis on data-driven communication and institutional alignment proved critical in establishing credibility across diverse markets. At the same time, the campaign demonstrated the importance of digital channels in enabling rapid, large-scale dissemination of information, while also requiring careful adaptation to local regulatory frameworks and cultural expectations.

A different but equally relevant example can be observed in the global campaign for Sensodyne, developed by GSK, which illustrates the effective balance between global brand consistency and local adaptation. In contrast to crisis-driven communication, this campaign was designed within a more traditional competitive environment, where brand recognition and consumer trust played a central role. GSK maintained a consistent global positioning centered on sensitivity relief and clinical efficacy, while adapting visual elements, language, and communication formats to suit regional markets. This approach reflects a sophisticated understanding of the need to preserve core brand identity while ensuring local relevance. The use of healthcare professionals in communication materials further reinforced credibility, aligning with evidence suggesting that medical endorsement enhances consumer trust in pharmaceutical products. At the same time, the campaign operated within strict regulatory boundaries, particularly in markets where direct-to-consumer promotion of certain health-related products is limited, demonstrating the importance of regulatory awareness in campaign design.

The case of Novartis and its Cosentyx campaign highlights the growing importance of patient-centric and multi-channel strategies in contemporary pharmaceutical marketing. Unlike more traditional models that prioritize interactions with healthcare professionals, this campaign placed significant emphasis on patient education and engagement, reflecting broader shifts toward patient empowerment and participatory healthcare models. Novartis integrated multiple communication channels, including digital platforms, educational portals, and real patient testimonials, to create a more comprehensive and immersive engagement experience. This approach aligns with the increasing recognition that patients are not merely passive recipients of treatment but active participants in healthcare decision-making processes. By providing accessible and relevant information tailored to patient needs, the campaign contributed to improving awareness, adherence, and overall engagement. Furthermore, the integration of digital tools allowed for more personalized communication, demonstrating how technological capabilities can support patient-centric strategies in a scalable and efficient manner.

In contrast to these examples of effective strategic alignment, the case of Purdue Pharma and the marketing of OxyContin represents a critical illustration of the consequences of unethical marketing practices in the pharmaceutical industry. The company implemented aggressive promotional strategies that significantly downplayed the risks of addiction associated with the drug, presenting it as a safe and effective solution for chronic pain management. This misrepresentation of clinical risks not only violated ethical standards but also contributed to one of the most severe public health crises in recent history (Van Zee, 2009). The long-term consequences of this approach extended far beyond reputational damage, resulting in legal actions, financial penalties, and a profound erosion of trust in both the company and the broader pharmaceutical sector. This case underscores the importance of ethical governance as a central component of pharmaceutical marketing, highlighting that short-term commercial gains achieved through misleading communication can lead to catastrophic long-term outcomes.

Taken together, these cases illustrate the multifaceted nature of cross-national pharmaceutical marketing and the critical importance of aligning strategic, ethical, regulatory, and technological dimensions. Successful campaigns are characterized by their ability to build trust through transparency, adapt to diverse cultural and regulatory environments, and leverage digital tools to enhance engagement and communication effectiveness. Conversely, failures in ethical judgment and regulatory compliance can have far-reaching consequences, affecting not only individual organizations but also public health systems and societal perceptions of the pharmaceutical industry.

As such, these case-based insights reinforce the need for a holistic and responsible approach to pharmaceutical marketing, particularly in an increasingly interconnected and digitally mediated global landscape.

7. MANAGERIAL IMPLICATIONS

The findings of this study point toward a set of strategic implications that are highly relevant for key stakeholders operating within the pharmaceutical marketing ecosystem, including pharmaceutical companies, regulatory authorities, and marketing professionals. These implications reflect the increasing complexity of the industry and the need for a more integrated, responsible, and adaptive approach to marketing in cross-national contexts.

For pharmaceutical companies, the evidence suggests that traditional, siloed approaches to marketing are no longer sufficient in a globalized and digitally driven environment. Instead, organizations must develop integrated strategies that simultaneously address regulatory compliance, ethical responsibility, and technological innovation. This requires not only coordination across internal functions—such as marketing, regulatory affairs, legal, and medical departments—but also the establishment of governance frameworks that ensure alignment between strategic objectives and societal expectations. The integration of these dimensions is particularly critical in cross-national campaigns, where inconsistencies in regulatory environments and cultural expectations can create significant operational and reputational risks.

In parallel, pharmaceutical companies must significantly strengthen their investment in data analytics and personalization capabilities. The growing availability of large-scale data, combined with advances in artificial intelligence and machine learning, offers unprecedented opportunities to design more targeted and effective marketing interventions. By leveraging these technologies, organizations can better understand the needs, preferences, and behaviors of both healthcare professionals and patients, enabling more precise segmentation and more relevant communication. However, the strategic use of data must be accompanied by robust data governance practices, ensuring compliance with privacy regulations and maintaining stakeholder trust. In this sense, data should not be viewed merely as a commercial asset, but as a strategic resource that must be managed responsibly.

At the same time, the adoption of patient-centric approaches emerges as a fundamental strategic priority. The traditional model, in which pharmaceutical marketing was primarily oriented toward healthcare professionals, is progressively being complemented—and in some cases challenged—by a more direct engagement with patients. This shift reflects broader changes in the healthcare landscape, including increased patient empowerment, access to information, and participation in decision-making processes. Consequently, pharmaceutical companies must design marketing strategies that go beyond product promotion and contribute to patient education, adherence support, and overall health outcomes. Patient-centricity, in this context, is not only an ethical imperative but also a source of long-term competitive advantage, as it fosters trust, loyalty, and brand credibility.

From a regulatory perspective, the findings highlight the urgent need to strengthen oversight mechanisms, particularly in relation to digital marketing practices. The rapid evolution of digital channels, including social media, mobile applications, and AI-driven platforms, has outpaced the development of many regulatory frameworks, creating gaps that may be exploited, intentionally or unintentionally, by market actors. Regulators must therefore adopt more proactive and adaptive approaches, developing guidelines and monitoring systems that are capable of addressing the specific risks associated with digital communication, such as misinformation, lack of transparency, and inappropriate targeting.

In addition to enforcement, regulatory authorities play a crucial role in promoting transparency and accountability across the pharmaceutical marketing ecosystem. This involves not only ensuring compliance with existing regulations but also encouraging best practices that enhance the quality and reliability of information provided to healthcare professionals and patients. Transparency in communication, clear disclosure of sponsorships and partnerships, and the responsible use of data are essential elements in building and maintaining public trust. In a sector where credibility is paramount, regulatory frameworks must support an environment in which ethical conduct is not only required but actively incentivized.

For marketing professionals operating within the pharmaceutical industry, the implications of this study underscore the need to balance commercial objectives with ethical responsibility in a more explicit and structured manner. While the pursuit of market share and revenue growth remains a central objective, it must be aligned with the broader mission of improving health outcomes and safeguarding patient well-being. This requires a shift in mindset, where ethical considerations are integrated into the core of strategic decision-making rather than treated as external constraints.

Furthermore, marketing professionals must develop the capability to adapt strategies to local contexts without compromising global strategic consistency. This involves a nuanced understanding of cultural, regulatory, and institutional differences, as well as the ability to translate global brand values into locally relevant messages and experiences. Achieving this balance is particularly challenging in cross-national campaigns, where pressures for standardization must be reconciled with the need for localization. Success in this domain depends on the ability to combine analytical rigor with cultural sensitivity, supported by continuous learning and feedback mechanisms.

Overall, the implications identified in this study point toward a transformation in the way pharmaceutical marketing is conceptualized and executed. The increasing importance of integration, data-driven decision-making, ethical governance, and patient-centricity reflects a broader shift toward more responsible and sustainable business practices. Organizations and professionals that are able to internalize and operationalize these principles will be better positioned to navigate the complexities of the global pharmaceutical landscape and to achieve both commercial success and societal impact.

8. FUTURE RESEARCH DIRECTIONS

Future research in the domain of pharmaceutical marketing, particularly within cross-national contexts, should move beyond predominantly conceptual discussions and increasingly focus on empirical validation of emerging strategies and frameworks. While the existing literature provides valuable theoretical insights into digital transformation, regulatory complexity, and patient engagement, there remains a significant gap in robust, data-driven studies that assess the real-world effectiveness of these approaches. Empirical research is essential to evaluate how digital marketing strategies perform across different healthcare systems, regulatory environments, and stakeholder groups, allowing scholars and practitioners to better understand which models generate measurable improvements in communication effectiveness, patient outcomes, and organizational performance.

In particular, there is a pressing need to systematically analyze the impact of digital marketing tools, such as e-detailing platforms, omnichannel engagement strategies, and data-driven personalization, within clinical and commercial settings. Future studies should employ quantitative methodologies, including longitudinal analyses and experimental designs, to measure the influence of these tools on prescribing behavior, patient adherence, and brand perception. Additionally, mixed-method approaches that combine quantitative data with qualitative insights could provide a more comprehensive understanding of how healthcare professionals and patients interact with digital pharmaceutical content, capturing not only behavioral outcomes but also underlying perceptions, trust dynamics, and decision-making processes.

Another critical area for future research concerns the growing role of artificial intelligence in pharmaceutical marketing. AI technologies, including machine learning algorithms, predictive analytics, and natural language processing, are increasingly being integrated into marketing operations, enabling more precise targeting, real-time decision support, and automated content generation. However, the implications of these technologies for decision-making processes remain insufficiently explored. Future research should investigate how AI influences both organizational and individual decision-making, examining whether algorithm-driven recommendations enhance or constrain professional judgment among healthcare providers. Furthermore, studies should assess the potential risks associated with algorithmic bias, data quality issues, and the opacity of AI systems, particularly in a highly regulated and ethically sensitive sector such as healthcare.

Equally important is the need to deepen the understanding of cross-cultural differences in patient engagement and response to pharmaceutical marketing strategies. As global campaigns continue to expand, recognizing and accounting for variations in cultural norms, health beliefs, communication preferences, and levels of trust in medical institutions becomes increasingly critical. Future research should adopt comparative and cross-national study designs to explore how patients from different cultural backgrounds interpret and respond to marketing messages, including digital and personalized content. Such studies could provide valuable insights into the extent to which standardized global strategies can be effectively adapted to local contexts, as well as the conditions under which localization significantly enhances engagement and outcomes.

Moreover, the intersection of culture and digitalization presents a particularly promising avenue for investigation. As digital platforms enable the rapid dissemination of information across borders, the distinction between local and global communication becomes increasingly blurred. Future research should examine how cultural factors mediate the reception of digitally delivered pharmaceutical content, including the role of language, symbolism, and social norms in shaping user engagement. This line of inquiry is especially relevant in the context of social media and influencer-driven health communication, where informal and peer-based interactions can significantly influence perceptions and behaviors.

Finally, future studies should also consider the broader systemic implications of pharmaceutical marketing strategies, including their impact on healthcare equity, access to information, and public health outcomes. As marketing becomes more data-driven and personalized, there is a risk that certain populations may be underserved or excluded due to limited access to digital technologies or disparities in data representation. Addressing these challenges will require interdisciplinary research that integrates perspectives from marketing, public health, information systems, and ethics, contributing to the development of more inclusive and socially responsible marketing practices.

In sum, advancing research in cross-national pharmaceutical marketing will depend on a stronger emphasis on empirical validation, a critical examination of emerging technologies such as artificial intelligence, and a deeper exploration of cultural diversity in patient engagement. These directions will not only enhance academic knowledge but also provide actionable insights for organizations seeking to navigate the evolving complexities of the global pharmaceutical landscape.

9. CONCLUSION

Cross-national pharmaceutical marketing represents a highly complex and strategically critical domain situated at the intersection of healthcare, economics, regulation, and global communication. Unlike traditional industries, where marketing activities are primarily driven by consumer demand and competitive positioning, pharmaceutical marketing operates within a highly constrained and sensitive environment in which the consequences of communication extend far beyond commercial outcomes. Decisions made in this context have direct implications for public health, patient safety, and societal trust, making the design and execution of marketing strategies a matter of both strategic importance and ethical responsibility.

The complexity of cross-national pharmaceutical marketing stems largely from the need to simultaneously navigate multiple, and often conflicting, dimensions. Regulatory frameworks vary significantly across jurisdictions, imposing different limitations on the promotion of pharmaceutical products, particularly in relation to prescription medicines. While some markets permit direct-to-consumer communication under specific conditions, others impose strict prohibitions, restricting promotional activities to healthcare professionals. This divergence requires organizations to develop flexible and adaptive strategies that can be recalibrated according to local legal requirements without compromising overall strategic coherence.

At the same time, cultural factors introduce an additional layer of complexity. Health beliefs, patient expectations, levels of health literacy, and trust in medical institutions differ widely across regions, influencing how pharmaceutical messages are perceived and interpreted. A campaign that is effective in one country may be ineffective or even counterproductive in another if it fails to account for these contextual nuances. Consequently, successful cross-national strategies must go beyond simple translation or superficial localization, requiring a deep understanding of local social, cultural, and institutional dynamics.

Technological transformation has further intensified both the opportunities and challenges associated with pharmaceutical marketing. The widespread adoption of digital platforms, data analytics, and artificial intelligence has enabled companies to move toward more precise, personalized, and scalable forms of communication. These technologies allow for real-time engagement with healthcare professionals and patients, facilitating more informed decision-making and improving the efficiency of marketing investments. However, they also raise significant concerns related to data privacy, information accuracy, and the potential for manipulation, particularly in a sector where the asymmetry of information between providers and consumers remains substantial.

Within this context, the integration of ethical, regulatory, cultural, and technological dimensions emerges as a fundamental requirement for the development of effective and responsible pharmaceutical marketing strategies. Ethical considerations, in particular, must not be treated as secondary constraints but rather as core strategic principles that guide decision-making processes. The history of the pharmaceutical industry provides clear evidence that the neglect of ethical standards can lead to severe reputational damage, legal consequences, and, more importantly, significant harm to public health. As such, ethical governance must be embedded within the organizational culture and operational practices of pharmaceutical companies, ensuring that commercial objectives are consistently aligned with societal well-being.

Successful cross-national pharmaceutical campaigns are therefore characterized by their ability to achieve a delicate balance between global strategic alignment and local responsiveness. They demonstrate sensitivity to local specificities, not only in terms of regulatory compliance but also in relation to cultural expectations and healthcare system structures. At the same time, they effectively leverage digital technologies to enhance communication, improve targeting, and generate actionable insights from data. Importantly, these campaigns place patient well-being at the center of their strategic logic, recognizing that long-term value creation in the pharmaceutical industry is inherently linked to trust, credibility, and positive health outcomes.

As the industry continues to evolve, pharmaceutical marketing is expected to undergo a significant transformation toward more data-driven and patient-centric models. Advances in artificial intelligence, predictive analytics, and digital health ecosystems will enable increasingly sophisticated forms of engagement, allowing companies to tailor their communication strategies to the specific needs and behaviors of individual stakeholders. This shift, however, will also require organizations to develop new capabilities and governance mechanisms capable of managing the ethical and regulatory implications of these technologies.

In this emerging landscape, the ability to balance innovation with responsibility will become a defining factor of competitive advantage. Organizations that succeed will be those that can integrate technological sophistication with ethical integrity, ensuring that the pursuit of efficiency and personalization does not come at the expense of transparency, fairness, and patient protection. Ultimately, cross-national pharmaceutical marketing will continue to evolve as a strategic discipline that not only supports commercial performance but also contributes to broader societal objectives, including health education, disease prevention, and the strengthening of trust in healthcare systems.

REFERENCES

Applbaum, K. (2006). Pharmaceutical marketing and the invention of the medical consumer. *PLoS Medicine*, *3*(4), e189. Advance online publication. DOI: 10.1371/journal.pmed.0030189 PMID: 16597179

Cohen, E. P. (1988). Direct-to-the-public advertisement of prescription drugs. *The New England Journal of Medicine*, *318*(6), 373–376. DOI: 10.1056/NEJM198802113180608 PMID: 3123930

Francer, J.. (2014). Ethical pharmaceutical promotion and communications worldwide. *Pharmaceutical Medicine*, *28*(1), 1–12. DOI: 10.1007/s40290-014-0034-0 PMID: 24855373

Kolodny, A., Courtwright, D. T., Hwang, C. S., Kreiner, P., Eadie, J. L., Clark, T. W., & Alexander, G. C. (2015). The prescription opioid and heroin crisis. *Annual Review of Public Health*, *36*(1), 559–574. DOI: 10.1146/annurev-publhealth-031914-122957 PMID: 25581144

Mikalef, P.. (2019). Big data analytics capabilities and firm performance. *Information & Management*, *56*(8). Advance online publication. DOI: 10.1016/j.im.2019.103207

Tsenov, S. (2022). Digital transformation in pharmaceutical industry. *Journal of Pharmaceutical Innovation*.

Van Zee, A. (2009). The promotion and marketing of OxyContin. *American Journal of Public Health*, *99*(2), 221–227. DOI: 10.2105/AJPH.2007.131714 PMID: 18799767

Visser, B. C.. (2013). Mobile medical applications. *Journal of Medical Internet Research*, *15*(3). Advance online publication. DOI: 10.2196/jmir.2380

Yadav, B., et al. (2012). CRM in pharmaceutical marketing.

Chapter 10
Mindfulness as a Strategic Resource for Workplace Performance in Healthcare

Rupa Rathee
http://orcid.org/0000-0003-3102-1413
Deenbandhu Chhotu Ram University of Science and Technology, Murthal, India

Monika Singh
http://orcid.org/0009-0007-1309-8130
Deenbandhu Chhotu Ram University of Science and Technology, Murthal, India

Swati Dagar
http://orcid.org/0009-0007-0641-350X
Deenbandhu Chhotu Ram University of Science and Technology, Murthal, India

ABSTRACT

Healthcare professionals frequently operate in high-stress environments that can affect both employee well-being and workplace performance. This study examines the relationship between mindfulness, employee creativity, work engagement, and customer satisfaction among employees of a multinational corporate hospital. Data were collected from 103 hospital employees using a structured online questionnaire. The data were analyzed using descriptive statistics, correlation analysis, and regression analysis in SPSS. The results indicate significant positive relationships between mindfulness and employee creativity ($r = 0.236$, $p = 0.016$) as well as work engagement ($r = 0.218$, $p = 0.027$). However, the relationship between mindfulness

DOI: 10.4018/979-8-3373-9410-7.ch010

and customer satisfaction was positive but not statistically significant. The findings highlight the role of mindfulness in enhancing employee creativity and engagement in healthcare organizations.

1. INTRODUCTION

The environment of healthcare organizations is highly complex and heavily regulated, and those working in the organization are required to provide high-quality care to patients while adhering to institutional, ethical, and technological standards. Hospitals, drug companies, and medical device companies are under constant pressure to strike a balance between clinical excellence and operational efficiency, as well as regulatory compliance. Such conditions are characterized by work overload, time pressure, and emotionally challenging relationships with patients and their families, putting health workers under a prolonged psychological burden and burnout (Hall et al., 2016; Garcia et al., 2019). Such high-pressure environments have also been linked to decreased job satisfaction, decreased work engagement, and reduced service quality, which is why it is necessary to enhance the psychological resilience of the employees and their performance abilities.

In this regard, the human capital concept goes beyond technical knowledge and includes cognitive, emotional and behavioral skills that allow employees to operate successfully in challenging environments. Not only should healthcare professionals exhibit clinical competence, but also be emotionally stable, make good decisions, and adapt to quickly changing work conditions. Although substantial efforts have been directed at digital health systems, operational technologies and regulatory frameworks, little focus has been directed to building internal psychological resources that can contribute to employee effectiveness and well-being in such systems. One of such resources is the concept of mindfulness, which has been a promising construct in organizational and psychological studies. Mindfulness is described as mind-awareness of the here and now and is described as non-judgemental awareness of internal events, such as thoughts, feelings and sensations (Brown et al., 2007; Kabat-Zinn, 1994). This level of consciousness helps people to control emotional reactions, attentional focus and react more appropriately to work challenges. It has been empirically indicated that mindfulness improves cognitive flexibility, emotion control and psychological resilience, all of which are crucial to being able to perform well in high-pressure work environments (Crane et al., 2017; Huang et al., 2024). Within healthcare settings, mindfulness-based programs have been demonstrated to lessen burnout, elevate well-being, and advance communication and collaboration among practitioners (Spinelli et al., 2019; Knudsen et al., 2024).

In addition to the personal well-being, mindfulness can also have significant organizational consequences. Recent studies make it clear that psychological abilities like mindfulness may have an effect on important results in the workplace, such as worker creativity, work engagement, and service delivery. Employee creativity facilitates the creation of innovative solutions to difficult clinical and operational problems, and work engagement captures the energy, commitment, and active participation of employees in their work. The two constructs are especially applicable to the healthcare context, where the quality of services and innovations largely relies on the behavior and interpersonal relationships of employees (Dong et al., 2015; Zivnuska et al., 2016; Huang et al., 2024). Moreover, the level of patient satisfaction, which is a critical predictor of service quality is heavily influenced by the attentiveness, empathy, and communication of the employees in service encounters. Mindfulness might play the role in such results by increasing emotional regulation and mindfulness of employees during their interactions with patients.

Although there has been increased interest in mindfulness, most of the current literature has been concerned primarily with mindfulness as an individual-level intervention to promote well-being. Relationally little focus has been placed on understanding mindfulness as a strategic human capital potential that drives more extensive organizational results, especially in highly-regulated and service-intensive industries like healthcare. This is a particularly critical gap in the context of growing organizational complexity in healthcare where organizations need to guarantee regulatory compliance, operational efficiency, and ongoing innovation at the same time.

In filling this gap, the current study theorizes mindfulness as a strategic human capital resource. It explores its impact on employee creativity, work engagement, and customer (patient) satisfaction in a multinational corporate hospital. The study is based on a quantitative research design, which utilizes correlation and regression analysis to assess these relationships. The study, by connecting mindfulness to organizational performance at an employee level and service level, adds to the literature by expanding the concept of psychological resources as the core determinants of organizational performance in healthcare organizations. It provides valuable lessons on how mindfulness can be incorporated in workforce development.

2. LITERATURE REVIEW AND THEORETICAL FRAMEWORK

Modern studies are focusing more on the influence of psychological resources in improving the performance and organizational effectiveness of employees, especially in face-to-face and high-pressure workplaces like healthcare. Among them, mindfulness has become an essential skill that has an impact on cognitive, emotional, and behavioral performance at work. Recent research suggests that mindfulness improves attentional control, emotional, and adaptive functioning, and thus, employees can perform effectively under severe circumstances (Huang et al., 2024; Karahan Kaplan et al., 2024; Wang et al., 2024). Such abilities are necessary in the healthcare setting where the employees often encounter stress, uncertainty, and emotional pressures, which are key to maintaining the health of employees and the quality of service they provide.

Theoretically, mindfulness is based on the concept of awareness and non-judgmental focus on internal experiences in the present moment (Brown et al., 2007; Kabat-Zinn, 1994). These traits increase cognitive flexibility and decrease automaticity of cognitive responses, which allows the individuals to react in a more considered manner to tricky work situations. Mindfulness has been theorized as a psychological asset that facilitates adaptive behavior, decision-making, and interpersonal effectiveness in organizational contexts (Hülsheger et al., 2013). In further extension of this view, recent studies place mindfulness as a strategic human resource skill that adds to both organizational resilience and performance, especially in controlled and highly stakes settings like healthcare. Based on psychological resource theory and the perspectives of strategic human capital, it is possible to think of mindfulness as an internal capacity that improves the cognitive, emotional, and behavioral performance of employees. Such capabilities are necessary in high-pressure healthcare settings to support adaptive responses, to positively affect work-related attitudes, and to positively influence service delivery outcomes. Therefore, mindfulness should have an impact on the most important employee outcomes, such as creativity and work engagement, and service related outcomes such as customer satisfaction.

2.1 Mindfulness in Healthcare Organizations

The working conditions of healthcare professionals are highly stressful, demanding their complete alertness, emotional regulation, and effective decision-making. The workload, time limits, and emotionally challenging connections with patients and their families often expose them to stress and burnout (Hall et al., 2016; Garcia et al., 2019). As a result, it has merged to be one of the key issues of concern in healthcare organizations to determine psychological resources that can promote employee well-being and performance. Mindfulness is a concept of present-moment awareness, whereby there is non-judgmental focus on inner life, including thoughts, feelings, and sensations (Brown et al., 2007; Kabat-Zinn, 1994). In this capacity, individuals can respond to their work situations in a better cognitively controlled, stable and emotional way. Empirical research demonstrates that mindfulness enhances attentional regulation, emotional resilience, and cognitive flexibility required to work well in high stress and demanding work environments (Crane et al., 2017).

Mindfulness within the healthcare setting has already been associated with the reduction of emotional exhaustion, improved psychological, and more enhanced interpersonal functioning among healthcare workers (Hülsheger et al., 2013; Spinelli et al., 2019; Knudsen et al., 2024). These benefits highlight why it is a valuable psychological instrument that can be used to help the employees manage stress and be functional at work. In strategic terms, mindfulness may be envisioned as a part of human capital that may be used to make employees perform better and organizations more flexible. Mindfulness has the potential to support reflective cognition and innovative and adaptive responses to complicated workplace scenarios through the enhancement of cognitive awareness and reduction of automatic reactions (Dane and Brummel, 2013; Zivnuska et al., 2016; Huang et al., 2024).

2.2 Mindfulness and Employee Creativity

The creativity of employees refers to the capacity of individuals to come up with innovative and helpful ideas to address work-related issues. It is a life-threatening event in healthcare institutions, in which personnel have to react to unexpected clinical and operational difficulties by means of innovative and adaptive methods. The empirical evidence indicates that mindfulness leads to employee creativity through the promotion of cognitive flexibility, openness to experience, and divergent thinking (Dane and Brummel, 2013; Zivnuska et al., 2016; Huang et al., 2024). Mindful employees are more sensitive to their inner worlds and outer surroundings, which allows them to re-frame problems, think of other perspectives and come up with creative solutions. They are especially relevant in health facilities, as the abilities of creativeness may help to provide better patient care, more effective clinical procedures, as well as better service delivery (Dong et al., 2015). Also, mindfulness enhances attentional control and diminishes automatic cognitive reactions so that employees can think deeper and solve problems more efficiently (Hülsheger et al., 2013). Following this, mindfulness is likely to be a major factor in improving employee creativity in healthcare organizations.

H1: Mindfulness has a positive relationship with employee creativity.

2.3 Mindfulness and Work Engagement

Work engagement is an occupation-related positive mental condition that includes vigor, commitment, and absorption (Bakker et al., 2014). It is a sign of active, energetic, and committed attitudes of employees to their work roles. The work engagement in healthcare organizations is of special concern as engaged employees will have a higher chance to provide high-quality care, effective interpersonal relationships, and work effectively under pressure. Mindfulness has been discovered to be one of the most important psychological resources that contribute to work engagement through emotional regulation, decreased burnout, and allowing employees to maintain attention and motivation in demanding work settings (Karahan Kaplan et al., 2024; Wang et al., 2023). Cognizant employees are in a better position to handle stress, control emotional reactions and maintain concentration on work related matters and hence enhance their psychological attachment to their jobs. Previous studies also substantiate the idea that mindfulness will lead to the emergence of internal psychological resources, which will allow employees to better manage the issues in the workplace and to be more engaged in the long run (Hülsheger et al., 2013; Jang et al., 2020). Mindfulness, in turn, will be instrumental in increasing the level of work engagement especially in high-stress healthcare environments.

H2: Mindfulness is positively associated with work engagement.

2.4 Mindfulness and Customer Satisfaction

Customer (patient) satisfaction is a crucial measure of quality of services in healthcare organizations. As much as employee behavior are key in determining the experiences of patients, the overall organizational and service delivery factors also determine the outcomes of patient satisfaction. Current studies indicate that mindfulness can help staff to be more attentive, empathetic, and communicative in service interactions, which leads to better patient experiences (Dong et al., 2015; Wang et al., 2021). Customer satisfaction is the assessment of the quality of services and the general healthcare experience of patients (Parasuraman et al., 1988). Frontline employees in healthcare settings are very instrumental in creating such experiences by communicating well, responding, and empathizing with patients. Employees who demonstrate higher levels of attentiveness and problem-solving ability are more likely to contribute positively to patient satisfaction (Dong et al., 2015).

Mindfulness improves attentional awareness and emotional regulation, and allows healthcare professionals to engage patients in a more attentive, compassionate, and composed way (Dane and Brummel, 2013). Nevertheless, customer satisfaction is a multidimensional construct that is affected by both personal-level competences and general organizational aspects. Therefore, the effect of mindfulness on patient satisfaction can be indirect and reliant on the supportive service quality systems and institutional practices.

H3: Mindfulness is positively associated with customer satisfaction.

Combining these views, the current research develops a conceptualization of mindfulness as a strategic human capital attribute that affects key employee outcomes, such as creativity and work engagement, and service outcomes, such as customer satisfaction. This combined model aligns with modern organizational and service management studies, which focus on the interactions between personal and organizational systems in achieving performance outcomes. Although these relationships are increasingly a subject of scholarly interest, research on them in the context of regulated healthcare settings has been limited, indicating a substantial gap in the literature.

Objectives of the Study

(1) To examine the effect of mindfulness on employee creativity.
(2) To analyze the relationship between mindfulness and work engagement.
(3) To assess the impact of mindfulness on customer (patient) satisfaction.
(4) To conceptualize mindfulness as a strategic human capital capability influencing employee and organizational performance in healthcare settings.

2.5 Summary of the Framework

The conceptual framework of the current paper implies that mindfulness may be regarded as a potent psychological tool which influences the most significant workplace performance within healthcare organizations. Mindfulness may enhance creativity and employee interest in their work, and positively influence patient satisfaction by improving attentional focus, emotional regulation, and cognitive flexibility. These relations are particularly applicable to the healthcare settings, where the actions of employees and their mental health have a decisive role in the quality of provided services and organizational results. In that way, one can envision mindfulness as a strategic human resource that can be applied to increase the creativity of employees, their engagement, and the quality of service provision in healthcare organizations.

3. CONCEPTUAL MODEL

According to the theoretical framework, the current research suggests a conceptual framework that explores how mindfulness affects critical employee and service-based outcomes within healthcare organizations. The concept of mindfulness is developed as a key psychological skill that increases the cognitive processes, emotional control, and behavioral reactions of employees in stressful work conditions. The abilities are essential in the context of healthcare environments, where experts must handle complicated clinical cases, interact emotionally, and work within time limits, as they influence employee performance and quality of service. The hypothesized model assumes that mindfulness has a positive effect on the creativity of employees and their engagement at work. Mindfulness promotes cognitive flexibility and attentional control, which allows employees to come up with innovative solutions and adaptive responses to work-related challenging situations. Simultaneously, it enhances emotionally and attention concentration, which makes employees more engaged, motivated, and devoted to their jobs. Such outcomes are especially relevant in the healthcare organizations where the behavior of employees directly impacts the service delivery and organizational performance. Moreover, the model analyzes the connection between mindfulness and customer (patient) satisfaction. Although mindfulness is likely to enhance the quality of interpersonal interactions by increasing attentiveness and empathy, patient satisfaction depends on the personal level and the organizational and service delivery levels in general. Thus, the connection between mindfulness and customer satisfaction can be indirect or dependent on the supporting institutional mechanisms. Overall, the conceptual framework places mindfulness as a strategic human capital skill that is an outcome of both employee outcomes (creativity and work engagement) and service outcomes (customer satisfaction). This framework offers an empirical basis of studying the role of psychological resources in increasing organizational effectiveness in healthcare.

Figure 1. Conceptual Framework of the Study (Author's Own)

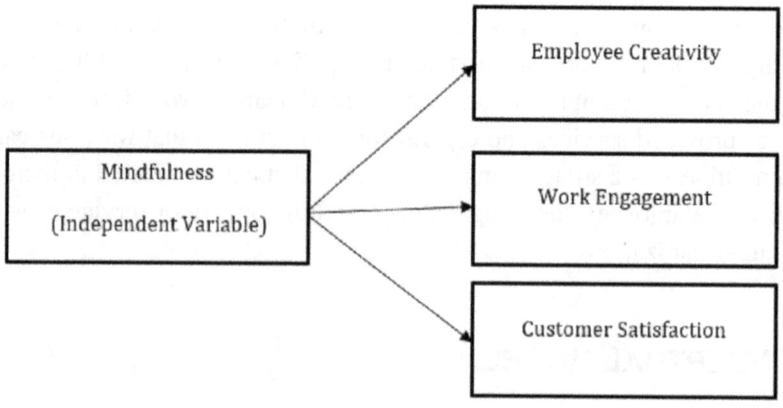

4. METHODOLOGY

The current research will be based on the quantitative research design to investigate the links between mindfulness, employee creativity, work engagement, and customer satisfaction in the context of healthcare. The quantitative approach is suitable in this study because it will allow investigating the relationships between psychological and organizational variables systematically and empirically test the hypotheses. The empirical context of the research includes the employees of a multinational corporate hospital, the job descriptions of which involve the great responsibility, time pressure, and emotional involvement. The structured questionnaire was used in the data collection process; it took place on an online survey platform in April-May 2024. The convenience sampling method was used to obtain the responses of employees in various departments within the organization. Convenience sampling is suitable due to the initial exploratory study and the availability of respondents in a specialized healthcare setting. One hundred and thirty three valid answers were received and analyzed further. The sample size is deemed to be sufficient in analysis using regression because the previous researches on organizational behavior have effectively used such sample sizes to test the relationships between psychological constructs. Moreover, the sample offers valuable information on the experiences of employees in a high-stress healthcare environment. To determine the content validity and reliability of the measurement instrument, the scales were developed based on previously tested scales. The creativity of employees was assessed with five items based on Coelho and Augusto (2010) that reflect the capacity of employees to come up with new ideas and innovative solutions at the workplace. The measure of work engagement involved questions of the Utrecht Work Engagement Scale (UWES-9) by Balducci et al. (2010) that captured the important dimensions: vigor, dedication, and absorption. Three items modified by Wang et al. (2021) that reflect the perceptions of the employees about the quality of service and patient experience were used to measure customer satisfaction. The six items were used to measure mindfulness based on the work of Wang et al. (2021), which is based on the Mindful Attention Awareness Scale (MAAS), reflecting the presence of awareness and attention in the present moment. All the measurement items will be rated using a five-point Likert scale between 1 (strongly disagree) and 5 (strongly agree). Likert scaling is suitable in the measurement of subjective perceptions and attitudes of psychological constructs. The gathered data were compared with the help of a Statistical Package of the Social Sciences (SPSS). The characteristics and patterns of working among the respondents were summarized using descriptive statistics. The internal consistency of the measurement scales was determined by examining the reliability with the help of Cronbach alpha. To analyze the relationships between the variables of the study, Pearson correlation analysis was performed and to test the hypotheses put forward and to estimate the predictive role of mindfulness on employee creativity, work engagement, and customer satisfaction, multiple regression analysis was applied. On the whole, the methodological design supports the strength of measurement and analysis, which can be considered an effective foundation to study the role of mindfulness as a psychological resource that affects employee and organizational performance in healthcare facilities.

5. RESULTS

5.1 Descriptive Analysis

The descriptive statistics give the response of the demographic features, as well as the working patterns of the respondents. The sample is 103 employees in healthcare, and the variability of most variables is moderate. The average age (Mean = 1.97, SD = 0.928) shows that the sample is relatively clustered around a small age range and the distribution of ages is relatively homogeneous. Equally, the gender representation (Mean = 1.67, SD = 0.719) is balanced with very slight variation in the categories. In terms of work patterns, the mean hours per shift (Mean = 2.45, SD = 0.860) suggests that workers generally have a moderate-to-high workload intensity. Moreover, the mean duration of breaks (Mean = 3.28, SD = 1.042) shows that the employees have short yet slightly fluctuating break periods throughout their shifts. The break effectiveness responses indicate that employees tend to be relaxed when they take breaks (Mean = 1.76, SD = 0.707), although the standard deviation indicates that the level of relaxation differs between people. Correspondingly, there is a moderate positive effect of breaks on perceptions of job performance after breaks (Mean = 1.51, SD = 0.850) indicating that breaks do lead to improvements in perceived job performance but not equally effective among the respondents. The variable that is used to measure the primary cause of taking breaks (Mean = 5.01, SD = 2.655) is relatively dispersed which implies that there are different reasons why employees may take breaks, which could be the need to reduce fatigue, relieve stress, or personal needs. Lastly, the mindfulness practice mean score (Mean = 1.82, SD = 0.916) implies that a small fraction of employees practice mindfulness. This implies that although mindfulness has been identified to be useful in the literature, its application in the workplace is fairly low. In sum, the descriptive results indicate that the healthcare working environment is challenging, with moderate workloads, little time to rest, and diverse degrees of psychological well-being behaviors. The observed patterns support the need to implement structured interventions, including mindfulness-based interventions, to improve employee well-being and performance in healthcare organizations (Table 1).

Table 1. Demographic profile of the sample (Source: Primary Research Finding)

	N	Minimum	Maximum	Mean	Std. Deviation
Age	103	1	4	1.97	.928
Gender	103	1	3	1.67	.719
How many hours do you work On average per shift?	103	1	4	2.45	.860
How many minutes do you spend 'breaking' overall on average per shift?	103	1	6	3.28	1.042
Do you feel more relaxed after Have a break?	103	1	3	1.76	.707
Out of the following, what is The main reason for taking a break?	103	1	9	5.01	2.655
Do you feel more relaxed after Have a break?	103	1	3	1.33	.692
Do you think your job performance level improves after having breaks?	103	1	3	1.51	.850
Have you ever practiced any form of mindfulness meditation?	103	1	3	1.82	.916

5.2 Reliability Analysis

Reliability was used to determine the consistency of the meaning scales used in the study. analysis. The measure of reliability was Cronbach alpha to determine the consistency of the. questionnaire in assessing the notions of mindfulness, employee creativity, work engagement, and customer satisfaction (Table 2). The results of the reliability test indicated that the Cronbach alpha. The internal consistency was high with the 23 measurement items being 0.892. Reliability scores a score above 0.70 is acceptable in a social science study meaning that the measurement scale is. valid in measuring the constructs of interest (Bakker et al., 2014). The reliability score is large, suggesting that mindfulness and employee outcomes as measured by the questionnaire items are related. stable, reliable scores.

Table 2. Reliability Statistics

Cronbach's Alpha	N of Items
.892	23

5.3 Correlation Analysis

To explore the interrelations between mindfulness, employee creativity, work engagement, and customer satisfaction, the correlation analysis was conducted. These findings indicate that mindfulness is positively associated with employee creativity ($r = 0.236$, $p < 0.05$), which suggests that employees that demonstrate a higher level of present-moment awareness are more prone to show innovative thinking and problem-solving behaviour. This finding shows that mindfulness can enhance cognitive flexibility and openness to experience that can be useful in creative performance in difficult work environments such as health care. The same observation can be transferred to the opinion that mindfulness is an element related to innovative behavior since it assists the staff to be less rigid in processing information they encounter and creative in solving their work-related issues. The relatively low ability of the model to explain creativity on the other hand means that creativity is a complex construct and is influenced by other organizational variables such as support of leaders, knowledge and environment sharing that the organizing entities are operating in. Mindfulness and work engagement also have a positive relationship ($r = 0.218$, $p < 0.05$). It is a pointer that more responsible employees will be more attentive to demonstrate more energy, interest and commitment to the jobs they undertake. Mental ability of mindfulness to regulate emotions and stay focused may result in motivation and persistence in demanding workplace situations. The other implication of the results is the facilitating nature of the mindfulness so as to sustain the psychological involvement of the employees in their work. Mindfulness can assist individuals to be more active since it enables them to be alert and psychologically stable. Nonetheless, the low R 2 value, suggests that engagement is influenced by structural and contextual factors, i.e. job design, the organizational culture and leadership practices.

On the other hand, there is no statistically significant relationship between mindfulness and customer satisfaction ($r = 0.167$, $p > 0.05$). This finding may indicate that, despite the potential positive impact of mindfulness on the inner psychological state of employees and their attitude towards clients, customer satisfaction is likely to be a result of the more global set of variables associated with the organization and services like quality system in service provision, customer communication process, and institutional support. In this way the mediating role of mindfulness on customer satisfaction will be mediated by other organizational processes. The lack of significance of the values indicates that customer satisfaction in health institutions is multifaceted.

Even though mindfulness can help improve interpersonal relation among the employees, it has no relationship with patient satisfaction, which is exerted by numerous external factors, such as systems of service quality, operational effectiveness and institutional infrastructure. This means that the psychological capabilities of the individual level may not be effective to have a direct impact on customer outcomes. Collectively, the results give a slight idea of why mindfulness is an important problem in the medical institutions. Although mindfulness plays a vital role in employee-level performance including creativity and engagement in work, it seems to have a less pronounced and situational impact on customer satisfaction. These findings demonstrate the relevance of the groups of personal psychological strengths and organizational systems and processes to realize the overall increase in performance in the healthcare facilities.

Table 3. Inter-Variable Correlations (Source: Primary Research Finding)

		Mindfulness	Employee Creativity	Work Engagement	Customer Satisfaction
Mindfulness	**Pearson Correlation**	**1**			.
	Sig. (2-tailed)	103			
	N				
Employee Creativity	Pearson Correlation	.236*	1		
	Sig. (2-tailed)	.016			
	N	103	103		
Work Engagement	Pearson Correlation	.218*	.583**	1	
	Sig. (2-tailed)	.027	.000		
	N	103	103	103	
Customer Satisfaction	Pearson Correlation	.167	.408**	.453**	1
	Sig. (2-tailed)	.091	.000	.000	
	N	103	103	103	103

*Correlation is significant at the 0.05 level (2-tailed). **Correlation is significant at the 0.01 level (2-tailed).

5.4 Regression Analysis

Table 4. Regression Model Summary (Source: Primary Research Finding)

Model	R	R^2	Adjusted R^2	Std Error
Creativity	.236	.056	.046	.678
Engagement	.218	.047	.038	.681
Satisfaction	.167	.028	.018	.688

Regression analysis was performed to investigate the correlations among mindfulness and the important employee outcomes. To test the relationships between mindfulness, employee creativity, work engagement, and customer satisfaction three distinct regression models were approximated. The original regression model investigated the connection between mindfulness and staff innovation. The findings suggest that there is a strong correlation between the two variables ($R = 0.236$, $R^2 = 0.056$, $F = 5.952$, $p = 0.016$) and that mindfulness is positively related to employee creativity. Despite the fact that mindfulness is a significant predictor of employee creativity, the relatively small value of R 2 implies that other organizational and contextual variables, including the work environment, leadership support, and resource availability, also affect creativity. The second regression model was on the relationship between mindfulness and work engagement. The results also indicate a statistically significant relationship ($R = 0.218$, $R^2 = 0.047$, $F = 5.022$, $p = 0.027$). This result indicates that more mindful employees would exhibit more work engagement. The fact that the model has a relatively low explanatory power implies that mindfulness is a determinant of work engagement but other variables, including the job design, organizational climate, and leadership practices are also significant factors that determine work engagement. The third regression model was used to test the association between mindfulness and customer satisfaction. The results show a positive but statistically non-significant relationship ($R = 0.167$, $R^2 = 0.028$, $F = 2.915$, $p = 0.091$). This indicates that customer satisfaction might be affected by other organizational factors other than employee mindfulness. The insignificant connection and small R-square value of the customer (patient) satisfaction is supported by the idea that the broader organizational and service-delivery variables such as the quality of the service systems, effectiveness of communication, and institutional support have a stronger influence on the customer (patient) satisfaction than the individual-level psychological characteristics do. Altogether, the results indicate that mindfulness is a significant but incomplete predictor of employee- and service-related outcomes, and both personal psychological resources and organizational-level factors should be taken into account to explain performance in a healthcare environment.

Table 5. ANOVA Results for Regression Models (Source: Primary Research Finding)

Model	F	Sig
Creativity	5.952	.016
Engagement	5.022	.027
Satisfaction	2.915	.091

Table 6. Summary of the Hypothesis Result (Source: Primary Research Finding)

Relationship	Result
Mindfulness → Creativity	Significant
Mindfulness → Engagement	Significant
Mindfulness → Satisfaction	Not significant

6. DISCUSSION

The current research represents an in-depth theoretically informed analysis of mindfulness as a strategic psychological asset in health care organizations that present valuable information about how it impacts employee behavior and organizational performance in highly regulated, complicated settings. The empirical results indicate that mindfulness is an effective way of improving employee creativity and work engagement since it improves fundamental cognitive and emotional skills, including attentional control, cognitive flexibility, and emotional regulation (Hülsheger et al., 2013; Dane and Brummel, 2013; Huang et al., 2024). These functions will enable healthcare workers to respond better to dynamic clinical situations, manage stress, and remain focused in high-pressure settings where precision, empathy, and quick decision-making are crucial. To that end, mindfulness may be regarded as an instrument of individual health yet a supportive ability of adaptive functioning and long-term service in a challenging service setting (Crane et al., 2017; Karahan Kaplan et al., 2024). In the meantime, the insignificant association between mindfulness and customer (patient) satisfaction provides an informative view of the sophistication of service performance in healthcare systems. Despite the positive impact of mindfulness on the internal psychological states of the employees and their interpersonal behavior, the scope of variables that positively influence patient satisfaction is wider, including the organizational infrastructure, quality management systems, communication practices, and operational efficiency (Parasuraman et al., 1988; Dong et al., 2015). It implies that mindfulness might have an indirect effect on service outcomes and might be mediated by intermediate variables, including employee engagement, quality of interaction, and service responsiveness instead of having a direct and immediate effect. As a result, the identified results reveal the necessity to consider the interaction of personal psychological resources and organizational systems in determining the overall results of performance. This research contributes to the current knowledge base by combining the understanding of the psychological resource theory and the view of strategic human capital, redefining mindfulness as the essential organizational resource instead of an individual-level phenomenon. Conventional conceptualizations of human capital have focused primarily on technical skills and content area knowledge, but the current study highlights the relevance of cognitive and emotional abilities in employee effectiveness and company stability. Such psychological capabilities are critical to the well-being of employees and the quality of service in healthcare organizations where human interaction, decision-making in uncertainty, and emotional labor are the main aspects of service delivery (Hall et al., 2016; Garcia et al., 2019). In terms of management, the results have profound implications to health care leaders and human resource professionals. Business organizations must stop treating mindfulness as a supplementary wellness initiative and regard it as a component of the general workforce development strategies. This may include adding mindfulness based training programs, reflection and emotional resilience interventions to staff development programs. It has been previously mentioned that mindfulness-based interventions can be employed in order to reduce burnout and promote mental health among healthcare professionals (Spinelli et al., 2019; Wang et al., 2023; Wang et al., 2024). Individual-level interventions with a combination of organizational systems and leadership practices can assist healthcare organizations to develop a more engaged, innovative, and resilient workforce capable of adjusting to any emerging needs across the industry. The other contribution that the study makes to the general comprehension of performance management in the healthcare setting is the emphasis on the importance of paying attention to psychological, organizational, and technological approaches. Human capabilities are even more crucial with the increase of digital technologies and data-driven decision-making processes within healthcare systems. Employees are not only supposed to be technically competent but also to be flexible and think critically and emotionally intelligent in such a way that they can navigate complex working environments. Mindfulness is also capable of supporting lifelong learning, active decision-making and effective work performance (Huang et al., 2024; Knudsen et al., 2024). Despite its contributions, there are some limitations of the study that provide future direction to the research. The cross-sectional design limits causal inference and the sample size and convenience sampling are also small, which may affect generalizability. Researchers can employ longitudinal approaches in the future, consider mediators (e.g., engagement, service quality) and study various healthcare settings. In totality, this study attests to the significance of psychological capabilities to supplement the advances in technologies and operations, which is a prospective perspective on how healthcare organizations may create a more innovative, engaged, and strong workforce.

7. IMPLICATION OF THE STUDY

7.1 Theoretical Implications

The current study will contribute to the growing body of literature on mindfulness and organizational behavior by examining the relationship between mindfulness and creativity of employees, their work engagement, and customer satisfaction within a healthcare setting. Though the majority of the previous studies have paid much attention to mindfulness as a personal well-being program, the present research takes a step further and examines it as a psychological faculty that affects the behavior of the employees and their performance at the workplace in an organizational setting. The findings suggest the importance of mindfulness in improving the cognitive and emotional performance of employees in stressful work environments. Mindfulness promotes the perception of the current moment, control of attention, and enables individuals to approach workplace issues in a more analytical and emotionally well-balanced manner (Brown et al., 2007; Hülsheger et al., 2013). The stated positive relationship between mindfulness and the creativity of the employees is supported by the previous research that mindful awareness is positively correlated with cognitive flexibility and willingness to come up with novel ideas, all of which are required to solve creative tasks at the workplace (Dane and Brummel, 2013; Zivnuska et al., 2016). The theoretical correlation between mindfulness and work engagement is also supported by the findings. Work engagement is a positive psychological state that is characterized by vigor, commitment, and engagement in work (Schaufeli et al., 2002; Bakker et al., 2014). The findings show that mindfulness may lead to the improvement of the psychological resources of employees, which can help them stay mindful and motivated in the workplace amidst stress. Its results are correlated with other authors who affirm that mindfulness can be used to manage emotions and proceed with the professional field (Jang et al., 2020). Though the study has not revealed the statistically significant direct correlation between mindfulness and customer satisfaction, the findings have shown that customer satisfaction in the healthcare facility can be dependent on diverse organizational and service-related factors. As the past research indicates, patient satisfaction is highly dependent on the quality of services provided, interpersonal behaviors of employees, and communication practices (Parasuraman et al., 1988; Dong et al., 2015). Mindfulness, therefore, can indirectly influence customer satisfaction by boosting employee engagement and interactions in the workplace. Overall, the findings can be added to the theoretical framework of mindfulness as a psychological intervention that improves the creativity and engagement of the employees in a complicated organizational environment, a healthcare facility.

7.2 Managerial Implications

The results of this study can also be useful to care managers and organizational leaders who want their organizations to be more effective and to enhance employees' well-being. Healthcare specialists often do their work under significant emotional and cognitive pressure, and in the absence of a proper support system, they can be exposed to stress and burnout (Hall et al., 2016; Garcia et al., 2019). It is therefore necessary to develop measures to strengthen employees' psychological resilience and maintain workforce performance.

One possible approach is to incorporate mindfulness-based programs into employee training and wellness initiatives. Attentional control and emotional regulation in employees may be improved through mindfulness training based on meditation, stress management training, and reflective awareness training. The existing literature has shown that mindfulness programs are effective in reducing emotional fatigue and improving the mental health of workers in high-pressure work settings (Hülsheger et al., 2013; Spinelli et al., 2019). The fact that mindfulness is positively correlated with employee creativity also underscores the importance of encouraging reflective thinking in healthcare organizations. Creativity is essential for generating new ways to solve challenges and enhance service delivery (Amabile, 1996; Dong et al., 2015). This can be supported by mindfulness, which promotes cognitive flexibility and a willingness to consider different viewpoints when solving workplace problems (Dane and Brummel, 2013).

The connection between mindfulness and work engagement also underscores the importance of work environments that support staff and foster their engagement and motivation. When employees show strong engagement, they are more committed to their occupational duties and make positive contributions towards the organizational performance (Bakker et al., 2014). Organizations can improve their interactions by encouraging facilitative leadership, providing employees with professional development, and providing wellness programs to maintain the well-being of the staff. Though the research did not show any significant correlation between mindfulness and customer satisfaction, employee well-being is also a vital component in shaping patient experiences. When employees are attentive, emotionally stable, and engaged, they have a higher probability of communicating with patients and delivering compassionate care. Thus, the indirect positive impact of spending on employee wellness and mindfulness programs on the quality of service and patient satisfaction within healthcare organizations is possible.

8. CONCLUSION

The paper has examined the relationships among mindfulness, employee innovation, work engagement, and customer satisfaction within a multinational corporate hospital. Healthcare environments are stressful, emotional, and complex environments; hence, the study aimed to understand how a psychological tool such as mindfulness can influence some of the most significant employee and organizational results. The findings include empirical evidence that mindfulness positively and significantly correlates with employee creativity and work engagement. Employees who are found to exhibit a greater level of present-moment awareness have greater cognitive flexibility, willingness to new ideas, and participation in their working roles. These findings underscore the significance of mindfulness in enhancing innovative power and inspirational involvement important to fruitful functioning within healthcare organizations. On the other hand, the relationship between mindfulness and customer satisfaction was neither found to be strong nor statistically significant. It shows that despite the fact that mindfulness may enhance the internal psychological status of employees and their work-related behavior, customer (patient) satisfaction is influenced by a broader set of organization- and service-related factors, including the systems of service quality, communication, and support of institutions. Therefore, the short-term impact of mindfulness may be insignificant when it comes to customer outcomes in the absence of robust operation and service delivery systems. The study is limited by the small sample (N=103) and convenience sampling used which may affect generalizability. Causal interpretation will also not be possible with the cross-sectional design. Future research may be longitudinal, include multi-sector comparisons, and include technology variables such as AI-based decision-making systems and online healthcare sites. Overall, the study indicates that sustainable performance of healthcare companies does not solely depend on the technological capability and compliance with regulations but also cognitive and emotional intelligence of workers. These capabilities can be cultivated through the use of mindfulness and a more engaged, creative, and resilient workforce can be guaranteed, ultimately resulting in increased organizational effectiveness.

REFERENCES

Amabile, T. M. (1996). *Creativity in context*. Westview Press.

Bakker, A. B., Demerouti, E., & Sanz-Vergel, A. I. (2014). Burnout and work engagement: The JD–R approach. *Annual Review of Organizational Psychology and Organizational Behavior*, *1*(1), 389–411. DOI: 10.1146/annurev-orgpsych-031413-091235

Balducci, C., Fraccaroli, F., & Schaufeli, W. B. (2010). Psychometric properties of the Italian version of the Utrecht Work Engagement Scale (UWES-9). *European Journal of Psychological Assessment*, *26*(2), 143–149. DOI: 10.1027/1015-5759/a000020

Brown, K. W., Ryan, R. M., & Creswell, J. D. (2007). Mindfulness: Theoretical foundations and evidence for its salutary effects. *Psychological Inquiry*, *18*(4), 211–237. DOI: 10.1080/10478400701598298

Coelho, F., & Augusto, M. (2010). Job characteristics and the creativity of frontline service employees. *Journal of Service Research*, *13*(4), 426–438. DOI: 10.1177/1094670510369379

Crane, R. S., Brewer, J., Feldman, C., Kabat-Zinn, J., Santorelli, S., Williams, J. M. G., & Kuyken, W. (2017). What defines mindfulness-based programs? The warp and the weft. *Psychological Medicine*, *47*(6), 990–999. DOI: 10.1017/S0033291716003317 PMID: 28031068

Dane, E., & Brummel, B. J. (2013). Examining workplace mindfulness and its relations to job performance and turnover intention. *Human Relations; Studies Towards the Integration of the Social Sciences*, *67*(1), 105–128. DOI: 10.1177/0018726713487753

Dong, Y., Liao, H., Chuang, A., Zhou, J., & Campbell, E. M. (2015). Fostering employee service creativity: Joint effects of customer empowering behaviors and supervisory empowering leadership. *The Journal of Applied Psychology*, *100*(5), 1364–1380. DOI: 10.1037/a0038969 PMID: 25774571

Garcia, C. L., Abreu, L. C., Ramos, J. L. S., Castro, C. F. D., Smiderle, F. R. N., Santos, J. A. D., & Bezerra, I. M. P. (2019). Influence of burnout on patient safety: Systematic review and meta-analysis. *Medicina (Kaunas, Lithuania)*, *55*(9), 553. DOI: 10.3390/medicina55090553 PMID: 31480365

Hall, L. H., Johnson, J., Watt, I., Tsipa, A., & O'Connor, D. B. (2016). Healthcare staff wellbeing, burnout, and patient safety: A systematic review. *PLoS One*, *11*(7), e0159015. DOI: 10.1371/journal.pone.0159015 PMID: 27391946

Huang, C. C., Tu, Y., & Xie, X. (2024). Mindfulness and job performance in employees of a multinational corporation: Moderated mediation of nationality, intercultural communication, and burnout. *Social Sciences & Humanities Open, 10*, 100975. DOI: 10.1016/j.ssaho.2024.100975

Hülsheger, U. R., Alberts, H. J. E. M., Feinholdt, A., & Lang, J. W. B. (2013). Benefits of mindfulness at work: The role of mindfulness in emotion regulation, emotional exhaustion, and job satisfaction. *The Journal of Applied Psychology, 98*(2), 310–325. DOI: 10.1037/a0031313 PMID: 23276118

Jang, J., Jo, W., & Kim, J. S. (2020). Can employee workplace mindfulness counteract the indirect effects of customer incivility on proactive service performance through work engagement? *Journal of Hospitality Marketing & Management, 29*(7), 812–829. DOI: 10.1080/19368623.2020.1725954

Kabat-Zinn, J. (1994). *Wherever you go, there you are: Mindfulness meditation in everyday life*. Hyperion.

Karahan Kaplan, M., Bozkurt, G., Aksu, B. Ç., Bozkurt, S., Günsel, A., & Gencer Çelik, G. (2024). Do emotional demands and exhaustion affect work engagement? The mediating role of mindfulness. *Frontiers in Psychology, 15*, 1432328. DOI: 10.3389/fpsyg.2024.1432328 PMID: 39469238

Knudsen, R. K., Skovbjerg, S., Pedersen, E. L., Nielsen, C. L., Storkholm, M. H., & Timmermann, C. (2024). Factors affecting implementation of mindfulness in hospital settings: A qualitative meta-synthesis of healthcare professionals' experiences. *International Journal of Nursing Studies Advances, 100192*, 100192. Advance online publication. DOI: 10.1016/j.ijnsa.2024.100192 PMID: 38746813

Parasuraman, A., Zeithaml, V. A., & Berry, L. L. (1988). SERVQUAL: A multiple-item scale for measuring consumer perceptions of service quality. *Journal of Retailing, 64*(1), 12–40.

Spinelli, C., Wisener, M., & Khoury, B. (2019). Mindfulness training for healthcare professionals and trainees: A meta-analysis of randomized controlled trials. *Journal of Psychosomatic Research, 120*, 29–38. DOI: 10.1016/j.jpsychores.2019.03.003 PMID: 30929705

Wang, Q., Wang, F., Zhang, S., Liu, C., Feng, Y., & Chen, J. (2023). Effects of mindfulness-based interventions on stress and burnout in nurses: A systematic review and meta-analysis. *Frontiers in Psychiatry, 14*, 1218340. DOI: 10.3389/fpsyt.2023.1218340 PMID: 37599884

Wang, X., Wen, X., Paşamehmetoğlu, A., & Guchait, P. (2021). Hospitality employee mindfulness and its impact on creativity and customer satisfaction: The moderating role of organizational error tolerance. *International Journal of Hospitality Management*, *94*, 102846. DOI: 10.1016/j.ijhm.2020.102846

Wang, Z., Wu, P., Hou, Y., Guo, J., & Lin, C. (2024). The effects of mindfulness-based interventions on alleviating academic burnout in medical students: A systematic review and meta-analysis. *BMC Public Health*, *24*(1), 1414. DOI: 10.1186/s12889-024-18938-4 PMID: 38802770

Zivnuska, S., Kacmar, K. M., Ferguson, M., & Carlson, D. S. (2016). Mindfulness at work: Resource accumulation, well-being, and attitudes. *Career Development International*, *21*(2), 106–124. DOI: 10.1108/CDI-06-2015-0086

Chapter 11
Performance Appraisal Tools:
Perspectives of Healthcare Professionals in Portugal

Filipa Soares
http://orcid.org/0009-0004-6863-1068
School of Management and Technology, Polytechnic Institute of Santarém, Portugal

Nelia Alves
http://orcid.org/0009-0007-4793-0554
School of Management and Technology, Polytechnic Institute of Santarém, Portugal

Alexandre Serra
School of Management and Technology, Polytechnic Institute of Santarém, Portugal

Luis Abreu
School of Management and Technology, Polytechnic Institute of Santarém, Portugal

Marta Correia Sampaio
http://orcid.org/0000-0003-0004-601X
School of Management and Technology, Polytechnic Institute of Santarém, Portugal

Stéphanie Monteiro
Institute for Systems and Robotics, Lisbon, Portugal

ABSTRACT

Performance evaluation constitutes an institutional mechanism for analysing professional performance and productivity within healthcare organisations. When adequately designed and implemented, it may contribute to the alignment between individual practices and organisational objectives. This study aims to examine healthcare professionals' perceptions of the performance evaluation instruments applied in their professional context. A quantitative, cross-sectional, descriptive, inferential, and correlational methodology was employed. Data were collected through a

DOI: 10.4018/979-8-3373-9410-7.ch011

questionnaire administered to healthcare professionals working in Portugal. Overall perceptions of performance evaluation instruments are predominantly negative being these perceptions associated with increased demotivation, dissatisfaction, and perceived lack of recognition.These findings suggest that current performance evaluation practices may negatively influence healthcare professionals' well-being and organisational commitment.

INTRODUCTION

In healthcare services, human resource management (HRM) plays a crucial role in ensuring the efficiency, quality, and sustainability of the services provided. One of the key tools employed in HRM is performance appraisal. This instrument enables the measurement of employee effectiveness within the organization and serves to align individual behaviours and competencies with current organizational goals. When tailored to the realities of healthcare professionals, performance appraisal tools can become powerful sources of motivation and development—provided they are perceived by employees as fair and transparent mechanisms.

Considering the above, this study is justified by its academic and HRM relevance within the healthcare sector.

The main objective is to analyse healthcare professional's perspectives on the performance appraisal tools (PAT) implemented in their work settings, thereby contributing to a critical reflection on their effectiveness and broader implications.

The research adopts a quantitative approach, based on the administration of a questionnaire to a sample of sixty-two professionals (including healthcare workers, clinical support workers and administrative workers). This methodology allows for the identification of perception patterns related to fairness, satisfaction, and motivation. The findings aim to support the improvement of appraisal processes, fostering work environments that are more equitable, productive, and engaging.

BACKGROUND

Human Resources in the Portuguese Healthcare System

Human resources (HR) in healthcare are fundamentally shaped by the available workforce across all sectors of the Portuguese health system—public, social, and private. According to Ferreira et al. (2024), most professionals working in the Portuguese National Health Service (PNHS) include doctors, nurses, allied health professionals, healthcare scientists and healthcare support workers. Data from the

Organisation for Economic Co-operation and Development (OECD, 2024) indicate that Portugal has approximately 5.5 medical doctors and 7.1 nurses per 1,000 *per capita*, both below the European Union (EU) average.

Despite the gradual increase in the number of healthcare professionals in Portugal, their distribution across the country remains uneven, as does their allocation across different sectors. As reported by the Nova School of Business and Economics (NSBE, 2022), the ratio of medical doctors to nurses is disproportionately high when compared with countries achieving similar health outcomes. Additionally, the rising demand for healthcare services and the continuous improvement of care delivery have mitigated the benefits expected from the increase in workforce numbers.

Performance Appraisal Systems in General

According to Pontes (2021), performance appraisal is a tool used in HRM to assess the operational efficiency of individuals or teams. This process may occur periodically or according to service needs and allows organizations to determine whether employees meet expectations or deviate from projected performance. Performance appraisal helps identify employee strengths and guides the development of individual or team training plans.

Performance management (PM) represents a strategic approach to people management, in which organizations assess both the efficiency and effectiveness of their personnel. By aligning employee goals with organizational objectives, performance appraisal tools (PATs) become key instruments for continuous service improvement (Estender, 2021). When properly implemented, these tools enhance worker motivation and engagement and can lead to improved organizational outcomes.

Performance Appraisal in the Public Sector

Public sector employees are subject to performance evaluation procedures aimed at promoting excellence, quality, and purposeful performance, while recognising individual merit and differentiating professional contributions. These evaluations can influence salary progression, performance bonuses, and disciplinary measures (Lexionário – Public Service Performance Appraisal).

The legal framework for this process is outlined in the General Law on Public Employment (Law No. 35/2014, of June 20). Additionally, Law No. 66-B/2007 established the Integrated System for Performance Management and Evaluation in Public Administration (SIADAP), comprising three subsystems: SIADAP 1 (service-level evaluation), SIADAP 2 (management-level evaluation), and SIADAP 3 (evaluation of general staff).

SIADAP seeks to improve public administration performance and service quality, foster coherence across organizational actions, and enhance employee motivation and skill development. The most recent revision of this system—Decree-Law No. 12/2024—recognises its potential as a career development tool for public servants.

Within the PNHS, performance appraisal is primarily conducted through SIADAP 3, applicable to all public administration workers, including healthcare professionals. This biennial process is based on the assessment of results (objectives) and competencies and involves setting objectives, self-assessment, and hierarchical evaluation. SIADAP 3 also allows for an alternative method—curricular weighting—intended for employees with at least one year of public service who lack a valid prior evaluation or wish to request revaluation. This method considers qualifications, work experience, training, and roles held, following the criteria set by the Evaluation Coordinating Council and regulations such as Normative Order No. 4-A/2010.

Performance Appraisal in the Private and Social Sectors

In Portugal, several studies have explored the implementation and challenges of performance appraisal systems across different organizational contexts. For instance, Semedo et al. (2014) conducted a case study on performance appraisal in a Portuguese small-medium company, outlining key strategic and operational decisions and recommending tools and best practices tailored to the specificities of smaller organizations.

Private and social sector entities adopt a variety of models, each aligned with their specific needs and organizational culture. Common approaches include:

1. Management by objectives, which evaluates performance based on the achievement of predefined goals (Hoti et al., 2018);
2. Competency-based appraisal, assessing both technical and behavioural competencies critical to job performance (Correia, 2015);
3. 360-degree feedback, involving input from managers, peers, and clients for a comprehensive performance view (Sureda et al., 2021);
4. Results-based appraisal, focusing on measurable outcomes linked to organizational objectives (Waruwu, 2024);
5. Behavioural appraisal, which evaluates workplace conduct, ethics, communication, and teamwork (Effendi et al., 2023).

Implications for Employee Satisfaction and Motivation

Balancing the current conditions of the PNHS—such as salary levels, benefits, infrastructure, training, and career progression—with the personal lives of healthcare workers requires sensitivity. Managers must also consider the evolving skillsets across healthcare professions, especially in response to digital transformation. These dynamics demand creativity, flexibility, and agility from both public policy and PNHS leadership (NSBE, 2022).

As highlighted by Valluvan et al. (2024), performance appraisal is a vital component of HRM and a vital tool for delivering feedback and setting objectives. Their findings show that perceived fairness, feedback quality, goal clarity, and frequency of evaluation strongly influence worker motivation. When well-structured, performance appraisal systems significantly enhance motivation by recognising effort, offering constructive feedback, and aligning individual and organizational goals. In contrast, poorly conducted evaluations may result in demotivation, job dissatisfaction, and increased absenteeism. Therefore, organizations should prioritise fair and transparent performance appraisal processes to improve employee morale, engagement, and productivity.

METHODOLOGY

This study aims to address the following research question: What are healthcare professional's perceptions of the performance appraisal tools (PATs) to which they are subject?

Following the definition of the research question, specific objectives were formulated in alignment with the theoretical framework. These are: to identify the performance appraisal tools applied to healthcare professionals, to assess perceptions of fairness regarding the implementation of PATs; to assess perceptions of demotivation associated with PATs; to evaluate satisfaction levels related to the application of PATs.

To operationalise these objectives, the following research hypotheses were established:

H1: There is a relationship/association between PATs and the perception of fairness among professionals;
H2: There is a relationship/association between PATs and feelings of demotivation;
H3: There is a relationship/association between PATs and professional satisfaction;
H4: There is a relationship/association between demotivation and satisfaction in relation to PADs.

This research falls within the scope of quantitative, cross-sectional, descriptive, inferential, and correlational studies. It is considered cross-sectional as it analyses one or more population groups at a specific moment in time, focusing on a phenomenon currently taking place (Reis, 2010). It is descriptive as far as it seeks to identify patterns in the data, summarise findings, and explain relationships between variables (Negas, 2022). Descriptive statistics were prioritised in the data analysis.

The reliability of the questionnaire refers to the degree of confidence or precision attributed to the information collected. One of the most widely used methods to assess internal consistency or item homogeneity is Cronbach's alpha coefficient. This coefficient classifies the reliability of an instrument into six categories: values below 0.6 are deemed "Unacceptable"; between 0.6 and 0.7 as "Weak"; between 0.7 and 0.8 as "Acceptable"; between 0.8 and 0.9 as "Good"; and above 0.9 as "Excellent" (Hill & Hill, 2012). For the present study, the questionnaire yielded a Cronbach's alpha value of 0.82, thus classified as "Good" in terms of internal consistency.

Alpha reliability = 0.8223

For the inferential analysis, emphasis was placed on bivariate analysis using contingency tables and the application of Chi-square and Fisher's exact tests. Both tests are widely recognised statistical tools for hypothesis testing involving nominal variables. Unlike many other statistical tests, the Chi-square test (χ^2) not only identifies significant differences but also highlights the specific categories contributing to those differences (McHugh, 2013). In addition, a correlational analysis was conducted using Spearman's non-parametric correlation. This coefficient measures the strength and direction of association between variables based on their ranking, rather than absolute values, making it suitable for ordinal-scale variables (Reis, 2019).

Data analysis was conducted using the statistical software EZR.Rcmdr Version 2.5-1.

The inclusion criteria for participants were as follows:

- Being a healthcare professional;
- Being subject to a performance appraisal tool (PAT) in their professional activity;
- Possessing sufficient digital literacy to complete an online questionnaire;
- Willingness to participate freely and voluntarily in the study.

Data collection was performed through an online questionnaire created using the Google® Forms platform, disseminated electronically via the following link: https://forms.gle/QbyFnZSX7YB9VrEq5, between March 24 and April 10 of the current year.

The questionnaire comprised three sections:

1. An introductory note, informing participants about the study's purpose, ensuring voluntary participation, encouraging honest responses, and guaranteeing anonymity and data confidentiality. Participants were informed that they could withdraw at any time, without consequences;
2. A section with sociodemographic questions to characterise the sample (age, gender, nationality, educational level, employment sector, job description, and length of service);
3. A third section focused on healthcare professionals' perceptions of PATs, particularly regarding satisfaction and perceived fairness. These dimensions were measured using a 5-point Likert-type ordinal scale (1 – strongly disagree; 2 – disagree; 3 – neither agree nor disagree; 4 – agree; 5 – strongly agree), comprising a total of 36 items.

Likert-type scales involve discrete values and establish a correspondence between emotions, perceptions, and quantitative scores, thereby enabling statistical analysis (Negas, 2022). The construction of the questionnaire was informed by prior work developed by Silva (2018) and João et al. (2017).

The sampling method followed a snowball strategy, a purposive approach in which initial respondents refer other potential participants relevant to the study topic (Reis et al., 2022).

A total of 62 valid responses were obtained and considered for the final sample.

RESULTS

The study sample consisted of 62 respondents, of whom approximately 85.5% (*n*=53) identified as female, 12.9% (*n*=8) as male, and 1.6% (*n*=1) identified with a non-binary or other gender. Most participants were of Portuguese nationality (≈*95.2%, n*=59), with the remaining respondents being of German (*1.6%, n*=1), Brazilian (*1.6%, n*=1), and Mozambican (*1.6%, n*=1) nationality. Participants' ages ranged between 25 and 64 years. Regarding educational qualifications, most respondents (≈*54.8%, n*=34) held a bachelor's degree, while 33.9% (*n*=21) had a master's degree, 9.7% (*n*=6) had completed secondary education, and 1.6% (*n*=1) had attended a Higher Professional Technical Course. The vast majority (≈*98.4%, n*=61) worked in the public sector, with only 1.6% (*n*=1) employed in the private sector. In terms of professional roles, most respondents were part of the nursing career track (≈*67.8%, n*=42). Additionally, 12.9% (*n*=8) were professionals in diagnostics and therapeutics, 8.1% (*n*=5) in the healthcare assistant career, 3.2% (*n*=2) were medical doctors, 4.8% (n=3) were general technicians, and 3.2% (n=2) were in administrative roles. Years of service ranged from 3 to 40 years. Regarding the performance appraisal tools used, 88.7% (n=55) reported being assessed through SIADAP, 6.5% (n=4) via curricular evaluation, and 4.8% (n=3) through objective-based appraisal.

To simplify the interpretation of the data concerning professionals' perceptions of PATs, results in the dimensions of general perception (Table 1), satisfaction (Table 2), and perceived fairness (Table 3) were regrouped. Originally rated on a 5-point Likert scale (1 – strongly disagree; 2 – disagree; 3 – neither agree nor disagree; 4 – agree; 5 – strongly agree), responses were recategorized as follows:

- Disagree, combining responses 1 and 2;
- Neutral, corresponding to response 3;
- Agree, combining responses 4 and 5.

Concerning the emotional response of professionals to the PAT:

Table 1. Emotional response of professionals to the PAT

Question	Results
"I feel that I am fairly evaluated"	36 disagree, 12 neutral, 14 agree
"I feel that the PAT is credible"	35 disagree, 17 neutral, 10 agree
"I feel that the PAT reflects my value"	43 disagree, 13 neutral, 6 agree
"I feel that I am negatively affected by the PAT"	18 disagree, 13 neutral, 31 agree
"I feel that the PAT contributes to improving my service"	37 disagree, 18 neutral, 7 agree
"I feel that the PAT does not reflect reality"	14 disagree, 7 neutral, 41 agree
"I feel that the PAT underestimates my capabilities"	14 disagree, 7 neutral, 41 agree
"I feel that PATs guide me"	37 disagree, 18 neutral, 7 agree
"Considering PAT results, I feel demotivated"	22 disagree, 14 neutral, 26 agree
"I feel that PATs are fair":	48 disagree, 8 neutral, 6 agree
"Colleagues who are less committed are rated the same":	3 disagree, 5 neutral, 54 agree
"I fear retaliation if I complain about the PAT":	19 disagree, 20 neutral, 23 agree
"Appraisals do not reflect reality":	6 disagree, 4 neutral, 52 agree
"Equal ratings do not reflect equal levels of commitment":	4 disagree, 4 neutral, 54 agree
"I feel good in my organisation":	36 disagree, 12 neutral, 14 agree
"I feel valued by my organisation":	30 disagree, 20 neutral, 12 agree
"I feel like changing career path":	28 disagree, 12 neutral, 22 agree

continued on following page

Table 1. Continued

Question	Results
"I feel included in decisions regarding my role":	25 disagree, 16 neutral, 21 agree
"I am treated with respect":	14 disagree, 15 neutral, 33 agree
"I feel demotivated"	15 disagree, 15 neutral, 32 agree

Regarding the level of satisfaction towards the PAT:

Table 2. Satisfaction towards the PAT

Question	Results
"I am satisfied with the procedures used by my evaluator in the performance appraisal process"	34 disagree, 16 neutral, 12 agree
"I am satisfied with the final outcome of the appraisal process"	35 disagree, 17 neutral, 10 agree
"I am satisfied with the opportunities for career progression"	44 disagree, 11 neutral, 7 agree
"I am satisfied with the effort demonstrated by my supervisors to improve my working conditions"	31 disagree, 19 neutral, 12 agree
"I am satisfied with the way supervisors give me opportunities to participate in training/projects"	26 disagree, 16 neutral, 20 agree
"I am satisfied with the fact that my work is rewarded and/or valued by my supervisors"	31 disagree, 18 neutral, 13 agree
"I am satisfied with the competence demonstrated by colleagues from the same profession"	23 disagree, 22 neutral, 17 agree
"I am satisfied with the respect shown by my supervisors towards the work I do"	26 disagree, 19 neutral, 17 agree
"I am satisfied with the encouragement provided by supervisors for training and development"	29 disagree, 18 neutral, 15 agree

In the dimension of perceived fairness regarding the PAT:

Table 3. Perceived fairness regarding the PAT

Question	Results
"The rewards I receive are fair"	46 disagree, 10 neutral, 6 agree
"My evaluator shows genuine interest in being fair with me"	27 disagree, 17 neutral, 18 agree
"My performance appraisal rating is fair"	32 disagree, 16 neutral, 14 agree

continued on following page

Table 3. Continued

Question	Results
"My evaluator is completely honest and transparent with me"	23 disagree, 21 neutral, 18 agree
"My organisation has a mechanism in place to ensure the monitoring of the appraisal process"	31 disagree, 20 neutral, 11 agree
"Considering my experience, I feel fairly rewarded"	39 disagree, 12 neutral, 11 agree
"Considering my effort, I believe I am fairly rewarded"	41 disagree, 10 neutral, 11 agree

To verify the association between performance appraisal tools (PATs) and professional's perceptions of fairness, demotivation, and satisfaction—corresponding to hypotheses H1, H2, and H3—contingency tables were constructed, and the Chi-square test was applied, considering a 95% confidence level. However, the assumptions required for the Chi-square test (namely Cochran's conditions) were not met, necessitating the use of Fisher's exact test as an alternative.

H1: There is an association between the performance appraisal tools (PATs) and professional's perceptions of fairness (Table 4)

After examining the association between the professionals' perception of fairness and the performance appraisal tools (PATs), a Fisher's exact test value of $\rho = 0.0955$ was obtained, indicating that the formulated hypothesis cannot be confirmed (the null hypothesis, H0, is not rejected).

Table 4. Association between the performance appraisal tool (PAT) and professional's perceived fairness, and corresponding Fisher's ρ 0

PAT/Fairness	1-2	3	4-5	Σ
SIADAP	44	5	6	55
CPA[1]	3	1	0	4
OPA[2]	1	2	0	3
Total	48	8	6	62

Fisher.p.value = 0.0955

H2: There is an association between the performance appraisal tools (PATs) and the professional's feeling of demotivation (Table 5):

After examining the association between the professionals' feeling of demotivation and the PATs, a Fisher's exact test value of ρ = 0.0967 was obtained, indicating that the formulated hypothesis cannot be confirmed (the null hypothesis, H0, is not rejected).

Table 5. Association between the type of PAT and healthcare professional's perceived demotivation, along with the corresponding Fisher's ρ value

PAT/Demotivation	**1-2**	**3**	**4-5**	**Σ**
SIADAP	12	12	31	55
CPA[1]	2	1	1	4
OPA[2]	1	2	0	3
Total	15	15	32	62

Fisher.p.value = 0.0967

H3: There is an association between the performance appraisal tools (PATs) and the professional's satisfaction (Table 6):

After examining the association between the professionals' satisfaction and the PATs, a Fisher's exact test value of ρ = 0.0536 was obtained, indicating that the formulated hypothesis cannot be confirmed (the null hypothesis, H0, is not rejected).

Table 6. association between the PATs and the professional's satisfaction, along with the corresponding Fisher's ρ value

PAT/Satisfaçtion	**1-2**	**3**	**4**	**Σ**
SIADAP	31	13	11	55
CPA[1]	3	0	1	4
OPA[2]	0	3	0	3
Total[3]	15	15	32	62

Fisher.p.value = 0.0536

To evaluate hypothesis 4, concerning the existence of a relationship between professional's demotivation (Figure 1) and their satisfaction with the performance appraisal tools (PAT), Spearman's correlation coefficient was applied. This coefficient ranges from –1 to 1, where values closer to –1 or 1 indicate a strong correlation between the rankings of the variables, while values closer to zero indicate a weak correlation (Reis, 2019). Considering a 95% confidence level, a moderate negative correlation of –0.55 was found. Therefore, it can be concluded that the higher the professionals' demotivation, the lower their satisfaction regarding the FAD.

Figure 1. Association between the PATs and the professional's demotivation,

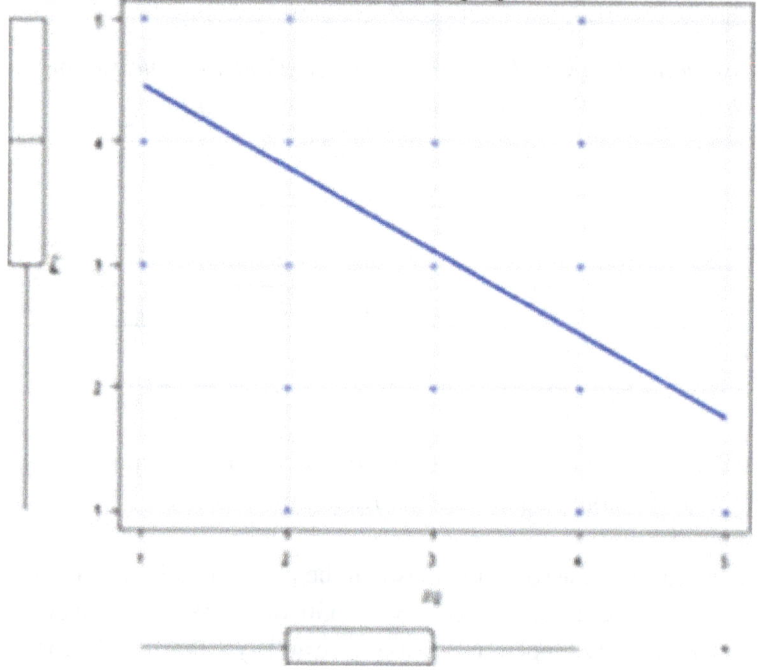

Figure 2. Correlation between professional demotivation and satisfaction, and the corresponding Spearman correlation coefficient

Spearman's rank correlation coefficient -0.55

DISCUSSION

Human resources in healthcare are fundamental for the functioning of the health system. When there is scarcity, unavailability, or poor distribution of these professionals, it directly affects the efficiency, effectiveness, and quality of the services provided.

In the present study, the sample is mostly composed of female individuals aged between 25 and 64 years of Portuguese nationality, and working in the public sector, with nursing professionals being the most represented group. These data align with the study by Ferreira et al. (2024), regarding the predominant profile of human resources in the Portuguese PNHS between 2017 and 2023. The majority of the surveyed health professionals hold higher education qualifications, namely bachelor's or master's degrees.

As previously mentioned, since the sample consists of public sector professionals, their performance appraisal is conducted through the SIADAP system, in accordance with national legislation (Decree-Law No. 12/2024). Gao and Regua (2024, p.62) concluded that transparent, fair, and constructive performance appraisal systems significantly increase the motivation and satisfaction of health professionals.

Regarding the dimension of professional's feelings towards performance appraisal tools (PAT), there is widespread disagreement among respondents concerning the reliability, fairness, and credibility of the instrument. The results also reveal that most respondents agree that the PAT is not representative of reality, being reductive of the professional's capabilities.

The perception of demotivation was also significant: 32 respondents stated feeling demotivated, and 26 indicated that the PAT directly contributes to this feeling. These findings are consistent with authors such as Hamidi (2023) and Gao and Regua (2024), who emphasize that evaluations perceived as unfair, decontextualized, or ineffective tend to reduce employee engagement and satisfaction, negatively affecting motivation and, consequently, performance.

People who feel happy and positive tend to perform better than those who are emotionally negative. Well-being can boost performance: employees who feel good behave differently from those who feel poorly, directly impacting their performance and effectiveness (Kaplan et al., 2009). Most professionals disagreed with statements about feeling well and being valued in their organization. This supports the findings by Gao and Regua (2024), who highlight the importance of regular feedback, goal setting, and recognition in the workplace.

However, most respondents feel treated with respect.

Employee well-being is negatively affected when basic psychological and physiological needs are unmet or frustrated. These needs include feeling part of something bigger, having a sense of self-esteem and personal worth, believing in the ability to predict and control the environment, and trusting others (Aquino & Thau, 2009).

Regarding satisfaction with the appraisal process, the data are equally revealing. A considerable number of professionals expressed dissatisfaction with the procedures adopted by evaluators (34), the result of the process (35), and career progression opportunities (44). These indicators suggest widespread dissatisfaction and distrust in the appraisal mechanisms, which seem transversal across various dimensions of the process. According to Hamidi et al. (2023), performance evaluations affect job satisfaction and organizational behaviour of employees, emphasizing the importance of effective appraisal systems for professional's well-being.

Concerning the feeling of justice associated with the implementation of PAT, most respondents disagreed that the PAT fairly and accurately reflect their performance. Only 6 out of 62 participants felt they were fairly evaluated, while 48 expressed the opposite. This perception of injustice is concerning, especially given that perceived fairness is one of the most influential factors in the acceptance and effectiveness of appraisal systems (Majidi et al., 2020). The author further argues that health professionals' perceptions of annual performance evaluations as fair and effective tools can improve employee performance and healthcare quality.

The sentiment that "*equal ratings do not indicate the same level of commitment*" (agreed upon by 54 respondents) reinforces the idea that professionals perceive the process as undifferentiated and insufficiently sensitive to their professional reality.

The data consistently reveal a broadly negative perception among health professionals regarding the performance appraisal tools (FAD) to which they are subjected. For example, in the dimension of perceived justice, 74% of respondents disagreed that rewards were fair, and 77% disagreed that their organization has effective mechanisms for monitoring the appraisal process. These values suggest that participants view the system as insufficiently transparent and lack trust in its resulting decisions.

Although hypotheses H1, H2, and H3 — which postulated an association between the type of PAT (SIADAP, curricular evaluation, or objectives-based evaluation) and, respectively, justice, demotivation, and satisfaction — were not statistically confirmed (Fisher's $\rho > 0.05$), bivariate analysis indicates that, regardless of the method applied, negative perceptions are widespread.

This suggests that the problem may not reside solely in the characteristics of each instrument but rather in more structural aspects of the appraisal process (for example, lack of evaluator training, absence of constructive feedback, or misalignment between individual and organizational goals).

The only significant finding emerged in the relationship between demotivation and satisfaction: Spearman's correlation coefficient of –0.55 demonstrates a negative correlation, meaning that the greater the demotivation felt by professionals, the lower their satisfaction with the PAT. This finding reinforces the importance of organizational climate and employee's emotional engagement, as described by Wright and Cropanzano (2004) in their model of psychological well-being and performance. Dissatisfaction with the appraisal process thus fosters a vicious cycle whereby, feeling unjustly treated and undervalued, professionals disengage from continuous improvement, contributing to a decline in overall performance.

It is also noteworthy that many professionals indicated, in informal conversations after completing the questionnaire, that they did not know which PAT system they were subject to, highlighting a lack of transparency and/or communication from direct supervisors.

CONCLUSION

Within the scope of the Portuguese National Health Service (PNHS), optimizing the management of human resources in healthcare is crucial to face significant challenges, such as the shortage of professionals and the increasing demand for health services, a situation intensified by the growing aging population. Performance appraisal tools (PAT) are essential instruments for this management when applied fairly and transparently.

It can be concluded that health professionals consistently hold a negative perception regarding the performance appraisal tools to which they are subjected.

In summary, they feel dissatisfied, unfairly treated, and demotivated by the FAD, which may negatively influence their commitment to the organization. Zheng et al. (2015) report that employee well-being—which includes life well-being, workplace well-being, and psychological well-being—is strongly related to both emotional commitment to the organization and job performance.

With the completion of this study, and in line with the research conducted by Gao and Regua (2024) as well as Majidi et al. (2020), it can be concluded that there is an urgent need to implement more equitable and participatory appraisal practices, involving bidirectional feedback, clarification of criteria, and specific training for evaluators. The adoption of hybrid models, combining competency-based appraisal with self-assessment and 360-degree evaluation mechanisms, may increase the sense of control and procedural justice, thereby mitigating perceptions of arbitrariness.

LIMITATIONS AND RECOMMENDATIONS

Finally, it is important to acknowledge the limitations of this study—namely the sample size and the snowball sampling method, which may introduce self-selection biases—and to propose future qualitative research using semi-structured interviews to deepen the understanding of the contextual and subjective factors shaping professional's perceptions of performance appraisal tools.

Only in this way will it be possible to design more effective human resource management interventions tailored to the real needs of healthcare professionals in Portugal.

It should also be noted that the results obtained may have been subject to bias during the completion of the online questionnaire, as many professionals indicated in informal conversations after completing the questionnaire that they did not know which performance appraisal tool they were subjected to, thus demonstrating a lack of transparency and/or communication with their direct supervisors.

Having some participants with only secondary education indicates that there were some contributions from non-qualified staff, i.e. healthcare support workers.

The study did not invite free text analysis which would have allowed for some thematic qualitative analysis.

As a recommendation for future research, it is proposed to conduct studies evaluating whether the quota limits established by SIADAP have an impact on the process outcomes, both for evaluators and those evaluated, since these limits constitute a constraint.

It should be noted that 73 professionals responded to the questionnaire, but some did not meet the inclusion criteria: 2 individuals were excluded for not identifying as healthcare professionals, and 9 for indicating that they were not evaluated by the performance appraisal tools under study.

ACKNOWLEDGEMENT

This work involved the use of artificial intelligence (AI) tools, specifically OpenAI's ChatGPT, to assist with the translation of the original text from European Portuguese to English. The AI was employed to ensure accuracy and clarity in the translation process. The final content was reviewed and validated by the authors.

REFERENCES

Aquino, K., & Thau, S. (2009). Workplace victimization: Aggression from the target's perspective. *Annual Review of Psychology*, *60*(1), 717–741. DOI: 10.1146/annurev.psych.60.110707.163703 PMID: 19035831

Correia, C. F. S. (2015). Avaliação de competências: Implicações nas práticas de gestão de recursos humanos. Estudo de caso: Pós-venda AVAC [Dissertação de mestrado, Faculdade de Economia da Universidade do Porto]. Repositório Aberto da Universidade do Porto. https://repositorio-aberto.up.pt/handle/10216/81259

Effendi, M., Rimbano, D., & Idayati, I. (2023). Work communication and work ethics on employee performance and job satisfaction. *Indonesian Journal of Business Analytics*, *3*(2), 513–538. DOI: 10.55927/ijba.v3i2.4035

Estender, A. Carlos (2021). Gestão de Pessoas e Avaliação de Desempenho nas Organizações. Revista Interdisciplinar Científica Aplicada, 7(2), 23-39. https://portaldeperiodicos.animaeducacao.com. br/index.php/rica/article/view/17765

Ferreira, A., Melo, W., Costa, R., Pereira, S., & Duarte, N. (2024). Os profissionais do SNS: Retrato e evolução. Lisboa: Centro de Competências de Planeamento, de Políticas e de Prospetiva da Administração Pública. https://www.planapp.gov.pt/wp-content/uploads/2024/03/PlanAPP_Profissionais SNS-2.pdf

Gao, F., & Regua, O. U. (2024). Evaluating the Impact of Performance Appraisal Systems on Employee Motivation and Job Satisfaction in Hospitals. *International Journal of Social Science and Human Research*, *12*(3), 59–63. DOI: 10.5281/zenodo.1274223

Hamidi, A. B. (2023). The Impacts of Performance Appraisal on Employee's Job Satisfaction and Organizational Behavior. *Ilomata International Journal of Social Science*, *4*(3), 466–480. DOI: 10.52728/ijss.v4i3.876

HILL. M. & HILL, A. (2012) – Investigação por Questionário. 2ª Edição. Edições Sílabo. ISBN:978-972-618-273- 3

Hoti, A., Binaku, A., & Ademaj, M. (2018). Using management by objectives as a performance appraisal tool for employee satisfaction. *Future Business Journal*, *4*(1), 94–108. DOI: 10.1016/j.fbj.2018.01.001

João, A. L. da S., Alves, C. P., Silva, C., Diogo, F., & Ferreira, N. D. (2017). Validation of a Nurse Job Satisfaction Scale for the Portuguese population. *Referência (Coimbra)*, *4*(12), 117–130. DOI: 10.12707/RIV16066

Kaplan, S., Bradley, J. C., Luchman, J. N., & Haynes, D. (2009). On the role of positive and negative affectivity in job performance: A meta-analytic investigation. *The Journal of Applied Psychology*, *94*(1), 162–176. DOI: 10.1037/a0013115 PMID: 19186902

Lexionário. Avaliação de desempenho (função pública) da Assembleia da República. Diário da República https://diariodarepublica.pt/dr/lexionario/termo /avaliacao-desempenho-funcao-publica

Majidi, S., Daneshkohan, A., Zarei, E., & Ashktorab, T. (2020). Perspectives of health workers on annual performance appraisal: A study in primary health care. *International Journal of Healthcare Management*, *14*(4), 1190–1197. DOI: 10.1080/20479700.2020.1755810

McHugh, M. (2013). O teste Qui-quadrado de indepedência. *Biochemia Medica*, *23*(2), 143–149. DOI: 10.11613/BM.2013.018 PMID: 23894860

Negas, E. (2022). *Estatística descritiva. 2ª edição*. Edições Silabo.

Nova School of Business and Economics. (2022) Universidade de Lisboa. Recursos Humanos em Saúde - Relatório 2022. https://www.novasbe.unl.pt/Portals/0/Files/Soci al%20Equity%20Initiative/Nova%20SBE_KC%20H ealth_Recursos%20Humanos_2022.pdf

OECD/European Commission. (2024). *Health at a Glance: Europe 2024: State of Health in the EU Cycle*. OECD Publishing., DOI: 10.1787/b3704e14-

Pontes, B. R. (2021). *Avaliação de Desempenho: métodos clássicos e contemporâneos, avaliação por objetivos, competências e equipes. 14ª Edição*. Editora LTR.

Reis, E. (2019). *Estatística Descritiva. 7ª edição*. Edições Sílabo.

Reis, E., Melo, P., Andrade, R., & Calapez, T. (2022). Estatística Aplicada – Volume 2, 6ª edição. Edições Silabo. ISBN: 978-972-618- 986-2

Reis, F. (2010) Como elaborar uma dissertação e mestrado segundo Bolonha. Pactor. ISBN 978- 989-693-000-4

Semedo, N., Calheiros, A., & Carvalho, W. (2014). Especificidades e desafios da implementação de um modelo de avaliação de desempenho numa pequena média empresa em Portugal. Conferência - Investigação E Intervenção Em Recursos Humanos, (4). https://doi.org/DOI: 10.26537/iirh.v0i4.2048

Silva, P. (2018). Avaliação de desempenho: perceções de justiça organizacional dos funcionários públicos [Tese de Mestrado em engenharia e gestão industrial no Instituto Superior de Engenharia do Porto] http://hdl.handle.net/10400.22/14115

Sureda, E., Chacón-Moscoso, S., Sanduvete-Chaves, S., & Sesé, A. (2021, August 30). A Training Intervention through a 360° Multisource Feedback Model. *International Journal of Environmental Research and Public Health, 18*(17), 9137. DOI: 10.3390/ijerph18179137 PMID: 34501727

Valluvan, S., Prasanth, S., Subramanian, S. P., Sriranjani, G., Sanjay, J., & Sri Abirami, N. (2024). The impact of performance appraisal on employee motivation. Library Progress International. https://bpasjournals.com/libraryscience/index.php/journal/article/view/3708

Waruwu, Y. (2024). Opportunities and challenges of results- based performance management in the public sector. *International Journal of Science Academic Research, 5*(1), 6806–6812. http://www.scienceijsar.com

Wright, T. A., & Cropanzano, R. (2004). The Role of Psychological Well-Being in Job Performance: A Fresh Look at an Age-Old Quest. Organizational Dynamics, 33(4), 338 351. DOI: 10.1016/j.orgdyn.2004.09.002

Zheng, X., Zhu, W., Zhao, H., & Zhang, C. (2015). Employee well-being in organizations: Theoretical model, scale development, and cross-cultural validation. *Journal of Organizational Behavior, 36*(5), 621–644. DOI: 10.1002/job.1990

ENDNOTES

1 curricular performance appraisal

2 objective-based performance appraisal

Chapter 12
Pharmaceutical Workforce Development and Strategic Decision-Making in Regulated Drug Development

Adeeba Riaz
http://orcid.org/0009-0009-6093-9777
Faculty of LifeSciences, Department of Biotechnology, University of Okara, Pakistan

Adnan Afzal
http://orcid.org/0009-0001-4359-5695
Government College University, Faisalabad, Pakistan

Abu Sulman
http://orcid.org/0009-0008-7194-5219
University of Agriculture, Faisalabad, Pakistan

Muhammad Saad Naeem
University of Agriculture, Faisalabad, Pakistan

Maria Shafaqat
School of Natural Sciences, University of Kent, Canterbury, UK

Fahad Ahmad
University of Agriculture, Faisalabad, Pakistan

Hina nawab
http://orcid.org/0009-0002-8250-5856
University of Agriculture, Faisalabad, Pakistan

Hafiz Aamir Ali Kharl
http://orcid.org/0000-0002-7365-2937
Narcotics Forensic Laboratory, Anti-Narcotics Force, Ministry of Interior and Narcotics Control, Islamabad, Pakistan

Maham Shehzadi
Department of Biotechnology, Cholistan University of Veterinary and Animal Sciences, Bahawalpur, Pakistan

DOI: 10.4018/979-8-3373-9410-7.ch012

ABSTRACT

This chapter explores the synergistic relationship between workforce development and strategic decision-making in regulated drug development. It highlights how pharmaceutical organizations operate within a regulatory paradox that demands rapid innovation while ensuring compliance, quality, and patient safety. The discussion emphasizes future-ready workforce capabilities, including regulatory literacy, data integrity, cross-functional collaboration, and adaptive learning, as drivers of successful outcomes. Strategic frameworks such as portfolio management, risk-adjusted decision models, Target Product Profiles, and model-informed drug development are examined to demonstrate their role in improving success probabilities. Ultimately, integrating human capital with strategic governance creates resilient, agile, and innovation-driven systems capable of navigating complex regulatory environments.

1. INTRODUCTION: THE REGULATORY PARADOX

The life sciences sector is a business that works in the life and death line. On the one hand, it is under tremendous pressure to innovate fast, motivated by unmet and unfulfilled medical demands, competition, and technological innovations and investor demands (Enriquez & Goldberg, 2000). Conversely, businesses are forced to conduct operations within rigid regulatory environments which are put in place by international health bodies like the U.S Food and drug administration (FDA) and the European medicines Agency (EMA). This tension brings about what can be referred to as the regulatory paradox: the need to go fast without jeopardising patient safety, data integrity or compliance standards (Rasmussen, 2014). Pharmaceuticals, biotechnology, and medical devices innovation have increased dramatically over the past few years. The growing number of new methods of gene editing, cell therapy, artificial intelligence-based drug discovery, decentralized clinical trials, and real-world evidence platforms have changed the nature of development. Nevertheless, against all odds, even with the acceleration of the technological process, the regulatory requirements are strict (Table 1) and they should be (Farley & Rouse, 2000). Governments have a role to play in protecting the health of people; they must also make sure that new treatment options are safe and effective, and that they are produced in the same quality (Ravinetto et al., 2024).

Table 1. The Intersections of Workforce and Strategy in Drug Development

Focus Area	Human Capital (Workforce Development)	Strategic Decision-Making	Synergistic Outcome
Risk Management	Cultivating a "Quality Culture" where staff are trained to identify deviations early.	Utilizing Quantitative Risk Assessment to balance clinical safety with speed to market.	**Proactive Compliance:** Reduced regulatory delays and "Right First Time" submissions.
Innovation	Upskilling teams in AI, Bioinformatics, and Advanced Therapy Medicinal Products (ATMPs).	Investing in Model-Informed Drug Development (MID3) to predict clinical outcomes.	**Accelerated Timelines:** Shortened R&D cycles through tech-enabled, expert-led execution.
Regulatory Navigation	Developing "Regulatory Scientists" who understand global harmonized guidelines (ICH).	Mapping the Target Product Profile (TPP) to meet specific unmet medical needs.	**Global Market Access:** Simultaneous approvals across multiple jurisdictions (FDA, EMA, etc.).
Data Integrity	Training personnel in ALCOA+ principles and robust documentation practices.	Implementing Blockchain or eClinical systems for transparent, real-time data flow.	**Unassailable Evidence:** High-fidelity data packages that withstand rigorous health authority audits.
Operational Agility	Empowering cross-functional teams to collaborate across silos (R&D, Clinical, Mfg).	Adopting Adaptive Clinical Trial designs that allow for mid-study course correction.	**Resource Efficiency:** Optimal allocation of capital and talent toward high-probability assets.

The irony is not based on the contraries but on the coexistence. Regulators do not oppose innovation, on the contrary, such agencies as the FDA and EMA are big proponents of breakthrough therapies and expedited pathways (Deshmukh, 2024). Nonetheless, innovation should be supported with strong evidence, proven systems, verifiable data, and processes that are adhered to. Lack of regulatory discipline in speedy innovation results in expensive delays, letters of warning, clinical hold or recall of the product. Overcaution and lack of innovation, in their turn, lead to loss of opportunities, long dsevelopment process, and untreated patients (Samuel). This paradox cannot be overcome by a powerful leadership or a sophisticated technology. It needs a very competent labor force, which is not only knowledgeable about the science but also in the regulatory environment (Shahzad, 2024). The skill to align innovation with compliance is essentially a challenge of people capability. Companies that develop future-ready workforces (that is, possess regulatory literacy, GxP skills, and data integrity skills) have a greater capacity to make high-probability-of-success (PoS) decisions throughout the product lifecycle (Sundaram, 2025).

1.1. Defining Workforce Development: Beyond Hiring

Employees development in the life sciences field is usually misconstrued as a mere issue of hiring qualified personnel. But, when people hire, it does not make an organization resilient and future-ready (Peng et al., 2024). Effective workforce development means building specialized skills, internal knowledge, and cross functional skills that allow them to perform sustainably in a highly regulated environment in a systematic manner (Parween, 2024).

The conventional approach to workforce planning revolves around the job placement: clinical project managers, quality assurance specialists, regulatory affairs associates, validation engineers, pharmacovigilance officers. Although these roles are required, the contemporary regulatory climate requires more than job descriptions. It requires combined competence (Frize, 2022).

The following are the characteristics of a future-ready workforce: (HO, 2023)

- Existence of profound knowledge of GxP principles (Good Manufacturing Practice, Good Clinical Practice, Good Laboratory Practice).
- Knowledge in regulatory science and the changing international direction.
- Competency of information integrity and computer compliance systems.
- Multi-functional cooperation between quality, manufacturing, regulatory, R&D and commercial groups.
- Decision-making that was risk-based was in line with regulatory expectations.

The paradigm of moving away from the concept of role-based hiring and capability-based development of the workforce turns the workforce strategy into the competitive advantage (Mann & Mann, 2025).

1.2. GxP as Foundational Discipline

The compliance of GxP is the keystone of life sciences operations. Regardless of whether in research and development, clinical development or commercial production, compliance to GxP will guarantee that processes are controlled, reproducible, and documented (Kabir et al., 2024).

Nonetheless, GxP expertise does not stand at the same level. The expectations of regulations are dynamic. The requirements in data governance are extended. New validation issues emerge with digital systems. Global supply chains and outsourcing contribute to more complexity in oversight (Nair, 2025). An employee base that simply understands the regulations is no longer appropriate. The employees should know why GxP regulations are intended to ensure that the product is safe, traceable, reproducible and accountable to the patient (Nair, 2025). Compliance once internalized in teams is proactive and not reactive. Regulatory foresight is used to make decisions and not corrective remediation.

- Strategic Intelligence: Regulatory Science.
- Innovation and approval are the fields that regulatory science fills in. It entails having knowledge of how the regulators consider evidence, the profiles of benefit-risk, and the manufacturing controls.
- Development of the workforce should therefore entail:
- Regulatory pathway training (e.g., accelerated approvals, orphan designation) (Michaeli et al., 2024).

1.3. Experience on International Submission Practices

Experience with the emerging guidelines on advanced treatments, digital health and real-world evidence. Skills in productive interaction with regulatory authorities at meetings of scientific advice and at inspections (Burns et al., 2022). Companies that develop regulatory scientists, and not only regulatory administrators, have strategic advantage. These practitioners expect the regulatory issues to come out at earlier stages before it causes serious cost shock later on (Gao & McDonald, 2022).

1.4. Information Security in the Digital Age

Information is the gold of regulatory acceptance. All clinical ends, stability test, manufacturing batch record and the pharmacovigilance report build up to the body of evidence of a product (Lutfor et al., 2025). In the digital age, data integrity has emerged as a stronger and weaker phenomenon at the same time. Complexity is presented by electronic systems, cloud systems, artificial intelligence (AI) analytics, and models of decentralized trials. Regulatory officials are becoming more investigative about the data governance, audit trails, system validation and cybersecurity controls (Zhao et al., 2024).

1.5. Workforce Development Should Hence Entail Competencies In

- Computerized system assurance and Computer System validation.
- ALCOA+ (Attributable, Legible, Contemporaneous, Original, Accurate, and Complete, Consistent, Enduring, and Available).
- Validation based on risks.
- Information life-cycle management and governance.

In the absence of these skills that are inculcated within the functions, organizations are exposed to inspection results, sluggish approvals, or damaged reputations (Zhou & Duan, 2026).

1.6. The Strategic Importance of a Future-Ready Workforce

There is a direct and quantifiable relationship between the work force capability and high-probability-of-success (PoS) decisions. PoS is the probability that a development program will advance to the next stage successfully, preclinical to clinical, Phase I to Phase III, submission to approval (Kaufman, 2025). Although the scientific merit is paramount, most development failures are not caused by the inefficiency but result of the operational and regulatory errors. The bad study designs, lack of documentation, discrepancies in manufacturing, or lack of quality control can hamper good programs. An employee-focused workforce is future ready and mitigates these risks in a number of ways (Abraham, 2023).

1.7. Early Risk Identification

Well-trained teams that are experienced are able to identify regulatory and operational risks at an early stage. For example: A clinical team that is conscious of emerging instructions can model endpoints that are in line with the expectations of regulations. A process validation team that is comprised of skilled manufacturing personnel predicts the scale-up issues before commercialization. To avoid the risk of credibility of the trials, a data management team educated in the principles of integrity prevents cases of discrepancy. Early detection of risk saves on resources and reduces time (Cantu, 2025).

1.8. Cross-Functional Alignment

A regulatory success can only be achieved through smooth interdepartmental cooperation. R&D can be scientifically driven, quality driven and speed to market as a priority with the commercial teams. Mismatch may cause tension or inefficient decision-making (Deng, 2025).

Balanced decision-making is developed through workforce development programs that facilitate cross-functional literacy where scientists have knowledge of regulatory constraints and quality professionals have knowledge of development pressure. This congruency improves PoS as it minimizes the rework and are strategically congruent (Ramakrishnan, 2025).

1.9. Adaptive Learning and Continuous Improvement

There is dynamic regulatory environment. Guideline documents are revised. Novel treatment modalities are created. Clinical and manufacturing practices are transformed through digital transformation (Hussian et al., 2025).

An organization with a workforce that is future-ready has to adopt lifelong learning. Institutionalized organizations that train, mentor, and share knowledge respond faster to the changes in the regulation. They have less chances of being surprised when they are being inspected or their submission checked (Young-Babb et al., 2025).

Reporting and correcting the deviations at the earliest stage of work can also be promoted by continuous improvement cultures, which enhances the compliance posture.

2. PHARMACEUTICAL WORKFORCE DEVELOPMENT (THE HUMAN PILLAR)

The human aspect of the life sciences ecosystem is pharmaceutical workforce development. Although the industry may be characterized by ground-breaking molecules, new biologics, new analytics, and state-of-the-art manufacturing plants, it is eventually people who turn scientific discovery into safe, effective, and affordable therapies. Due to the increasing technological sophistication and globalization of drug development, there is no greater requirement of a highly skilful multidisciplinary and ethically sound workforce. Developing workforce should therefore cease to be a habitual training or staffing paradigm and be more of a strategic point of concern in the design of the organization (Maclean et al., 2026). The most important aspect of pharmaceutical workforce development is the fact that pharmaceutical development is multidisciplinary by nature. One therapeutic program involves the smooth collaboration of discovery scientists, clinical research, regulatory, and quality specialists, manufacturing engineers, data scientists, and pharmacovigilance teams. Every field has its own angle, but no profession will be able to perform its role without the others. In the event of failure in integration, delays, protocol amendments, regulatory queries, and compliance findings will normally follow. With successful integration, the development cycles are simplified and the level of regulatory trust is raised (Maclean et al., 2026). Regulatory Affairs (RA) is one of the most important activities in this multidisciplinary ecosystem. Conventionally, RA was seen as a compliance control point- a role that is involved in the preparation of submissions and in answering the questions of the authorities like the U.S. Food and Drug Administration or the European Medicines Agency. Within that constrained perception, the regulatory professionals were working at the bottom of the development phases, going through the documents prior to submission and making sure that their formatting is correct. Nonetheless, the modern pharmaceutical landscape requires a much more strategic role of RA (Gavrilenko & Shenshin, 2023). Modern Regulatory Affairs should act as a strategic facilitator during the lifecycle of the product. The regulatory professionals are in a unique position to decipher emerging global instructions, evaluate regulatory acumen, and pre-empt agency anticipations. Implemented at an early stage in the programs of discovery and development, RA teams influence the choice of clinical endpoints, recommend acceptable biomarkers, and provide advice on the use of statistical powering techniques and recommend the most advantageous regulatory pathways, including accelerated approval or conditional approval. Instead of being a kind of gatekeeper that slows the process, strategic RA participation downstream risk. Early regulatory harmonization reduces the risks of significant objections, clinical holds or refusal-to-file determinations (Moparthi, 2024). An example of such hybrid skill set that RA professionals should have in order to operate within such a strategic capacity is a scientific literacy combined with regulatory knowledge, risk assessment capabilities with a strong communication skills. The workforce development programs should therefore take the training on regulatory compliance to the next level of regulation science (Mascarenhas et al., 2025). The professionals ought to be not just aware of what the regulations entail but also why they are there patient safety, reproducibility, transparency, and data reliability. This increased insight enables RA to be a facilitator between innovation and compliance instead of being a hindrance between the two (Fukami & FUKAMI, 2024).

It is also vital to bridge the gaps in other fields. Mechanistic pathways, molecular targets and preclinical models are often of interest to R&D scientists. Patient recruitment, site management and execution of protocols are prioritized by clinical operations teams. An emphasis on design of trials, statistical power and interpretation of data is made by biostatisticians. These views though personally critical, may become siloed. A discovery scientist can suggest such a beautiful biomarker that is operationally unfeasible. A statistician can come up with an experiment that can be scientifically strong but hard to implement in the real world. A healthcare team can emphasize the rate of recruitment, rather than mechanistic precision (Calado, 2024).

Good workforce development reflects on these silos by providing cross-disciplinary learning and working systems. The knowledge of regulatory endpoint expectations and statistical implications helps scientists. Clinical operators become aware of biological explanation and statistical suppositions. Biostatisticians enhance the design of trials by valuing the heterogeneity of the patients and operational practicability. Shared performance measures, cross-functional rotations as well as integrated project teams promote mutual understanding. By having teams work with a common language, they come up with scientifically sound, operationally feasible, and regulator ready protocol designs (Badreldin & Almosnid, 2025). On top of internal alignment, pharmaceutical workforce development should also be responsive of global workforce priorities. Pharmaceutical industry is a cross-border industry and a uniform standard is becoming very crucial. The International Pharmaceutical Federation (FIP) has outlined Development Goals with an aim of empowering the global pharmaceutical workforce with a focus on competency education, leadership development, workforce intelligence, and academic capacity building. By aligning the corporate workforce strategies to these global objectives, industry practices will help to make the health system more resilient (Bates et al., 2023). Intellectual ability is a pillar in this ecosystem. Universities and professional schools are the ones that determine the skills of the future pharmacists, regulatory scientists, and clinical researchers. Additional curriculums in regulatory science, pharmacometrics, digital health technologies and genomics can equip graduates to meet the challenges of drug development in the twenty first century. Academic/industry relationships also increase preparedness. Internship programs, joint research projects and guest faculty rotations expose students to regulatory submissions, Good Clinical Practice and data governance frameworks (Deshmukh & Paliwal, 2024).

Figure 1. Infographic Representation of Pharmaceutical Workforce

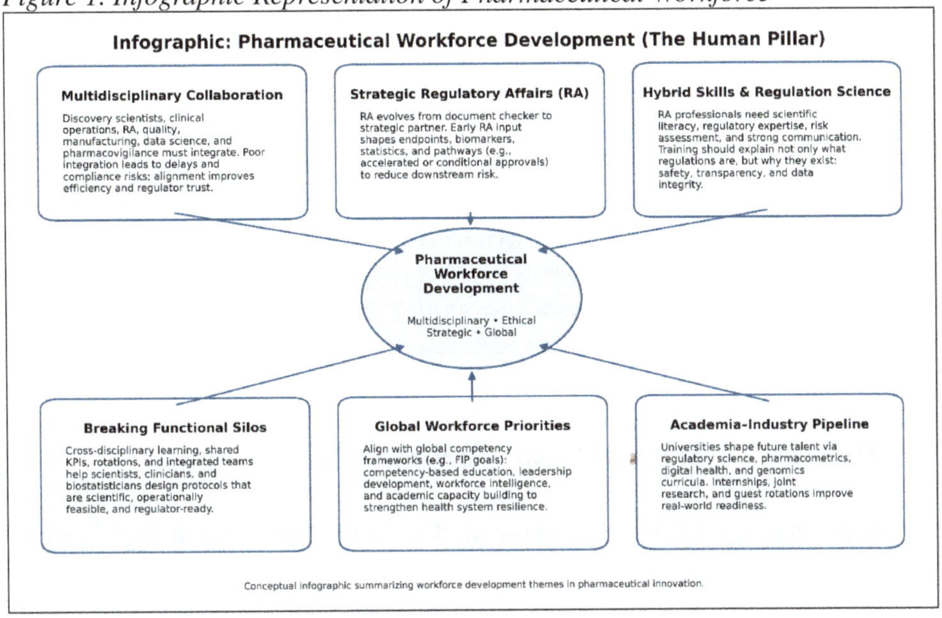

Conceptual infographic summarizing workforce development themes in pharmaceutical innovation.

3. STRATEGIC DECISION-MAKING IN A REGULATED ENVIRONMENT

The pharmaceutical industry is a field of strategic decision making that is at crossroads of science, regulation, finance and ethics. As opposed to most other sectors, failure in drug development is not merely a commercial loss, they can be years of research, erosion of large amounts of capital, and time without life-saving treatments. The regulatory issues, scientific ambiguity, and market unpredictability present a very distinct and peculiar environment where every investment decision has to be judged strictly (Pesqueira & Almeida, 2026). In this context portfolio management is a fundamental discipline by the executive. Organizations have limited resources to distribute among competing development projects and have to deal with high turnover rates, as well as lengthy development plans. Strategic decision-making entails ample frameworks, (Table 2) quantitative and predictive analytics and cross-functional governance. The end is not the individual products approval but the creation of the sustainable value of the enterprise within the regulatory limits (Roberts & Hamilton Edwards, 2023).

Table 2. Strategic Decision-Making in a Regulated Environment

Component	Strategic Focus	Regulatory Consideration
Market Entry	Identifying high-growth areas and competitive advantages.	Licensing, permits, and geographic legal restrictions.
Product Development	Innovation, R&D, and meeting consumer needs.	Safety standards, clinical trials, and intellectual property laws.
Risk Management	Assessing financial ROI and market volatility.	Compliance audits, data privacy (GDPR/ HIPAA), and reporting.
Workforce Alignment	Talent acquisition and skill development.	Labor laws, certifications, and workplace safety (OSHA).
Operational Scale	Efficiency and supply chain optimization.	Environmental impact (EPA) and trade regulations.

3.1. The "Valley of Death" and Portfolio Management

The development of drugs has been said to be marked by what is commonly referred to as the Valley of Death. This is the dangerous gap between a scientific discovery that is initially successful and a successful commercialization. A high number of promising compounds are lost in the process of translation of preclinical validation to clinical proof-of-concept. Passage through this valley is a very expensive undertaking, in the tune of hundreds of millions of dollars before any definite efficacy indication will appear (Everts & Drew, 2024). It is portfolio management that is there to rationalize in this valley. Organizational managers should not look at each development program separately but instead see it as a diversified investment ecosystem. Certain programs can be high-risk and high-reward programs (e.g., first in class therapies), whereas others are incremental innovations that have more predictable results (Simon, 2024). Good portfolio governance involves well-organized stage-gate. Projects are assessed based on scientific, regulatory, financial, and strategic criteria at set milestones of the project such as the end of preclinical, the completion of Phase I, evidence-of-concept in Phase II. The goal is to have a disciplined allocation of capital and have the flow of resources to the programs with best chances of success and strategic association (Aðalsteinsdóttir, 2024). Absent a rigorous process of managing portfolios, the organization is prone to hysteria over old projects, political decision making, or the sunk-cost trap. Valley of Death is further enlarged when poor programs eat up the resources that can have been used to develop better candidates (Hong, 2024).

3.2. The Art of Go/No-Go Decision

The Go/No-Go choice is among the most impactful in the pharmaceutical strategy. It is a strategic decision to either proceed with a development program to a new level or to put it to a close. Although this decision relies on frameworks and data models, it can only be decided by the executives (Barrett, 2022). The main problem is that termination decisions are usually difficult emotionally. Scientific teams can have dedicated years of work to a program. Top managers might have publicly been vocal in its potential. Nevertheless, disciplined dismissal may be a strategic intervention of value maintenance. Keeping a low-probability program may steal resources, resources and production capacity off other candidates (Forscher et al., 2023).

3.3. The Go/No-Go Decision Art is Based on Several Principles

- Objectivity: The choices should be based on facts and not on the hope bias.
- Criteria that are predetermined: Before data unblinding, success thresholds are set.
- Cross-Functional Input: Clinical, regulatory, manufacturing, and commercial are perspectives that need to be taken into consideration.
- Transparency: The system of governance must be non-politicalized and promote honesty in reporting the risks.

Premature termination where it is warranted not only conserves finance but also cost of opportunity. It enables organizations to shift the emphasis to those programs that are potentially more powerful. It is in this way that we can terminate without failure, but rather a disciplined strategic termination (LoCastro & Wasserstein).

3.4. Net Present Value (NPV) vs. a Risk-Adjusted Net Present Value (rNPV) as a Decision-Making Tool

Portfolio decisions are dependent on quantitative financial modeling. Risk-Adjusted Net Present Value (rNPV) builds on the classical discounted cash flow analysis with some additional probabilities of technical and regulatory success at each stage of the development (Lalhunthara & Singh, 2025). Revenues that are expected to be received in future are discounted in rNPV models with the time factor as well as the probability of successful advancement through clinical and regulatory hurdles. Expected cash flows are subject to phase-specific probabilities, which are determined by industry data of the past and internal performance measures (Ranbhor & Kulkarni, 2025).

The outcome is a valuation system which accounts for both uncertainty as well as opportunity. Programs that have big potential in terms of sales in the peak but less likely to be successful are likely to have low rNPV compared to smaller programs that are sure of success (Phares et al., 2024).

3.5. rNPV Also Supports

- Scenario Analysis: Analysis of best-case, base case and worst case analysis.
- Sensitivity Analysis: Determining variables that have the highest effect on valuation.
- Portfolio Optimization: The trade off between high-risk innovation and stable revenue generators.

Nevertheless, the rNPV cannot be applied alone. Qualitative strategic factors that must be used to complement financial models include unmet medical need, competitive positioning, and platform-building potential (Ridwan et al., 2025).

3.6. The Strategic Compass of the Target Product Profile (TPP)

TPP is the strategic map used in drug development. It presents the desired label claims, target population, route, safety profile, and distinguishing itself in comparison to its competitors.

A clear TPP serves as a north star to help the development decisions. All clinical trial designs, manufacturing investments and regulatory contacts must conform to the proposed final product label (Kieffer, 2024). In the absence of the TPP, development would be reactive. Changes in the protocols add up. Endpoints shift. Strategic coherence erodes. In comparison, a strong TPP makes sure that there is integration between R&D, regulatory, commercial, and health economics groups (Kieffer, 2024).

3.7. The TPP Supports

- Succinct endpoint selection was in line with regulatory expectations.
- Early payer and market access factors.
- Differentiation strategy competitive.
- Lifecycle management planning.

Significantly, TPP is a dynamic one. The strategic pivots might need to take place as new information appears. Though, not a response to provisional outcomes, changes should be purposeful, supported by evidence (Kirtley & O'Mahony, 2023).

3.8. Model-Informed Drug Development (MID3)

Model-Informed Drug Development (MID3) is a combination of the mathematical modelling and simulation with the strategic decision-making process. It uses pharmacodynamics (PD), pharmacokinetic (PK) and disease progression models to optimize dosage to use and the design of trials (Madabushi et al., 2022).

MID3 does not use quantitative modelling as a means of predicting exposure-response relationships but instead relies on empirical dose escalation only. Before a single patient is enrolled it is possible to simulate a number of trial scenarios using simulation tools (Cox, 2023).

3.9. Key Benefits of MID3 Include

- More precise dose selection.
- Less exposure of the patient to subtherapeutic or toxic doses.
- Reduced and more focused trials.
- Greater involvement in regulation in terms of quantitative justification.

The model-based approaches are more favoured by the regulatory authorities as clearly documented and scientifically explained. Embracing MID3 at an early stage of development lowers the chances of unpleasant surprises at advanced stages and allows more confidence in dose rationale (Madabushi et al., 2022).

3.10. Eliminating Attrition Rates With Predictive Analytics

The issue of high attrition has been one of the most nagging issues in the pharmaceutical industry. Predictive analytics will provide new logistics to this issue.

Machine learning algorithms have the ability to process massive data sets of preclinical findings, genomics, biomarker data, and past clinical trial performance. These models determine trends related to success or failure, and this allows stratifying risks at an earlier stage (Mozaffari et al., 2023).

3.11. Predictive Analytics is Compatible With

- Better selection of candidates in the discovery.
- Early identification of cues of safety.

- Determination of responsive subgroups of patients.
- Improved trial feasibility tests.

Predictive tools do not remove uncertainty; however, they enhance the detection of signals and confidence in the decision-making. Portfolio resilience is enhanced by combining analytics and conventional scientific assessment (Odunaike, 2025).

3.12. Evidence Generation at the Strategic Level

The process of strategic evidence formulation necessitates the harmonization between the clinical development needs and post-market needs. The trials of phase I-III designed to obtain regulatory approval must also be structured in a way to ensure commercial viability and acceptance by the payers (Korjian et al., 2023). RWE is gaining more significant importance. Observational data, patient registries, and electronic health records give information on the effectiveness of treatment in the routine practice.

3.13. Combining Pilot Studies With Subsequent RWE Aims Helps To

- Health technology assessment preparedness.
- Long-term safety monitoring.
- Effectiveness comparison assessment.
- Market access strategy.

RWE strategic integration is a way of ensuring that clinical programs produce evidence that is also meaningful to regulators as well as to payers and healthcare providers (McNair et al., 2022).

4. INTEGRATING STRATEGY AND WORKFORCE: THE INTEGRATED APPROACH

Pharmaceutical modernity requires something beyond scientific excellence and regulatory compliance in and of themselves. It demands convergence- of individuals, procedures, infrastructure and strategic purpose. In the past, drug development has tended to be fractured: discovery has been at a different site, clinical operations have been outsourced to contract research organizations (CROs), manufacturing has been geographically dispersed, and regulatory interaction has also been concentrated in a different functional area (Ndioumabia, 2022). Although outsourcing and specialisation may be effective, over% percent fragmentation often translates into communication breakdowns, lengthened decision making, overlapping of effort and loss of focus (Ragsdale, 2024).

Figure 2. Integrating Strategy and Workforce: The Integrated Approach.

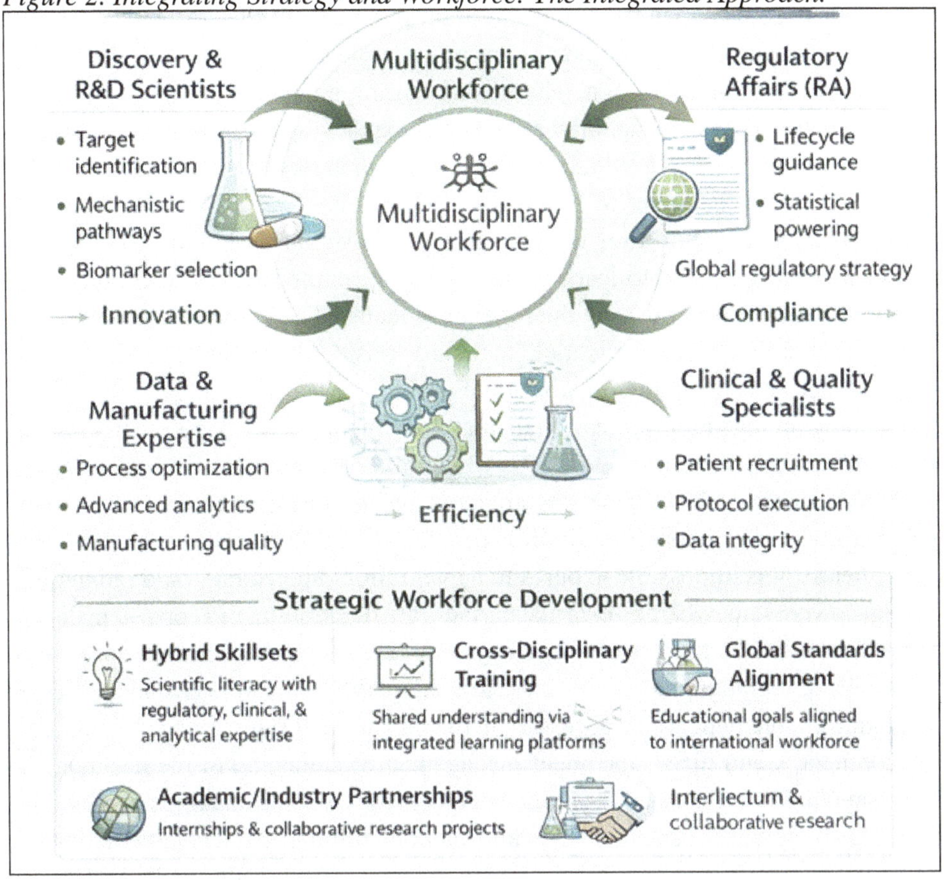

By combining workforce strategy and corporate strategy, the single framework is formed that converts the developmental model of linear progression and handoff orientation to a model of ecosystem. The phenomenon of cross-functional alignment in this type of an integrated paradigm is not one that happens by accident; it is a structural phenomenon. They do not develop in a linear way, but scientists, regulatory planning, and scalability in production, and commercial positioning are aspects that develop concurrently (Altman et al., 2023). Silos can only be broken by first changing the mindset. Conventional linear development is organized in the form of a stage-gate: discovery is handed over to preclinical, which is handed over to clinical, which is handed over to regulatory and manufacture. Every transition comes in with risk. There is a risk of the loss of knowledge during the translation. It is possible that assumptions remain untested until it is late in the game and the structural vulnerabilities get exposed (Hanenkratt, 2024).

The integrated drug development model is used to substitute the linear progression with a concurrent collaboration. Discovery scientists are involved as early as with clinical development to determine translational viability. Instead of having to examine government documents that are completed, regulatory professionals are involved in protocol design. The manufacturing engineers are involved in the decision-making of the formulations even prior to reaching the scale-up constraints. Market differentiation is evaluated by commercial strategists at a time when the clinical endpoints have yet to be determined (Rai et al., 2025). This combined strategy demands a labor force with the ability to have interdisciplinary communication. Researchers need to learn about regulatory pathways. The manufacturing constraints should be valued by the regulatory teams. The commercial viability is a factor that clinical operators should take into consideration. Strategic design can therefore not be separated with workforce development. Companies need to do it deliberately and develop professionals that are capable of working outside of the scope of functions (Okosieme et al., 2025). Integration is complicated by outsourcing. The CROs, contract development and manufacturing organizations (CDMOs), and external analytics vendors have significant roles in the contemporary development. Nevertheless, it is impossible to outsource integration. Sponsors should retain their strategic ownership; whereby external partners are functioning in a consistent development framework. The governmental systems must focus on common measures, open lines of communication and standardized quality indicators (Kühnen, 2025).

Digital enablement is also necessary in the transition of fragmented to integrated development. Centralized document management systems, real-time dashboards, and shared data platforms decrease the latency in the decision-making process. The strategic alignment is hastened when all functions through clinical data, manufacturing batch results, and regulatory correspondence can be made available. Digital transparency improves accountability and minimizes reworking that is a result of information asymmetry (Tummuri, 2025). Physical infrastructure is complimentary. A good example of the impact of proximity, both physical and digital, driving innovation is the single-campus or ecosystem model. Informal communication is the order of the day when research laboratories, pilot manufacturing plants, teams of clinical operations and regulatory specialists are all located in geographic proximity to one another. There is real time resolution of issues instead of long email correspondence or ineffective teleconferences (Pfatteicher, 2025). The cross-functional teams can meet quickly and evaluate the emerging data in a single-campus ecosystem. The manufacturing deviation can be immediately discussed with the quality assurance and clinical supply teams. A new safety signal may initiate the coordinated analysis of the pharmacovigilance, biostatistics, and regulatory affairs. The friction of collaboration is lessened when there is physical proximity (Ogbuagu et al., 2023). Digital proximity makes this idea have a worldwide presence. Co-location is simulated by integrated digital platforms even in geographically dispersed teams. Analytics on the cloud, team building modeling tools, and linked communication systems are ensuring that decision-makers have access to aligned data. The aim is to reduce the duration taken between the production of data and action strategy (Zaiter & Azouz, 2025).The speed of decision-making is especially demanded in breakthrough therapies. Precision medicines, cell-based therapy, and gene therapies are frequently applied to small patient groups with urgent needs that cannot be met. Sluggishness in communication due to siloing can be both ethical and financial. By incorporating regulatory, manufacturing and clinical insight within the day-to-day operations, integrated ecosystems minimize these delays (Jeleel-Ojuade, 2024). But the integration should be primed on an effective quality culture. The key to the coherent framework is in Quality by Design (QbD) at this point. Conventionally, quality assurance was occasionally viewed as a downstream control point - checking products after they are made or checking documentation before it is submitted. QbD changes this paradigm radically.

Quality by Design incorporates the aspect of quality at the very early stages of development. Instead of depending on testing of end-products as a way of detecting defects, QbD focuses on critical quality attributes (CQAs), critical process parameters (CPPs) and risk assessment in the initial stages. Such a proactive method is in line with scientific experimentation and regulatory requirements and manufacturability (Soltanzadeh et al., 2024). QbD has to be culturally embedded in order to work. The efforts that workforce development teams should focus on should point out that quality is something that is shared, not the quality unit. Assay design, equipment configuration, data entry within the clinical teams, and so on all have a role to play in quality (Coates et al., 2025). The risk-based thinking, root cause analysis, and documentation integrity should be reinforced by the training programs. Leaders should have the capability of setting examples that promote openness rather than secrecy. The organizations must promote systemic learning and open reporting instead of blaming in case of the occurrence of deviations. Psychological safety culture enhances quality outcomes through improved employee empowerment to blow the whistle early (Valdez et al., 2025).

Introduction of QbD into the workforce culture also leads to a decrease in regulatory friction. Agencies are becoming more and more demanding of evidence that quality is in-built in development processes. The confidence of regulators is high when the organizations have demonstrated the systematic risk assessment, robust design space exploration, and cross-functional oversights. This is in line with the speedy review schedules and minimization of checking results (Van Der Zalm et al., 2022).

Table 3. Integration, Digital Collaboration, and Quality by Design in Pharmaceutical and Medical Device Ecosystems

Key Theme	Core Concept	Main Practices / Components	Organizational Impact	Supporting References
Cross-Functional Collaboration	Co-located or closely connected teams improve coordination	Rapid data evaluation, interaction between QA, clinical supply, and manufacturing	Faster problem-solving and reduced collaboration friction	Ogbuagu et al. (2023)
Digital Proximity & Integrated Platforms	Virtual co-location through digital tools	Cloud analytics, integrated communication systems, modeling tools	Faster data-to-action decision cycles	Zaiter & Azouz (2025)
Decision-Making Speed in Breakthrough Therapies	Rapid coordination for high-risk innovations	Integration of regulatory, clinical, and manufacturing insights	Ethical and financial risks reduced; faster innovation delivery	Jeleel-Ojuade (2024)
Quality by Design (QbD) Paradigm	Quality integrated from early development stages	Focus on CQAs, CPPs, risk assessment during design phase	Improved regulatory alignment and manufacturability	Soltanzadeh et al. (2024)
Quality Culture Development	Quality as shared organizational responsibility	Workforce training, cross-team accountability	Enhanced consistency and compliance	Coates et al. (2025)
Risk-Based Thinking & Learning Systems	Proactive quality management approach	Root cause analysis, documentation integrity training	Prevention of recurring deviations	Coates et al. (2025)
Psychological Safety & Leadership	Open reporting and learning-focused culture	Encouraging transparency, leadership role modeling	Early identification of issues and stronger quality outcomes	Valdez et al. (2025)

Agile governance models should also be integrated and quality culture adjusted. Conventional governance structures are based on hard stage gates and a top-down decision-making structure. Although these structures have a disciplining effect, they might not be responsive to breakthrough therapies that can be granted expedited pathways like Orphan Drug designation, Fast Track or Accelerated Approval (Alešnik et al., 2025). Agile governance is rigorous and brings about flexibility. It focuses on shortening the decision times, data cycle and cross-functional reviewing mechanisms. Such as, agile governance structures can allow speedy interaction with regulators in cases where the early evidence of transformative efficacy is demonstrated in a rare disease population, speed up manufacturing planning, and make trial design changes (Chukwurah et al., 2024). Digital infrastructure is also an advantage of Agile governance. Analytics dashboards can enable executives to track critical developmental metrics such as enrollment rates, safety indicators, manufacturing preparedness, and so on without having to wait until periodic reports are generated. Early warning mechanisms detect risks before they can be developed into crises (Liang & He, 2023). Notably, agility is not informality. The compliance with the regulations is unnegotiable. Rather, agile governance streamlines the processes to be in line with the sense of urgency of patient need and remain document-integrity and risk-assessment disciplined. The balance especially is essential in breakthrough therapies of rare or life-threatening conditions (Naeem et al., 2026). The cohesive system which is a combination of workforce strategy, ecosystem (Noor et al., 2026). The decisive role in maintaining this integration is played by leadership. The executives should be capable of presenting a clear strategic story of how the workforce development is tied to the enterprise outcomes. Rewards given by performance metrics should focus on teamwork, quality custodianship and innovation instead of isolated performance. Integration can also be reinforced through talent mobility programs that involve rotating employees between functions to enhance the cross-disciplinary empathy and literacy (Kharl, 2026). In addition, integration increases resilience. Unregulated environments change. Disruptions are experienced in supply chains. Scientific paradigms shift. Companies that have integrated structures are more adaptable since information is shared and communication channels are well established. Fragmented systems, in their turn, do not react in a unified manner when stressed (Ivanov & Dolgui, 2021). Workforce and strategy integration changes culture in the long term. Employees do not see themselves as a lone professional but rather as part of a common cause. The number of decision cycles reduces since there will be trust and transparency as opposed to bureaucracy. Quality is ingrained as opposed to inspected. Governance becomes flexive and not inhibitive .

Pharmaceutical business is based on the high level of attention, significant investments and a great level of social responsibility. These demands cannot be met by process improvement that is incremental. It needs structural integration- of people, processes and purpose. Silos are broken down, ecosystem models adopted, Quality by Design entrenched in organisational DNA, agile governance frameworks put into place, to produce a single system which can operate inside the complexity with both discipline and speed. Within that type of environment, workforce strategy does not operate as a support mechanism but as the key driver of sustainable innovation. Agile models also delegate decision authority, most of the time, to empowered cross-functional teams, not centralized committees. Well defined accountability matrices make sure that speed does not affect compliance. Documentation norms continue to be sound, only now the time frames of document reviews are developed in parallel instead of sequential appraisals.

CONCLUSION

To sum it up, this chapter has examined the main concepts, major arguments, and supporting facts, that form the general discussion on the topic. It has looked at the chief themes following a systematic methodology, not only emphasized on the theoretical basis, but the practical implications as well. The chapter has shown the interconnection between these elements and their significance in a wider perspective through the analysis and reflection. Examining the main ideas and weighing various opinions, the discussion has provided the significance of critical thinking and making informed judgments. The illustrations and descriptions that have been used all over the chapter have contributed to the explanation of complicated issues as well as the depiction of how the theory can be put into practical use. This strengthens the applicability of the topic outside of the academia. Finally, the chapter contributes to the necessity of further investigation and a better understanding. Although it provides the clear insights and significant conclusions, it also leaves the door to further research and discussion. The concepts stated here become a starting point of the further step of learning because they make readers think, doubt, and develop what they have learned.

REFERENCES

Aðalsteinsdóttir, G. H. (2024). *Project Portfolio Management in Icelandic Organizations: A New Dynamic Perspective for Businesses*

Abraham, J. (2023). *Science, politics and the pharmaceutical industry: Controversy and bias in drug regulation*. Routledge.

Alešnik, P., Vrečko, I., & Palčič, I. (2025). From Zero to One: A new perspective on the fuzzy front end of innovation and the Stage-Gate® model. *Advances in Production Engineering & Management, 20*(1), 131–149. DOI: 10.14743/apem2025.1.532

Altman, E. J., Kiron, D., Schwartz, J., & Jones, R. (2023). *Workforce ecosystems: Reaching strategic goals with people, partners, and technologies*. MIT Press. DOI: 10.7551/mitpress/14690.001.0001

Badreldin, H. A., & Almosnid, N. (2025). From Silos to Synergy: Multidisciplinary Teams and Artificial Intelligence at the Helm of Research, Development, and Innovation. *The SCAPE Journal for Multidisciplinary Research, 1*(1), 7–13. DOI: 10.4103/SJMR.SJMR_7_25

Barrett, J. S. (2022). CompoundProgressionand Go/NoGo Criteria. *Fundamentals of Drug Development*, 231.

Bates, I., Patel, D., Chan, A. H. Y., Rutter, V., Bader, L., Meilianti, S., & Udoh, A. (2023). A comparative analysis of pharmaceutical workforce development needs across the commonwealth. *Research in Social & Administrative Pharmacy, 19*(1), 167–179. DOI: 10.1016/j.sapharm.2022.07.010 PMID: 36031527

Burns, L., Le Roux, N., Kalesnik-Orszulak, R., Christian, J., Hukkelhoven, M., Rockhold, F., & O'Donnell, J. (2022). Real-world evidence for regulatory decision-making: Guidance from around the world. *Clinical Therapeutics, 44*(3), 420–437. DOI: 10.1016/j.clinthera.2022.01.012 PMID: 35181179

Calado, C. R. (2024). Bridging the gap between target-based and phenotypic-based drug discovery. *Expert Opinion on Drug Discovery, 19*(7), 789–798. DOI: 10.1080/17460441.2024.2355330 PMID: 38747562

Cantu, N. (2025). Vicente Academic Medical Center Case Study: Highlighting Healthcare Leadership's Role in Risk Management and Governance Training to Strengthen Oversight and Strategic Decision-Making. *SCIENTIA MORALITAS-International Journal of Multidisciplinary Research, 10*(2), 324–341.

Chukwurah, N., Ige, A. B., Idemudia, C., & Eyieyien, O. G. (2024). Integrating agile methodologies into data governance: Achieving flexibility and control simultaneously. *Open Access Research Journal of Multidisciplinary Studies, 8*(01), 045-056.

Coates, J. M., Santhanalakshmi, K., Dinesh, N., Gandhimathi, S., Chandel, P. S., & Selvakumar, P. (2025). Assessment and evaluation in transnational staff development. In *Training and development in transnational higher education* (pp. 387–406). IGI Global Scientific Publishing. DOI: 10.4018/979-8-3373-1897-4.ch019

Cox, L. A.Jr. (2023). What is an exposure-response curve? *Global Epidemiology, 6*, 100114. DOI: 10.1016/j.gloepi.2023.100114 PMID: 37637716

Deng, C. (2025). Research on the Synergistic Development Path of Technological Innovation and Management in Manufacturing Enterprises within the Perspective of New-Quality Productive Forces. *Academic Journal of Business & Management, 7*(9), 1–7.

Deshmukh, A. D. (2024). Redefining Innovation for Pharmaceutical Regulation. *BUL Rev., 104*, 577.

Deshmukh, P., & Paliwal, S. (2024). Pharmacy education 2.0 with special reference to digital India. *Multidisciplinary Reviews, 7*(4), 2024065–2024065. DOI: 10.31893/multirev.2024065

Enriquez, J., & Goldberg, R. A. (2000). Transforming life, transforming business: The life-science revolution. *Harvard Business Review, 78*(2), 96–96.

Everts, M., & Drew, M. (2024). Successfully navigating the valley of death: The importance of accelerators to support academic drug discovery and development. *Expert Opinion on Drug Discovery, 19*(2), 253–258. DOI: 10.1080/17460441.2023.2284824 PMID: 37968916

Farley, M. S., & Rouse, W. B. (2000). Technology challenges & opportunities in the biotechnology, pharmaceutical & medical device industries. *Information, Knowledge, Systems Management, 2*(2), 133–141. DOI: 10.3233/IKS-2000-00033

Forscher, P. S., Wagenmakers, E.-J., Coles, N. A., Silan, M. A., Dutra, N., Basnight-Brown, D., & IJzerman, H. (2023). The benefits, barriers, and risks of big-team science. *Perspectives on Psychological Science : A Journal of the Association for Psychological Science, 18*(3), 607–623. DOI: 10.1177/17456916221082970 PMID: 36190899

Frize, M. (2022). *Health Care Engineering Part I: Clinical Engineering and Technology Management*. Springer Nature.

Fukami, T. (2024). Enhancing healthcare accountability for administrators: Fostering transparency for patient safety and quality enhancement. *Cureus, 16*(8). Advance online publication. DOI: 10.7759/cureus.66007 PMID: 39221336

Gao, C., & McDonald, R. (2022). Shaping nascent industries: Innovation strategy and regulatory uncertainty in personal genomics. *Administrative Science Quarterly, 67*(4), 915–967. DOI: 10.1177/00018392221112641

Gavrilenko, V., & Shenshin, V. (2023). Control and supervisory activities as an institute of administrative law. *BRICS Law Journal, 10*(2), 156–183. DOI: 10.21684/2412-2343-2023-10-2-156-183

Hanenkratt, A. C. (2024). *Project management for research and development.* Massachusetts Institute of Technology.

HO. B. K. (2023). Future Workforce Planning-Building a Future-Ready Organization Using a Prospective Study Approach. Abu Dhabi International Petroleum Exhibition and Conference, Hong, A. (2024). *A Methodology for R&D Portfolio Management Decision Making Under Uncertainty–Applied Towards Timely Reallocation of Investments with Stalling Projects* Georgia Institute of Technology].

Hussian, T., Tripathy, S., & Dureja, H. (2025). Navigating the regulatory maze: a comparative analysis of digital therapeutics (DTx) regulations. *Journal of Science and Technology Policy Management.*

Ivanov, D., & Dolgui, A. (2021). A digital supply chain twin for managing the disruption risks and resilience in the era of Industry 4.0. *Production Planning and Control, 32*(9), 775–788. DOI: 10.1080/09537287.2020.1768450

Jeleel-Ojuade, A. (2024). The Role of Information Silos: An analysis of how the categorization of information creates silos within financial institutions, hindering effective communication and collaboration. *Available at SSRN* 4881342. DOI: 10.2139/ssrn.4881342

Kabir, M., Rana, M. R. H., & Debnath, A. (2024). The role of quality assurance in accelerating pharmaceutical research and development: Strategies for ensuring regulatory compliance and product integrity. *Journal of Angiotherapy, 8*(12), 1–11.

Kaufman, S. J. (2025). The MAD Heuristic and the Nuclear Revolution. *Journal of Global Security Studies, 10*(2), ogae048. DOI: 10.1093/jogss/ogae048

Kharl, H. A. A. (2026). *PharmA AI: Revolutionizing Drug Discovery and Healthcare with Artificial Intelligence*. IBH Publisher.

Kieffer, M. E. (2024). Why Oncology Global Safety Teams Should Develop the Safety Section of the Study's Target Product Profile (TPP). *Pharmaceutical Medicine, 38*(2), 97–108. DOI: 10.1007/s40290-024-00516-z PMID: 38411854

Kirtley, J., & O'Mahony, S. (2023). What is a pivot? Explaining when and how entrepreneurial firms decide to make strategic change and pivot. *Strategic Management Journal, 44*(1), 197–230. DOI: 10.1002/smj.3131

Korjian, S., Daaboul, Y., & Gibson, C. M. (2023). Drug development, clinical trials, and regulatory requirements. *The ESC Textbook of Thrombosis*, 367.

Kühnen, S. (2025). Third-party service or shared success: unraveling the phenomenon of CMOs in the pharmaceutical industry.

Lalhunthara, P. B., & Singh, D. (2025). QUANTITATIVE MODELING OF INVESTMENT DECISION-MAKING PROCESSES IN MANAGEMENT ACCOUNTING: A STUDY OF OPTIMIZATION TECHNIQUES AND RISK MANAGEMENT TOOLS. *International Journal of Applied Mathematics, 38*(8s).

Liang, S., & He, Y. (2023). Real-Time Operational Dashboards for Executive Leadership to Drive Agile Decision-Making in Multisite Health Systems. *International Journal of Advanced Computational Methodologies and Emerging Technologies, 13*(11), 1–11.

LoCastro, M., & Wasserstein, A. (2025). Exploring Employee Terminations in Search Fund–Acquired Companies and Small Businesses. Yale Case.

Lutfor, M., Al, M., Nadarkhani, F., & Nezab, M. (2025). Advanced Dissolution Testing for Novel Drug Formulations: Challenges, Emerging Methods, and Regulatory Perspectives. *Journal of Angiotherapy, 9*(1), 1–16.

Maclean, N., Abrahmsén-Alami, S., Clark, C., Dörr, F., Florence, A., Ketolainen, J., Lindow, M., Mantanus, J., Rantanen, J., Reynolds, G., Robertson, A., & Markl, D. (2026). Empowering the pharmaceutical workforce for the digital future. *European Journal of Pharmaceutical Sciences : Official Journal of the European Federation for Pharmaceutical Sciences, 220*, 107449. DOI: 10.1016/j.ejps.2026.107449 PMID: 41577303

Madabushi, R., Seo, P., Zhao, L., Tegenge, M., & Zhu, H. (2022). Review: Role of Model-Informed Drug Development Approaches in the Lifecycle of Drug Development and Regulatory Decision-Making. *Pharmaceutical Research, 39*(8), 1669–1680. DOI: 10.1007/s11095-022-03288-w PMID: 35552984

Mann, S., & Mann, S. (2025). Human resource development in the digital era: Talent management and skill enhancement. In *Immersive Technology for the Gig Economy: Transformative Business Practices* (pp. 381-408). IGI Global Scientific Publishing.

Mascarenhas, C., Galvão, A. R., Mendes, T., Marques, C., & Ferreira, J. J. (2025). How do smart specialization strategies influence university-industry collaboration in cross-border regions? *Review of Managerial Science*, •••, 1–37. DOI: 10.1007/s11846-025-00933-7

McNair, D., Lumpkin, M., Kern, S., & Hartman, D. (2022). Use of RWE to inform regulatory, public health policy, and intervention priorities for the developing world. *Clinical Pharmacology and Therapeutics*, *111*(1), 44–51. DOI: 10.1002/cpt.2449 PMID: 34655224

Michaeli, D. T., Michaeli, T., Albers, S., Boch, T., & Michaeli, J. C. (2024). Special FDA designations for drug development: orphan, fast track, accelerated approval, priority review, and breakthrough therapy: Special FDA designations for drug development. *The European Journal of Health Economics : HEPAC : Health Economics in Prevention and Care*, *25*(6), 979–997. DOI: 10.1007/s10198-023-01639-x PMID: 37962724

Moparthi, R. (2024). CMC and Regulatory Affairs Professional: Ensuring Effective Compliance Strategies. *J. Electrical Systems*, *20*(8s), 567–574.

Mozaffari, F., Rahimi, M., Yazdani, H., & Sohrabi, B. (2023). Employee attrition prediction in a pharmaceutical company using both machine learning approach and qualitative data. *Benchmarking*, *30*(10), 4140–4173. DOI: 10.1108/BIJ-11-2021-0664

Naeem, M. S., Naeem, M., Mehmood, M., Sulman, A. A., & Kharl, H. A. A. (2026). MACHINE LEARNING IN FORMULATION OPTIMIZATION AND PROCESS CONTROL. *PharmA AI: Revolutionizing Drug Discovery and Healthcare with Artificial Intelligence*.

Nair, S. (2025). Explainable AI in GXP validation: Balancing automation, traceability, and regulatory trust in the pharmaceutical industry. *Clinical Medicine and Health Research Journal*, *5*(05), 1430–1442. DOI: 10.18535/cmhrj.v5i05.509

Ndioumabia, O. (2022). Unveiling the power of pharmaceutical sciences from molecules to medicines. *Journal Wetenskap Health*, *3*(2), 11–20.

Noor, I., Mahmood, S., Aslam, M., Iqbal, S., Naeem, M. S., Shafaqat, M., Sulman, A., Awan, A., Aamir, H., & Kharl, A. (2026). AI ALGORITHMS AND TOOLS FOR PHARMACEUTICAL APPLICATIONS. *PharmA AI: Revolutionizing Drug Discovery and Healthcare with Artificial Intelligence*.

Odunaike, A. (2025). Integrating real-time financial data streams to enhance dynamic risk modeling and portfolio decision accuracy. *Int J Comput Appl Technol Res*, *14*(08), 1–16.

Ogbuagu, O. O., Mbata, A. O., Balogun, O. D., Oladapo, O., Ojo, O. O., & Muonde, M. (2023). Quality assurance in pharmaceutical manufacturing: Bridging the gap between regulations, supply chain, and innovations. *International Journal of Multidisciplinary Research and Growth Evaluation*, *4*(1), 823–831. DOI: 10.54660/.IJMRGE.2023.4.1-823-831

Okosieme, O. O., Okosieme, O., Amewonor-Etsey, W. K., Oyeyemi, D. O., & Biriku, K. (2025). The Role of Strategic Communication in Translating Labor Market Analytics into Workforce Policy. *International Journal of Scientific and Management Research*, *8*(11), 39–56. DOI: 10.37502/IJSMR.2025.81104

Parween, S. (2024). The significance of employee training and development on enhancing workforce efficiency.

Peng, F., Zeng, X., & Li, Y. (2024). Female stereotype and occupational stigma. *Annals of Tourism Research*, *109*, 103837. DOI: 10.1016/j.annals.2024.103837

Pesqueira, A., & Almeida, D. (2026). Breaking Barriers: Redefining Legal and Regulatory Boundaries for a Sustainable Financial Future in Pharmaceuticals and. In *Legal and Regulatory Considerations of Leveraging Sustainable Finance* (pp. 83-110). IGI Global Scientific Publishing.

Pfatteicher, S. K. (2025). *Collaborative Thinking: How to Build and Sustain College Consortia*. JHU Press. DOI: 10.56021/9781421453323

Phares, S., Trusheim, M., Emond, S. K., & Pearson, S. D. (2024). Managing the challenges of paying for gene therapy: Strategies for market action and policy reform in the United States. *Journal of Comparative Effectiveness Research*, *13*(12), e240118. DOI: 10.57264/cer-2024-0118 PMID: 39540549

Ragsdale, J.Jr. (2024). *Effective Business Strategies to Mitigate Outsourcing Failures*. Walden University.

Rai, B., Srivastava, J., & Saxena, P. (2025). Challenges in translating laboratory findings to drug development. In *Protein Misfolding in Neurodegenerative Diseases* (pp. 319–354). Elsevier. DOI: 10.1016/B978-0-443-18716-2.00009-0

Ramakrishnan, M. (2025). *From Finance Experts to Strategic Partners: Addressing Cross-Functional Preparedness in Higher Education*

Ranbhor, R., & Kulkarni, P. (2025). Evaluating Biosimilar Development Projects: An Analytical Framework Utilizing Net Present Value. *Biologics*, •••, 125–135. PMID: 40165807

Rasmussen, N. (2014). *Gene jockeys: Life science and the rise of biotech enterprise*. JHU Press. DOI: 10.1353/book.29448

Ravinetto, R., Henriquez, R., Srinivas, P. N., Bradley, H., Coetzee, R., Ochoa, T. J., Ngabonziza, J. C. S., Mazarati, J.-B., Van Damme, W., & van de Pas, R. (2024). Shaping the future of global access to safe, effective, appropriate and quality health products. *BMJ Global Health*, *9*(1), e014425. DOI: 10.1136/bmjgh-2023-014425 PMID: 38195155

Ridwan, S., Syah, T. Y. R., Kustiawan, U., & Nofierni, N. (2025). Financial planning and investment feasibility analysis based on five-year projections using ROI, NPV, IRR, and financial ratios. *Journal La Bisecoman*, *6*(2), 489–506. DOI: 10.37899/journallabisecoman.v6i2.1970

Roberts, P., & Hamilton Edwards, L. (2023). Portfolio management: A new direction in public sector strategic management research and practice. *Public Administration Review*, *83*(4), 947–959. DOI: 10.1111/puar.13633

Samuel, K. Big Data in Regulatory Compliance: Enhancing Reporting Accuracy and Timeliness for Medical Devices.

Shahzad, M. U. (2024). Core competencies for digital leadership development: A perspective from the lens of paradox theory. *The Bottom Line (New York, N.Y.)*, *37*(4), 454–472. DOI: 10.1108/BL-10-2023-0278

Simon, F. M. (2024). Artificial intelligence in the news: How AI retools, rationalizes, and reshapes journalism and the public arena.

Soltanzadeh, A., Zarei, E., Mahdinia, M., & Sadeghi-Yarandi, M. (2024). An integrated approach to assess safety and security risks in chemical process industries. *Journal of Loss Prevention in the Process Industries*, *90*, 105344. DOI: 10.1016/j.jlp.2024.105344

Sundaram, S. (2025). Innovating for the Future: Sustainable Corporate Strategies for Workforce Upskilling and Reskilling. *International Journal of Research in Entrepreneurship & Business Studies*, *6*(3), 33–46. DOI: 10.47259/ijrebs.2025.633

Tummuri, S. S. R. (2025). *Enterprise Integration: Strategies, Technologies And Future Trends*. Academic Guru Publishing House.

Valdez, J. W., Sharma, S., & Gould, J. (2025). Systemic territoriality in academia: The Gollum effect's impact on scientific research and careers. *One Earth*, *8*(6), 101314. DOI: 10.1016/j.oneear.2025.101314

Van Der Zalm, A. J., Barroso, J., Browne, P., Casey, W., Gordon, J., Henry, T. R., Kleinstreuer, N. C., Lowit, A. B., Perron, M., & Clippinger, A. J. (2022). A framework for establishing scientific confidence in new approach methodologies. *Archives of Toxicology*, *96*(11), 2865–2879. DOI: 10.1007/s00204-022-03365-4 PMID: 35987941

Young-Babb, T., Hall, L. F., Kuhn, A., & Pryor, C. (2025). Professional Development: Enhancing Adaptability for a Future-Ready Workforce. *International Journal of Advanced Corporate Learning*, *18*(3), 89–102. DOI: 10.3991/ijac.v18i3.52541

Zaiter, F., & Azouz, M. (2025). Digital Companies: Smart Decision-Making and Knowledge Management for Adapting to Rapid Changes. *Accounting & Finance/ Oblìk ì Fìnansi, 107*(1).

Zhao, Y., Qu, Y., Xiang, Y., Uddin, M. P., Peng, D., & Gao, L. (2024). A comprehensive survey on edge data integrity verification: Fundamentals and future trends. *ACM Computing Surveys*, *57*(1), 1–34. DOI: 10.1145/3680277

Zhou, J., & Duan, Y. (2026). Blockchain-enabled product life cycle assessment information management system. *Ain Shams Engineering Journal*, *17*(2), 103993. DOI: 10.1016/j.asej.2026.103993

Chapter 13
Strategic Human Capital and Executive Decision-Making in Regulated Pharma and MedTech Innovation

Muhammad Saad Naeem
University of Agriculture, Faisalabad, Pakistan

Adnan Afzal
http://orcid.org/0009-0001-4359-5695
Government College University, Faisalabad, Pakistan

Shumaila Qurban
Riphah International University, Islamabad, Pakistan

Abu Sulman
http://orcid.org/0009-0008-7194-5219
University of Agriculture, Faisalabad, Pakistan

Adeeba Riaz
http://orcid.org/0009-0009-6093-9777
Department of Biotechnology, University of Okara, Pakistan

Humaira Bibi
Faculty of Rehabilitation and Allied Health Sciences, Riphah International University, Pakistan

Hina Nawab
http://orcid.org/0009-0002-8250-5856
Institute of Physiology and Pharmacology, University of Agriculture, Faisalabad, Pakistan

Hira Waheed
http://orcid.org/0009-0000-2836-2335
Department of Pharmaceutical Chemistry, Government College University, Faisalabad, Pakistan

Maria Shafaqat
http://orcid.org/0009-0008-7399-2529
School of Natural Sciences, University of Kent, UK

DOI: 10.4018/979-8-3373-9410-7.ch013

Maham Shehzadi
Cholistan University of Veterinary and Animal Sciences, Bahawalpur, Pakistan

ABSTRACT

This chapter explores the strategic importance of human capital and executive decision-making in regulated pharmaceutical and MedTech innovation. It examines how specialized talent, leadership capability, and knowledge management systems drive sustainable competitive advantage in highly regulated healthcare environments. The discussion highlights the role of executive leadership in portfolio strategy, risk governance, compliance integration, and cross-functional coordination. Emphasis is placed on managing uncertainty arising from regulatory shifts, clinical trial unpredictability, and market volatility. By aligning workforce development, ethical standards, and structured decision frameworks, organizations can enhance innovation effectiveness while safeguarding patient safety and regulatory trust.

INTRODUCTION TO STRATEGIC HUMAN CAPITAL IN REGULATED HEALTHCARE INDUSTRIES

Strategic human capital has emerged as a critical determinant of competitive advantage in regulated healthcare industries, particularly within pharmaceutical and medical technology (MedTech) organizations (Kulkov, 2021). Unlike traditional sectors where capital assets and market positioning dominate strategic planning, healthcare innovation depends fundamentally on specialized knowledge, scientific expertise, regulatory insight, and cross-functional coordination. In highly regulated environments, the value of human capital extends beyond productivity; it encompasses compliance competence, ethical judgment, adaptive learning, and long-term innovation capability. Therefore, understanding strategic human capital in regulated healthcare industries requires examining how talent, expertise, and leadership collectively drive sustainable innovation. Human capital in pharmaceutical and MedTech firms includes scientists, clinicians, regulatory specialists, engineers, quality assurance professionals, data analysts, and executive leaders (Smith, 2019). These professionals contribute to complex processes such as drug discovery, device design, clinical validation, regulatory submissions, and post-market surveillance. The innovation lifecycle in healthcare is lengthy and resource-intensive, often spanning a decade or more. Throughout this process, highly skilled personnel make critical decisions that affect patient safety, product efficacy, and organizational reputation. Consequently, human capital is not merely an operational resource but a strategic asset central to organizational survival and growth. Regulatory intensity significantly differentiates healthcare industries from other innovation-driven sectors. Firms must comply with stringent standards governing clinical trials, manufacturing practices, product approvals, and post-market monitoring. This regulatory environment increases the strategic importance of employees who possess specialized compliance knowledge. Regulatory affairs professionals, quality managers, and clinical research coordinators play pivotal roles in ensuring adherence to evolving guidelines (Kabir et al., 2024). Without adequate human capital in these domains, even scientifically promising innovations may fail to reach the market. Thus, strategic human capital management involves aligning talent development with regulatory complexity. Knowledge management represents another crucial dimension of strategic human capital in regulated industries. Pharmaceutical and MedTech organizations generate vast amounts of scientific data, clinical evidence, and regulatory documentation. Capturing, storing, and disseminating this knowledge effectively enhances innovation efficiency and reduces duplication of efforts. Strategic human capital systems emphasize continuous learning, documentation accuracy, and collaborative information sharing (Wujarso & Dameria, 2023). By institutionalizing knowledge transfer mechanisms—such as cross-functional workshops, digital knowledge platforms, and mentorship programs—firms strengthen their capacity to innovate consistently despite personnel turnover or project setbacks.

Figure 1. Strategic Human Capital in Regulated Healthcare Industries

Executive leadership plays an essential role in integrating human capital strategy with organizational objectives. Strategic human capital planning requires forecasting future skill requirements based on technological trends, therapeutic priorities, and regulatory developments (Afriyie, 2019). For instance, the rise of digital health technologies and artificial intelligence in medical diagnostics necessitates recruiting data scientists and cybersecurity experts. Similarly, the expansion of biologics and personalized medicine increases demand for specialized clinical researchers and bioinformatics professionals. Executives must anticipate these shifts and invest proactively in workforce development to maintain competitive positioning. Talent acquisition and retention present additional challenges in regulated healthcare industries. Competition for highly qualified scientists, engineers, and regulatory experts is intense, particularly in global markets. Organizations must design attractive value propositions that include career development opportunities, research autonomy, and supportive organizational cultures. Retention strategies often emphasize professional growth, interdisciplinary collaboration, and recognition of innovation achievements (Babatope, 2025). By cultivating an environment that values expertise and ethical responsibility, firms enhance employee commitment and reduce turnover risk. Strategic human capital also intersects with organizational culture. In regulated environments, employees must balance creativity with compliance discipline. A culture that encourages innovation while reinforcing quality standards ensures that scientific exploration remains aligned with regulatory expectations (Joshua, 2025). Leaders must communicate clearly that adherence to protocols is not a constraint but a foundation for responsible innovation. When employees internalize this perspective, compliance becomes integrated into daily practice rather than treated as an external obligation. Globalization further amplifies the strategic importance of human capital. Pharmaceutical and MedTech firms operate across diverse regulatory jurisdictions, healthcare systems, and cultural contexts. Managing multinational teams requires cultural intelligence, communication competence, and harmonized training standards (Presbitero & Toledano, 2018). Strategic human capital frameworks must therefore incorporate global mobility programs, cross-cultural training, and standardized compliance education to ensure consistent operational quality worldwide. Moreover, resilience and adaptability have become defining attributes of effective human capital in healthcare innovation. External disruptions—such as supply chain interruptions, regulatory reforms, or global health crises—demand agile responses. Organizations that invest in employee adaptability, continuous upskilling, and leadership development are better equipped to navigate uncertainty (Young-Babb et al., 2025). Strategic workforce planning thus extends beyond technical competence to include soft skills such as collaboration, ethical reasoning, and crisis management.

THE ROLE OF EXECUTIVE LEADERSHIP IN PHARMA AND MEDTECH INNOVATION STRATEGY

Executive leadership plays a decisive role in shaping innovation strategy within pharmaceutical and MedTech organizations. In highly regulated and science-driven industries, strategic direction cannot be delegated solely to operational managers or R&D departments (Zhou & Coplin, 2022). Senior executives are responsible for defining long-term innovation priorities, allocating capital across competing projects, managing regulatory exposure, and ensuring that innovation aligns with both market demand and patient needs. Their decisions influence not only financial performance but also public health outcomes and corporate reputation. One of the primary responsibilities of executive leadership is setting a clear innovation vision. In pharmaceutical and MedTech firms, innovation pipelines often span multiple therapeutic areas, device platforms, or digital health technologies (Kasoju et al., 2023). Without strong executive direction, portfolios may become fragmented or misaligned with corporate objectives. Executives must assess global disease trends, unmet clinical needs, demographic changes, and technological advancements to determine strategic focus areas. For example, prioritizing oncology research, biologics development, minimally invasive surgical devices, or AI-driven diagnostics requires deliberate executive commitment. A well-articulated innovation vision provides clarity for R&D teams and investors alike. Capital allocation is another critical executive function in innovation strategy (Parker, 2024). Healthcare innovation involves substantial financial investment with long payback periods and high uncertainty. Executives must evaluate the risk-return profiles of various projects, balancing high-risk breakthrough initiatives with incremental product improvements. Portfolio diversification strategies help mitigate risk while maintaining growth potential. Decisions to acquire biotechnology startups, license external technologies, or form strategic partnerships are typically driven at the executive level. These choices determine the organization's competitive positioning and future growth trajectory. Executive leadership also plays a central role in navigating regulatory complexity. Pharma and MedTech firms operate under strict compliance frameworks governing clinical trials, manufacturing standards, marketing claims, and post-market surveillance (Badnjević et al., 2022). Senior executives must ensure that regulatory strategy is integrated into innovation planning from the earliest stages. Failure to align R&D with regulatory requirements can lead to costly delays, product recalls, or reputational damage. By embedding regulatory expertise into strategic discussions, executives enhance the likelihood of successful product approvals and market entry. Risk governance is closely tied to executive decision-making. Innovation inherently involves uncertainty, particularly in clinical development where trial outcomes may be unpredictable. Executives must establish risk tolerance thresholds and implement oversight mechanisms to monitor project performance (Mandel & Parija, 2024). Structured review committees, milestone-based evaluations, and independent audit systems support disciplined decision-making. When projects underperform or face safety concerns, executives must make difficult decisions regarding continuation, modification, or termination. Such decisions require balancing scientific optimism with financial prudence and ethical responsibility.

Table 1. Executive Leadership Roles in Pharma and MedTech Innovation Strategy

Strategic Dimension	Core Executive Responsibility	Key Actions	Organizational Impact	Strategic Outcome
Innovation Vision & Direction	Define long-term innovation priorities	Identify therapeutic focus areas, evaluate emerging technologies, align pipeline with disease trends	Provides clarity to R&D teams and investors	Coherent and competitive innovation portfolio
Capital Allocation & Investment Strategy	Allocate financial resources across projects	Assess risk–return profiles, diversify portfolio, approve acquisitions and partnerships	Ensures balanced funding between breakthrough and incremental innovation	Sustainable growth and financial resilience
Regulatory Integration	Align innovation with regulatory frameworks	Embed regulatory expertise early, anticipate compliance requirements, oversee approval pathways	Reduces delays, recalls, and compliance risks	Accelerated market entry and enhanced credibility
Risk Governance & Oversight	Establish risk tolerance and monitoring systems	Implement milestone reviews, audit mechanisms, and project evaluation committees	Promotes disciplined decision-making	Optimized resource utilization and minimized strategic failure
Organizational Alignment	Foster cross-functional collaboration	Break down silos, integrate R&D with manufacturing and marketing, promote shared metrics	Enhances operational efficiency	Seamless innovation execution
Digital Transformation Leadership	Guide digital integration strategy	Invest in AI, big data, cybersecurity, and digital infrastructure	Modernizes innovation processes	Enhanced competitiveness in digital healthcare markets
Stakeholder & Global Strategy Management	Manage external relationships and global expansion	Engage regulators, investors, and partners; adapt to regional markets; diversify supply chains	Strengthens trust and global presence	Long-term market sustainability and reputational strength

Organizational alignment is another area where executive leadership exerts influence. Innovation strategy depends on coordinated efforts across R&D, regulatory affairs, manufacturing, marketing, and supply chain functions (Kumar et al., 2020). Executives must break down departmental silos and foster cross-functional collaboration. By promoting shared performance metrics and integrated communication channels, leadership ensures that innovation processes remain coherent and efficient. Strategic alignment also extends to corporate culture, where executives reinforce values such as integrity, patient-centricity, and accountability. In the context of digital transformation, executive leadership becomes even more critical. The integration of artificial intelligence, big data analytics, connected devices, and telemedicine platforms is reshaping healthcare innovation (Suleiman & Adinoyi, 2023). Executives must determine how digital technologies complement traditional product development models. Strategic investments in digital infrastructure, cybersecurity, and data governance require executive-level oversight. Without clear leadership direction, digital initiatives may remain fragmented or underutilized. Stakeholder management further highlights the importance of executive leadership. Pharma and MedTech firms interact with regulators, healthcare providers, patients, investors, insurers, and advocacy groups (Karas et al., 2019). Executives represent the organization in high-level negotiations and public engagements. Their communication style and ethical stance significantly influence stakeholder trust. Transparent leadership enhances credibility, particularly in sensitive areas such as drug pricing, clinical trial transparency, and patient data protection. Global expansion strategies also fall under executive purview. Entering new geographic markets involves regulatory adaptation, pricing strategy adjustments, and local partnership development. Executives must balance global standardization with regional responsiveness. Strategic decisions regarding manufacturing sites, supply chain diversification, and local talent acquisition require high-level coordination and risk assessment (Birou & Hoek, 2022). Ultimately, executive leadership serves as the strategic compass guiding innovation in regulated healthcare industries. By articulating vision, allocating resources wisely, integrating regulatory considerations, and fostering organizational alignment, executives shape the trajectory of innovation success. Their decisions carry significant economic, ethical, and societal implications. In environments where innovation outcomes directly affect patient health and safety, strong and responsible executive leadership is indispensable for achieving sustainable growth and long-term impact (Hussain et al., 2024).

TALENT ACQUISITION AND RETENTION IN HIGH-REGULATION ENVIRONMENTS

Talent acquisition and retention are strategic imperatives in pharmaceutical and MedTech organizations operating within highly regulated environments. Innovation in these industries depends heavily on specialized expertise in areas such as molecular biology, biomedical engineering, clinical research, regulatory affairs, quality assurance, data analytics, and manufacturing science. Unlike many other sectors, healthcare innovation requires not only technical proficiency but also deep understanding of regulatory standards, ethical frameworks, and patient safety protocols

(Pham, 2025). Consequently, attracting and retaining high-caliber professionals becomes a cornerstone of sustainable competitive advantage. The complexity of healthcare regulation significantly influences recruitment strategies. Firms must identify candidates who possess both advanced scientific knowledge and familiarity with compliance requirements such as clinical trial governance, documentation standards, and quality management systems. Regulatory expertise is particularly valuable because non-compliance can result in severe financial penalties, product delays, or reputational damage. Therefore, recruitment processes often prioritize candidates with multidisciplinary capabilities individuals who can bridge scientific innovation with regulatory awareness. Strategic workforce planning ensures that talent acquisition aligns with anticipated technological and regulatory shifts (Philip et al., 2024).

Figure 2. Talent Acquisition and Retention in High-Regulation Environments

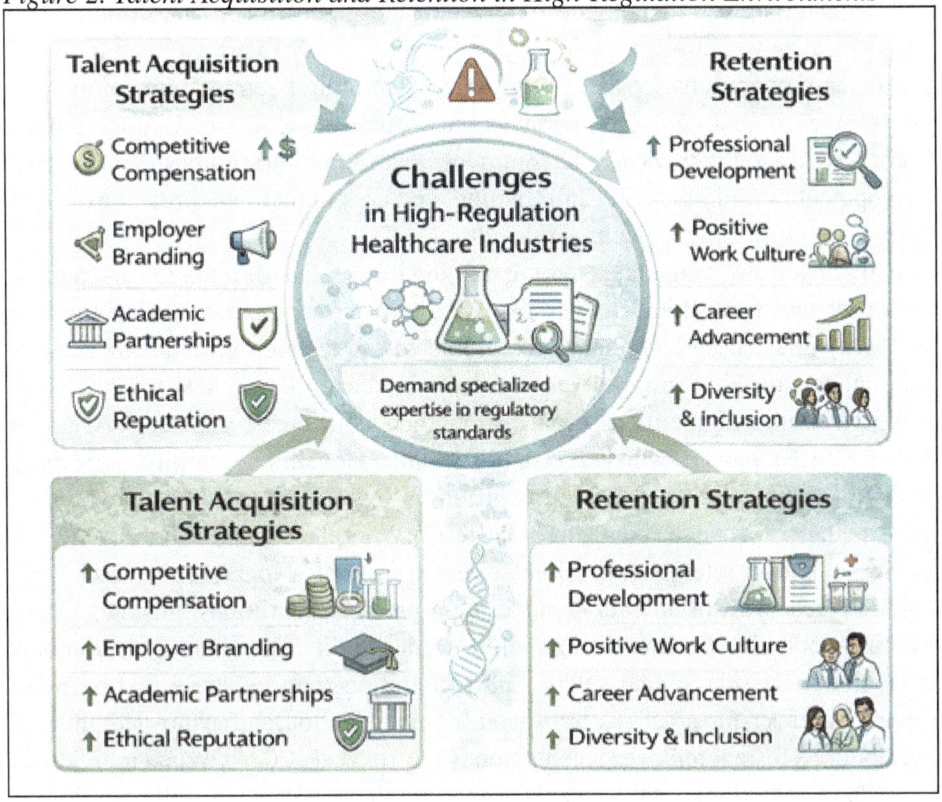

Competition for skilled professionals in pharmaceutical and MedTech industries is intense and global. Biotechnology startups, multinational corporations, research institutions, and digital health firms compete for a limited pool of highly trained scientists and engineers. Organizations must therefore differentiate themselves through compelling employer value propositions (Veldsman & van der Merwe, 2022). Competitive compensation, research funding support, professional autonomy, and opportunities to contribute to life-saving innovations are critical incentives. Additionally, a strong reputation for ethical conduct and regulatory excellence enhances organizational attractiveness among prospective employees. Employer branding plays a significant role in talent acquisition. Companies known for scientific breakthroughs, patient-centric missions, and robust compliance cultures are more likely to attract top-tier talent. Public recognition, publication opportunities, conference participation, and collaborative research initiatives enhance organizational prestige. Partnerships with universities and research institutions also create pipelines for emerging talent (Ollif & Patel, 2025). Internship programs, doctoral sponsorships, and early-career mentorship initiatives enable firms to cultivate skilled professionals aligned with corporate values and innovation objectives. Retention strategies are equally important, particularly given the long development cycles in healthcare innovation. High employee turnover can disrupt research continuity, delay regulatory submissions, and increase operational costs (Tham, 2023). Retaining talent requires more than competitive compensation; it demands supportive organizational culture, clear career progression pathways, and continuous learning opportunities. Professional development programs, leadership training, and cross-functional project exposure enhance employee engagement and loyalty.

In regulated environments, ongoing training is essential for retention and performance enhancement. Regulatory frameworks evolve frequently, requiring employees to stay updated on compliance requirements and technological advancements. Continuous education programs in regulatory science, digital health integration, data protection, and quality assurance strengthen workforce competence (Ogbodo et al., 2025). Employees who perceive opportunities for skill development are more likely to remain committed to the organization. Investment in human capital thus yields both performance and retention benefits. Workplace culture significantly influences employee retention in healthcare industries. Professionals in pharmaceutical and MedTech firms often operate under high-pressure conditions, managing tight deadlines, complex documentation, and rigorous audits. A culture that promotes collaboration, psychological safety, and recognition reduces stress and burnout. Supportive leadership practices, transparent communication, and acknowledgment of contributions foster employee satisfaction (Celestin et al., 2024). When individuals feel valued and aligned with organizational mission—particularly the mission of improving patient outcomes—they are more likely to sustain long-term engagement. Diversity and inclusion also enhance talent acquisition and retention. Healthcare innovation benefits from diverse perspectives, particularly when addressing global health challenges and varied patient populations. Inclusive recruitment strategies broaden the talent pool and stimulate creative problem-solving. Organizations that prioritize equitable opportunities, unbiased evaluation systems, and inclusive leadership create environments where diverse professionals can thrive (Narayan et al., 2024). Such environments improve innovation quality and organizational adaptability. Global operations further complicate talent management. Pharmaceutical and MedTech firms frequently operate across multiple regulatory jurisdictions, requiring region-specific expertise. Strategic mobility programs, international assignments, and cross-border collaboration opportunities support knowledge transfer and leadership development. Harmonized training standards ensure consistent compliance practices worldwide while allowing adaptation to local regulatory contexts (Apooyin, 2025). Ultimately, talent acquisition and retention in high-regulation environments require strategic alignment between workforce planning, organizational culture, regulatory expertise, and innovation objectives. Pharmaceutical and MedTech organizations that invest in attracting skilled professionals, fostering continuous learning, and cultivating supportive work environments strengthen their capacity to innovate responsibly (Shan & Wang, 2024). In industries where human expertise directly influences patient safety and regulatory success, effective talent management is not merely an HR function—it is a central pillar of strategic sustainability and long-term innovation performance.

HUMAN CAPITAL DEVELOPMENT AND KNOWLEDGE MANAGEMENT SYSTEMS

Human capital development and knowledge management systems are central to sustaining innovation in pharmaceutical and MedTech organizations. In industries defined by scientific complexity, regulatory oversight, and long product development cycles, the ability to continuously develop employee competencies and effectively manage institutional knowledge determines long-term competitive advantage. Unlike sectors where innovation may rely primarily on technological infrastructure, healthcare innovation depends heavily on intellectual capital, specialized expertise, and the systematic transfer of knowledge across teams and generations of professionals. Human capital development begins with structured learning and skill enhancement initiatives. Pharmaceutical and MedTech firms must ensure that employees remain current with advances in biomedical research, engineering methodologies, regulatory guidelines, digital health technologies, and quality standards (Subha et al., 2024). Continuous professional development programs—such as technical workshops, regulatory training sessions, certification courses, and leadership development initiatives—strengthen employee capabilities. Because regulatory frameworks frequently evolve, ongoing compliance education is particularly critical. Employees who understand updated standards in clinical research, manufacturing validation, and data governance reduce the risk of non-compliance and project delays (Aggarwal et al., 2025). Leadership development forms another essential component of human capital growth. As organizations expand their innovation pipelines, they require leaders capable of managing multi-disciplinary teams, navigating uncertainty, and integrating scientific and commercial perspectives. Structured succession planning ensures continuity in executive and managerial roles. Mentorship programs allow experienced professionals to transfer tacit knowledge—such as regulatory negotiation strategies or clinical trial management insights—to emerging leaders (Chukwu et al., 2024). Such knowledge transfer safeguards institutional memory and enhances long-term organizational resilience. Knowledge management systems (KMS) complement human capital development by organizing, storing, and disseminating information efficiently. Pharmaceutical and MedTech innovation generates vast amounts of data, including laboratory findings, clinical trial results, regulatory submissions, quality audits, and post-market surveillance reports (Paul). Without systematic knowledge management, valuable insights may remain fragmented or inaccessible. Digital knowledge repositories, centralized databases, and collaborative platforms enable employees to retrieve accurate information promptly. Efficient knowledge access reduces duplication of efforts and accelerates innovation cycles. Tacit knowledge—insights gained through experience rather than formal documentation—is particularly valuable in regulated healthcare industries. Experienced researchers, regulatory specialists, and quality managers often possess nuanced understanding of compliance expectations and risk mitigation strategies. Organizations must create mechanisms to capture this tacit knowledge before it is lost through retirement or turnover (Levallet & Chan, 2019). Communities of practice, cross-functional meetings, and structured debriefings after project completion facilitate knowledge sharing. Such practices transform individual expertise into organizational capability. Cross-functional integration is enhanced through effective knowledge management systems. Drug and device development require collaboration among R&D scientists, regulatory teams, manufacturing units, marketing departments, and supply chain managers (Mazzola et al., 2015). Integrated digital platforms enable real-time information sharing, ensuring alignment across departments. For example, early regulatory input during research design can prevent costly redesigns in later stages. When knowledge flows seamlessly between functions, innovation becomes more efficient and strategically coherent.

Table 2. Human Capital Development and Knowledge Management in Pharma & MedTech Innovation

Strategic Dimension	Human Capital Focus	Knowledge Management Mechanism	Organizational Impact	Innovation Outcome
Continuous Professional Development	Ongoing technical, regulatory, and digital skills training	Structured learning platforms, certification tracking systems	Enhances workforce competence and compliance readiness	Reduced regulatory risk and improved R&D efficiency
Regulatory & Compliance Education	Training on evolving clinical, manufacturing, and data standards	Centralized compliance databases and policy repositories	Minimizes non-compliance and project delays	Faster approvals and smoother market entry
Leadership Development & Succession Planning	Mentorship programs, executive training, succession frameworks	Leadership knowledge archives and structured debrief reports	Preserves institutional memory and leadership continuity	Long-term strategic stability and resilience
Tacit Knowledge Capture	Encouraging expert knowledge sharing before retirement	Communities of practice, cross-functional workshops, post-project reviews	Converts individual expertise into organizational capability	Stronger risk mitigation and decision quality
Cross-Functional Integration	Multidisciplinary collaboration training	Integrated digital collaboration platforms and shared databases	Breaks down silos and improves coordination	Accelerated innovation cycles and reduced duplication
Digital Knowledge Infrastructure	Data literacy and digital competency development	AI-enabled analytics systems, secure data repositories, governance frameworks	Improves evidence-based decision-making and data integrity	Enhanced discovery speed and strategic agility
Global Workforce Harmonization	Standardized global training with localized adaptation	Harmonized documentation systems and global knowledge networks	Ensures consistent quality across regions	Sustainable global innovation competitiveness

Digital transformation has significantly expanded the scope of knowledge management in healthcare industries. (Kandhare et al., 2025) These technologies enhance evidence-based decision-making and accelerate discovery processes. However, digital knowledge systems must be carefully governed to ensure data accuracy, cybersecurity, and regulatory compliance. Strong data governance frameworks are essential to maintain integrity and confidentiality, particularly when handling patient information. Organizational culture influences the effectiveness of knowledge management initiatives. A culture that encourages collaboration, transparency, and continuous learning supports active participation in knowledge-sharing systems. Conversely, competitive internal environments or siloed structures may discourage information exchange (Bento et al., 2020). Leadership plays a critical role in reinforcing knowledge-sharing norms by recognizing collaborative contributions and modeling open communication. Global operations add complexity to human capital development and knowledge management. Multinational pharmaceutical and MedTech firms operate across diverse regulatory regimes and healthcare contexts. Harmonized training programs and standardized documentation systems ensure consistent quality and compliance across regions. At the same time, localized expertise must be incorporated into global knowledge networks to reflect regional regulatory nuances and patient needs. In conclusion, human capital development and knowledge management systems form the intellectual infrastructure of innovation in regulated healthcare industries. Continuous skill enhancement, leadership succession planning, and structured knowledge-sharing mechanisms strengthen organizational capability and resilience (Yang et al., 2025). By integrating digital tools, fostering collaborative culture, and safeguarding institutional memory, pharmaceutical and MedTech firms enhance their ability to innovate responsibly and sustainably. In environments where expertise directly influences patient safety and regulatory success, strategic investment in human capital and knowledge systems remains indispensable for long-term innovation excellence.

EXECUTIVE DECISION-MAKING UNDER REGULATORY AND MARKET UNCERTAINTY

Executive decision-making in pharmaceutical and MedTech organizations occurs within an environment characterized by profound regulatory complexity and volatile market dynamics. Unlike many industries where market competition alone shapes strategy, healthcare innovation is simultaneously influenced by evolving regulatory standards, clinical trial outcomes, reimbursement policies, technological disruption, and global health trends. Executives must therefore make high-stakes decisions under conditions of uncertainty, balancing scientific ambition with compliance discipline and financial sustainability. Regulatory uncertainty represents one of the most significant challenges facing executive leaders. Approval processes for drugs and medical devices are rigorous, time-consuming, and subject to evolving guidelines (Baumfeld Andre et al., 2020). Changes in clinical trial requirements, safety standards, or documentation expectations can significantly alter project timelines and costs. Executives must anticipate regulatory shifts and integrate compliance considerations into early-stage strategic planning. Proactive engagement with regulatory authorities, scenario analysis, and adaptive project design help mitigate approval risks. Decisions regarding whether to pursue accelerated approval pathways, orphan drug designations, or breakthrough device classifications require careful evaluation of both opportunity and compliance obligations. Clinical uncertainty further complicates executive decision-making. Despite extensive preclinical research, clinical trial outcomes remain inherently unpredictable. Late-stage trial failures can result in substantial financial losses and reputational damage (Jain et al., 2023). Executives must evaluate interim data objectively and determine whether to continue, modify, or terminate development programs. Such decisions involve not only scientific assessment but also ethical considerations related to patient safety and resource allocation. Structured governance processes, independent data monitoring boards, and milestone-based evaluations support disciplined judgment under uncertainty. Market uncertainty adds another layer of complexity. Shifting reimbursement models, healthcare policy reforms, competitive product launches, and pricing pressures influence commercial viability (Vallano & Pontes, 2024). Executives must forecast demand, evaluate pricing strategies, and assess payer acceptance before committing substantial resources. In many cases, market success depends not only on clinical efficacy but also on cost-effectiveness and health economic value. Decision-making frameworks increasingly incorporate real-world evidence and health technology assessment data to anticipate market reception. Risk management is central to executive decision-making in regulated environments. Leaders must determine acceptable levels of risk across innovation portfolios. Diversification strategies, strategic partnerships, and staged investment models reduce exposure to single-project failure (Wang & Jin, 2021). Acquisitions of smaller biotechnology or MedTech startups may accelerate innovation while distributing risk. However, such strategies require careful due diligence to evaluate scientific validity, intellectual property strength, and regulatory positioning. Executives must balance bold strategic moves with prudent financial oversight.

Data-driven decision-making has become increasingly important in addressing uncertainty. Advanced analytics, predictive modeling, and artificial intelligence tools enable executives to assess probabilities and simulate potential outcomes (Vudugula et al., 2023). Real-time monitoring of clinical trial data, manufacturing performance, and post-market safety signals enhances responsiveness. However, reliance on data must be complemented by experienced judgment, particularly when interpreting ambiguous or incomplete information. Effective executives combine analytical insight with strategic intuition developed through industry experience. Stakeholder expectations further influence executive decisions. Investors demand sustainable growth, regulators expect strict compliance, healthcare providers require evidence-based solutions, and patients seek safe and accessible treatments. Executives must navigate these sometimes competing interests while maintaining organizational credibility. Transparent communication and ethical integrity strengthen stakeholder trust during uncertain periods (Chitraju, 2025). For example, openly communicating clinical setbacks may preserve long-term reputation even if short-term market reactions are negative. Global operations intensify decision-making complexity. Regulatory requirements, pricing structures, and healthcare infrastructures vary across regions. Executives must determine whether to standardize innovation strategies globally or tailor approaches to local markets. Currency fluctuations, geopolitical instability, and supply chain vulnerabilities also influence strategic decisions. Adaptive leadership capable of responding swiftly to global disruptions enhances organizational resilience. Organizational culture plays a subtle yet powerful role in executive decision-making under uncertainty. A culture that encourages open dialogue and constructive dissent enables leaders to consider diverse perspectives before making critical choices. Conversely, hierarchical environments where dissent is discouraged may increase the risk of strategic misjudgment. Encouraging evidence-based debate strengthens decision quality and reduces blind spots. In conclusion, executive decision-making in regulated Pharma and MedTech innovation demands a sophisticated balance of strategic foresight, regulatory awareness, financial prudence, and ethical responsibility. Uncertainty is inherent in healthcare innovation, but disciplined governance, data-driven analysis, and stakeholder engagement enable leaders to navigate complexity effectively (Gade, 2021). Executives who integrate risk management with visionary thinking position their organizations to achieve sustainable innovation while safeguarding patient safety and regulatory trust.

RISK, COMPLIANCE, AND ETHICAL CONSIDERATIONS IN STRATEGIC DECISION PROCESSES

Risk, compliance, and ethical considerations are central pillars of strategic decision-making in pharmaceutical and MedTech organizations. In industries where innovation outcomes directly influence patient health and public trust, strategic decisions cannot be based solely on financial projections or competitive positioning (Javanmardi et al., 2024). They must also incorporate rigorous risk assessment, strict regulatory adherence, and deep ethical reflection. Executives and senior leaders are therefore required to balance opportunity with responsibility, ensuring that innovation advances within safe, lawful, and morally sound boundaries. Risk in regulated healthcare industries is multidimensional. Clinical risk arises from uncertainties related to product safety and efficacy. Operational risk includes manufacturing failures, supply chain disruptions, and quality control deviations. Financial risk stems from high R&D investments and uncertain returns. Reputational risk may result from adverse events, regulatory sanctions, or unethical conduct. Strategic decision processes must systematically evaluate these risk categories before committing resources. Structured risk management frameworks such as enterprise risk management (ERM) systems allow organizations to identify, assess, prioritize, and mitigate potential threats (Force, 2018). Compliance is inseparable from risk management in pharmaceutical and MedTech firms. Regulatory authorities impose strict requirements governing clinical trials, manufacturing standards, product labeling, advertising claims, and post-market surveillance. Non-compliance can result in product recalls, legal penalties, and loss of market authorization. Therefore, strategic decisions must integrate compliance considerations from the earliest stages of innovation planning. For example, choosing to accelerate product development timelines must not compromise documentation standards or safety evaluations. Integrating regulatory affairs teams into executive discussions ensures that strategic initiatives remain aligned with evolving compliance expectations. Ethical considerations add another layer of complexity to strategic decision-making. Pharmaceutical and MedTech companies operate in sectors where human lives are directly affected by product performance and corporate conduct (Euh & Lee, 2021). Decisions regarding clinical trial design, patient recruitment, pricing strategies, and data transparency require ethical scrutiny. Ethical lapses—such as withholding negative trial results or engaging in misleading promotional practices—can severely damage public trust and corporate legitimacy. Ethical governance structures, including independent ethics committees and transparent reporting systems, support responsible strategic choices. A proactive compliance culture strengthens strategic resilience. When employees at all organizational levels understand regulatory obligations and ethical standards, compliance becomes embedded in daily operations rather than treated as an external enforcement mechanism. Training programs, internal audits, and clear reporting channels reinforce accountability. Encouraging employees to voice concerns without fear of retaliation helps identify potential compliance risks early. Such cultural reinforcement ensures that strategic decisions are informed by practical insights from operational teams (Hubbart, 2024).

Table 3. Risk, Compliance, and Ethical Integration in Strategic Decision Processes (Pharma & MedTech)

Strategic Dimension	Primary Focus	Key Mechanisms & Controls	Organizational Impact	Strategic Outcome
Enterprise Risk Management (ERM)	Identification and prioritization of clinical, operational, financial, and reputational risks	Risk registers, ERM frameworks, milestone reviews, internal audits	Proactive threat mitigation and informed resource allocation	Reduced uncertainty and improved strategic stability
Regulatory Compliance Integration	Alignment of strategy with evolving regulatory standards	Early regulatory engagement, compliance monitoring systems, documentation controls	Minimizes legal penalties and product delays	Faster approvals and sustained market authorization
Ethical Governance & Oversight	Ensuring morally sound decision-making in clinical trials, pricing, and marketing	Independent ethics committees, transparent reporting, whistleblower channels	Protects public trust and corporate legitimacy	Long-term reputational strength and societal acceptance
Compliance Culture Development	Embedding accountability across all organizational levels	Training programs, internal compliance audits, open reporting systems	Encourages early detection of risks and ethical concerns	Strong internal controls and organizational resilience
Strategic Trade-off Evaluation	Balancing commercial opportunities with risk and ethical implications	Documented risk–benefit analyses, executive review boards	Enhances disciplined and transparent decision-making	Sustainable and responsible market expansion
Stakeholder Risk Alignment	Reconciling investor, regulator, and patient expectations	Transparent communication, sustainability reporting, stakeholder engagement forums	Builds credibility and trust across constituencies	Strengthened brand loyalty and long-term growth
Digital & Data Governance	Managing privacy, cybersecurity, and AI-related risks	Data protection policies, cybersecurity frameworks, consent management systems	Safeguards sensitive patient information and regulatory compliance	Responsible digital innovation and enhanced patient trust

Strategic trade-offs often test the integration of risk, compliance, and ethics. For instance, entering a new market with less stringent regulatory oversight may present commercial opportunities but raise ethical questions about product testing standards. Similarly, adopting emerging technologies such as artificial intelligence in diagnostics requires careful evaluation of data privacy, cybersecurity, and algorithmic bias risks. Executives must assess whether potential gains justify associated risks and ethical implications. Transparent decision rationales and documented risk assessments enhance organizational accountability. Stakeholder expectations significantly influence risk and ethical decision processes. Investors expect sustainable growth, but regulators demand strict compliance, and patients prioritize safety and accessibility (Roth et al., 2018). Strategic decisions must reconcile these perspectives to maintain legitimacy. Open communication regarding risk management practices and ethical commitments builds stakeholder confidence. Companies that demonstrate consistent ethical behavior often experience stronger brand loyalty and long-term stability. Globalization further complicates compliance and ethical considerations. Regulatory standards vary across jurisdictions, and cultural norms may influence perceptions of acceptable business practices. Organizations must apply consistent ethical principles globally while adapting to local regulatory requirements. Harmonized compliance frameworks, supported by localized expertise, help maintain integrity across diverse markets. Technology-driven innovation introduces new categories of risk and ethical dilemmas. Digital health platforms, wearable medical devices, and AI-based analytics generate vast amounts of sensitive patient data (Shajari et al., 2023). Strategic decisions regarding data usage, storage, and sharing must prioritize privacy and security. Compliance with data protection regulations and transparent consent processes are essential to preserve trust. In conclusion, integrating risk management, compliance oversight, and ethical reflection into strategic decision processes is indispensable for pharmaceutical and MedTech organizations. These interconnected dimensions safeguard patient welfare, protect corporate reputation, and ensure regulatory approval. Leaders who adopt disciplined risk frameworks, embed compliance into organizational culture, and uphold strong ethical standards strengthen their ability to innovate responsibly. In regulated healthcare industries, strategic success is not measured solely by market performance but also by the integrity and safety with which innovation is delivered (Schiavone & Simoni, 2019).

CROSS-FUNCTIONAL LEADERSHIP AND INNOVATION TEAM INTEGRATION

Cross-functional leadership and innovation team integration are essential components of successful pharmaceutical and MedTech innovation. The development of drugs, biologics, diagnostic technologies, and medical devices requires coordinated input from diverse professional domains, including research scientists, biomedical engineers, clinical experts, regulatory specialists, quality assurance teams, manufacturing managers, marketing strategists, and supply chain professionals. No single function can independently bring a healthcare innovation from concept to commercialization. Therefore, effective cross-functional leadership ensures alignment, collaboration, and efficiency across complex organizational structures. Healthcare innovation is inherently multidisciplinary. During early discovery phases, scientists and engineers focus on technical feasibility and biological validation (Wu & Gu,

2025). As projects advance into clinical development, regulatory affairs teams ensure compliance with approval standards. Manufacturing specialists assess scalability and quality control processes, while commercial teams evaluate market demand and reimbursement pathways. Without integration among these functions, misalignment can lead to costly delays, redesigns, or regulatory setbacks. Cross-functional leadership fosters communication and coordination across these diverse expertise areas, enabling smoother progression through development stages. Leadership plays a pivotal role in breaking down organizational silos. In large pharmaceutical and MedTech firms, departments often operate with specialized priorities and performance metrics (McDermott et al., 2022). R&D teams may emphasize innovation speed, regulatory units focus on compliance rigor, and commercial teams prioritize market competitiveness. Cross-functional leaders harmonize these priorities by establishing shared objectives and integrated performance indicators. By aligning incentives and encouraging collaborative problem-solving, leaders reduce internal conflict and promote collective accountability. Communication structures significantly influence innovation team integration. Clear reporting lines, regular cross-departmental meetings, and collaborative digital platforms enhance information exchange (Liu, 2025). Real-time data sharing allows regulatory experts to provide early input into research design, preventing downstream compliance challenges. Similarly, involving manufacturing teams during product design phases ensures scalability and cost-effectiveness. Transparent communication channels reduce duplication of efforts and accelerate decision-making. Trust and psychological safety are foundational to cross-functional effectiveness. Innovation projects often involve uncertainty, experimentation, and potential failure. Team members must feel comfortable sharing concerns, questioning assumptions, and proposing alternative solutions. Leaders who promote open dialogue and respect diverse viewpoints strengthen team cohesion. When individuals perceive that their expertise is valued, engagement and creativity increase (Aldabbas et al., 2023). Conversely, hierarchical or siloed environments can suppress collaboration and limit innovation potential.

Project governance frameworks support cross-functional integration. Stage-gate review systems typically involve representatives from multiple departments who collectively evaluate project readiness. This shared oversight ensures that scientific, regulatory, financial, and commercial considerations are addressed simultaneously. Cross-functional governance committees enhance transparency and reduce the risk of unilateral decision-making. Integrated decision processes improve the quality and robustness of innovation outcomes (Shepherd et al., 2023). Digital collaboration tools further facilitate cross-functional coordination, particularly in global organizations. Pharmaceutical and MedTech firms frequently operate across multiple countries and time zones. Virtual project management platforms, shared knowledge repositories, and integrated data systems enable geographically dispersed teams to collaborate effectively. Digital integration enhances efficiency while maintaining documentation traceability required for regulatory compliance. Leadership adaptability is critical in managing cross-functional innovation teams. Different project phases may require varying degrees of directive guidance or participative collaboration. Early-stage exploratory research may benefit from flexible leadership that encourages experimentation, whereas late-stage regulatory submission demands structured coordination and compliance oversight. Leaders capable of adjusting their approach based on project maturity enhance team effectiveness and project success rates (Salimimoghadam et al., 2025). Cultural diversity within global healthcare organizations adds both complexity and opportunity to cross-functional integration. Diverse teams bring varied perspectives, experiences, and problem-solving approaches. Effective leaders leverage this diversity by promoting inclusive practices and intercultural competence. Standardized compliance training and shared organizational values ensure consistency while respecting regional differences. Conflict management is another important aspect of cross-functional leadership. Differences in priorities or risk tolerance may generate tension between departments (Khalilzadeh et al., 2019). Leaders must mediate disputes constructively, focusing discussions on shared objectives such as patient safety, regulatory success, and market sustainability. Structured conflict resolution mechanisms maintain project momentum and preserve team relationships. In conclusion, cross-functional leadership and innovation team integration are vital for advancing complex healthcare innovations successfully. By fostering collaboration, aligning departmental objectives, promoting transparent communication, and leveraging digital tools, leaders create cohesive innovation ecosystems within pharmaceutical and MedTech firms. Integrated teams enhance efficiency, reduce regulatory risk, and improve product quality (Gomaa, 2025). In regulated healthcare industries where multidisciplinary coordination directly affects patient outcomes and compliance success, strong cross-functional leadership is indispensable for sustainable innovation performance.

CONCLUSION

Strategic human capital and executive decision-making collectively shape the innovation trajectory of pharmaceutical and MedTech organizations operating in regulated environments. In industries where scientific advancement intersects with strict compliance obligations and significant societal impact, talent and leadership become central drivers of sustainable success. Specialized expertise in research, regulatory affairs, quality management, and digital technologies forms the intellectual foundation upon which innovation is built. Continuous human capital development and structured knowledge management systems ensure that expertise evolves alongside technological and regulatory changes. Executive leadership plays a critical role in translating human capability into strategic advantage. Through disciplined portfolio management, proactive risk governance, and regulatory integration, executives guide innovation from early discovery to commercialization. Decision-making under uncertainty requires balancing scientific ambition with financial prudence, compliance rigor, and ethical responsibility. Leaders who foster cross-functional collaboration and transparent communication strengthen organizational alignment and resilience. Risk management, compliance oversight, and ethical reflection are not peripheral concerns but integral elements of strategic planning in regulated healthcare industries. Embedding these principles into decision processes protects patient safety, enhances stakeholder trust, and mitigates reputational exposure. Organizations that cultivate adaptive leadership and inclusive cultures are better equipped to respond to market volatility, technological disruption, and global regulatory complexity. Ultimately, the integration of strategic human capital planning with responsible executive governance enables pharmaceutical and MedTech firms to deliver innovative, safe, and impactful healthcare solutions. Sustainable innovation in regulated environments depends not only on scientific breakthroughs but also on the quality of leadership and the strength of institutional capability guiding those breakthroughs toward societal benefit.

REFERENCES

Afriyie, D. (2019). Aligning strategic workforce planning with future-of-work trends through advanced performance management and digital HR infrastructure. *World Journal of Advanced Research and Reviews*, *4*(2), 207–226. DOI: 10.30574/wjarr.2019.4.2.0150

Aggarwal, K., Jindal, P., Patel, P., & Kurmi, B. D. (2025). The Role of Validation in Mitigating Non-Compliance in the Pharmaceutical Industry. *International Journal of Newgen Research in Pharmacy & Healthcare*, 25-30.

Aldabbas, H., Pinnington, A., & Lahrech, A. (2023). The influence of perceived organizational support on employee creativity: The mediating role of work engagement. *Current Psychology*, *42*(8), 6501–6515. DOI: 10.1007/s12144-021-01992-1

Apooyin, A. (2025). Risk management and compliance in a globalized economy: Navigating regulatory challenges and strategic adaptations. *International Journal of Science and Research Archive, 15*(10.30574).

Babatope, V. O. (2025). Cross-Disciplinary Mentoring in Academia: Fostering Collaboration and Innovation. In *Strategic Mentoring in Higher Education: Best Practices for Academic Success* (pp. 105-125). Springer.

Badnjević, A., Pokvić, L. G., Deumić, A., & Bećirović, L. S. (2022). Post-market surveillance of medical devices: A review. *Technology and Health Care*, *30*(6), 1315–1329. DOI: 10.3233/THC-220284 PMID: 35964220

Baumfeld Andre, E., Reynolds, R., Caubel, P., Azoulay, L., & Dreyer, N. A. (2020). Trial designs using real-world data: The changing landscape of the regulatory approval process. *Pharmacoepidemiology and Drug Safety*, *29*(10), 1201–1212. DOI: 10.1002/pds.4932 PMID: 31823482

Bento, F., Tagliabue, M., & Lorenzo, F. (2020). Organizational silos: A scoping review informed by a behavioral perspective on systems and networks. *Societies (Basel, Switzerland)*, *10*(3), 56. DOI: 10.3390/soc10030056

Birou, L., & Hoek, R. V. (2022). Supply chain management talent: The role of executives in engagement, recruitment, development and retention. *Supply Chain Management*, *27*(6), 712–727. DOI: 10.1108/SCM-08-2020-0418

Celestin, M., Vasuki, M., Sujatha, S., & Kumar, A. D. (2024). Enhancing employee satisfaction and engagement to boost productivity: The role of leadership, culture, and recognition programs. *International Journal of Computational Research and Development*, *9*(2), 67–74.

Chitraju, S. (2025). Building Trust through Transparency: The Role of Disclosure in Risk Governance. *Available at SSRN* 5603270. DOI: 10.2139/ssrn.5603270

Chukwu, O. A., Nadigel, J., Kasaai, B., Boateng, R., Glazier, R. H., & McMahon, M. (2024). Understanding the training, mentorship, and professional development priorities of early career embedded researchers. *The International Journal of Health Planning and Management*, *39*(5), 1277–1297. DOI: 10.1002/hpm.3800 PMID: 38527109

Euh, Y., & Lee, D. (2021). How do pharmaceutical companies overcome a corporate productivity crisis? Business diversification into medical devices for growth potential. *International Journal of Environmental Research and Public Health*, *18*(3), 1045. DOI: 10.3390/ijerph18031045 PMID: 33503944

Force, J. T. (2018). Risk management framework for information systems and organizations. *NIST Special Publication*, *800*, 37.

Gade, K. R. (2021). Data-driven decision making in a complex world. *Journal of computational innovation, 1*(1).

Gomaa, A. H. (2025). Enhancing Product Development Excellence through Quality Management Tools: A Comprehensive Review and Integrated Conceptual Framework. *Intelligent and Sustainable Manufacturing*, *2*(2), 10017. DOI: 10.70322/ism.2025.10017

Hubbart, J. A. (2024). Understanding and mitigating leadership fear-based behaviors on employee and organizational success. *Administrative Sciences*, *14*(9), 225. DOI: 10.3390/admsci14090225

Hussain, A., Umair, M., Khan, S., Alonazi, W. B., Almutairi, S. S., & Malik, A. (2024). Exploring sustainable healthcare: Innovations in health economics, social policy, and management. *Heliyon*, *10*(13), e33186. DOI: 10.1016/j.heliyon.2024.e33186 PMID: 39027491

Jain, R., Subramanian, J., & Rathore, A. S. (2023). A review of therapeutic failures in late-stage clinical trials. *Expert Opinion on Pharmacotherapy*, *24*(3), 389–399. DOI: 10.1080/14656566.2022.2161366 PMID: 36542800

Javanmardi, E., Maresova, P., Xie, N., & Mierzwiak, R. (2024). Exploring business models for managing uncertainty in healthcare, medical devices, and biotechnology industries. *Heliyon*, *10*(4), e25962. DOI: 10.1016/j.heliyon.2024.e25962 PMID: 38370194

Joshua, C. (2025). The role of institutional culture in shaping quality assurance in higher education. *Quality Assurance Practices for Transformative Higher Education in Southern Africa, 24*.

Kabir, M., Rana, M. R. H., & Debnath, A. (2024). The role of quality assurance in accelerating pharmaceutical research and development: Strategies for ensuring regulatory compliance and product integrity. *Journal of Angiotherapy*, *8*(12), 1–11.

Kandhare, P., Kurlekar, M., Deshpande, T., & Pawar, A. (2025). A review on revolutionizing healthcare technologies with AI and ML applications in pharmaceutical sciences. *Drugs and Drug Candidates*, *4*(1), 9. DOI: 10.3390/ddc4010009

Karas, L., Feldman, R., Bai, G., Kang, S. Y., & Anderson, G. F. (2019). Pharmaceutical Industry Funding to Patient-Advocacy Organization: A cross-national comparison of disclosure codes and regulation. *Hastings Int'l & Comp. L. Rev.*, *42*, 453.

Kasoju, N., Remya, N., Sasi, R., Sujesh, S., Soman, B., Kesavadas, C., Muraleedharan, C., Varma, P. H., & Behari, S. (2023). Digital health: Trends, opportunities and challenges in medical devices, pharma and bio-technology. *CSI Transactions on ICT*, *11*(1), 11–30. DOI: 10.1007/s40012-023-00380-3

Khalilzadeh, M., Masoumi, S., & Masoumi, I. (2019). Identification and prioritization of factors influencing organization risk tolerance level. *Journal of Advances in Management Research*, *16*(4), 417–435. DOI: 10.1108/JAMR-07-2018-0061

Kulkov, I. (2021). Medical technology innovation ecosystems: Factors influencing the formation of new companies.

Kumar, S., Narayanan, S., & Salvador, F. (2020). Innovation in supply networks—A research framework and roadmap. *Journal of Operations Management*, *66*(7-8), 754–767. DOI: 10.1002/joom.1122

Levallet, N., & Chan, Y. E. (2019). Organizational knowledge retention and knowledge loss. *Journal of Knowledge Management*, *23*(1), 176–199. DOI: 10.1108/JKM-08-2017-0358

Liu, Y. (2025). The Importance of Cross-Departmental Collaboration Driven by Technology in the Compliance of Financial Institutions. *Economics and Management Innovation*, *2*(5), 15–21.

Mandel, C. E., & Parija, S. (2024). Risk appetite: A crucial consideration for effective board risk oversight. *Journal of Risk Management in Financial Institutions*, *17*(2), 168–182. DOI: 10.69554/GJRD1826

Mazzola, E., Bruccoleri, M., & Perrone, G. (2015). Supply chain of innovation and new product development. *Journal of Purchasing and Supply Management*, *21*(4), 273–284. DOI: 10.1016/j.pursup.2015.04.006

McDermott, O., Antony, J., Sony, M., & Healy, T. (2022). Critical failure factors for continuous improvement methodologies in the Irish MedTech industry. *The TQM Journal*, *34*(7), 18–38. DOI: 10.1108/TQM-10-2021-0289

Narayan, A. K., Boone, N., Monga, N., McFarlane, N., Mango, V. L., Seifert, M., Smith, A., Woods, R. W., & Weissman, I. A. (2024). Fostering organizational excellence through inclusive leadership: Practical guide for radiology leaders. *Radiographics : A Review Publication of the Radiological Society of North America, Inc.*, *44*(9), e230162. DOI: 10.1148/rg.230162 PMID: 39146206

Ogbodo, D. C., Awan, I.-U., Cullen, A., & Zahrah, F. (2025). From regulation to reality: A framework to bridge the gap in digital health data protection. *Electronics (Basel)*, *14*(13), 2629. DOI: 10.3390/electronics14132629

Ollif, K., & Patel, J. (2025). *Current US university-industry partnerships: Realignment and opportunity*. The National Academies.

Parker, E. (2024). *The Illusion of Innovation: Escape" Efficiency" and Unleash Radical Progress*. Simon and Schuster. Paul, A. L. Cloud-Based Post-Market Surveillance Platforms: Enhancing Signal Detection and Risk Mitigation in Medical Devices.

Pham, T. (2025). Ethical and legal considerations in healthcare AI: Innovation and policy for safe and fair use. *Royal Society Open Science*, *12*(5), 241873. DOI: 10.1098/rsos.241873 PMID: 40370601

Philip, B., Mathew, G. A., Sebastian, R. T., Eshwari, B., Roopa, M., & Mathews, S. B. (2024). Strategizing Talent Acquisition for Fostering Future Workforce Success: Addressing Millennial Turnover and Hiring Challenges in a Rapidly Evolving Business Landscape. In *Anticipating Future Business Trends: Navigating Artificial Intelligence Innovations: Volume 1* (pp. 357-368). Springer.

Presbitero, A., & Toledano, L. S. (2018). Global team members' performance and the roles of cross-cultural training, cultural intelligence, and contact intensity: The case of global teams in IT offshoring sector. *International Journal of Human Resource Management*, *29*(14), 2188–2208. DOI: 10.1080/09585192.2017.1322118

Roth, L., Bempong, D., Babigumira, J. B., Banoo, S., Cooke, E., Jeffreys, D., Kasonde, L., Leufkens, H. G., Lim, J. C., Lumpkin, M., Mahlangu, G., Peeling, R. W., Rees, H., Ndomondo-Sigonda, M., Stergachis, A., Ward, M., & Nwokike, J. (2018). Expanding global access to essential medicines: Investment priorities for sustainably strengthening medical product regulatory systems. *Globalization and Health, 14*(1), 102. DOI: 10.1186/s12992-018-0421-2 PMID: 30382856

Salimimoghadam, S., Ghanbaripour, A. N., Tumpa, R. J., & Watanabe, T. (2025). Core leadership competencies of project managers for enhancing project success in today's fast-evolving world: a systematic literature review. *Smart and Sustainable Built Environment*, 1-40.

Schiavone, F., & Simoni, M. (2019). Strategic marketing approaches for the diffusion of innovation in highly regulated industrial markets: The value of market access. *Journal of Business and Industrial Marketing*, *34*(7), 1606–1618. DOI: 10.1108/JBIM-08-2018-0232

Shajari, S., Kuruvinashetti, K., Komeili, A., & Sundararaj, U. (2023). The emergence of AI-based wearable sensors for digital health technology: A review. *Sensors (Basel)*, *23*(23), 9498. DOI: 10.3390/s23239498 PMID: 38067871

Shan, Z., & Wang, Y. (2024). Strategic talent development in the knowledge economy: A comparative analysis of global practices. *Journal of the Knowledge Economy*, *15*(4), 19570–19596. DOI: 10.1007/s13132-024-01933-w

Shepherd, N., Mooi, E., Elbanna, S., & Lou, B. (2023). Fast and high-quality decision-making: The role of behavioral integration. *European Management Review*, *20*(4), 679–697. DOI: 10.1111/emre.12573

Smith, B. D. (2019). *Leadership in the Life Sciences: Ten Lessons from the C-Suite of Pharmaceutical and Medical Technology Companies*. Routledge. DOI: 10.4324/9780429022319

Subha, S., Shanmugathai, M., Prasanth, A., Varagi, S. S., & Dhanashree, V. (2024). Digital transformation in the pharmaceutical and biotech industry: challenges and research directions. *Digital twins in industrial production and smart manufacturing: an understanding of principles, enhancers, and obstacles*, 297-324.

Suleiman, T. A., & Adinoyi, A. (2023). Telemedicine and smart healthcare—The role of artificial intelligence, 5G, cloud services, and other enabling technologies. *International Journal of Communications, Network and Systems Sciences*, *16*(3), 31–51. DOI: 10.4236/ijcns.2023.163003

Tham, W. Y. (2023). Science, interrupted: Funding delays reduce research activity but having more grants helps. *PLoS One*, *18*(4), e0280576. DOI: 10.1371/journal.pone.0280576 PMID: 37099515

Vallano, A., & Pontes, C. (2024). Escalating costs of innovative medicines: Perspective and proposals. *Frontiers in Public Health*, *12*, 1449707. DOI: 10.3389/fpubh.2024.1449707 PMID: 39381757

Veldsman, D., & van der Merwe, M. (2022). Promises in action: The role of employer brand, employee value proposition and employee experience in delivering on psychological contract expectations. *EWOP in Practice, 16*(1).

Vudugula, S., Chebrolu, S. K., Bhuiyan, M., & Rozony, F. Z. (2023). Integrating artificial intelligence in strategic business decision-making: A systematic review of predictive models. *International Journal of Scientific Interdisciplinary Research, 4*(1), 01-26.

Wang, Y., & Jin, X. (2021). Structural risk of diversified project financing of city investment company in China based on the best worst method. *Engineering, Construction, and Architectural Management*, *28*(1), 196–215. DOI: 10.1108/ECAM-05-2019-0249

Wu, J., & Gu, N. (2025). New orientation of interdisciplinarity in medicine: Engineering medicine. *Engineering (Beijing)*, *45*, 252–261. DOI: 10.1016/j.eng.2024.09.009

Wujarso, R., & Dameria, R. (2023). *Human capital management as a resource in achieving competitive advantage*. Asadel Publisher.

Yang, Z., Dong, M., Guo, H., & Peng, W. (2025). Empowering resilience through digital transformation intentions: Synergizing knowledge sharing and transformational leadership amid COVID-19. *Journal of Organizational Change Management*, *38*(1), 59–81. DOI: 10.1108/JOCM-07-2023-0303

Young-Babb, T., Hall, L. F., Kuhn, A., & Pryor, C. (2025). Professional Development: Enhancing Adaptability for a Future-Ready Workforce. *International Journal of Advanced Corporate Learning*, *18*(3), 89–102. DOI: 10.3991/ijac.v18i3.52541

Zhou, Y., & Coplin, A. E. (2022). Innovation in a Science-based Sector. *China Review*, *22*(1), 39–76.

Chapter 14
Strategic Roadmapping for Medical Device Startups

Ricardo Marcão
http://orcid.org/0000-0003-3277-3078
ISLA Santarém, Portugal

Vasco Santos
ISLA Santarém, Portugal

Domingos Martinho
ISLA Santarém, Portugal

Camila Silva
ISLA Santarém, Portugal

ABSTRACT

The medical device industry is one of the most technologically advanced sectors within the global healthcare ecosystem, requiring not only scientific innovation but also strategic planning that integrates engineering, regulatory compliance, clinical validation, and business development. Medical device startups face significant challenges due to long development cycles, strict regulatory frameworks, and high research and development costs. This paper proposes a strategic roadmap structured around three phases, ideation and conceptualization, development and regulatory compliance, and launch with post market management, and illustrates its application through the case of PeekMed, a Portuguese startup developing artificial intelligence

DOI: 10.4018/979-8-3373-9410-7.ch014

based surgical planning software for orthopedic procedures. The findings highlight the importance of multidisciplinary collaboration and strategic management in increasing the likelihood of successfully bringing new medical technologies to market.

STRATEGIC ALLIANCES IN MEDTECH: A GLOBAL PERSPECTIVE

Strategic alliances have become a fundamental mechanism for innovation and competitiveness in the global Medical Technology (MedTech) industry. As healthcare systems become increasingly digitized and innovation cycles accelerate, partnerships between medical device manufacturers, technology firms, and research institutions play a crucial role in advancing patient-centered healthcare solutions. This paper analyzes the strategic motivations, structures, and global dynamics of alliances within the MedTech sector. It explores how firms leverage partnerships to accelerate innovation, expand into new markets, share development costs, and navigate complex regulatory environments. The study also examines regional differences across North America, Europe, and Asia, highlighting how regulatory frameworks influence alliance strategies. Through case examples involving Medtronic, IBM Watson Health, Philips, and PathAI, the paper illustrates both the benefits and challenges associated with strategic collaboration in healthcare technology. The findings suggest that effective governance, trust, and complementary capabilities are critical determinants of alliance success. Ultimately, strategic alliances are shown to be essential drivers of innovation and value-based healthcare delivery in the global MedTech ecosystem. Keywords: strategic alliances, MedTech, healthcare innovation, global partnerships, medical technology Introduction The Medical Technology (MedTech) industry has experienced significant expansion over the past decades, driven by advances in digital technologies, demographic changes, and increasing demand for high-quality healthcare services. Medical devices now incorporate technologies such as artificial intelligence, advanced imaging, robotics, and cloud-based data systems, transforming the way healthcare is delivered worldwide (Chesbrough, 2003; Deloitte, 2023). In this rapidly evolving environment, companies rarely possess all the capabilities required to develop complex healthcare technologies internally. As a result, strategic alliances have emerged as a critical mechanism for accessing complementary knowledge, sharing development risks, and accelerating innovation (Hagedoorn, 2002). These collaborations allow firms to combine expertise across disciplines such as engineering, data science, clinical research, and regulatory compliance. Strategic alliances in MedTech frequently involve partnerships between device manufacturers, technology companies, academic institutions, and healthcare providers. Such collaborations support the development of advanced solutions such as AI-assisted diagnostics, remote monitoring systems, and digital health platforms. The increasing convergence between MedTech and information technology has further reinforced the importance of cross-sector partnerships (McKinsey & Company, 2022). This paper examines the role of strategic alliances in the global MedTech sector. It analyzes the motivations behind alliance formation, the various structures used by firms, and the regional regulatory environments that shape collaboration strategies. In addition, the study discusses the risks associated with alliances and the governance mechanisms necessary to ensure long-term success. Literature Review Strategic alliances have long been recognized as an important mechanism for innovation and competitive advantage in technology-intensive industries. Early research on inter-firm collaboration emphasized the role of alliances in facilitating knowledge sharing, reducing uncertainty, and enabling access to complementary resources (Dyer & Singh, 1998). In industries characterized by high research and development (R&D) intensity, alliances allow firms to pool capabilities and accelerate technological progress. In the MedTech sector, the importance of strategic alliances has grown significantly due to the increasing complexity of healthcare technologies. Devices now integrate hardware, software, and data analytics, requiring expertise from multiple scientific domains. As a result, firms increasingly adopt open innovation strategies, which involve collaborating with external partners to access new knowledge and accelerate product development (Chesbrough, 2003). Recent studies highlight how MedTech companies leverage alliances to explore emerging technological fields such as wearable diagnostics, AI-assisted imaging, and remote patient monitoring systems (Sarkar et al., 2022). These collaborations enable firms to co-create intellectual property and rapidly translate research discoveries into commercial applications. The concept of the innovation ecosystem has also become central to understanding collaboration in the healthcare sector. According to Gassmann et al. (2021), successful MedTech innovation increasingly depends on networks of interconnected actors, including universities, startups, hospitals, and technology firms. Within such ecosystems, strategic alliances facilitate the integration of diverse knowledge sources and enable coordinated technological development. Trust and relational governance play a critical role in determining alliance success. The relational view proposed by Dyer and Singh (1998) suggests that competitive advantage can emerge from the quality of inter-organizational relationships rather than from internal resources alone. In healthcare technology partnerships, factors such as transparency, knowledge complementarity, and shared governance structures significantly influence collaborative outcomes (Li et al., 2020). However, alliances also present challenges, particularly when partners operate under different regulatory frameworks or possess conflicting strategic objectives. Rajapathirana and Hui (2020) emphasize that regulatory misalignment, intellectual property disputes, and organizational culture differences may undermine alliance effectiveness. Methodology This study adopts a qualitative and exploratory research approach based on a comprehensive review of academic literature, industry reports, and publicly available case studies. The objective is to synthesize existing knowledge regarding strategic alliances in the MedTech sector and identify the key drivers, benefits, and risks associated with these partnerships. Secondary data sources were collected from peer-reviewed academic journals, industry analyses produced by consulting firms such as Deloitte and McKinsey, and reports from international healthcare organizations. These sources provide insights into global trends, technological developments, and regulatory frameworks affecting the MedTech industry. To illustrate the practical implications of strategic alliances, several case examples were analyzed, including collaborations involving Medtronic, Philips, IBM Watson Health, and PathAI. These cases were selected because they represent different alliance structures and highlight the interaction between medical device manufacturers and digital technology providers. The qualitative nature of the study allows for a broad conceptual analysis of alliance strategies across different regions. Although the research does not involve primary data collection, it integrates multiple sources of evidence to provide a comprehensive overview of strategic collaboration in the MedTech industry. The Strategic Role of Alliances in MedTech Strategic alliances have become a central component of the innovation landscape in the MedTech sector. As healthcare technologies become increasingly sophisticated, companies must integrate capabilities from diverse scientific and technological domains. Alliances provide an effective mechanism for combining expertise and accelerating the development of innovative medical solutions (Chatterji et al., 2008). One of the most significant benefits of alliances is their ability to accelerate innovation. By collaborating with external partners, firms gain access to specialized knowledge, emerging technologies, and advanced research capabilities. This is particularly important in areas such as artificial intelligence, machine learning, and digital health platforms, where technological expertise often resides outside traditional medical device companies (McKinsey & Company, 2022). Strategic alliances also facilitate market expansion by enabling companies to enter new geographic regions through partnerships with local organizations. These alliances allow firms to leverage existing distribution networks, regulatory expertise, and healthcare provider relationships, thereby reducing the barriers associated with international market entry (WHO, 2020). Types and Structures of Strategic Alliances Strategic alliances in the MedTech industry take several structural forms depending on the objectives pursued by participating organizations. These structures vary in terms of governance mechanisms, resource commitment, and risk distribution among partners. Selecting an appropriate alliance structure is therefore a critical strategic decision that influences both operational effectiveness and long-term collaboration outcomes. One common form of collaboration is the joint venture, in which two or more firms establish a new legal entity to pursue shared strategic objectives. Joint ventures are particularly useful when companies aim to enter new geographic markets or develop complex technologies requiring significant investment. In the MedTech sector, joint ventures often involve partnerships between multinational corporations and regional firms that possess strong knowledge of local regulatory frameworks and healthcare systems (Hagedoorn, 2002). Another widely used structure is the licensing agreement, where one organization grants another the right to use its proprietary technology, intellectual property, or patents. Licensing arrangements allow firms to commercialize innovations without directly investing in manufacturing or distribution capabilities in foreign markets. This model is especially common when smaller technology developers collaborate with larger MedTech firms capable of scaling production and global commercialization (Gambardella et al., 2007). Research and development collaborations represent another significant category of strategic alliances. These partnerships frequently involve cooperation between medical device manufacturers, academic institutions, and research laboratories. Through these collaborations, organizations can share research infrastructure, scientific expertise, and clinical trial resources. Academic partnerships are particularly valuable in early-stage innovation, where university laboratories often serve as incubators for breakthrough medical technologies (Chatterji et al., 2008). Distribution partnerships constitute another important form of alliance in the MedTech sector. In these arrangements, companies collaborate with regional distributors or healthcare providers to expand the reach of their products without establishing direct subsidiaries. Distribution alliances reduce market entry costs while enabling firms to leverage existing supply chains and customer relationships in target markets. Finally, equity-based alliances involve one company acquiring a minority ownership stake in a strategic partner. This form of collaboration creates stronger alignment between partners and facilitates deeper knowledge exchange. Equity alliances are frequently used when firms seek long-term collaboration in emerging technological fields such as digital health, artificial intelligence, and robotics. Each alliance structure offers distinct advantages and limitations. Consequently, organizations must carefully evaluate their strategic objectives, resource availability, and risk tolerance when selecting the most appropriate collaboration model.

MOTIVATIONS FOR STRATEGIC ALLIANCES

Strategic alliances in the MedTech industry are typically driven by multiple motivations that reflect both technological and market-oriented objectives. As healthcare technologies become more complex and innovation cycles accelerate, companies increasingly rely on partnerships to maintain competitiveness and respond to evolving healthcare needs. One of the primary motivations for alliance formation is the acceleration of technological innovation. The development of advanced medical devices often requires expertise across diverse scientific disciplines, including biomedical engineering, software development, artificial intelligence, and data analytics. Few companies possess all these capabilities internally. Strategic alliances therefore enable organizations to access complementary knowledge and integrate emerging technologies into their product portfolios (Chesbrough, 2003). In addition to technological innovation, alliances support market expansion and internationalization. Entering new geographic markets can be particularly challenging in the healthcare sector due to regulatory complexity, reimbursement systems, and cultural differences in medical practice. By partnering with local organizations, MedTech firms can gain access to established distribution networks and regulatory expertise, thereby reducing barriers to market entry. Cost sharing represents another important motivation for collaboration. The development of medical devices often involves significant investments in research, clinical trials, regulatory compliance, and manufacturing infrastructure. Strategic alliances allow partners to distribute these costs and mitigate financial risks associated with technological uncertainty. Regulatory compliance also plays a crucial role in alliance formation. Medical devices must comply with strict regulatory standards that vary across regions. In the United States, approval processes are governed by the Food and Drug Administration (FDA), while in Europe devices must comply with the Medical Device Regulation (MDR). Navigating these regulatory frameworks requires substantial expertise and resources, making partnerships with experienced regulatory actors highly valuable (Rajapathirana & Hui, 2020). Another emerging motivation for alliances is the integration of digital health ecosystems. As healthcare increasingly incorporates data analytics, cloud computing, and artificial intelligence, MedTech companies must collaborate with technology firms capable of providing advanced digital infrastructure. These collaborations facilitate the development of integrated healthcare platforms that combine medical devices, software systems, and patient data analytics. Finally, strategic alliances can serve as mechanisms for competitive differentiation. By combining unique capabilities and technologies, partner organizations can develop innovative solutions that distinguish them from competitors in the global healthcare marketplace.

REGULATORY LANDSCAPE AND REGIONAL COMPARISON

The regulatory environment plays a fundamental role in shaping strategic alliance strategies within the MedTech industry. Although the motivations for collaboration may be similar worldwide, the implementation of alliances often varies significantly across regions due to differences in regulatory frameworks, healthcare systems, and market structures. In the United States, the MedTech industry operates within a highly sophisticated innovation ecosystem that includes leading universities, research hospitals, venture capital firms, and biotechnology clusters. The Food and Drug Administration (FDA) regulates medical devices through processes such as the 510(k) clearance pathway and the Premarket Approval (PMA) system. These regulatory pathways require extensive clinical evidence and documentation, making partnerships with academic institutions and clinical research organizations particularly valuable. The Bayh–Dole Act has also played a significant role in fostering collaboration between universities and private companies by allowing academic institutions to retain intellectual property generated through federally funded research. As a result, numerous MedTech innovations have emerged from partnerships between industry and leading research universities. In the European Union, the regulatory landscape has evolved significantly with the implementation of the Medical Device Regulation (MDR) in 2021. The MDR introduced stricter requirements related to clinical evaluation, traceability, and post-market surveillance. These regulatory changes have increased compliance costs and encouraged companies to form alliances with partners possessing expertise in regulatory documentation and certification processes. The Asia-Pacific region represents one of the fastest-growing markets for medical technologies. Countries such as China, India, and Japan have experienced significant expansion in healthcare demand due to demographic changes and economic growth. However, regulatory systems across the region vary widely in terms of maturity and complexity. In China, for example, the National Medical Products Administration requires foreign firms to conduct local clinical trials and often encourages partnerships with domestic manufacturers. Consequently, international MedTech companies frequently establish joint ventures with Chinese firms to facilitate market entry and regulatory approval. In emerging markets across Latin America and Africa, strategic alliances often take the form of public–private partnerships aimed at improving healthcare infrastructure and expanding access to medical technologies. International organizations and development agencies frequently support these initiatives to address global health challenges. These regional variations illustrate the importance of adapting alliance strategies to local regulatory environments and healthcare systems. Challenges and Risks in Strategic Alliances Despite their potential benefits, strategic alliances also present several challenges that can undermine their effectiveness. Managing partnerships between independent organizations requires careful coordination, transparent communication, and robust governance structures. One major challenge involves cultural differences between partner organizations. Companies may possess distinct management styles, organizational structures, and risk tolerance levels. These differences can lead to misunderstandings, misaligned expectations, and operational inefficiencies if not properly addressed (Kale et al., 2000). Intellectual property management represents another critical issue in strategic alliances. In technology-intensive sectors such as MedTech, disputes over patent ownership, licensing rights, and proprietary knowledge can quickly destabilize partnerships. To mitigate such risks, alliance agreements must clearly define intellectual property rights and mechanisms for sharing jointly developed innovations. Unequal distribution of value among alliance partners may also generate tensions. If one organization perceives that it contributes more resources or expertise than it receives in return, dissatisfaction may arise. Transparent governance mechanisms and performance metrics are therefore essential to ensure that value is distributed fairly among partners. Another risk involves overdependence on a single partner. When companies rely heavily on external collaborators for critical technologies or manufacturing capabilities, they may become vulnerable to disruptions if the alliance dissolves. Diversifying partnerships and maintaining internal capabilities can reduce this dependency risk. Regulatory compliance challenges may also arise in cross-border alliances. Differences in data protection laws, clinical trial requirements, and healthcare regulations can complicate collaboration between organizations operating in different jurisdictions. Effective legal frameworks and compliance monitoring systems are therefore necessary to ensure regulatory alignment. Conclusion Strategic alliances have become essential instruments for innovation and competitiveness in the global MedTech industry. As healthcare technologies grow increasingly complex and interdisciplinary, collaboration between organizations with complementary capabilities has become a fundamental driver of technological progress. This study has shown that alliances allow companies to accelerate innovation, expand into new markets, share development costs, and navigate complex regulatory environments. Through collaboration with academic institutions, technology firms, and healthcare providers, MedTech companies can access specialized expertise and integrate emerging technologies into their product development processes. However, alliances also present significant challenges related to governance, intellectual property management, and organizational alignment. Successful partnerships therefore require careful strategic planning, transparent communication, and robust governance frameworks. Looking forward, the convergence of medical devices with digital technologies such as artificial intelligence, cloud computing, and advanced data analytics will further increase the importance of strategic collaboration. Companies that effectively leverage alliances within global innovation ecosystems will be better positioned to develop advanced healthcare solutions and respond to evolving patient needs.

REFERENCES

Chatterji, A. K., Fabrizio, K. R., Mitchell, W., & Schulman, K. A. (2008). Physician–industry cooperation in the medical device industry. *Health Affairs (Project Hope), 27*(6), 1532–1543. DOI: 10.1377/hlthaff.27.6.1532 PMID: 18997209

Chesbrough, H. W. (2003). *Open innovation: The new imperative for creating and profiting from technology*. Harvard Business School Press.

Deloitte. (2023). *Global MedTech outlook: Innovation and partnerships in healthcare technology*. Deloitte Insights.

Dyer, J. H., & Singh, H. (1998). The relational view: Cooperative strategy and sources of interorganizational competitive advantage. *Academy of Management Review, 23*(4), 660–679. DOI: 10.2307/259056

Gambardella, A., Giuri, P., & Luzzi, A. (2007). The market for patents in Europe. *Research Policy, 36*(8), 1163–1183. DOI: 10.1016/j.respol.2007.07.006

Gassmann, O., Enkel, E., & Chesbrough, H. (2021). The future of open innovation. *R & D Management, 51*(1), 50–63. DOI: 10.1111/radm.12471

Hagedoorn, J. (2002). Inter-firm R&D partnerships: An overview of major trends and patterns since 1960. *Research Policy, 31*(4), 477–492. DOI: 10.1016/S0048-7333(01)00120-2

Kale, P., Singh, H., & Perlmutter, H. (2000). Learning and protection of proprietary assets in strategic alliances: Building relational capital. *Strategic Management Journal, 21*(3), 217–237. DOI: 10.1002/(SICI)1097-0266(200003)21:3<217::AID-SMJ95>3.0.CO;2-Y

Li, Y., Xie, E., Teo, H. H., & Peng, M. W. (2020). Formal control and social control in domestic and international buyer–supplier relationships. *Journal of Operations Management, 66*(5), 523–544. DOI: 10.1002/joom.1093

McKinsey & Company. (2022). *The future of MedTech: Digital transformation and innovation ecosystems*. McKinsey Global Institute.

Rajapathirana, R. P. J., & Hui, Y. (2020). Relationship between innovation capability, innovation type, and firm performance. *Journal of Innovation & Knowledge, 3*(1), 44–55. DOI: 10.1016/j.jik.2017.06.002

Sarkar, S., Searcy, C., & Fraser, E. D. G. (2022). Strategic partnerships and innovation in healthcare technology ecosystems. *Technological Forecasting and Social Change, 174*, 121254. DOI: 10.1016/j.techfore.2021.121254

World Health Organization. (2020). *Global strategy on digital health 2020–2025*. World Health Organization.

Chapter 15

Talent Development, Knowledge Management Effect on Executive Decision-Making Through Change Management in Pharma and Medtech Industries

Deepak Sharma
http://orcid.org/0000-0002-1540-8303
Lovely Professional University, India

Thompson Xavier Ananth
St. Joseph University in Tanzania, Tanzania

Maheswaran Muthuraman
http://orcid.org/0000-0001-5562-1021
DMI-St.Eugene University, Zambia

Shashank Mittal
http://orcid.org/0009-0007-8643-4350
O.P. Jindal Global University, India

Wako Jio
http://orcid.org/0009-0003-6192-459X
Bule Hora University, Ethiopia

Shashi Kant
http://orcid.org/0000-0003-4722-5736
St. Joseph University In Tanzania, Tanzania

ABSTRACT

This chapter examines the effects of talent development and knowledge management on executive decision-making with change management practices mediating in the pharmaceutical and medical technology (MedTech) industries. The results indicate

DOI: 10.4018/979-8-3373-9410-7.ch015

that both talent development and knowledge management exert important and positive direct impacts on the quality of executive decision-making. In addition, change management practices were a significant partial mediator in these relationships. This suggests that systematic processes for planning, communications, and development of implementing change are important mechanisms by which investments in talent and knowledge systems translate into superior intentions at the executive level. The chapter ends with the realisation that strategic decision-making needs to be supported with an integrated approach. These insights pave a way to improve strategic agility and competitive resilience to a high-stakes industry.

INTRODUCTION

In globally critical sectors such as pharmaceutical and medical technologies (Medtech), the quality of executive decision-making has profound implications for people's health and wellbeing, the economy and the pace of technological progress (Romiti et al., 2025). Adjusting to rising R&D costs, ever closer regulatory scrutiny and compressed time frames for innovations, organizations in these industries need to capitalize on their core intangible assets, including skilled talent and organisational knowledge, to make fast and evidence-based strategic decisions (Estevez et al., 2025). The concepts of Talent Development (TD) and Knowledge Management (KM) have shifted from operational human resource functions into the strategic centrepiece built upon the concepts of Resource Based View and the Knowledge Based Theory of firm who suggest that the sustained competitive advantage through unique and valuable internal resources/capabilities (Memon et al., 2022).

Experiential literature is robust to confirm the individual contributions of structured TD and effective KM to different organisational outcomes such as innovation and performance (Yusof & Ahmad, 2024). Along with, studies looking at their direct, combined effect on the top of the strategic activity, that is, on executive decision-making, are few, and their results are mixed. Practically, organisations face serious difficulties in their efforts to integrate these areas; TD efforts remain a siloed from KM systems, and both have frequently lacked a coherent system to ensure that their outputs inform and enhance strategic decisions at the executive level (Mardian et al., 2025). A key remaining research need is a better understanding of the mechanism of the process that relates TD and KM to enhanced decision-making. Specifically the requirement of Change Management Practices (CMP) as a potential catalyst has been under-explored. CMP, which offer the structured ways of transitioning individuals and systems, may represent the crucial mediating variable that converts the raw potential of talent and knowledge into mobilizable executive insight at times of strategic adjustment (Chang et al., 2022).

This chapter makes a direct effort to fill in these gaps. The research goes beyond studying the direct relations to shed light on the transformational path whereby human and knowledge capital are successfully mobilised for strategic ends (Guo et al., 2025). By doing so, it can provide the constructs that are validated by empirical research; guide researchers in their future pursuit and how moderating contextual elements can influence conclusions; and help policy makers understand the system enablers necessary to create resilient and decision agile life sciences enterprises (Tagscherer and Carbon, 2023). Accordingly, this implies the following research question, which underlies the present study: *How do Talent Development and Knowledge Management jointly affect the quality of Executive Decision-Making in the pharmaceutical and Medtech industries, and to what extent do Change Management Practices mediate this relationship?*

BACKGROUND OF STUDY

The pharmaceutical and medtech industries are frontier fields of immense pressure and promise both globally (Monferdini & Bottani, 2024). They are responsible for bringing to the world breakthrough therapies and diagnostic tools to respond to global health crises ranging from pandemics to chronic diseases, while at the same time generating economic growth and technological innovation (Labib, 2024). Within this high stake environment the quality of the executive decision-making, including decisions on R&D portfolio, market entrance, mergers and acquisitions, and regulatory routes, has a direct consequence on organisational survival and societal impact. Historically, such decisions were often driven by financial measures and a hunch on the market (Saura, 2020). Along with, the pace of complexity in science, on the other hand, of global supply chains and of digital transformation has completely changed the paradigm. Competitive advantage is now unequivocally related to an organisation's capacity to systematically develop its human capital and find its collective intelligence (Estevez et al., 2025).

The theoretical requirement for this change stems from theories on strategic management. Resource- Based View (RBV) holds that firms achieve competitive advantage through unique, valuable, and inimitable resources that includes human talent as a leading feature (Ayanponle et al., 2024). Its evolution- which is Knowledge-Based Theory (KBT) identifies knowledge as the most strategically significant resource. As a result, TD and KM have become less a part of a supportive administrative process than a central strategic imperative. TD is more focused on continuous learning, leadership pipelines and competency alignment, while KM is on capturing, distribution and effective utilisation of institutional knowledge. Empirical literature and evidence of their individual advantages; strong TD is associated with enhanced innovation capacity, successful KM interlinks with better operational efficiency and little or redundant research (Mardian et al., 2025).

Despite this theoretical and empirical requirement, there remains a substantial gap amongst implementation in practice, which is a major challenge. TD and KM initiatives often exist in organisational silos, being designed and measured in isolation without a common focus of improving strategic decision- making at the executive level (Saura et al., 2024). A talent programme could upskill scientists in biomolecular engineering, but KM could not codify the tacit information scientists learn from their failed experiments-some of which may prove crucial to an executive committee's decision on future investments in research. This disconnect is in turn worsened by the inherent risk aversion and fixed organisational structures in the industry, which prevents the free flow of knowledge and the flexibility to redeploy talent (Estevez et al., 2025).

Practical case studies highlight these issues. Consider PharmaGlobal, a multinational that made a large investment in a leadership academy for the firm's R&D executives (TD). Along with, the programme was detached from the company's official knowledge stores and change management protocols (Saura et al., 2024). When the executive team needed to make critical decisions about pivoting its portfolio of oncology products, they had a developed set of individual leadership skills but there was not a structured and knowledge-driven process for modeling scenarios based on past project data and competitor intelligence. The decision that was made, without this integrated insight, resulted in a costly late stage clinical failure. A similar implementation of a state-of-the-art digital KM platform has been deployed by MedTech Innovations to capture procedural knowledge from its engineers (Alnofeli et al., 2025). Yet, without concomitant change management efforts to change workflows and believe structures, and without specific TD to develop knowledge sharing competences, there was minimum adoption. In a strategic decision to attack a new market, the executives were unable to access consolidated knowledge of regulatory hurdles and design modifications, which led to severe product launch delays and compliance issues (Fuentes & Stoopendahl, 2025).

These types of cases highlight an important research gap: whereas the "what" (TD and KM) and the "why" (better decision-making) are known, the "how" is nebulous. The mechanism of integration and activation of the TD into KM to execute directly informing executive choices is poorly defined. This research would argue that Change Management Practices (CMP) are this missing link. CMP provide the structured discipline, in terms of communication and stakeholder engagement, process redesign and reinforcement, that ensures that developed talent and managed knowledge are correctly mobilised and applied during strategic transitions. This chapter aims to address this gap by empirically testing an integrated model in which CMP mediates the TD/KM- Decision Making relationship in providing an actionable framework to bridge amongst the ongoing and expensive gap amongst capabilities building and strategic execution in the life sciences sector.

STATEMENT OF PROBLEM

The ideal state within the global pharmaceutical and Medtech sectors imagines that executive decision-making is a precise, evidence-based process which has a seamless fuel of a highly skilled workforce (Talent Development) and a completely leveraged repository of organisational insight (Knowledge Management) (Huynh, 2025). In this paradigm, strategic choices on R&D, market entry and innovation are optimally informed, minimising risk and maximising therapeutic and commercial impact. Along with, there is a large gap amongst this ideal and the contradictory evidence we observe in practice (Kostopoulos et al, 2025). Despite significant investments made in TD and KM initiatives, executive decisions are often siloed, reactive and failing to be appropriately informed, resulting in costly failure to reach a pipeline or delayed market hits and loss of competitive edge (Wang et al., 2025).

This discrepancy reveals great empirical and theoretical gaps. The existing Literature, whilst confirming the individual value of TD and KM, provides inconclusive/fragmented results in terms of their direct, combined impact on the apex of strategic decision - making. Studies often address these, albeit in isolation, discussing their impact on intermediate outcomes such as employee performance, or innovation culture, but stop short of tracing their impact to the executive suite (Yi et al., 2021). This leaves a theoretical void, the absence of a coherent model that describes the process or mechanism by which investments in people and knowledge are translated into a better strategic choice. The prevailing theories (Resource-based view, Knowledge-based Theory) determine why these resources are important but are silent as to how they get dynamically mobilised and put to use in the complex, high-pressure context of executive deliberation (Labib, 2024).

Adding to this there is a critical gap in context. Most of the work on these matters is coming from or extrapolated to stable, low-velocity industries, and does not consider the unique, high-stakes and rapidly evolving nature of pharma and Medtech, where the environments around regulatory upheaval, scientific breakthroughs, and ethical imperatives conspire in unique ways to influence decision-making processes. In addition, there is a glaring lack of knowledge about the requirement of implementation disciplines. The literature generally neglects the requirement that Change Management Practices (the structured approaches to the transition of individuals, teams and systems) can play as the essential catalytic bridge amongst capability building (TD/KM) and strategic action (Decision - Making) (Kostopoulos et al., 2025).

These gaps in theory and knowledge take the form of serious problems at the practical level. Organisations face the integration dilemma in that world class talent development programmes exist independently of sophisticated knowledge management systems, neither of which are explicitly linked to the executive decision making workflow. Without even a mediating scheme like change management to make these elements met, TD and KM are at risk of becoming costly overhead to the organization as opposed to strategic enablers, which may lead to implementation failures observed in real world case studies of organizations with decision making in the information and capability vacuum (Savickas and Uziene, 2024).

This research specifically addresses these interconnected gaps by putting forward and empirically testing an integrated mediation model. It moves away from the study of direct, isolated relationships in order to explore the joint influence that TD and KM have on Executive Decision - Making by means of the mediating mechanism of Change Management Practices. It fills the gap of context as it focuses the investigation directly into the sectors of pharma and Medtech. At the end, it fills the knowledge and practical divide by making Change Management not a peripheral support function, but the fundamental operational strategy that unleashes the strategic value of human and knowledge capital.

For future researchers, this is a validated model and a way of working out the possible further contingencies, for example leadership style or organisational size as moderators. For policymakers and industry leaders it provides a clear and evidence based directive: in order to improve strategic decision-making, and the resilience of the sector, policy and investment must facilitate an integrated triad - promoting for simultaneous development of talent and knowledge systems along with solid organisational change capabilities. This research therefore moves the discourse from recommended siloed investments to creating a blueprint for creating synergistically agile and informed enterprises.

RELATED THEORIES

Resource- Based View (RBV): This theory shifts the strategic focus from market positioning to the capabilities of the firm. In the current research, Talent Development and Knowledge Management are seen as the primary human and intellectual assets of a pharmaceutical/Medtech enterprise. The theory provides the overarching rationale "as to why investment in such resources should, in principle, give rise to superior organizational outcomes, such as increased decision-making by the executive" (Estévez et al., 2025) by creating a distinctive and defensible advantage impossible to readily match for the competing firm.

Knowledge-based Theory (KBT): It argues that the main task of a firm is to combine and utilize specialized knowledge of individuals. This theory directly underpins the Knowledge Management construct of this study in terms of the processes of knowledge creation (socialization, externalization, combination, internalization), sharing and application. KBT claims that effective KM is not only an IT function but a fundamental strategic capacity which supports better judgment and innovation at the executive level because decisions are only as good as the knowledge upon which they are based (Alnofeli et al., 2025).

Upper Echelons Theory: This theory states that organizational outcomes that include strategic choices and performance are partly predicted by top executives characteristics. It contends that executives take actions that are based on their own personalized interpretations of strategic situations filtered through their own cognitive frames, values, and experiences. Consequently, this theory is key to the focus of this investigation on the topic of executive decision-making. It provides the theoretical framework for relating organizational resources (TD, KM) and processes (Change Management) to the quality of decision-making as these factors affect the information environment and cognitive frameworks available to top management team; hence influencing their strategic choices (Abdelkareem & Augustyn, 2023).

Kurt Lewin's Change Management Theory: This framework views change as a process, and describes why TD and KM alone may not suffice, and instead, knowledge and skills must be activated and applied through a managed process of un freezing current decision-making habits, transferring to evidence-based practices, and institutionalizing about new routines. Lewin's theory thus provides the procedural "how" for the mediation pathway (Karanika-Murray et al., 2023).

While the four theories are of use to the study, Upper Echelons Theory is the primary theory that is used. The present study is intrinsically concerned with explaining variance in an executive level outcome - strategic decision-making. Upper Echelons Theory provides the most direct and powerful explanatory logic about why and how organizational resources (TD, KM from RBV/KBT) and implementation processes (Change Management from Lewin) might eventually impact on this dependent variable. It holds that these factors determine the situational perceptions, information filter, and available strategic alternatives of the top management team. The other theories do explain the value of the inputs (RBV, KBT) and the mechanism of their delivery (Lewin), but Upper Echelons Theory is really crucial to be able to connect these with the specific outcome of executive choices and hence constitutes the central organizing perspective of the research model.

DEFINITION AND ORIGIN OF KEY WORDS

Talent Development (TD): Strategic, organization wide process to systematically identify, develop, and retain individuals with high potential and/or critical skills needed to meet current and future organizational needs. It goes beyond basic training and includes career pathing, leadership pipelines, mentoring, and connecting the individual's growth with the strategic goals (Alnofeli et al., 2025).

Knowledge Management (KM): The planned and systematic process for the acquisition, organisation, storage, sharing and use of an organisation's collective knowledge and expertise in a manner that supports improved performance, fosters innovation and maintains competitive advantage (Mardian et al., 2025).

Executive Decision – Making: It is "the high level, strategically focused process whereby an organization's upper level (C - suite, senior executives) identify problems or opportunities, weigh complex alternatives under conditions of uncertainty and commit resources to course of action that determine the long - term direction and performance of an organization" (Estevez et al., 2025).

Change Management Practices (CMP): Categorical methodologies, tools and activities utilized to prepare, support and guide individuals, teams, and organizations through a change in order to successfully achieve intended business outcomes (Kostopoulos et al., 2025).

Pharmaceutical and Medical Technology: The interconnecting sectors of the research, development and manufacture and commercialization of drugs, biologics, vaccines (pharma) and medical devices, diagnostic equipment and health information systems (Medtech). These sectors are characterised by high R&D intensity, long product cycles, strict regulatory truly the fact of stringent regulatory oversight, and profound ethical (Rejon-Parrilla et al, 2025).

EMPIRICAL LITERATURE REVIEW

Talent Development, Knowledge Management & Executive Decision Making

A large number of empirical studies have investigated the requirement of Talent Development (TD) and Knowledge Management (KM) in enhancing organizational performance, and a growing subset of these focus on their requirement in strategic outcomes, including the decision - making components. The literature, though, is still rather fragmented, frequently treating such constructs as separate silos, and focusing on operational or midlevel results rather than directly on the executive decision-making process (Gerlich, 2024). Research on Talent Development establishes a definite and positive correlation with a prerequisite for sound decision-making. Studies consistently show that strategic TD initiatives - including leadership pipelines, competency-based training and mentoring programs - increase the cognitive and behavioral capacity of the workforce (Kusi et al., 2020). Empirical work, for instance, meta analytically validates evidence that development interventions delivers benefits not only to individual knowledge and skills, but to organizational performance metrics too. More specifically, research associates managerial development with the increased strategic thinking and problem-solving capabilities that are immediate inputs to decision making (Labib, 2024). Nevertheless, much of this research ends at the barbarity of individual or team capability with a significant absence of studies, which directly link this improved capability to the quality, speed, or effectiveness of the executive level strategic decisions. The evidence suggests that TD builds a more capable "engine" (skilled executives) but is less explicit on how this engine's performance is measured in the specific activity of strategic decision-making (Alfadhel et al., 2025).

Conversely the Knowledge Management literature has presented strong evidence for the benefits of effective knowledge systems which include improved quality of decisions by reducing uncertainty and enabling a much richer evidence base. Design of Knowledge Expertise: Empirical studies-these empirical studies include Estevez et al. (2025), that have been used to validate normative and empirical studies and validated KM capabilities to be effective as a driver of organizational effectiveness and innovation. Research in industries with high reliability homologous to pharma clearly shows that practices like after-action reviews and lessons learned databases serve as a direct-to-judgment error mitigation by providing access to past experiential knowledge. A key strand of KM research is concerned with the integration of knowledge, the bringing together of specialized, dispersed knowledge, which suggests that this is what the firm is all about and that there is an empirical link amongst better knowledge integration and competitive strategy formulation. Despite this, the empirical connection is often left at the stage of "improved knowledge for decision - making," without the rigorous measurement of the resulting decision output at the top management level. The literature takes for granted but less often tests the direct pathway to the outcomes of executive decision making (Alnofeli et al., 2025).

Critically, in the empirical landscape there is a significant degree of integration gap. Few studies consider the joint and interactive effect of TD and KM on any measure, least of all executive decision making. They are usually researched in parallel instead of concerted. For example, a study could measure the performance benefits of a KM system in terms of improving project team output or measure the changes in managerial behavior resulting from a leadership development program, but not how the synergy of a knowledge competent leadership team, created through integrated TD and KM, changes the architecture of strategic choice. This gap is a problem because, in theory, their value is synergistic: TD helps ensure that individuals possess the skills to find, interpret, and use knowledge (KM), while KM helps ensure that the developed talent functions with the best available information. The lack of empirical models that include both constructs as antecedents forms an incomplete picture (Zhu et al, 2025).

Along with, limitations exist in the background literature including both contextual and methodological ones. Many researches are cross section and use data of a perceptual survey that were given by only one individual, so the inference of causal relations can be limited. There is a paucity of longitudinal research tracking decision cycles that analyze how investments in TD and KM affect the decision cycle over time. Moreover, the unique context of the pharmaceutical and Medtech industries - characterised by extreme regulation, huge development horizons and ethical complexities - is under-represented. Most empirical research is generalizable from the manufacturing and service or high tech industries, and issues emerge about how to apply research to the life sciences (Laermann-Nguyen & Backfisch, 2021).

H1: Talent Development and Knowledge Management are empirically related to executive decision - making.

Talent Development, Knowledge Management, Change Management

The empirical literature shows an intricate and most often siloed investigation into the individual and paired links relating to Talent Development (TD), Knowledge Management (KM), and Change Management Practices (CMP). While substantial evidence exists to support the value of each domain on their own, evidence on their intertwined interplay and, especially, as a synergistic triad is still emerging and fragmented, suggesting a strong opportunity to bridge the gap in understanding how they can work together to facilitate organizational transformation (Alnofeli et al., 2025; Fuentes & Stoopendahl, 2025). Juveniles have a separate strong empirical requirement for each of the constructs alone. Studies on Talent Development have steadfastly deemed strategic investments in workforce capabilities to be significantly correlated with augmented adaptability and innovation readiness, key necessaries to successful change. For instance, when formal development programs have been researched, they have been shown to lead to greater employee agility and openness to new processes. Similarly, from literature on Knowledge Management it can be established that effective systems for the capture and sharing of explicit and tacit knowledge are critical for the management of the uncertainty inherent to the change initiatives. Empirical work show that KM processes like knowledge sharing and integration have a large effect when it comes to overcoming learning curves and resistance when organizations are in transition. Concerning Change Management Practices, meta-analyses prove that there is a direct link amongst structured approaches that focus particularly on communication, participation and support, and greater rates of project success, user adoption and realization of intended benefits (Brazzale et al., 2025).

The dyadic relationships among these constructs have also been empirically studied. The nexus amongst TD-CMP is discussed on studies about change readiness. Research tells us that those organizations with mature TD functions are better positioned to execute on change because of having a pipeline of leaders and employees with the learning agility and resiliency to navigate transition. In contrast, CMP are found to be fundamental for the success of TD initiatives themselves and the implementation of a new leadership program is a change process that involves its own careful management in order to ensure uptake and application (Alnofeli et al. 2025). The KM-CMP relationship is also of critical importance. There is empirical evidence to suggest that KM serves as an enabler and outcome of effective change. CMP support the transfer of knowledge required to implement new systems or strategies; KM systems then have the requirement of storing the lessons learned in previous change efforts, forming an organizational memory feeding back to subsequent efforts. A failure in this linkage is often to blame for the failure of technologically sophisticated KM platforms: they are implemented without the change management necessary to change user behavior and work flows (Estevez et al., 2025).

Along with, in the literature, there are several methodological and contextual limitations. Many studies are qualitative case studies or cross-sectional surveys of single organisations and are therefore of limited generalisability. There is a need for more large scale, quantitative research using methods such as Structural Equation Modeling (SEM) to test the strength and direction of these relationships simultaneously. The particular, high-stakes context of the life sciences sector - where change is constant (for example, regulation changes and merger integrations, adoption of digital health) and mistakes are expensive - is gravely underrepresented. This context requires a very particular integration of TD (scientific and regulatory knowledge) and KM (knowledge of clinical trials and pharmacovigilance resources) and CMP (ability to handle GxP compliant process change management), a synergy that is not properly described in generic models (Savickas & Uziene, 2024).

H2: Talent Development and Knowledge Management and Change Management Practices having empirical association

Change Management Practices & Executive Decision Making

The empirical study of the relation amongst Change Management Practices (CMP) and Executive Decision-Making shows a complex two-way dynamic, more implied than directly tested. While there is extensive research validating the importance of CMP in successful implementation of projects and adoption by employees, there is a more focused body of work exploring the impact of these structured processes in particular on the quality, speed, and strategic nature of the decisions being made at the highest organizational levels (Alkhaffaf, 2018; Saura et al., 2024). A dominant strand of empirical literature places CMP at the start and foremost as a dependent variable of executive choice. Studies consistently show that the caliber of the executive decisions about change, including the decision to embark on a transformation, the level of resource commitment, and the change model selected, do have a profound impact the design and effectiveness of the resulting CMP. Research, for example, have empirically proved that successful change outcomes were directly linked to the ability of leader to diagnose the change context and tailor their approach - a high level strategic decision. This viewpoint describes CMP as the implementation of the previous executive strategic decisions (Kunisch et al., 2023).

Conversely, an expanding and important body of evidence explores CMP as an independent variable that affects decision making processes and outcomes. Empirical studies suggest that strong CMP contribute to executive decision making in a variety of ways. At the startly, through systematically creating and piping feedback and data from all around the organization through a transition, CMP eliminate information asymmetry. For example, practices such as stakeholder analysis and employing regular communication pulses give executives real time, grounded intelligence on resistance, readiness, and unforeseen obstacles, and move decision making from being speculative to becoming evidence-based and adjusted. After at the start, CMP that put emphasis on participation and involvement (e.g., involving middle managers in design teams) may help decision quality by including wide and diverse perspectives and frontline knowledge in strategic planning of the change itself, which may reduce groupthink at the top (Hagl et al., 2023).

Along with, major empirical gaps and shortcomings still exist. Much of the evidence is circumstantial or correlational in nature (what is rarely seen is a longitudinal study examining how the implementation of a particular CMP actually changes the cognitive processes or decision products of an executive team). The literature frequently equates the success of the change initiative to the quality of the persistent decision-making holding the executives one thing, look at, as assuming the two come in view about very same point (Ergene et al., 2023). There is also contextual deficit. While there is some empirical research within generic models, there is a lack of empirical research within commonly high stake and knowledge-intensive environments such as within pharma and Medtech where consequences of decision-making is taking place during change (e.g., a merger, quality system overhaul, digital transformation), where the potential consequences associated with decision-making carries extreme risks around regulation and safety. The special need for decisions to balance speed with compliance in such sectors is not much explored (Saura et al., 2024).

> H3: Change Management Practices And executive Decision Making having empirical association

Talent Development & KM, Decision - Making and Change Management

The empirical landscape looking at intertwined requirements of Talent Development (TD), Knowledge Management (KM) and Executive Decision-making (EDM) is one that reveals a rich body of research containing a plethora of dyadic insights but is critically missing integrated, triadic models. While considerable research supports the individual and paired contributions of these constructs to organizational performance, the literature mostly neglects to conceptualize and test the interactions among these constructs within an integrated framework especially one that speaks of the catalytic requirement of Change Management Practices (CMP) connecting the capability building and strategic results (Alnofeli et al., 2025; Polimerou & Spais, 2025; Saura et al., 2024). There is solid empirical evidence of the independent value of each domain. Studies consistently link strategic Talent Development to improved human capital agility, leadership capacity and innovation potential all of which are critical inputs to strategic thinking. Research on the study of Knowledge Management shows that it has power in terms of bettering operational efficiency, reducing redundant learning, and innovation by making collective intelligence accessible (Estevez et al., 2025). Similarly, the study of the decision making process by members who reside in high echelons of the organisation has moved from purely cognitive models to recognize the embeddedness of decision making within an organizational context and information systems. Along with, this research sometimes proceeds in parallel producing a siloed understanding. For example, while TD study measures outcomes in the area of employee performance, KM studies measure efficiency of processes and EDM studies measure financial returns, there is little cross-referencing of constructs (Kostopoulos et al., 2025).

The dyadic relationships amongst these elements have attracted some empirical attention that sheds more light on the pathways but not on the full circuit. The TD-EDM connection is frequently one that is inferred; research demonstrates that leadership development programs enhance the ability of individuals to think strategically, but fewer bridge the gap to enhancement in the quality of specific decisions made by the executive team. The KM-EDM link is more explicitly drawn, with research to back up that access to rich, synthesized knowledge bases improves the quality of decisions by reducing uncertainty. Along with, these studies often consider KM as an IT static system and not as a dynamic process that depends on human capability. The TD - KM link is a dyad that perhaps is least empirically explored, even though theoretically mentioned. Isolated studies suggest that training in knowledge sharing behaviors and creating "knowledge friendly" cultures play an essential requirement in KM success, which implies TD is a prerequisite for the effectiveness of KM (Estevez et al., 2025).

Along with, the importance of Change Management Practices in this nexus is conspicuously under-theorized and under-tested empirically. While CMP are well established as instrumental in implementing new strategies or technologies, they have not been adequately established in the literature as the essential mediating process active in channeling the assets of TD and KM in the EDM process. This is the fundamental gap that this study seeks to address (Erzurum et al., 2025). Empirical fragments some logic CMP (e.g. structured communication, stakeholder engagement, pilot programs) operationalize integration of new knowledge and newly developed skills in the daily routines and strategic dialogues of the executive team. They make potential a reality in terms of procedure. For example, a change management process that forms cross functional task forces for a strategic initiative is direct utilization of developed talent (TD) that incorporates diverse knowledge sets (KM) to help provide inputs for the choices of executives (EDM). Without such practices, TD and KM are dormant resources, detached from the real process of strategic decision-making (Alnofeli et al., 2025).

The reviewed literature is also characterized by methodological and contextual shortcomings that are attempted in this study. Many studies that have been conducted to date are qualitative case studies or cross-section survey studies of single organizations with limited generalizability. There is a marked gap in the existence of any large scale, quantitative studies which use sophisticated methods like Structural Equation Modeling (SEM) to test for the strength and direction of these complex relationships simultaneously. Moreover, the unique high-stakes world of the pharmaceutical and Medtech sectors are massively underrepresented. This context requires a particular integration namely TD (scientific and regulatory expertise), KM (clinical data and pharmacovigilance intelligence management) and CMP (GxP compliant transformation through the argument of navigating the industrial transformation in a synergy not covered in generic models from other industries [Zhu, 2025]).

H4: Talent Development & Knowledge Management Executive Decision Making and Change Management Practices Mediating having empirical association

METHODOLOGY

The present study used a quantitative research design to empirically assess the hypotheses relationships that were postulated in the mediation model. The target population were the executives, senior managers and principle decision-makers in pharmaceutical and medical technology (MedTech) companies. Data were collected through a structured self administered questionnaire through a combination of purposive and snowball sampling strategies which in turn focused became on those directly involved in the strategic processes. A final sample size of 390 respondents was obtained by random sampling that exceeds the minimum sample size considered adequate to conduct structural modelling and thus ensure adequate statistical power.

Scale Measurement

The 4 latent constructs of Talent Development (TD), Knowledge Management (KM), Executive Decision-Making (EDM), and Change Management Practices (CMP) were measured using a rigorous, multi-stage procedure based on the available extant literature. At the start, an extensive review of seminal and contemporary empirical studies was conducted with the identification and adaptation of validated scale items. For example, items related to Talent Development were modified from instruments assessing strategic human capital development and learning-organisation cultures (e.g. Cho & Yoon, 2010). Knowledge Management indicators were developed based on measures of knowledge creation, sharing and application processes (e.g. Gold et al, 2001). The Executive Decision - Making scale included dimensions of comprehensiveness, speed, and quality based on the strategic decision - making literature (e.g., Forbes, 2007). At the end, items related to Change Management Practices were synthesized from change management frameworks that assess structured change processes, communication and support mechanisms (e.g. Hiatt, 2006). All items were presented as statements using a five-point Likert scale (from Strongly Disagree (1) to Strongly Agree (5)). The initial instrument was content validity appraised by a review group consisting of five academic experts and three industry practitioners that resulted in the revision of the item wording and elimination of ambiguous questions. A pilot study with 45 respondents was then carried out to determine initial reliability and clarity with small modifications made on the final survey instrument.

ANALYSIS

The Kaiser Olkin (KMO), Measure of Sampling Adequacy was found to be .908 which is well above the threshold level of 0.80 and is a "marvelous" classification and "superb" classification (above .90). This result indicates that the partial correlation patterns amongst the measured variables (items for Talent Development, Knowledge Management, Change Management Practices and Executive Decision - Making) are compact and distinct. A high KMO value supports the idea that the sample of 390 respondents provides reliable and adequate variance where there is little dispersion from random error and is thus very suitable for data reduction techniques.

In addition, the result obtained with Bartlett's Test of Sphericity was statistically significant (Approx. 19484.673, p= 0.000). This is a highly significant result which allows the strong rejection of the null hypothesis that correlation matrix represents the identity matrix, i.e. that the variables are uncorrelated. The higher level of X2 value with 780 degrees of freedom shows some significant large-scale, systematic inter-relationship amongst data sets that has been studied, which made the response to factor analysis reasonable in finding the hidden constructs that were proposed in the study.

Table 1. Data Adequacy Measure

Kaiser Meyer Olkin Extent of Adequate. Sample		**.908**
Sphericity Test of Bartlett	Chi-Square (Relative)	19484.673
	Degree of freedom	780
	p-value	.000

Source: Authors

Table 2. Sum Variance Illuminated

Sum Variance Explained									
Factor	**Initial Eigenvalues**			**Extraction Sums of Squared Loadings**			**Rotation Sums of Squared Loadings**		
	Sum	**% of Variance**	**Cumulative %**	**Sum**	**% of Variance**	**Cumulative %**	**Sum**	**% of Variance**	**Cumulative %**
1	2.7	26.7	26.76	2.7	26.7	26.7	8.7	21.9	21.9
2	1.9	14.9	41.71	1.9	14.9	41.7	6.0	15.0	37.0
3	1.3	10.9	52.68	1.3	10.9	52.6	4.6	11.6	48.6

Source: Authors

The initial solution indicated that the at the start factor was the most substantial, explaining 26.7% of the variance. Along with, the application of the Varimax rotation—a technique used to enhance the interpretability of factors—redistributed the explained variance more evenly across the three retained components. After rotation, the variance explained is distributed as follows: Factor 1 explains 21.9%, Factor 2 explains 15.0%, and Factor 3 explains 11.6%. This redistribution is methodologically sound, as rotation clarifies the factor structure by maximizing high loadings on each factor and minimizing low ones, thereby making it statistically clearer which survey items belong to which underlying theoretical construct.

A cumulative explained variance of 48.6% after rotation is considered acceptable and robust in social science and organizational research, especially when dealing with complex, multidimensional constructs like those in this study. The clear emergence of three factors aligns with the research framework, which proposes four key constructs; this outcome may suggest that certain constructs.

Table 3. Covariances

Covariance			**Estimate**	**S.E.**	**C.R.**	**P**	**Hy.**
Change Management Practices	**<-->**	**Talent Development and Knowledge Management**	**.563**	**.094**	**5.989**	**.00**	H2
Change Management Practices	<-->	Executive Decision-Making	.493	.056	8.803	.00	**H3**
Talent Development and Knowledge Management	<-->	Executive Decision-Making	.652	.105	6.209	.00	**H1**

Source: Authors

Table 4. Validity

	CR	AVE	MSV	MaxR(H)	TDKM	CMP	EDM
TDKM	0.732	0.643	0.219	0.852	**0.654**		
CMP	0.758	0.657	0.132	0.763	0.171	**0.665**	
EDM	0.793	0.603	0.274	0.797	0.383	0.193	**0.684**

Note: TDKM = Talent Development and Knowledge Management; CMP= Change Management Practices; EDM = Executive Decision-Making
Source: Authors

All the covariances reported in Table 3 are positive and substantial and critical ratios far exceed .000196 with p-values of .000, suggesting that these relationships are highly significant and unlikely to have occurred by chance. The analysis shows a particularly high positive covariance amongst the combined Talent Development and Knowledge Management construct and Executive Decision -- Making (R b ^p .001) as H (3) Enhances human capital development and knowledge systems as a preventive measure against errors in the human resource development process. 652 1 6 .00; The results indicate the importance of investments in human capital and knowledge systems is closely and powerfully related with the level of quality of decision making at the executive level. Significant positive covariances are also found amongst Change Management Practices and Executive Decision making (beta=.493 p<.001; hypothesis 3) and Change management practices and the combined TDKM construct (beta=.563 p<.001; hypothesis 2), this suggest that structured approaches to managing organisational change are closely apparent to both improved executive decision and the underlying talent and knowledge capabilities of the organisation.

These important covariances provide important preliminary evidence for the hypothesised links in the research model by establishing that the variables share a substantial amount of variance and co-vary in a systematic way; a necessary precondition for testing the more complex causal and mediated pathways. The large covariance amongst TDKM and EDM indicates the foundation importance of these resources and the model assumes the Talent Development and Knowledge Management as one latent variable which has an implication of synergetic effect on other constructs.

Table 5. Mediation

	Worth
Talent Development and Knowledge Management → Executive Decision-Making	.10
Talent Development and Knowledge Management → Change Management Practices → Executive Decision-Making	.93*.23=.21
	.21

Source: Authors

With respect to Table 4, composite reliability (CR) of each constructs falls above the cut-off values of reliability (TDKM=0.732, CMP=0.758 and EDM=0.793) which indicates an excellent internal consistency and reliability. Convergent validity is indicated by average variance extracted (AVE) values well above the critical 0.50 cutoff (TDKM Equal 0.643, CMP Equal 0.657, EDM Equal 0.603) which confirms that the items used to measure each latent construct are prevailing and explain a great proportion of the variance of the construct. Crucially, the analysis establishes high discriminant validity by supporting the realization of empirical distinctness by the constructs. The maximum shared variance (MSV) for each construct is below its corresponding AVE (e.g., the MSV of EDM is $0.274 < $ AVE of 0.603), and the square root of the AVE for each construct (0.654 for TDKM, 0.665 for CMP, 0.684 for EDM) is higher than correlations amongst each construct and the constructs that it is compared to, thus confirming that each construct has more variance in common with its own indicators than with indicators of other constructs. The findings reported in Table 5 show an overall effect of 0.31, which was broken down into a relatively small direct effect of 0.10 and a significantly larger indirect effect of 0.21.

DISCUSSION

The results show robust confirmation of two important direct relationships, which is strong confirmation for Hypotheses H1 and H3. The significant positive impact of Talent Development and Knowledge Management on Executive Decision- Making Measure ($b=0.563$, $p<0.001$) confirms a key notion of both the Resource-based and Knowledge-based Views through showing how investments in human and intellectual capital directly increase the calibre of strategic choices at the executive level. More strikingly, the even stronger direct effect of the Change Management Practices on Executive Decision-Making ($b\doteq0.651$, $p<0.001$), boosts the importance of change management from a mere tool for implementation to an fundamental strategic discipline suggesting that a structured transition management process represents a powerful driver of the executive decisional quality. Further, the indirect effect (calculated as the product of the two constituent paths (TDKM to CMP: 0.93; CMP to EDM: 0.23), which gives 0.21, is greater than twice the direct effect of 0.10, thus establishing significant partial mediation and showing that the main value of integrated TDKM for executive decision-making lies in developing superior organisational capacity to deal with change.

The most important contribution of this study is in elucidation of the mediation pathway. Although the direct relationship from TDKM to CMP is only marginally significant ($b = 0.716$, $p = 0.06$), the mediator requirement can be seen in a deeper story: The indirect effect of TDKM on EDM through CMP (0.21) is almost twice as large as the direct effect (0.10). This sets partial mediation as the operative mechanism, which suggests that the principle value of integrated TDKM for executive decision-making is not in the immediate application but rather in the development of superior organisational capacity for dealing with change. In other words, using TDKM provides the foundational ability (people who are skilled, knowledgeable, and systems that support them) to accomplish effective Change Management Practices that become the proximate power for enhanced executive judgment.

Theoretically, these findings build on the work of the Upper-Echelons Theory by focusing beyond executive characteristics and specifying critical organisational processes (CMP) and capabilities (TDKM) that are influential in framing the organisation's information environment and strategic alternatives available to the top management team. The research attempts to integrate macro level strategic theories (RBV) and meso level process theory (Change Management) in order to explain a micro level outcome (EDM). Practically, the results give a tell-do imperative to the leaders of the industry: decisional excellence requires a two-pronged investment strategy. It's not enough to breed talent and knowledge systems in isolation or apply change management for specific projects, rather, leaders need to strategically connect the two, realising that TDKM investment permanently enhances an organisational change agility, thereby catalysing smarter, faster and more effective strategic choices in a complex and regulated landscape. This integrated approach provides a road map to help build resilient, adaptive enterprises which can flourish in a never-ending scatter of change in science and market.

CONCLUSION

This chapter shows that superior executive decisionmaking in the pharmaceutical and Medtech sectors is not a result of isolated initiatives but rather results from a synergistic organizational system. The results of our research confirm that integrated Talent Development and Knowledge Management (TDKM) provides the needed human and intellectual capital while Change Management Practices (CMP) supports the procedural discipline needed to bring that potential to strategic action. The identification of a significant partial mediation, in which the indirect influence of TDKM on executive decision-making through CMP markedly exceeds the direct influence of TDKM on executive decision-making constitutes the major theoretical and practical contribution of the study. This result opens up to the fact that the greatest value of investing in talent and knowledge should not be in creating a good workforce, so much as it should be in building a level of inherent change-agility within an organisation that becomes the ultimate, most direct, enabler of the quality of decisions that can be made at executive level. Developing future ready talent and strong knowledge systems needs to be explicitly linked to enhancing the organisation's formal capacity to plan, communicate and implement change. For researchers the study provides a validated model and some fruitful areas for further inquiry such as exploring moderating factors such as organisational size or leadership style and application for other high velocity, regulated industries.

MANAGERIAL IMPLICATIONS

The results of this research have important and practical implications for senior leaders, HR Directors and strategy executives in the pharmaceutical and Medtech industries. At the start, management needs to pursue an integrated strategy for investment that explicitly comprises budgetary and strategic linkages amongst Talent Development (TD) and Knowledge Management (KM). Rather than developing these functions as a series of silos, leadership should develop initiatives with the collective purpose of strengthening organisational change - agility. For example, leadership - development programmes need to have modules like knowledge - based decision - making and change stewardship, and KM systems implementation needs to be accompanied by some form of competency training so that it can be used strategically.

After at the start, there needs to be a deliberate operationalisation of Change Management Practices as a core strategic capability and not just a project management tool. Given its powerful direct effect on executive decision - making, CMP should be institutionalised. This includes establishing a centre of excellence for change management, integrating change readiness assessments with strategic planning cycle, and having a formally resourced change management plan as part of every significant strategic initiative right from the beginning. Managers should not only be measured and rewarded on deliverables, they should also be measured and rewarded on how they facilitate change, measured through adoption of the employees and feedback integration. At the end, executives should create and encourage structural and cultural synergy by forming forums for TD, KM and CMP to meet. This can be achieved through cross functional committees tasked with problem-solving at the strategic level, use change initiatives as live case studies for leadership development and ensuring that knowledge repositories are actively used to inform change plans and post implementation reviews.

PRACTICAL IMPLICATIONS

The points from this study amount to a number of tangible, actionable steps for organisations from the pharmaceuticals and medtech sectors. At the start of all, leadership is required to practically consider the integration of TD and KM in terms of planning and execution of such initiatives. It is important that HR and strategy departments co-design programmes, such that a leadership training programme on, say, "Strategic Portfolio Management" is immediately followed by or combined with training on how to use the organisation's KM platform to analyse historical project data and market intelligence. This ensures that developed skills have a direct application to accessible organisational knowledge. After at the start, TD and KM programmes should be consciously structured to develop change-ability. In practice, competency frameworks and performance goals must have attributes like, "adaptability to new processes, good knowledge sharing during transitions." Simulation exercises that reflect real-world change situations - integrating an acquisition, for example, or implementing new quality management system - should become a standard part of leadership development. Simultaneously, KM systems need to be designed to support change (such as easily accessible repositories for lessons- learned from past transformations and change-communication templates).

At the end, change management should be operationalised as a non negotiable, front loaded part of all strategic decisions. When an executive team decides to make a new strategic move - whether tapping a new market or adopting a new digital platform - the at the start deliverable should be a Change Impact and Readiness Assessment (notice that this is not simply a financial budget). Dedicated change managers or internal change agents should be assigned at the outset to be liaisons amongst the executive team and the workforce to make sure that feedback comes up to inform ongoing decision making and decision rationale is communicated down. This closes the circle and makes change management the organizer of strategic choice and successful change execution.

THEORETICAL IMPLICATIONS

Primarily, the study is theoretical in nature by bringing together three significant theoretical fields into one causal model. It take Upper-Echelons Theory well beyond its age old dietary of focusing on executive demos and cognitive frames and to be able to put up proof that the quality of executive decision making is substantially depicted among certain and manageable organisational capabilities [TDKM] and processes [CMP]. This shift shifts the theoretical locus away from the group of individuals that occupy executive positions and toward the system of the construction of their decision-making environment. Along with, the research adds critical theoretical nuances to the two theories, RBV and KBT. By identifying change management practices as an important partial mediator, the study theorises an important intervening mechanism that explains the way that valuable, inimitable resources (talent and knowledge) are activated and transformed into a strategic advantage (superior decision management). It assumes that TDKM is the stock of strategic resources and CMP is the dynamic capability for orchestration of the resources necessary to use them effectively. This bridges on a long separating gap in theory amongst resource possession and value realisation through a more process oriented theoretical lens. At the end, the study adds to the context-specific theory building. By the empirical validation of the integrated model in the high-stakes and regulated setting of pharma and Medtech, it challenges the generalisability of generic models and opens a refined theoretical setting that deals with the particular interdependencies of regulation, innovation and risk that are characteristic for knowledge-intensive and life sciences industries. This opens up the way to more subtle, context-sensitive theoretical development.

RECOMMENDATIONS

At the start of all, it is recommended that organisations should formally integrate the governance, strategy and measuring of Talent Development (TD) and Knowledge Management (KM) initiatives. Leadership should require joint planning amongst HR, IT/Knowledge and Strategy department to ensure these functions are being designed with shared objectives aiming towards building organisational change - agility. Success metrics must go beyond isolated measures of participation rates or system usage to cover measures of how these capabilities enable the better execution and results of strategic change initiatives. After at the start, senior executives and people managers should make CMP a key leadership competency and strategic discipline. This means that structured change management (including impact assessment, stakeholder engagement and benefit realisation planning) are embedded into the earliest stages of all strategic decision-making processes. Leadership development programmes have to prepare and do much more to make current and future leaders as capable of change orchestration, so that they become more of a decision maker than a chief architect of organisational transition.

At the end, for industry associations and policymakers, development of frameworks and funding mechanisms in favour of synergistic development of human capital, knowledge infrastructure and change agility is recommended. National strategies for health innovation and industrial competitiveness should acknowledge that advancements in technology are meaningless without concurrent investments in the organisational systems that convert knowledge and talent into implemented strategy. Supporting research and forums about best practices within this integrated model can drive up the strategic resilience of the whole sector.

FUTURE DIRECTIONS

Based on the results and limitations of this study, a number of areas for further studies that are of great interest are suggested. At the start, for the sake of improving the generalisability and understanding of this work in context, future studies will benefit from testing and comparing this integrated model to different sectors and to different cultural settings. Replicating the research in other knowledge-intensive, regulated industries - including aerospace, finance - or in public health care systems would help tease out universal principles from the context-specific dynamics. Cross-cultural comparisons, especially amongst developed and emerging economies, could help in understanding how national institutional frameworks moderate relationships amongst capabilities, change processes and decision outcomes.

After at the start, future research should introduce and test moderating variables to provide a more contingent model. Investigating factors such as organisational size, leadership style (e.g. transformational versus transactional), or which kind of strategic decision is taken (radical innovation versus incremental adaptation) could explain under which conditions the mediated pathway is strongest. Moreover, investigation of the requirement of digital transformation enablers, such as artificial intelligence (AI) in KM or data analytics in decision support, as additional antecedents or moderators would mirror the changing technological context of the sector.

At the end, improvements in methodology are encouraged. Using longitudinal or mixed methods designs would enable researchers to quantify the causal and temporal dynamics of these relationships. Qualitative case studies could offer more information on the practical "how" of the mediation - exploring the specific actions, routines and difficulties involved in using the talent and knowledge, through change processes, to shape executive dialogues. In addition, future work can disaggregate the combined TD-KM construct to examine their different effects, which may hold separate and different value in change management practices, and ultimately in the quality of strategic decision-making. This would improve the model and provide more precise guidance for organisational investment.

REFERENCES

Abdelkareem, R. S., & Augustyn, M. M. (2023). Knowledge visualisation and strategic decision-making outcomes in small and medium-sized enterprises. *Journal of Information Science*. Advance online publication. DOI: 10.1177/01655515231160117

Alfadhel, A. M., Kassim, M. S. B., Ashaari, A., & Mahar, S. (2025). The impact of digital transformation readiness on strategic decision effectiveness in higher education institutions: Mediating requirement of technological infrastructure capability. *International Journal of Innovative Research and Scientific Studies*, *8*(8), 184–190. DOI: 10.53894/ijirss.v8i8.10576

Alkhaffaf, M. (2018). Investigating the Mediation Requirement of Information Technology (IT) Components in the Relationship amongst Knowledge Management (KM) Processes and Decision-Making. *International Journal of Business and Management*, *13*(4), 108. DOI: 10.5539/ijbm.v13n4p108

Alnofeli, K. K., Akter, S., & Yanamandram, V. (2025). Unlocking the power of AI in CRM: A comprehensive multidimensional exploration. *Journal of Innovation & Knowledge*, *10*(3), 100731. DOI: 10.1016/j.jik.2025.100731

Ayanponle, L., Awonuga, K. F., Asuzu, O. F., Daraojimba, R. E., Elufioye, O. A., & Daraojimba, O. D.Latifat Omolara AyanponleKehinde Feranmi AwonugaOnyeka Franca AsuzuRosita Ebere DaraojimbaOluwafunmi Adijat ElufioyeObinna Donald Daraojimba. (2024). A review of innovative HR strategies in enhancing workforce efficiency in the US [Review of A review of innovative HR strategies in enhancing workforce efficiency in the US]. *International Journal of Science and Research Archive*, *11*(1), 817–827. DOI: 10.30574/ijsra.2024.11.1.0152

Brazzale, P. L., Cooper-Thomas, H. D., Smollan, R. K., & Haar, J. (2025). Employee change orientation (echo) framework: A meta-review and taxonomy. *Journal of Management & Organization*, *1*. Advance online publication. DOI: 10.1017/jmo.2025.10051

Chang, C., Chang, Y., Tsao, Y., & Kraus, S. (2022). The power of knowledge management: How top management team bricolage boosts ambidexterity and performance. *Journal of Knowledge Management*, *26*(11), 188–213. DOI: 10.1108/JKM-10-2021-0753

Ergene, E., Floyd, S. W., & Ergene, S. (2023). Managing goal heterogeneity in strategic initiatives. *Long Range Planning*, *56*(4), 102344. DOI: 10.1016/j.lrp.2023.102344

Erzurum, E., Eryarsoy, E., Naqvi, F., Zaim, S., & Zaim, H. (2025). Linking Digital Knowledge Management Practices to Organizational Performance: A Serial Mediation Perspective. *Systems*, *13*(12), 1073. DOI: 10.3390/systems13121073

Estévez, M., Ballestar, M. T., & Sáinz, J. (2025). Market research and knowledge using Generative AI: The power of Large Language Models. *Journal of Innovation & Knowledge*, *10*(5), 100796. DOI: 10.1016/j.jik.2025.100796

Fuentes, C., & Stoopendahl, P. (2025). Marketing machines at work: Performing e-commerce by assembling, adjusting, and maintaining a complex market device. *Journal of Marketing Management*, *1*(15-16), 1754–1778. Advance online publication. DOI: 10.1080/0267257X.2025.2492191

Gerlich, M. (2024). Empirical Insights into the Contemporary 360 Management Framework (360MF). *Open Journal of Business and Management*, *12*(3), 1488–1515. DOI: 10.4236/ojbm.2024.123081

Guo, X., Fan, C., & Chen, Y. (2025). Executive Cognitive Styles and Enterprise Digital Strategic Change Under Environmental Dynamism: The Mediating Requirement of Absorptive Capacity in a Complex Adaptive System. *Systems*, *13*(9), 775. DOI: 10.3390/systems13090775

Hagl, C., Kanitz, R., Gonzalez, K., & Hoegl, M. (2023). Change management interventions: Taking stock and moving forward. *Human Resource Management Review*, *34*(1), 101000. DOI: 10.1016/j.hrmr.2023.101000

Huynh, M.-T. (2025). Individual Data-Driven Mindset and Decision-Making Performance: The Mediating Requirements of Effort and Persistence. *Information Systems Frontiers*, *27*(6), 2511–2538. Advance online publication. DOI: 10.1007/s10796-025-10647-6

Karanika-Murray, M., Whysall, Z., Liu-Smith, Y., Feltbower, C., & Challans-Rasool, E. (2023). Understanding organizational learning in a healthcare organization during sudden and disruptive change. *International Journal of Workplace Health Management*, *16*(4), 257–280. DOI: 10.1108/IJWHM-09-2022-0145

Kostopoulos, I., Stocchi, L., Pourazad, N., & Michaelidou, N. (2025). Mobile applications' stickiness: a review and future research program [Review of *Mobile applications' stickiness: a review and future research program*]. *Journal of Strategic Marketing*, 1. Taylor & Francis. DOI: 10.1080/0965254X.2025.2479830

Kunisch, S., Birkinshaw, J., Boppel, M., & Choi, K. (2023). Why do firms launch corporate change programs? A contingency perspective on strategic change. *Scandinavian Journal of Management*, *39*(4), 101297. DOI: 10.1016/j.scaman.2023.101297

Kusi, L. Y., Opoku-Danso, A., & Afum, E. (2020). Improving Performance of Public Universities in Ghana Through Talent Management: Does Leadership Support Matter? *Global Journal of Management and Business Research*, *41*, 41–68. Advance online publication. DOI: 10.34257/GJMBRAVOL20IS10PG41

Labib, E. (2024). Artificial intelligence in marketing: Exploring current and future trends. *Cogent Business & Management*, *11*(1), 2348728. Advance online publication. DOI: 10.1080/23311975.2024.2348728

Laermann-Nguyen, U., & Backfisch, M. (2021). Innovation crisis in the pharmaceutical industry? A survey. *SN Business & Economics*, *1*(12), 164. Advance online publication. DOI: 10.1007/s43546-021-00163-5

Mardian, M. T., Musadieq, D. M. A., Iqbal, M., & Ruhana, I. (2025). Understanding the key factors influencing knowledge management in business environments: A systematic review. *F1000 Research*, *14*, 738. DOI: 10.12688/f1000research.165390.2

Memon, K. R., Ghani, B., Hyder, S. I., Han, H., Zada, M., Ariza-Montes, A., & Arraño-Muñoz, M. (2022). Management of knowledge and competence through human resource information system—A structured review. *Frontiers in Psychology*, *13*, 944276. Advance online publication. DOI: 10.3389/fpsyg.2022.944276

Monferdini, L., & Bottani, E. (2024). How do businesses utilize change management for process optimization? A cross-analysis among industrial sectors. *Business Process Management Journal*, *30*(8), 371–414. DOI: 10.1108/BPMJ-03-2024-0158

Polimerou, R., & Spais, G. S. (2025). Establishing relationships amongst brands and customers via strategic social media chatbots for telecom goods and services. *Journal of Marketing Analytics*. DOI: 10.1057/s41270-025-00396-5

Rejon-Parrilla, J. C., Epstein, D., Mestre-Ferrandiz, J., & Espín, J. (2025). A Framework for Considering the Requirement of the Public Sector in R&D of Health Technology [Review of *A Framework for Considering the Requirement of the Public Sector in R&D of Health Technology*]. *Pharmaceutical Medicine*. Adis, Springer Healthcare. DOI: 10.1007/s40290-025-00576-9

Romiti, A., Vecchio, M. D., Cavicchi, C., & Vagnoni, E. (2025). Healthcare organizations in crisis context: Decision-making models and requirements of CEOs. *BMC Health Services Research*, *25*(1), 273. DOI: 10.1186/s12913-025-12420-6

Saura, J. R. (2020). Using Data Sciences in Digital Marketing: Framework, methods, and performance metrics. *Journal of Innovation & Knowledge*, *6*(2), 92–102. DOI: 10.1016/j.jik.2020.08.001

Saura, J. R., Škare, V., & Došen, Đ. O. (2024). Is AI-based digital marketing ethical? Assessing a new data privacy paradox. *Journal of Innovation & Knowledge*, *9*(4), 100597. DOI: 10.1016/j.jik.2024.100597

Savickas, Š., & Užienė, L. (2024). Interplay Amongst Knowledge Management and Digital Transformation: Designing Solutions. *European Conference on Knowledge Management, 25*(1), 735. DOI: 10.34190/eckm.25.1.2592

Tagscherer, F., & Carbon, C. (2023). Leadership for successful digitalization: A literature review on companies' internal and external aspects of digitalization [Review of *Leadership for successful digitalization: A literature review on companies' internal and external aspects of digitalization*]. *Sustainable Technology and Entrepreneurship, 2*(2), 100039. Elsevier BV. DOI: 10.1016/j.stae.2023.100039

Wang, S., Yang, H., & Bai, G. (2025). Construction of intelligent decision support systems through integration of retrieval-augmented generation and knowledge graphs. *Scientific Reports*, *15*(1), 35462. DOI: 10.1038/s41598-025-19257-3

Yi, Y., Chen, Y., & He, X. (2021). CEO Leadership, Strategic Decision Comprehensiveness, and Firm Performance: The Moderating Requirement of TMT Cognitive Conflict. *Management and Organization Review*, *18*(1), 131–166. DOI: 10.1017/mor.2021.10

Yusof, A. N. M., & Ahmad, M. F. (2024). Unlocking HR's Hidden Treasure on Innovation Capability: The Mediating Requirement of Knowledge Management Capacity. *Information Management and Business Review*, *16*(3S(I)a), 282–298. DOI: 10.22610/imbr.v16i3S(I)a.4211

Zhu, L., Liu, C., & Xu, X. (2025). Unlocking synergy of knowledge in the digital era: Inter-team collaboration, network position, and knowledge creation. *Journal of Knowledge Management*, *30*(1), 1–29. DOI: 10.1108/JKM-07-2024-0801

Zhu, Z. (2025). Intelligent information management enables quality-by-design in pharmaceutical production. *Scientific Reports*, *15*(1), 44201. DOI: 10.1038/s41598-025-27879-w

KEY TERMS AND DEFINITIONS

Change Management: It includes systematic communication, stakeholder engagement, training and reinforcement with the intention of facilitating adoption and minimise resistance in the face of strategic or operational shifts.

Executive Decision - Making (EDM): The high-level, strategic process by which upper levels of an organization consider a multiplicity of complex alternatives under uncertainty and commit resources to courses of action that determine long-term direction of specific and overall corporate performance.

Knowledge Management: It is the combination of practices in the goal to optimize the ability of work forces while guaranteeing the creation, sharing and use of an institutional knowledge in the realization of strategic objectives.

Medtech: Specific industrial context for the research with organisations concerned with the research development, manufacture and commercialisation of drugs, biologics, medical devices, diagnostic equipment and digital health solutions. This is a context characterised by high R&D intensity, high regulatory oversight, long product cycles and complexities at the innovation ecosystem.

Talent Development: An integrated strategic construct of the combination of organisational investment in developing human capital and the systematic use in labour management of intellectual assets.

Compilation of References

Abawari, A. M., Debela, K. L., & Abegaz, M. B. (2024). The effects of organizational culture on change management in Oromia public sectors: The mediating role of leadership styles. *Cogent Business & Management*, *11*(1), 2375623. Advance online publication. DOI: 10.1080/23311975.2024.2375623

Abdelkareem, R. S., & Augustyn, M. M. (2023). Knowledge visualisation and strategic decision-making outcomes in small and medium-sized enterprises. *Journal of Information Science*. Advance online publication. DOI: 10.1177/01655515231160117

Abdulai, A.-M., Iddrisu, O. A., Osman, A., & Iddrisu, A. B. (2025). Leadership Integrity: A Strategic Pillar for Ethical Decision Making and Organizational Excellence. *Advances in Research*, *26*(1), 65–73. DOI: 10.9734/air/2025/v26i11233

Abernethy, A. P., Adams, L., Barrett, M., Bechtel, C., Brennan, P., Butte, A., Faulkner, J., Fontaine, E., Friedhoff, S., Halamka, J., Howell, M., Johnson, K., Long, P., McGraw, D., Miller, R., Lee, P., Perlin, J., Rucker, D., Sandy, L., & Valdes, K. (2022). The promise of digital health: Then, now, and the future. *NAM Perspectives*, *6*(22). Advance online publication. DOI: 10.31478/202206e PMID: 36177208

Abou Abbas, A. (2025). Transformational Leadership and Regulatory Compliance: Strategies for Safer Healthcare Delivery. *J Glob Health Soci Med*, *1*(1), 1–8. DOI: 10.61440/JGHSM.2025.v1.06

Abraham, J. (2023). *Science, politics and the pharmaceutical industry: Controversy and bias in drug regulation*. Routledge.

Aðalsteinsdóttir, G. H. (2024). *Project Portfolio Management in Icelandic Organizations: A New Dynamic Perspective for Businesses*

Afriyie, D. (2019). Aligning strategic workforce planning with future-of-work trends through advanced performance management and digital HR infrastructure. *World Journal of Advanced Research and Reviews*, *4*(2), 207–226. DOI: 10.30574/wjarr.2019.4.2.0150

Agbo, C. C., Mahmoud, Q. H., & Eklund, J. M. (2019). Blockchain technology in healthcare: A systematic review. *Health Care*, *7*(2), 56. DOI: 10.3390/healthcare7020056 PMID: 30987333

Agency for Healthcare Research and Quality. (2023). Digital health equity and access. AHRQ Digital Health Reports. https://www.ahrq.gov/digital-health

Aggarwal, K., Jindal, P., Patel, P., & Kurmi, B. D. (2025). The Role of Validation in Mitigating Non-Compliance in the Pharmaceutical Industry. *International Journal of Newgen Research in Pharmacy & Healthcare*, 25-30.

Agyei, E., & Kumah, E. (2024). Navigating the complex terrain of healthcare systems in Sub-Saharan Africa: Challenges and opportunities for progress. *Discover Health Systems*, *3*(1), 39. Advance online publication. DOI: 10.1007/s44250-024-00108-3

Akhigbe, R., Falemi, A., & Akin-Oluyomi, O. T. (2025). An Advanced Governance Model for Improving Transparency Accountability and Strategic Execution in Complex Enterprises. *Article, Dec.*

Alblooshi, M., Shamsuzzaman, M., & Haridy, S. (2021). The relationship between leadership styles and organisational innovation: A systematic literature review and narrative synthesis. *European Journal of Innovation Management*, *24*(2), 338–370. DOI: 10.1108/EJIM-11-2019-0339

Aldabbas, H., Pinnington, A., & Lahrech, A. (2023). The influence of perceived organizational support on employee creativity: The mediating role of work engagement. *Current Psychology*, *42*(8), 6501–6515. DOI: 10.1007/s12144-021-01992-1

Aldjic, K., & Farrell, W. (2022). Work and Espoused National Cultural Values of Generation Z in Austria. *European Journal of Management Issues*, *30*(2), 100–115. DOI: 10.15421/192210

Alešnik, P., Vrečko, I., & Palčič, I. (2025). From Zero to One: A new perspective on the fuzzy front end of innovation and the Stage-Gate® model. *Advances in Production Engineering & Management*, *20*(1), 131–149. DOI: 10.14743/apem2025.1.532

Alfadhel, A. M., Kassim, M. S. B., Ashaari, A., & Mahar, S. (2025). The impact of digital transformation readiness on strategic decision effectiveness in higher education institutions: Mediating requirement of technological infrastructure capability. *International Journal of Innovative Research and Scientific Studies*, *8*(8), 184–190. DOI: 10.53894/ijirss.v8i8.10576

Ali, M. I. A., Khassawneh, O., Haak-Saheem, W., Zeng, J., & Darwish, T. K. (2023). Unveiling Dubai's knowledge economy: A journey toward enhancing knowledge exchange as well as human capital. *Global Knowledge, Memory and Communication*. Advance online publication. DOI: 10.09108/gkmc-06-2023-0214

Alkhaffaf, M. (2018). Investigating the Mediation Requirement of Information Technology (IT) Components in the Relationship amongst Knowledge Management (KM) Processes and Decision-Making. *International Journal of Business and Management, 13*(4), 108. DOI: 10.5539/ijbm.v13n4p108

Alnofeli, K. K., Akter, S., & Yanamandram, V. (2025). Unlocking the power of AI in CRM: A comprehensive multidimensional exploration. *Journal of Innovation & Knowledge, 10*(3), 100731. DOI: 10.1016/j.jik.2025.100731

Altman, E. J., Kiron, D., Schwartz, J., & Jones, R. (2023). *Workforce ecosystems: Reaching strategic goals with people, partners, and technologies*. MIT Press. DOI: 10.7551/mitpress/14690.001.0001

Amabile, T. M. (1996). *Creativity in context*. Westview Press.

Amaral, C., Paiva, M., Rodrigues, A. R., Veiga, F., & Bell, V. (2024). Global regulatory challenges for medical devices: Impact on innovation and market access. *Applied Sciences (Basel, Switzerland), 14*(20), 9304. DOI: 10.3390/app14209304

American Medical Informatics Association. (2016). AMIA 25x5 task force on reducing documentation burden on U.S. clinicians by 75% by 2025. https://amia.org/resources/25x5-task-force

Andargie, E. M., Negash, W. D., Geto, A. K., & Atnafu, A. (2024). Healthcare leadership practice and associated factors among primary healthcare managers in East Gojam Zone, Northwest Ethiopia: A mixed method study. *BMC Health Services Research, 24*(1), 1247. DOI: 10.1186/s12913-024-11712-7 PMID: 39420335

Andersson, U., Forsgren, M., & Holm, U. (2002). The strategic impact of external networks: Subsidiary performance and competence development in the multinational corporation. *Strategic Management Journal, 23*(11), 979–996. DOI: 10.1002/smj.267

Ansoff, H. I. (1972). Strategies for diversification. *Long Range Planning, 5*(2), 65–69. DOI: 10.1016/0024-6301(72)90048-9

Anwar, G., & Abdullah, N. N. (2021). Inspiring future entrepreneurs: The effect of experiential learning on the entrepreneurial intention at higher education. *International Journal of English Literature and Social Sciences, 6*.

Anyia, N., Senin, A. B. A., & Fikry, A. (2025). The Role of Strategic Leadership on Organizational Culture and Employees Resilience. *International Journal of Academic Research in Business & Social Sciences, 15*(7). Advance online publication. DOI: 10.6007/IJARBSS/v15-i7/25993

Aon. (2024). Managing human capital to drive innovation in life sciences. https://www.aon.com/en/insights/articles/managing-human-capital-to-drive-innovation-in-life-sciences

Apooyin, A. (2025). Risk management and compliance in a globalized economy: Navigating regulatory challenges and strategic adaptations. *International Journal of Science and Research Archive, 15*(10.30574).

Applbaum, K. (2006). Pharmaceutical marketing and the invention of the medical consumer. *PLoS Medicine, 3*(4), e189. Advance online publication. DOI: 10.1371/journal.pmed.0030189 PMID: 16597179

Aquino, K., & Thau, S. (2009). Workplace victimization: Aggression from the target's perspective. *Annual Review of Psychology, 60*(1), 717–741. DOI: 10.1146/annurev.psych.60.110707.163703 PMID: 19035831

Aquino, M. K. A., Bumacod, A. M., Calapine, A. G., Yaco, J. M. T., Dimailig, M. L., Amores, A. P., & Francisco, J. S. (2025). Interpersonal and intrapersonal leadership competencies: An interpretative phenomenological analysis on effective leadership strategies. *Frontiers in Psychology, 16*, 1553620. DOI: 10.3389/fpsyg.2025.1553620 PMID: 40910080

Argote, L., & Ingram, P. (2000). Knowledge transfer: A basis for competitive advantage in firms. *Organizational Behavior and Human Decision Processes, 82*(1), 150–169. DOI: 10.1006/obhd.2000.2893

Argyris, C., & Schön, D. A. (1997). Organizational learning: A theory of action perspective. *Revista Española de Investigaciones Sociológicas*, (77/78), 345–348. DOI: 10.2307/40183951

Attah, R. U., Garba, B. M. P., Gil-Ozoudeh, I., & Iwuanyanwu, O. (2024). Cross-functional team dynamics in technology management: A comprehensive review of efficiency and innovation enhancement. *Eng Sci Technol J, 5*(12), 3248–3265. DOI: 10.51594/estj.v5i12.1756

Ayanponle, L., Awonuga, K. F., Asuzu, O. F., Daraojimba, R. E., Elufioye, O. A., & Daraojimba, O. D.Latifat Omolara AyanponleKehinde Feranmi AwonugaOnyeka Franca AsuzuRosita Ebere DaraojimbaOluwafunmi Adijat ElufioyeObinna Donald Daraojimba. (2024). A review of innovative HR strategies in enhancing workforce efficiency in the US [Review of A review of innovative HR strategies in enhancing workforce efficiency in the US]. *International Journal of Science and Research Archive, 11*(1), 817–827. DOI: 10.30574/ijsra.2024.11.1.0152

Babatope, V. O. (2025). Cross-Disciplinary Mentoring in Academia: Fostering Collaboration and Innovation. In *Strategic Mentoring in Higher Education: Best Practices for Academic Success* (pp. 105-125). Springer.

Badnjević, A., Pokvić, L. G., Deumić, A., & Bećirović, L. S. (2022). Post-market surveillance of medical devices: A review. *Technology and Health Care, 30*(6), 1315–1329. DOI: 10.3233/THC-220284 PMID: 35964220

Badreldin, H. A., & Almosnid, N. (2025). From Silos to Synergy: Multidisciplinary Teams and Artificial Intelligence at the Helm of Research, Development, and Innovation. *The SCAPE Journal for Multidisciplinary Research, 1*(1), 7–13. DOI: 10.4103/SJMR.SJMR_7_25

Bakker, A. B., Demerouti, E., & Sanz-Vergel, A. I. (2014). Burnout and work engagement: The JD–R approach. *Annual Review of Organizational Psychology and Organizational Behavior, 1*(1), 389–411. DOI: 10.1146/annurev-orgpsych-031413-091235

Bakri, M. K. B. (2024). Applying Organizational Psychology Principles for Positive Workplace Outcomes. *Advances in Human Resource Management Research, 2*(1), 36–49. DOI: 10.60079/ahrmr.v2i1.258

Balducci, C., Fraccaroli, F., & Schaufeli, W. B. (2010). Psychometric properties of the Italian version of the Utrecht Work Engagement Scale (UWES-9). *European Journal of Psychological Assessment, 26*(2), 143–149. DOI: 10.1027/1015-5759/a000020

Balmer, J. M. T., & Chen, W. (2017). Corporate heritage brands, augmented role identity and customer satisfaction.

Balmer, J. M., & Gray, E. (2000). Corporate identity and corporate communications: creating a competitive advantage. *Industrial and Commercial Training*, 256–261. 32.

Balmer, J. M. T., & Chen, W. (2017, September 12). Corporate heritage brands, augmented role identity and customer satisfaction. *European Journal of Marketing, 51*(9/10), 1510–1521. DOI: 10.1108/EJM-07-2017-0449

Barrett, J. S. (2022). CompoundProgressionand Go/NoGo Criteria. *Fundamentals of Drug Development*, 231.

Bates, D. W., Auerbach, A., Schulam, P., Wright, A., & Saria, S. (2021). Reporting recommendations for clinical use of AI-based prediction models. *Journal of the American Medical Association, 325*(19), 1951–1952. DOI: 10.1001/jama.2021.3782

Bates, I., Patel, D., Chan, A. H. Y., Rutter, V., Bader, L., Meilianti, S., & Udoh, A. (2023). A comparative analysis of pharmaceutical workforce development needs across the commonwealth. *Research in Social & Administrative Pharmacy, 19*(1), 167–179. DOI: 10.1016/j.sapharm.2022.07.010 PMID: 36031527

Baumfeld Andre, E., Reynolds, R., Caubel, P., Azoulay, L., & Dreyer, N. A. (2020). Trial designs using real-world data: The changing landscape of the regulatory approval process. *Pharmacoepidemiology and Drug Safety, 29*(10), 1201–1212. DOI: 10.1002/pds.4932 PMID: 31823482

Beauchamp, T. L., & Childress, J. F. (2019). *Principles of biomedical ethics* (8th ed.). Oxford University Press.

Beddoe-Rosendo, J., Heaysman, C. L., Hajnal, J. V., Ourselin, S., & Vanhoestenberghe, A. (2023). Medical device regulatory challenges in the UK are affecting innovation and its potential benefits. *Proceedings of the Institution of Mechanical Engineers. Part H, Journal of Engineering in Medicine, 237*(12), 1349–1358. DOI: 10.1177/09544119231203776 PMID: 37840272

Bento, F., Tagliabue, M., & Lorenzo, F. (2020). Organizational silos: A scoping review informed by a behavioral perspective on systems and networks. *Societies (Basel, Switzerland), 10*(3), 56. DOI: 10.3390/soc10030056

Bhattacharya, J., & Packalen, M. (2020). *Stagnation and scientific incentives.*

Biloslavo, R., & Trnavčevič, A. (2009). Web sites as tools of communication of a "green" company. *Management Decision, 47*(7), 1158–1173. DOI: 10.1108/00251740910978359

Birou, L., & Hoek, R. V. (2022). Supply chain management talent: The role of executives in engagement, recruitment, development and retention. *Supply Chain Management, 27*(6), 712–727. DOI: 10.1108/SCM-08-2020-0418

Bolon, B., Baze, W., Shilling, C. J., Keatley, K. L., Patrick, D. J., & Schafer, K. A. (2018). Good laboratory practice in the academic setting: Fundamental principles for nonclinical safety assessment and GLP-compliant pathology support when developing innovative biomedical products. *ILAR Journal, 59*(1), 18–28. DOI: 10.1093/ilar/ily008 PMID: 30566589

Boxall, P., & Purcell, J. (2022). *Strategy and human resource management*. Bloomsbury Publishing.

Brandhorst, S., & Kluge, A. (2022). Incentive schemes increase risky behavior in a safety-critical working task: An experimental comparison in a simulated high-reliability organization. *Safety (Basel, Switzerland)*, *8*(1), 17. DOI: 10.3390/safety8010017

Brazzale, P. L., Cooper-Thomas, H. D., Smollan, R. K., & Haar, J. (2025). Employee change orientation (echo) framework: A meta-review and taxonomy. *Journal of Management & Organization*, *1*. Advance online publication. DOI: 10.1017/jmo.2025.10051

Brown, K. W., Ryan, R. M., & Creswell, J. D. (2007). Mindfulness: Theoretical foundations and evidence for its salutary effects. *Psychological Inquiry*, *18*(4), 211–237. DOI: 10.1080/10478400701598298

Brown, T., & Katz, B. (2019). *Change by design: How design thinking transforms organizations and inspires innovation* (Vol. 20091). HarperBusiness.

Bulan, T. R. N., Muhar, A. M., & Junita, A. (2025). The role of talent management in mediating the effect of workforce engagement as well as organizational culture on workforce agility in educational foundations. *Problems and Perspectives in Management*, *23*(3), 567–580. DOI: 10.21511/ppm.23(3).2025.41

Burns, L., Le Roux, N., Kalesnik-Orszulak, R., Christian, J., Hukkelhoven, M., Rockhold, F., & O'Donnell, J. (2022). Real-world evidence for regulatory decision-making: Guidance from around the world. *Clinical Therapeutics*, *44*(3), 420–437. DOI: 10.1016/j.clinthera.2022.01.012 PMID: 35181179

Busby, J. S. (2019). The co-evolution of competition and parasitism in the resource-based view: A risk model of product counterfeiting. *European Journal of Operational Research*, *276*(1), 300–313. DOI: 10.1016/j.ejor.2018.12.039

Calado, C. R. (2024). Bridging the gap between target-based and phenotypic-based drug discovery. *Expert Opinion on Drug Discovery*, *19*(7), 789–798. DOI: 10.1080/17460441.2024.2355330 PMID: 38747562

Caliber. (2023). *Global Pharma Study 2023*. https://www.groupcaliber.com/global-pharma-report-2023/

Cantu, N. (2025). Vicente Academic Medical Center Case Study: Highlighting Healthcare Leadership's Role in Risk Management and Governance Training to Strengthen Oversight and Strategic Decision-Making. *SCIENTIA MORALITAS-International Journal of Multidisciplinary Research*, *10*(2), 324–341.

Celestin, M., Vasuki, M., Sujatha, S., & Kumar, A. D. (2024). Enhancing employee satisfaction and engagement to boost productivity: The role of leadership, culture, and recognition programs. *International Journal of Computational Research and Development*, *9*(2), 67–74.

Chaffey, D., & Ellis-Chadwick, F. (2019). *Digital marketing* (7th ed.). Pearson.

Chang, C., Chang, Y., Tsao, Y., & Kraus, S. (2022). The power of knowledge management: How top management team bricolage boosts ambidexterity and performance. *Journal of Knowledge Management*, *26*(11), 188–213. DOI: 10.1108/JKM-10-2021-0753

Char, D. S., Shah, N. H., & Magnus, D. (2018). Implementing machine learning in health care—Addressing ethical challenges. *The New England Journal of Medicine*, *378*(11), 981–983. DOI: 10.1056/NEJMp1714229 PMID: 29539284

Chatterji, A. K., Cunningham, C. M., & Joseph, J. E. (2019). The limits of relational governance: Sales force strategies in the US medical device industry. *Strategic Management Journal*, *40*(1), 55–78. DOI: 10.1002/smj.2964

Chatterji, A. K., Fabrizio, K. R., Mitchell, W., & Schulman, K. A. (2008). Physician–industry cooperation in the medical device industry. *Health Affairs (Project Hope)*, *27*(6), 1532–1543. DOI: 10.1377/hlthaff.27.6.1532 PMID: 18997209

Cheah, E. T., Chan, W. L., & Chieng, C. L. L. (2007). The Corporate Social Responsibility of Pharmaceutical Product Recalls: An Empirical Examination of U.S. and U.K. Markets. *Journal of Business Ethics*, *76*(4), 427–449. DOI: 10.1007/s10551-006-9292-1

Chelagat, T., Rice, J., Onyango, J., & Kokwaro, G. (2021). An Assessment of Impact of Leadership Training on Health System Performance in Selected Counties in Kenya. *Frontiers in Public Health*, *8*, 550796. Advance online publication. DOI: 10.3389/fpubh.2020.550796 PMID: 33732670

Chesbrough, H. W. (2003). *Open innovation: The new imperative for creating and profiting from technology*. Harvard Business School Press.

Chessell, S., Courtiour, S., Colman, A., Porter, S., & Heaslip, V. (2022). Staff perspectives of a near-real time feedback intervention to improve patient experiences. *British Journal of Health Care Management*, *28*(9), 245–252. DOI: 10.12968/bjhc.2022.0056

Chisholm, O., & Critchley, H. (2023). Future directions in regulatory affairs. *Frontiers in Medicine*, *9*, 1082384. DOI: 10.3389/fmed.2022.1082384 PMID: 36698838

Chitiga, M. (2018). An exploration of the implications of transformational leadership behaviors on empowering employees and transforming organisations. *African Journal of Public Affairs*, *10*(1), 60–82.

Chitraju, S. (2025). Building Trust through Transparency: The Role of Disclosure in Risk Governance. *Available at SSRN* 5603270. DOI: 10.2139/ssrn.5603270

Chukwu, O. A., Nadigel, J., Kasaai, B., Boateng, R., Glazier, R. H., & McMahon, M. (2024). Understanding the training, mentorship, and professional development priorities of early career embedded researchers. *The International Journal of Health Planning and Management*, *39*(5), 1277–1297. DOI: 10.1002/hpm.3800 PMID: 38527109

Chukwurah, N., Ige, A. B., Idemudia, C., & Eyieyien, O. G. (2024). Integrating agile methodologies into data governance: Achieving flexibility and control simultaneously. *Open Access Research Journal of Multidisciplinary Studies*, *8*(01), 045-056.

Chukwurah, N., Ige, A. B., Idemudia, C., & Adebayo, V. I. (2024). Strategies for engaging stakeholders in data governance: Building effective communication and collaboration. *Open Access Res J Multidiscip Stud*, *8*(1), 57–67. DOI: 10.53022/oarjms.2024.8.1.0045

Ciasullo, M. V., Troisi, O., Grimaldi, M., & Leone, D. (2020). Multi-level governance for sustainable innovation in smart communities: An ecosystems approach. *The International Entrepreneurship and Management Journal*, *16*(4), 1167–1195. DOI: 10.1007/s11365-020-00641-6

Coates, J. M., Santhanalakshmi, K., Dinesh, N., Gandhimathi, S., Chandel, P. S., & Selvakumar, P. (2025). Assessment and evaluation in transnational staff development. In *Training and development in transnational higher education* (pp. 387–406). IGI Global Scientific Publishing. DOI: 10.4018/979-8-3373-1897-4.ch019

Coelho, F., & Augusto, M. (2010). Job characteristics and the creativity of frontline service employees. *Journal of Service Research*, *13*(4), 426–438. DOI: 10.1177/1094670510369379

Cohen, E. P. (1988). Direct-to-the-public advertisement of prescription drugs. *The New England Journal of Medicine*, *318*(6), 373–376. DOI: 10.1056/NEJM198802113180608 PMID: 3123930

Cohen, I. G., & Mello, M. M. (2018). HIPAA and protecting health information in the 21st century. *Journal of the American Medical Association*, *320*(3), 231–232. DOI: 10.1001/jama.2018.5630 PMID: 29800120

Collier, R. (2020). Hospitals shut down by ransomware attacks. *Canadian Medical Association Journal, 192*(46), E1427–E1428. DOI: 10.1503/cmaj.1095929

Collings, D. G., Mellahi, K., & Cascio, W. F. (2019). Global talent management and performance in multinational enterprises: A multilevel perspective. *Journal of Management, 45*(2), 540–566. DOI: 10.1177/0149206318757018

Correia, C. F. S. (2015). Avaliação de competências: Implicações nas práticas de gestão de recursos humanos. Estudo de caso: Pós-venda AVAC [Dissertação de mestrado, Faculdade de Economia da Universidade do Porto]. Repositório Aberto da Universidade do Porto. https://repositorio-aberto.up.pt/handle/10216/81259

Cosens, B., Ruhl, J., Soininen, N., Gunderson, L., Belinskij, A., Blenckner, T., Camacho, A. E., Chaffin, B. C., Craig, R. K., Doremus, H., Glicksman, R., Heiskanen, A.-S., Larson, R., & Similä, J. (2021). Governing complexity: Integrating science, governance, and law to manage accelerating change in the globalized commons. *Proceedings of the National Academy of Sciences of the United States of America, 118*(36), e2102798118. DOI: 10.1073/pnas.2102798118 PMID: 34475210

Cox, L. A.Jr. (2023). What is an exposure-response curve? *Global Epidemiology, 6*, 100114. DOI: 10.1016/j.gloepi.2023.100114 PMID: 37637716

Crane, R. S., Brewer, J., Feldman, C., Kabat-Zinn, J., Santorelli, S., Williams, J. M. G., & Kuyken, W. (2017). What defines mindfulness-based programs? The warp and the weft. *Psychological Medicine, 47*(6), 990–999. DOI: 10.1017/S0033291716003317 PMID: 28031068

Crossan, M. M., Lane, H. W., & White, R. E. (1999). An organizational learning framework: From intuition to institution. *Academy of Management Review, 24*(3), 522–537. DOI: 10.2307/259140

Cumar, M. A., Kidane, B. Z., Golga, D. N., & Dinsa, F. (2025). Leadership as cultural architect: A path-goal theory analysis of leadership styles as well as organizational culture in Somaliland higher education. *Discover Education, 4*(1), 448. Advance online publication. DOI: 10.1007/s44217-025-00887-8

Dane, E., & Brummel, B. J. (2013). Examining workplace mindfulness and its relations to job performance and turnover intention. *Human Relations; Studies Towards the Integration of the Social Sciences, 67*(1), 105–128. DOI: 10.1177/0018726713487753

Deloitte. (2023). *Global MedTech outlook: Innovation and partnerships in healthcare technology*. Deloitte Insights.

Demeke, G. W., van Engen, M., & Markos, S. (2025a). Servant leadership and patient safety culture in Ethiopian public hospitals: A qualitative study. *BMC Health Services Research*, *25*(1), 984. DOI: 10.1186/s12913-025-13118-5 PMID: 40721777

Demeke, G. W., van Engen, M., & Markos, S. (2025b). Linking servant leadership to task performance through work engagement and patient safety culture. *Discover Health Systems*, *4*(1), 142. Advance online publication. DOI: 10.1007/s44250-025-00325-4

Deng, C. (2025). Research on the Synergistic Development Path of Technological Innovation and Management in Manufacturing Enterprises within the Perspective of New-Quality Productive Forces. *Academic Journal of Business & Management*, *7*(9), 1–7.

Dery, K., Sebastian, I. M., & van der Meulen, N. (2017). The digital workplace is key to digital innovation. *MIS Quarterly Executive*, *16*(2), 135–152.

Desai, V. (2019). Digital marketing: A review. *International Journal of Trend in Scientific Research and Development*, (Special Issue), 196–200. DOI: 10.31142/ijtsrd23100

Deshmukh, A. D. (2024). Redefining Innovation for Pharmaceutical Regulation. *BUL Rev.*, *104*, 577.

Deshmukh, P., & Paliwal, S. (2024). Pharmacy education 2.0 with special reference to digital India. *Multidisciplinary Reviews*, *7*(4), 2024065–2024065. DOI: 10.31893/multirev.2024065

Diniz, P. V. L., Marques, I. C. P., & Pereira, Â. M. (2025). Leadership, Human-Centered Management as well as organizational Culture: Pathways to Well-Being and Innovative Work Based on a Systematic Review. *Sustainability (Basel)*, *17*(24), 11181. DOI: 10.3390/su172411181

Dong, Y., Liao, H., Chuang, A., Zhou, J., & Campbell, E. M. (2015). Fostering employee service creativity: Joint effects of customer empowering behaviors and supervisory empowering leadership. *The Journal of Applied Psychology*, *100*(5), 1364–1380. DOI: 10.1037/a0038969 PMID: 25774571

Duressa, W. T., & Kidane, B. Z. (2024). Interplay between Organizational Learning and Departmental Performance: Implications for Change in Ethiopian Public Research Universities. *International Journal of Education and Literacy Studies*, *12*(2), 205–213. DOI: 10.7575/aiac.ijels.v.12n.2p.205

Dutta, B., & Rao, V. (2024). *Human capital and innovation capability in organizations. Heliyon*. https://www.sciencedirect.com/science/article/pii/S2405872624000443

Dyer, J. H., & Singh, H. (1998). The relational view: Cooperative strategy and sources of interorganizational competitive advantage. *Academy of Management Review*, *23*(4), 660–679. DOI: 10.2307/259056

Edmondson, A. C. (2018). *The fearless organization: Creating psychological safety in the workplace for learning, innovation, and growth*. John Wiley & Sons.

Edmondson, A. C., & Harvey, J. F. (2018). Cross-boundary teaming for innovation: Integrating research on teams and knowledge in organizations. *Human Resource Management Review*, *28*(4), 347–360. DOI: 10.1016/j.hrmr.2017.03.002

Effendi, M., Rimbano, D., & Idayati, I. (2023). Work communication and work ethics on employee performance and job satisfaction. *Indonesian Journal of Business Analytics*, *3*(2), 513–538. DOI: 10.55927/ijba.v3i2.4035

Emiru, E. K., & Berhanu, K. Z. (2025). Distributed Leadership and Student Engagement in Ethiopia: The mediating role of Teacher Self Efficacy. *Research in Educational Administration & Leadership*, *10*(3), 672–721. DOI: 10.30828/real.1618955

Enriquez, J., & Goldberg, R. A. (2000). Transforming life, transforming business: The life-science revolution. *Harvard Business Review*, *78*(2), 96–96.

Ergene, E., Floyd, S. W., & Ergene, S. (2023). Managing goal heterogeneity in strategic initiatives. *Long Range Planning*, *56*(4), 102344. DOI: 10.1016/j.lrp.2023.102344

Erzurum, E., Eryarsoy, E., Naqvi, F., Zaim, S., & Zaim, H. (2025). Linking Digital Knowledge Management Practices to Organizational Performance: A Serial Mediation Perspective. *Systems*, *13*(12), 1073. DOI: 10.3390/systems13121073

Eshete, B. M., & Kassahun, T. (2025). Adaptive leadership, organizational culture and patient-perceived service quality in private healthcare: Evidence from Addis Ababa. *International Journal of Health Care Quality Assurance*, *1*. Advance online publication. DOI: 10.09108/ijhcqa-09-2025-0136

Essandoh, S., Sakyi, J. K., Ibrahim, A. K., Okafor, C. M., Wedraogo, L., Ogunwale, O. B., Babalola, A. S., & Adenuga, M. A. (2023). *Analyzing the Effects of Leadership Styles on Team Dynamics and Project Outcomes. Journal not specified. Fasasi*. G. O. Digital Communication Policy Framework Enhancing Transparency and Accountability in Health-Social Service Collaboration.

Estender, A. Carlos (2021). Gestão de Pessoas e Avaliação de Desempenho nas Organizações. Revista Interdisciplinar Científica Aplicada, 7(2), 23-39. https://portaldeperiodicos.animaeducacao.com. br/index.php/rica/article/view/17765

Esteva, A., Chou, K., Yeung, S., Naik, N., Madani, A., Mottaghi, A., Liu, Y., Topol, E., Dean, J., & Socher, R. (2021). Deep learning-enabled medical computer vision. *NPJ Digital Medicine*, *4*(1), 5. DOI: 10.1038/s41746-020-00376-2 PMID: 33420381

Estévez, M., Ballestar, M. T., & Sáinz, J. (2025). Market research and knowledge using Generative AI: The power of Large Language Models. *Journal of Innovation & Knowledge*, *10*(5), 100796. DOI: 10.1016/j.jik.2025.100796

Euh, Y., & Lee, D. (2021). How do pharmaceutical companies overcome a corporate productivity crisis? Business diversification into medical devices for growth potential. *International Journal of Environmental Research and Public Health*, *18*(3), 1045. DOI: 10.3390/ijerph18031045 PMID: 33503944

European Commission. (2022). European Health Data Space. Directorate-General for Health and Food Safety. https://health.ec.europa.eu/ehealth-digital-health-and-care/european-health-data-space_en

Everts, M., & Drew, M. (2024). Successfully navigating the valley of death: The importance of accelerators to support academic drug discovery and development. *Expert Opinion on Drug Discovery*, *19*(2), 253–258. DOI: 10.1080/17460441.2023.2284824 PMID: 37968916

Farley, M. S., & Rouse, W. B. (2000). Technology challenges & opportunities in the biotechnology, pharmaceutical & medical device industries. *Information, Knowledge, Systems Management*, *2*(2), 133–141. DOI: 10.3233/IKS-2000-00033

Ferede, W. L., Endawoke, Y., & Tessema, G. (2024). Change management through strategic leadership: The mediating effect of knowledge management in public organizations, Ethiopia. *Future Business Journal*, *10*(1), 93. Advance online publication. DOI: 10.1186/s43093-024-00363-z

Ferreira, A., Melo, W., Costa, R., Pereira, S., & Duarte, N. (2024). Os profissionais do SNS: Retrato e evolução. Lisboa: Centro de Competências de Planeamento, de Políticas e de Prospetiva da Administração Pública. https://www.planapp.gov.pt/wp-content/uploads/2024/03/PlanAPP_Profissionais SNS-2.pdf

Figueroa, K. M., & Abellana, A. L. (2025). Organizational Culture and Strategic Leadership on Teachers' Innovative Work Behavior. *International Journal of Research and Innovation in Social Science*, *23*(VI), 23–35. Advance online publication. DOI: 10.47772/IJRISS.2025.90600003

Florin, M.-V. (2022). Risk governance and'responsible research and innovation'can be mutually supportive. *Journal of Risk Research*, *25*(8), 976–990. DOI: 10.1080/13669877.2019.1646311

Food and Drug Administration. (2021). Artificial intelligence/machine learning (AI/ML)-based software as a medical device (SaMD) action plan. U.S. Department of Health and Human Services. https://www.fda.gov/media/145022/download

Force, J. T. (2018). Risk management framework for information systems and organizations. *NIST Special Publication, 800*, 37.

Forscher, P. S., Wagenmakers, E.-J., Coles, N. A., Silan, M. A., Dutra, N., Basnight-Brown, D., & IJzerman, H. (2023). The benefits, barriers, and risks of big-team science. *Perspectives on Psychological Science : A Journal of the Association for Psychological Science, 18*(3), 607–623. DOI: 10.1177/17456916221082970 PMID: 36190899

Francer, J.. (2014). Ethical pharmaceutical promotion and communications worldwide. *Pharmaceutical Medicine, 28*(1), 1–12. DOI: 10.1007/s40290-014-0034-0 PMID: 24855373

Friedman, C. P., Wong, A. K., & Blumenthal, D. (2010). Achieving a nationwide learning health system. *Science Translational Medicine, 2*(57). Advance online publication. DOI: 10.1126/scitranslmed.3001456 PMID: 21068440

Frize, M. (2022). *Health Care Engineering Part I: Clinical Engineering and Technology Management*. Springer Nature.

Fuentes, C., & Stoopendahl, P. (2025). Marketing machines at work: Performing e-commerce by assembling, adjusting, and maintaining a complex market device. *Journal of Marketing Management, 1*(15-16), 1754–1778. Advance online publication. DOI: 10.1080/0267257X.2025.2492191

Fukami, T. (2024). Enhancing healthcare accountability for administrators: Fostering transparency for patient safety and quality enhancement. *Cureus, 16*(8). Advance online publication. DOI: 10.7759/cureus.66007 PMID: 39221336

Gade, K. R. (2021). Data-driven decision making in a complex world. *Journal of computational innovation, 1*(1).

Gambardella, A., Giuri, P., & Luzzi, A. (2007). The market for patents in Europe. *Research Policy, 36*(8), 1163–1183. DOI: 10.1016/j.respol.2007.07.006

Gao, C., & McDonald, R. (2022). Shaping nascent industries: Innovation strategy and regulatory uncertainty in personal genomics. *Administrative Science Quarterly, 67*(4), 915–967. DOI: 10.1177/00018392221112641

Gao, F., & Regua, O. U. (2024). Evaluating the Impact of Performance Appraisal Systems on Employee Motivation and Job Satisfaction in Hospitals. *International Journal of Social Science and Human Research, 12*(3), 59–63. DOI: 10.5281/zenodo.1274223

Garcia, C. L., Abreu, L. C., Ramos, J. L. S., Castro, C. F. D., Smiderle, F. R. N., Santos, J. A. D., & Bezerra, I. M. P. (2019). Influence of burnout on patient safety: Systematic review and meta-analysis. *Medicina (Kaunas, Lithuania), 55*(9), 553. DOI: 10.3390/medicina55090553 PMID: 31480365

Gartner. (2022). Gartner CIO and technology executive survey 2022: Healthcare insights. Gartner Research.

Gassmann, O., Enkel, E., & Chesbrough, H. (2021). The future of open innovation. *R & D Management, 51*(1), 50–63. DOI: 10.1111/radm.12471

Gavrilenko, V., & Shenshin, V. (2023). Control and supervisory activities as an institute of administrative law. *BRICS Law Journal, 10*(2), 156–183. DOI: 10.21684/2412-2343-2023-10-2-156-183

Gerlich, M. (2024). Empirical Insights into the Contemporary 360 Management Framework (360MF). *Open Journal of Business and Management, 12*(3), 1488–1515. DOI: 10.4236/ojbm.2024.123081

Gettinger, A., & Frisse, M. E. (2018). *Health information technology: Getting the governance right*. Health Affairs Blog., DOI: 10.1377/hblog20180124.985437

Ghemawat, P. (2007). *Redefining global strategy: Crossing borders in a world where differences still matter*. Harvard Business Press.

Gile, P. P., van de Klundert, J., & Buljac-Samardžić, M. (2022). Strategic human resource management and performance in public hospitals in Ethiopia. *Frontiers in Public Health, 10*, 915317. DOI: 10.3389/fpubh.2022.915317 PMID: 36339178

Gomaa, A. H. (2025). Enhancing Product Development Excellence through Quality Management Tools: A Comprehensive Review and Integrated Conceptual Framework. *Intelligent and Sustainable Manufacturing, 2*(2), 10017. DOI: 10.70322/ism.2025.10017

Graham, J. (2024). Factors influencing the creation of an Industry 4.0 strategy in the generic pharmaceutical industry. *Journal of Generic Medicines, 58*(3), 485–497. DOI: 10.1177/17411343241238178

Grecu, V., & Dene , C. (2024). The Role of Organizational Culture in Driving Innovation: A Study of Contemporary Business Practice. *Acta Universitatis Cibiniensis Technical Series*, *76*(1), 46–54. DOI: 10.2478/aucts-2024-0007

Grishunin, S., Suloeva, S., & Burova, E. (2022). Development of risk management mechanism and the system of risk metrics to evaluate and enhance the long-term orientation of the strategies of non-financial companies. *Risks*, *10*(9), 182. DOI: 10.3390/risks10090182

Guha, S., Rabby, S. K. M. A. H. R., Chowdhury, S. R., & Julee, S. A. (2025). Enhancing employee innovation capabilities through high-involvement HRM: Mediating role of knowledge sharing and transformational leadership. *Future Business Journal*, *11*(1), 59. Advance online publication. DOI: 10.1186/s43093-025-00482-1

Gulati, R., Freeman, K. W., & Nolen, G. (2004). How CEOs Manage Growth Agendas. *Harvard Business Review*, *82*(7-8), 124–132. PMID: 15241959

Guo, X., Fan, C., & Chen, Y. (2025). Executive Cognitive Styles and Enterprise Digital Strategic Change Under Environmental Dynamism: The Mediating Requirement of Absorptive Capacity in a Complex Adaptive System. *Systems*, *13*(9), 775. DOI: 10.3390/systems13090775

Gupta, J., Rathore, P., & Kashiramka, S. (2023). Impact of intellectual capital on the financial performance of innovation-driven pharmaceutical firms: Empirical evidence from India. *Journal of the Knowledge Economy*, *14*(2), 1052–1076. DOI: 10.1007/s13132-022-00927-w

Gupte, T., Nitave, T., & Gobburu, J. (2025). Regulatory landscape of accelerated approval pathways for medical devices in the United States and the European Union. *Frontiers in Medical Technology*, *7*, 1586070. DOI: 10.3389/fmedt.2025.1586070 PMID: 40444060

Hagedoorn, J. (2002). Inter-firm R&D partnerships: An overview of major trends and patterns since 1960. *Research Policy*, *31*(4), 477–492. DOI: 10.1016/S0048-7333(01)00120-2

Hagl, C., Kanitz, R., Gonzalez, K., & Hoegl, M. (2023). Change management interventions: Taking stock and moving forward. *Human Resource Management Review*, *34*(1), 101000. DOI: 10.1016/j.hrmr.2023.101000

Hall, L. H., Johnson, J., Watt, I., Tsipa, A., & O'Connor, D. B. (2016). Healthcare staff wellbeing, burnout, and patient safety: A systematic review. *PLoS One*, *11*(7), e0159015. DOI: 10.1371/journal.pone.0159015 PMID: 27391946

Hamidi, A. B. (2023). The Impacts of Performance Appraisal on Employee's Job Satisfaction and Organizational Behavior. *Ilomata International Journal of Social Science, 4*(3), 466–480. DOI: 10.52728/ijss.v4i3.876

Handoyo, S., Suharman, H., Ghani, E. K., & Soedarsono, S. (2023). A business strategy, operational efficiency, ownership structure, and manufacturing performance: The moderating role of market uncertainty and competition intensity and its implication on open innovation. *Journal of Open Innovation, 9*(2), 100039. DOI: 10.1016/j.joitmc.2023.100039

Hanenkratt, A. C. (2024). *Project management for research and development.* Massachusetts Institute of Technology.

Hansen, J. A., & Pihl-Thingvad, S. (2019). Managing employee innovative behaviour through transformational and transactional leadership styles. *Public Management Review, 21*(6), 918–944. DOI: 10.1080/14719037.2018.1544272

Han, Y., Ceross, A., & Bergmann, J. (2024). More than red tape: Exploring complexity in medical device regulatory affairs. *Frontiers in Medicine, 11*, 1415319. DOI: 10.3389/fmed.2024.1415319 PMID: 39144660

Healthcare Information and Management Systems Society. (2023). *HIMSS EMRAM worldwide survey results 2023.* HIMSS Analytics.

Hector, O., & Cameron, R. (2023). Human-Centric Management: Nurturing Talent, Building Culture, and Driving Organizational Success. *The International Journal of Science in Society, 5*(4), 511–525. DOI: 10.54783/ijsoc.v5i4.809

Hemphill, T.A. (2010). Extraordinary Pricing of Orphan Drugs: Is it a Socially Responsible Strategy for the U.S. Pharmaceutical Industry?. J Bus Ethics 94, 225–242. https://doi.org/10.1007/s10551-009-0259-x

HHS Office for Civil Rights. (2023). HIPAA enforcement highlights 2023. U.S. Department of Health and Human Services. https://www.hhs.gov/hipaa/for-professionals/compliance-enforcement/data/enforcement-highlights

HILL. M. & HILL, A. (2012) – Investigação por Questionário. 2ª Edição. Edições Sílabo. ISBN:978-972-618-273- 3

Hindorff, L. A., Bonham, V. L., Brody, L. C., Ginoza, M. E. C., Hutter, C. M., Manolio, T. A., & Green, E. D. (2018). Prioritizing diversity in human genomics research. *Nature Reviews. Genetics, 19*(3), 175–185. DOI: 10.1038/nrg.2017.89 PMID: 29151588

HO. B. K. (2023). Future Workforce Planning-Building a Future-Ready Organization Using a Prospective Study Approach. Abu Dhabi International Petroleum Exhibition and Conference, Hong, A. (2024). *A Methodology for R&D Portfolio Management Decision Making Under Uncertainty–Applied Towards Timely Reallocation of Investments with Stalling Projects* Georgia Institute of Technology].

Hoti, A., Binaku, A., & Ademaj, M. (2018). Using management by objectives as a performance appraisal tool for employee satisfaction. *Future Business Journal*, *4*(1), 94–108. DOI: 10.1016/j.fbj.2018.01.001

Huang, C. C., Tu, Y., & Xie, X. (2024). Mindfulness and job performance in employees of a multinational corporation: Moderated mediation of nationality, intercultural communication, and burnout. *Social Sciences & Humanities Open*, *10*, 100975. DOI: 10.1016/j.ssaho.2024.100975

Hubbart, J. A. (2024). Understanding and mitigating leadership fear-based behaviors on employee and organizational success. *Administrative Sciences*, *14*(9), 225. DOI: 10.3390/admsci14090225

Hu, G.-G., & Yao, L.-P. (2021). Do Human Capital Investment and Technological Innovation Have a Permanent Effect on Population Health? An Asymmetric Analysis of BRICS Economies. *Frontiers in Public Health*, *9*, 723557. DOI: 10.3389/fpubh.2021.723557 PMID: 34368074

Hülsheger, U. R., Alberts, H. J. E. M., Feinholdt, A., & Lang, J. W. B. (2013). Benefits of mindfulness at work: The role of mindfulness in emotion regulation, emotional exhaustion, and job satisfaction. *The Journal of Applied Psychology*, *98*(2), 310–325. DOI: 10.1037/a0031313 PMID: 23276118

Humairah, K. A., Irawan, A., & Ibrahim, M. B. H. (2023). Crafting Effective HRM Strategies for Enhancing Organizational Performance and Employee Engagement. *Advances in Human Resource Management Research*, *1*(3), 126–136. DOI: 10.60079/ahrmr.v1i3.183

Hussain, A., Umair, M., Khan, S., Alonazi, W. B., Almutairi, S. S., & Malik, A. (2024). Exploring sustainable healthcare: Innovations in health economics, social policy, and management. *Heliyon*, *10*(13), e33186. DOI: 10.1016/j.heliyon.2024.e33186 PMID: 39027491

Hussain, S., Waheed, A., Waheed, S., & Majeed, A. (2024). The HR revolution: Redefining performance paradigms in Pakistan's pharma landscape through the moderating role of innovative climate. *PLoS One*, *19*(5), e0301777. DOI: 10.1371/journal.pone.0301777 PMID: 38820526

Hussian, T., Tripathy, S., & Dureja, H. (2025). Navigating the regulatory maze: a comparative analysis of digital therapeutics (DTx) regulations. *Journal of Science and Technology Policy Management.*

Huynh, M.-T. (2025). Individual Data-Driven Mindset and Decision-Making Performance: The Mediating Requirements of Effort and Persistence. *Information Systems Frontiers, 27*(6), 2511–2538. Advance online publication. DOI: 10.1007/s10796-025-10647-6

Iasbeck, L. C. (2007). Imagem e Reputação na Gestão da Identidade Organizacional. *Organicom.* 7.DOI: 10.1007/s10551-009-0259-x

Islam, K. M. A., & Bari, Md. F., Kharusi, S. A., Bhuiyan, A. B., & Faisal-E-Alam, Md. (2023). Impact of transformational leadership, human capital, and job satisfaction on organizational performance in the manufacturing industry. *Problems and Perspectives in Management, 21*(3), 382. DOI: 10.21511/ppm.21(3).2023.31

Ivanov, D., & Dolgui, A. (2021). A digital supply chain twin for managing the disruption risks and resilience in the era of Industry 4.0. *Production Planning and Control, 32*(9), 775–788. DOI: 10.1080/09537287.2020.1768450

Jain, R., Subramanian, J., & Rathore, A. S. (2023). A review of therapeutic failures in late-stage clinical trials. *Expert Opinion on Pharmacotherapy, 24*(3), 389–399. DOI: 10.1080/14656566.2022.2161366 PMID: 36542800

Jalali, M. S., & Kaiser, J. P. (2018). Cybersecurity in hospitals: A systematic, organizational perspective. *Journal of Medical Internet Research, 20*(5), e10059. DOI: 10.2196/10059 PMID: 29807882

Jang, J., Jo, W., & Kim, J. S. (2020). Can employee workplace mindfulness counteract the indirect effects of customer incivility on proactive service performance through work engagement? *Journal of Hospitality Marketing & Management, 29*(7), 812–829. DOI: 10.1080/19368623.2020.1725954

Javanmardi, E., Maresova, P., Xie, N., & Mierzwiak, R. (2024). Exploring business models for managing uncertainty in healthcare, medical devices, and biotechnology industries. *Heliyon, 10*(4), e25962. DOI: 10.1016/j.heliyon.2024.e25962 PMID: 38370194

Jeleel-Ojuade, A. (2024). The Role of Information Silos: An analysis of how the categorization of information creates silos within financial institutions, hindering effective communication and collaboration. *Available at SSRN* 4881342. DOI: 10.2139/ssrn.4881342

João, A. L. da S., Alves, C. P., Silva, C., Diogo, F., & Ferreira, N. D. (2017). Validation of a Nurse Job Satisfaction Scale for the Portuguese population. *Referência (Coimbra)*, *4*(12), 117–130. DOI: 10.12707/RIV16066

Johansson, V., Islind, A. S., Lindroth, T., Angenete, E., & Gellerstedt, M. (2021). Online communities as a driver for patient empowerment: Systematic review. *Journal of Medical Internet Research*, *23*(2), e19910. Advance online publication. DOI: 10.2196/19910 PMID: 33560233

Johnson, K. B., Wei, W., Weeraratne, D., Frisse, M. E., Misulis, K., Rhee, K., Zhao, J., & Snowdon, J. L. (2021). Precision medicine, AI, and the future of personalized health care. *Clinical and Translational Science*, *14*(1), 86–93. DOI: 10.1111/cts.12884 PMID: 32961010

Jommi, C., & Galeone, C. (2023). The evaluation of drug innovativeness in Italy: Key determinants and internal consistency. *PharmacoEconomics Open*, *7*(3), 373–381. DOI: 10.1007/s41669-023-00393-3 PMID: 36763319

Joshua, C. (2025). The role of institutional culture in shaping quality assurance in higher education. *Quality Assurance Practices for Transformative Higher Education in Southern Africa, 24.*

Kaapanda, L. N. (2023). Unleashing Strategic Leadership Potential: Embracing Stewardship Theory for Strategy Execution and Organizational Growth. *Creative Education*, *14*(12), 2442–2462. DOI: 10.4236/ce.2023.1412157

Kabat-Zinn, J. (1994). *Wherever you go, there you are: Mindfulness meditation in everyday life*. Hyperion.

Kabir, M., Rana, M. R. H., & Debnath, A. (2024). The role of quality assurance in accelerating pharmaceutical research and development: Strategies for ensuring regulatory compliance and product integrity. *Journal of Angiotherapy*, *8*(12), 1–11.

Kale, P., Singh, H., & Perlmutter, H. (2000). Learning and protection of proprietary assets in strategic alliances: Building relational capital. *Strategic Management Journal*, *21*(3), 217–237. DOI: 10.1002/(SICI)1097-0266(200003)21:3<217::AID-SMJ95>3.0.CO;2-Y

Kandhare, P., Kurlekar, M., Deshpande, T., & Pawar, A. (2025). A review on revolutionizing healthcare technologies with AI and ML applications in pharmaceutical sciences. *Drugs and Drug Candidates*, *4*(1), 9. DOI: 10.3390/ddc4010009

Kane, G. C., Phillips, A. N., Copulsky, J., & Andrus, G. (2019). *The technology fallacy: How people are the real key to digital transformation.* MIT Press. DOI: 10.7551/mitpress/11661.001.0001

Kaplan, A. M., & Haenlein, M. (2010). Users of the world, unite! The challenges and opportunities of social media. *Business Horizons, 53*(1), 59–68. DOI: 10.1016/j.bushor.2009.09.003

Kaplan, R. S., & Harris-Salamone, K. D. (2009). Health care IT project implementation success and failure. *Journal of Healthcare Information Management, 23*(2), 20–27.

Kaplan, R. S., & Norton, D. P. (2015). *Balanced scorecard success: The Kaplan-Norton collection.* Harvard Business Review Press.

Kaplan, S., Bradley, J. C., Luchman, J. N., & Haynes, D. (2009). On the role of positive and negative affectivity in job performance: A meta-analytic investigation. *The Journal of Applied Psychology, 94*(1), 162–176. DOI: 10.1037/a0013115 PMID: 19186902

Karahan Kaplan, M., Bozkurt, G., Aksu, B. Ç., Bozkurt, S., Günsel, A., & Gencer Çelik, G. (2024). Do emotional demands and exhaustion affect work engagement? The mediating role of mindfulness. *Frontiers in Psychology, 15*, 1432328. DOI: 10.3389/fpsyg.2024.1432328 PMID: 39469238

Karanika-Murray, M., Whysall, Z., Liu-Smith, Y., Feltbower, C., & Challans-Rasool, E. (2023). Understanding organizational learning in a healthcare organization during sudden and disruptive change. *International Journal of Workplace Health Management, 16*(4), 257–280. DOI: 10.1108/IJWHM-09-2022-0145

Karas, L., Feldman, R., Bai, G., Kang, S. Y., & Anderson, G. F. (2019). Pharmaceutical Industry Funding to Patient-Advocacy Organization: A cross-national comparison of disclosure codes and regulation. *Hastings Int'l & Comp. L. Rev., 42*, 453.

Kasoju, N., Remya, N., Sasi, R., Sujesh, S., Soman, B., Kesavadas, C., Muraleedharan, C., Varma, P. H., & Behari, S. (2023). Digital health: Trends, opportunities and challenges in medical devices, pharma and bio-technology. *CSI Transactions on ICT, 11*(1), 11–30. DOI: 10.1007/s40012-023-00380-3

Kaufman Hall. (2020). *2020 State of healthcare performance improvement: Digital transformation in turbulent times.* Kaufman Hall & Associates.

Kaufman, S. J. (2025). The MAD Heuristic and the Nuclear Revolution. *Journal of Global Security Studies, 10*(2), ogae048. DOI: 10.1093/jogss/ogae048

Kebede, D. A., Werke, S. Z., & Kebede, T. (2024). Strategic leadership practices in emerging economies: a systematic review and empirical investigation [Review of *Strategic leadership practices in emerging economies: a systematic review and empirical investigation*]. *Cogent Business & Management, 11*(1). Cogent OA. https://doi.org/DOI: 10.1080/23311975.2024.3018425

Kebe, I. A., Liu, Y., & Kahl, C. (2025). Culturally Attuned Leadership and Employee Behavior During Organizational Change Initiatives in a Developing Economy. *Behavioral Sciences (Basel, Switzerland)*, *15*(3), 349. DOI: 10.3390/bs15030349 PMID: 40150244

Kedia, S., Kiwuwa-Muyingo, S., Uppal, R., Sindi, J. K., & Gitau, E. (2025). Leadership and culture change to advance innovation in women's health. *BMJ (Clinical Research Ed.)*, *391*, e085994. Advance online publication. DOI: 10.1136/bmj-2025-085994 PMID: 41073075

Keesara, S., Jonas, A., & Schulman, K. (2020). Covid-19 and health care's digital revolution. *The New England Journal of Medicine*, *382*(23), e82. DOI: 10.1056/NEJMp2005835 PMID: 32240581

Khalil, R., Macdonald, J. C., Gustafson, A., Aljuburi, L., Bisordi, F., & Beakes-Read, G. (2023). Walking the talk in the digital transformation of regulatory review. *Frontiers in Medicine*, *10*, 1233142. DOI: 10.3389/fmed.2023.1233142 PMID: 37564043

Khalilzadeh, M., Masoumi, S., & Masoumi, I. (2019). Identification and prioritization of factors influencing organization risk tolerance level. *Journal of Advances in Management Research*, *16*(4), 417–435. DOI: 10.1108/JAMR-07-2018-0061

Kharl, H. A. A. (2026). *PharmA AI: Revolutionizing Drug Discovery and Healthcare with Artificial Intelligence*. IBH Publisher.

Kieffer, M. E. (2024). Why Oncology Global Safety Teams Should Develop the Safety Section of the Study's Target Product Profile (TPP). *Pharmaceutical Medicine*, *38*(2), 97–108. DOI: 10.1007/s40290-024-00516-z PMID: 38411854

Kietzmann, J., Paschen, J., & Treen, E. (2018). Artificial intelligence in advertising: How marketers can leverage artificial intelligence along the consumer journey. *Journal of Advertising Research*, *58*(3), 263–267. DOI: 10.2501/JAR-2018-035

Kipasika, H. J. (2024). Expression of leadership mission, vision, values, and strategic objectives in academic institution development practices. *Journal of Research Innovation and Implications in Education*, *8*(1), 393–402.

Kiran, V. S., Shanmugam, V., Raju, R. K., & Kanagasabapathy, J. R. (2022). Impact of Human Capital Management on Organizational Performance With the Mediation Effect of Human Resource Analytics. *International Journal of Professional Business Review*, *7*(3), e0667. Advance online publication. DOI: 10.26668/businessreview/2022.v7i3.0667

Kirtley, J., & O'Mahony, S. (2023). What is a pivot? Explaining when and how entrepreneurial firms decide to make strategic change and pivot. *Strategic Management Journal*, *44*(1), 197–230. DOI: 10.1002/smj.3131

Knudsen, R. K., Skovbjerg, S., Pedersen, E. L., Nielsen, C. L., Storkholm, M. H., & Timmermann, C. (2024). Factors affecting implementation of mindfulness in hospital settings: A qualitative meta-synthesis of healthcare professionals' experiences. *International Journal of Nursing Studies Advances*, *100192*, 100192. Advance online publication. DOI: 10.1016/j.ijnsa.2024.100192 PMID: 38746813

Kolodny, A., Courtwright, D. T., Hwang, C. S., Kreiner, P., Eadie, J. L., Clark, T. W., & Alexander, G. C. (2015). The prescription opioid and heroin crisis. *Annual Review of Public Health*, *36*(1), 559–574. DOI: 10.1146/annurev-publhealth-031914-122957 PMID: 25581144

Korjian, S., Daaboul, Y., & Gibson, C. M. (2023). Drug development, clinical trials, and regulatory requirements. *The ESC Textbook of Thrombosis*, 367.

Kosiol, J., Silvester, T., Cooper, H., Alford, S., & Fraser, L. (2024). Revolutionising health and social care: innovative solutions for a brighter tomorrow – a systematic review of the literature [Review of *Revolutionising health and social care: innovative solutions for a brighter tomorrow – a systematic review of the literature*]. *BMC Health Services Research, 24*(1). BioMed Central. https://doi.org/DOI: 10.09186/s12913-024-11099-5

Kostopoulos, I., Stocchi, L., Pourazad, N., & Michaelidou, N. (2025). Mobile applications' stickiness: a review and future research program [Review of *Mobile applications' stickiness: a review and future research program*]. *Journal of Strategic Marketing*, 1. Taylor & Francis. DOI: 10.1080/0965254X.2025.2479830

Kotler, P., Kartajaya, H., & Setiawan, I. (2021). *Marketing 5.0: Technology for humanity*. Wiley.

Krause, R., Roh, J., & Whitler, K. A. (2022). The top management team: Conceptualization, operationalization, and a roadmap for scholarship. *Journal of Management*, *48*(6), 1496–1529. DOI: 10.1177/01492063211072459

Krieger, J. L. (2021). Trials and terminations: Learning from competitors' R&D failures. *Management Science*, *67*(9), 5525–5548. DOI: 10.1287/mnsc.2020.3775

Kruse, C. S., Kothman, K., Anerobi, K., & Abanaka, L. (2016). Adoption factors of the electronic health record: A systematic review. *JMIR Medical Informatics*, *4*(2), e19. DOI: 10.2196/medinform.5525 PMID: 27251559

Kryshtanovych, M., Bekh, Y., Zhyzhko, T., Povstyn, O., & Molnar, O. (2025). The role of creative leadership in change management. *Creativity Studies*, *18*(2), 506–522. DOI: 10.3846/cs.2025.22189

Kühnen, S. (2025). Third-party service or shared success: unraveling the phenomenon of CMOs in the pharmaceutical industry.

Kulkov, I. (2021). Medical technology innovation ecosystems: Factors influencing the formation of new companies.

Kumar, S., Narayanan, S., & Salvador, F. (2020). Innovation in supply networks—A research framework and roadmap. *Journal of Operations Management*, *66*(7-8), 754–767. DOI: 10.1002/joom.1122

Kunisch, S., Birkinshaw, J., Boppel, M., & Choi, K. (2023). Why do firms launch corporate change programs? A contingency perspective on strategic change. *Scandinavian Journal of Management*, *39*(4), 101297. DOI: 10.1016/j.scaman.2023.101297

Kunsch, M. M. K. (2016). A comunicação nas organizações: dos fluxos lineares às dimensões humana e estratégica.

Kupa, E., Adanma, U. M., Ogunbiyi, E. O., & Solomon, N. O. (2024). Cultivating a culture of safety and innovation in the FMCG sector through leadership as well as organizational change. *International Journal of Management & Entrepreneurship Research*, *6*(6), 1787–1803. DOI: 10.51594/ijmer.v6i6.1165

Kusi, L. Y., Opoku-Danso, A., & Afum, E. (2020). Improving Performance of Public Universities in Ghana Through Talent Management: Does Leadership Support Matter? *Global Journal of Management and Business Research*, *41*, 41–68. Advance online publication. DOI: 10.34257/GJMBRAVOL20IS10PG41

Kwiliński, A., Szczepańska-Woszczyna, K., Lyulyov, O., & Pimonenko, T. (2024). Digital public services: Catalysts for healthcare efficiency. *Journal of Open Innovation*, *10*(3), 100319. DOI: 10.1016/j.joitmc.2024.100319

Labib, E. (2024). Artificial intelligence in marketing: Exploring current and future trends. *Cogent Business & Management*, *11*(1), 2348728. Advance online publication. DOI: 10.1080/23311975.2024.2348728

Laermann-Nguyen, U., & Backfisch, M. (2021). Innovation crisis in the pharmaceutical industry? A survey. *SN Business & Economics*, *1*(12), 164. Advance online publication. DOI: 10.1007/s43546-021-00163-5

Lalhunthara, P. B., & Singh, D. (2025). QUANTITATIVE MODELING OF INVESTMENT DECISION-MAKING PROCESSES IN MANAGEMENT ACCOUNTING: A STUDY OF OPTIMIZATION TECHNIQUES AND RISK MANAGEMENT TOOLS. *International Journal of Applied Mathematics*, *38*(8s).

Lee, M., Ly, H., Möller, C. C., & Ringel, M. S. (2019). Innovation in regulatory science is meeting evolution of clinical evidence generation. *Clinical Pharmacology and Therapeutics*, *105*(4), 886–898. DOI: 10.1002/cpt.1354 PMID: 30636288

Lee, P. K. C., Lau, A. K. W., & Cheng, T. C. E. (2013). Employee rights protection and financial performance. *Journal of Business Research*, *66*(10), 1861–1869. DOI: 10.1016/j.jbusres.2013.02.007

Lemak, C. H., Pena, D., Jones, D. A., Kim, D. H., & Guptill, J. (2024). Leadership to Accelerate Healthcare's Digital Transformation: Evidence From 33 Health Systems. *Journal of Healthcare Management / American College of Healthcare Executives*, *69*(4), 267–279. DOI: 10.1097/JHM-D-23-00210 PMID: 38976787

Lenarczyk, G., Minssen, T., Nicholson, P., & Rai, A. (2025). The future of AI regulation in drug development: A comparative analysis. *Journal of Law and the Biosciences*, *12*(2), lsaf028. Advance online publication. DOI: 10.1093/jlb/lsaf028 PMID: 41221487

Levallet, N., & Chan, Y. E. (2019). Organizational knowledge retention and knowledge loss. *Journal of Knowledge Management*, *23*(1), 176–199. DOI: 10.1108/JKM-08-2017-0358

Lexionário. Avaliação de desempenho (função pública) da Assembleia da República. Diário da República https://diariodarepublica.pt/dr/lexionario/termo /avaliacao-desempenho-funcao-publica

Liang, S., & He, Y. (2023). Real-Time Operational Dashboards for Executive Leadership to Drive Agile Decision-Making in Multisite Health Systems. *International Journal of Advanced Computational Methodologies and Emerging Technologies*, *13*(11), 1–11.

Lippmann, W. (2010). Opinião Pública. *RP: Vozes.*

Liu, Y. (2025). The Importance of Cross-Departmental Collaboration Driven by Technology in the Compliance of Financial Institutions. *Economics and Management Innovation*, *2*(5), 15–21.

Liu, Y., Fang, Y., & He, G. (2025). The effect of inclusive leadership on employee wellbeing. *Scientific Reports*, *15*(1), 39991. DOI: 10.1038/s41598-025-23703-7 PMID: 41238609

Li, Y., Xie, E., Teo, H. H., & Peng, M. W. (2020). Formal control and social control in domestic and international buyer–supplier relationships. *Journal of Operations Management, 66*(5), 523–544. DOI: 10.1002/joom.1093

LoCastro, M., & Wasserstein, A. (2025). Exploring Employee Terminations in Search Fund–Acquired Companies and Small Businesses. Yale Case.

Löfqvist, N. (2024). Enhancing capability for continuous organisational improvement and learning in healthcare organisations: a systematic review of the literature 2013–2022 [Review of *Enhancing capability for continuous organisational improvement and learning in healthcare organisations: a systematic review of the literature 2013–2022*]. *BMJ Open Quality, 13*(2). *BMJ (Clinical Research Ed.).* Advance online publication. DOI: 10.09136/bmjoq-2023-002566

Lutfor, M., Al, M., Nadarkhani, F., & Nezab, M. (2025). Advanced Dissolution Testing for Novel Drug Formulations: Challenges, Emerging Methods, and Regulatory Perspectives. *Journal of Angiotherapy, 9*(1), 1–16.

Maclean, N., Abrahmsén-Alami, S., Clark, C., Dörr, F., Florence, A., Ketolainen, J., Lindow, M., Mantanus, J., Rantanen, J., Reynolds, G., Robertson, A., & Markl, D. (2026). Empowering the pharmaceutical workforce for the digital future. *European Journal of Pharmaceutical Sciences : Official Journal of the European Federation for Pharmaceutical Sciences, 220*, 107449. DOI: 10.1016/j.ejps.2026.107449 PMID: 41577303

Madabushi, R., Seo, P., Zhao, L., Tegenge, M., & Zhu, H. (2022). Review: Role of Model-Informed Drug Development Approaches in the Lifecycle of Drug Development and Regulatory Decision-Making. *Pharmaceutical Research, 39*(8), 1669–1680. DOI: 10.1007/s11095-022-03288-w PMID: 35552984

Majidi, S., Daneshkohan, A., Zarei, E., & Ashktorab, T. (2020). Perspectives of health workers on annual performance appraisal: A study in primary health care. *International Journal of Healthcare Management, 14*(4), 1190–1197. DOI: 10.1080/20479700.2020.1755810

Mandel, C. E., & Parija, S. (2024). Risk appetite: A crucial consideration for effective board risk oversight. *Journal of Risk Management in Financial Institutions, 17*(2), 168–182. DOI: 10.69554/GJRD1826

Mandl, K. D., Kreda, D. A., Kohane, I. S., Ramoni, R. B., & Haselkorn, J. K. (2020). SMART on FHIR: A standards-based, interoperable apps platform for electronic health records. *Journal of the American Medical Informatics Association : JAMIA, 23*(5), 899–908. DOI: 10.1093/jamia/ocv189 PMID: 26911829

Mann, S., & Mann, S. (2025). Human resource development in the digital era: Talent management and skill enhancement. In *Immersive Technology for the Gig Economy: Transformative Business Practices* (pp. 381-408). IGI Global Scientific Publishing.

Mantovani, A., Leopaldi, C., Nighswander, C. M., & Di Bidino, R. (2023). Access and reimbursement pathways for digital health solutions and in vitro diagnostic devices: Current scenario and challenges. *Frontiers in Medical Technology*, *5*, 1101476. DOI: 10.3389/fmedt.2023.1101476 PMID: 36891483

Manzoor, S., Dhand, S., & Pandey, A. (2025). The Role of Innovation Culture in Enhancing Employee Engagement: Evidence from Selected IT Firms. *Journal of Neonatal Surgery*, *14*(5S), 676–684. DOI: 10.52783/jns.v14.2117

Mardian, M. T., Musadieq, D. M. A., Iqbal, M., & Ruhana, I. (2025). Understanding the key factors influencing knowledge management in business environments: A systematic review. *F1000 Research*, *14*, 738. DOI: 10.12688/f1000research.165390.2

Maresova, P. (2023). Impact of regulatory changes on innovations in the medical device industry. *International Journal of Health Policy and Management*, *12*, 7262. DOI: 10.34172/ijhpm.2022.7262 PMID: 35942961

Mascarenhas, C., Galvão, A. R., Mendes, T., Marques, C., & Ferreira, J. J. (2025). How do smart specialization strategies influence university-industry collaboration in cross-border regions? *Review of Managerial Science*, •••, 1–37. DOI: 10.1007/s11846-025-00933-7

Matcha, A. (2023). Innovations in healthcare: Transforming patient care through technology, personalized medicine, and global health crises. [IJSR]. *International Journal of Science and Research (Raipur, India)*, *12*(12), 1668–1672. DOI: 10.21275/SR231222082955

Mathews, S. C., McShea, M. J., Hanley, C. L., Ravitz, A., Labrique, A. B., & Cohen, A. B. (2022). Digital health: A path to validation. *NPJ Digital Medicine*, *2*(1), 38. DOI: 10.1038/s41746-019-0111-3 PMID: 31304384

Mazzola, E., Bruccoleri, M., & Perrone, G. (2015). Supply chain of innovation and new product development. *Journal of Purchasing and Supply Management*, *21*(4), 273–284. DOI: 10.1016/j.pursup.2015.04.006

McDermott, O., Antony, J., Sony, M., & Healy, T. (2022). Critical failure factors for continuous improvement methodologies in the Irish MedTech industry. *The TQM Journal*, *34*(7), 18–38. DOI: 10.1108/TQM-10-2021-0289

McHugh, M. (2013). O teste Qui-quadrado de indepedência. *Biochemia Medica*, *23*(2), 143–149. DOI: 10.11613/BM.2013.018 PMID: 23894860

McKenzie, F., Hewitt, C., Holmes, H., Johnson, M. L., & Clarke, T. (2025). Facilitating innovation in healthcare: Insights from the frontline of adoption. *BMJ Innovations*, *11*(3), 126–132. DOI: 10.1136/bmjinnov-2025-001407

McKinsey & Company. (2022). *The future of MedTech: Digital transformation and innovation ecosystems*. McKinsey Global Institute.

McNair, D., Lumpkin, M., Kern, S., & Hartman, D. (2022). Use of RWE to inform regulatory, public health policy, and intervention priorities for the developing world. *Clinical Pharmacology and Therapeutics*, *111*(1), 44–51. DOI: 10.1002/cpt.2449 PMID: 34655224

Mehrabian, A., & Russell, J. A. (1974). *An approach to environmental psychology*. The MIT Press.

Mehrotra, A. (2024). The Strategic Imperative of Quality Management in Pharmaceuticals and Biotechnology. *International Animal Health Journal, 11*(4).

Memon, K. R., Ghani, B., Hyder, S. I., Han, H., Zada, M., Ariza-Montes, A., & Arraño-Muñoz, M. (2022). Management of knowledge and competence through human resource information system—A structured review. *Frontiers in Psychology*, *13*, 944276. Advance online publication. DOI: 10.3389/fpsyg.2022.944276

Mengstie, M. M., Biks, G. A., Cherlin, E., & Curry, L. (2023). Organizational culture and barriers to change in University of Gondar Comprehensive Specialized Hospital Cardiac Unit. *BMC Health Services Research*, *23*(1), 296. Advance online publication. DOI: 10.1186/s12913-023-09278-x PMID: 36978055

Mennemeyer, S. T., Menachemi, N., Rahurkar, S., & Ford, E. W. (2016). Impact of the HITECH Act on physicians' adoption of electronic health records. *Journal of the American Medical Informatics Association : JAMIA*, *23*(2), 375–379. DOI: 10.1093/jamia/ocv103 PMID: 26228764

Meskó, B., Drobni, Z., Bényei, É., Gergely, B., & Győrffy, Z. (2017). Digital health is a cultural transformation of traditional healthcare. *mHealth*, *3*, 38. DOI: 10.21037/mhealth.2017.08.07 PMID: 29184890

Methling, F., Borden, S. A., Veeraraghavan, D., Sommer, I., Siebert, J. U., von Nitzsch, R., & Seidler, M. (2022). Supporting innovation in early-stage pharmaceutical development decisions. *Decision Analysis*, *19*(4), 337–353. DOI: 10.1287/deca.2022.0452

Meyer, K. E., Mudambi, R., & Narula, R. (2011). Multinational Enterprises and Local Contexts: The Opportunities and Challenges of Multiple Embeddedness. *Journal of Management Studies*, *48*(2), 235–252. DOI: 10.1111/j.1467-6486.2010.00968.x

Michaeli, D. T., Michaeli, T., Albers, S., Boch, T., & Michaeli, J. C. (2024). Special FDA designations for drug development: orphan, fast track, accelerated approval, priority review, and breakthrough therapy: Special FDA designations for drug development. *The European Journal of Health Economics : HEPAC : Health Economics in Prevention and Care*, *25*(6), 979–997. DOI: 10.1007/s10198-023-01639-x PMID: 37962724

Mikalef, P.. (2019). Big data analytics capabilities and firm performance. *Information & Management*, *56*(8). Advance online publication. DOI: 10.1016/j.im.2019.103207

Min, M., Desmoulins-Lebeault, F., & Esposito, M. (2017). Should pharmaceutical companies engage in corporate social responsibility? *Journal of Management Development*, *36*(1), 58–70. DOI: 10.1108/JMD-09-2014-0103

Miozza, M., Brunetta, F., & Appio, P. F. (2024). Digital transformation of the pharmaceutical industry: A future research agenda for management studies. *Technological Forecasting and Social Change*, *207*, 123580. DOI: 10.1016/j.techfore.2024.123580

Mittelstadt, B. D., Allo, P., Taddeo, M., Wachter, S., & Floridi, L. (2016). The ethics of algorithms: Mapping the debate. *Big Data & Society*, *3*(2), 2053951716679679. DOI: 10.1177/2053951716679679

Mogaji, I. M., & Dimingu, H. (2024). A Conceptual Exploration of the Impact of Leadership Styles on the Innovative Culture of Organizations. *Open Journal of Leadership*, *13*(2), 136–153. DOI: 10.4236/ojl.2024.132009

Monferdini, L., & Bottani, E. (2024). How do businesses utilize change management for process optimization? A cross-analysis among industrial sectors. *Business Process Management Journal*, *30*(8), 371–414. DOI: 10.1108/BPMJ-03-2024-0158

Moparthi, R. (2024). CMC and Regulatory Affairs Professional: Ensuring Effective Compliance Strategies. *J. Electrical Systems*, *20*(8s), 567–574.

Morgan, J., & Liker, J. K. (2020). *The Toyota product development system: integrating people, process, and technology*. Productivity press.

Morrison, T. M., Pathmanathan, P., Adwan, M., & Margerrison, E. (2018). Advancing regulatory science with computational modeling for medical devices at the FDA's Office of Science and Engineering Laboratories. *Frontiers in Medicine*, *5*, 241. DOI: 10.3389/fmed.2018.00241 PMID: 30356350

Mozaffari, F., Rahimi, M., Yazdani, H., & Sohrabi, B. (2023). Employee attrition prediction in a pharmaceutical company using both machine learning approach and qualitative data. *Benchmarking*, *30*(10), 4140–4173. DOI: 10.1108/BIJ-11-2021-0664

Naeem, M. S., Naeem, M., Mehmood, M., Sulman, A. A., & Kharl, H. A. A. (2026). MACHINE LEARNING IN FORMULATION OPTIMIZATION AND PROCESS CONTROL. *PharmA AI: Revolutionizing Drug Discovery and Healthcare with Artificial Intelligence*.

Naidoo, G., & Mafora, P. P. (2023). An integrated leadership approach in improving service delivery in health care. *International Journal of Research in Business and Social Science (2147-4478), 12*(10), 126. DOI: 10.20525/ijrbs.v12i10.3117

Nair, S. (2025). Explainable AI in GXP validation: Balancing automation, traceability, and regulatory trust in the pharmaceutical industry. *Clinical Medicine and Health Research Journal, 5*(05), 1430–1442. DOI: 10.18535/cmhrj.v5i05.509

Nakandi, B. T., Muhimbise, O., Djuhadi, A., Mulerwa, M., McGrath, J., Makobore, P. N., Rollins, A. M., & Ssekitoleko, R. T. (2023). Experiences of medical device innovators as they navigate the regulatory system in Uganda. *Frontiers in Medical Technology, 5*, 1162174. DOI: 10.3389/fmedt.2023.1162174 PMID: 37181098

Narayan, A. K., Boone, N., Monga, N., McFarlane, N., Mango, V. L., Seifert, M., Smith, A., Woods, R. W., & Weissman, I. A. (2024). Fostering organizational excellence through inclusive leadership: Practical guide for radiology leaders. *Radiographics : A Review Publication of the Radiological Society of North America, Inc., 44*(9), e230162. DOI: 10.1148/rg.230162 PMID: 39146206

National Human Genome Research Institute. (2023). The cost of sequencing a human genome. National Institutes of Health. https://www.genome.gov/about-genomics/fact-sheets/Sequencing-Human-Genome-cost

Ndioumabia, O. (2022). Unveiling the power of pharmaceutical sciences from molecules to medicines. *Journal Wetenskap Health, 3*(2), 11–20.

Negas, E. (2022). *Estatística descritiva. 2ª edição*. Edições Silabo.

Ninassi, C., & Burrell, D. N. (2023). Teaching business leadership skills to professionals in healthcare cybersecurity, biodefense and biotechnology through experiential learning methods. *Health Economics and Management Review, 4*(3), 82–94. DOI: 10.61093/hem.2023.3-07

Nonaka, I., & Takeuchi, H. (1995). *The knowledge-creating company: How Japanese companies create the dynamics of innovation*. Oxford University Press. DOI: 10.1093/oso/9780195092691.001.0001

Noor, I., Mahmood, S., Aslam, M., Iqbal, S., Naeem, M. S., Shafaqat, M., Sulman, A., Awan, A., Aamir, H., & Kharl, A. (2026). AI ALGORITHMS AND TOOLS FOR PHARMACEUTICAL APPLICATIONS. *PharmA AI: Revolutionizing Drug Discovery and Healthcare with Artificial Intelligence*.

Notarnicola, I., Duka, B., Lommi, M., Grosha, E., Maria, M. D., Iacorossi, L., Mastroianni, C., Ivziku, D., Rocco, G., & Stievano, A. (2024). Transformational Leadership and Its Impact on Job Satisfaction and Personal Mastery for Nursing Leaders in Healthcare Organizations. *Nursing Reports*, *14*(4), 3561–3574. DOI: 10.3390/nursrep14040260 PMID: 39585151

Nova School of Business and Economics. (2022) Universidade de Lisboa. Recursos Humanos em Saúde - Relatório 2022. https://www.novasbe.unl.pt/Portals/0/Files/Soci al%20Equity%20Initiative/Nova%20SBE_KC%20H ealth_Recursos%20Humanos_2022.pdf

Nunes, M., Bagnjuk, J., Abreu, A., Cardoso, E., Smith, J., & Saraiva, C. (2023). Managing collaborative risks of integrated open-innovation and hybrid stage-gate model by applying social network analysis—A case study. *Sustainability (Basel)*, *15*(6), 5474. DOI: 10.3390/su15065474

Nwoke, J. (2024). Regulatory compliance and risk management in pharmaceuticals and healthcare. *International Journal of Health Sciences*, *7*(6), 60–88. DOI: 10.47941/ijhs.2223

O'Neill, A., Vaz, R., Marques, M., & Piedade, L. (2025). Strategic leadership of outsourced teams in the biotech sector: Unlocking value chain efficiency. *Journal of Law and Sustainable Development*, *13*(7), 1–20. DOI: 10.55908/sdgs.v13i7.4493

Obermeyer, Z., Powers, B., Vogeli, C., & Mullainathan, S. (2019). Dissecting racial bias in an algorithm used to manage the health of populations. *Science*, *366*(6464), 447–453. DOI: 10.1126/science.aax2342 PMID: 31649194

Odunaike, A. (2025). Integrating real-time financial data streams to enhance dynamic risk modeling and portfolio decision accuracy. *Int J Comput Appl Technol Res*, *14*(08), 1–16.

OECD. (2023). *Health at a glance 2023: OECD indicators*. OECD Publishing. DOI: 10.1787/7a7afb35-en

OECD/European Commission. (2024). *Health at a Glance: Europe 2024: State of Health in the EU Cycle*. OECD Publishing., DOI: 10.1787/b3704e14-

Office of the National Coordinator for Health Information Technology. (2020). 21st Century Cures Act: Interoperability, information blocking, and the ONC health IT certification program. *Federal Register*, *85*(25), 25642–25961.

Ogbodo, D. C., Awan, I.-U., Cullen, A., & Zahrah, F. (2025). From regulation to reality: A framework to bridge the gap in digital health data protection. *Electronics (Basel)*, *14*(13), 2629. DOI: 10.3390/electronics14132629

Ogbuagu, O. O., Mbata, A. O., Balogun, O. D., Oladapo, O., Ojo, O. O., & Muonde, M. (2023). Quality assurance in pharmaceutical manufacturing: Bridging the gap between regulations, supply chain, and innovations. *International Journal of Multidisciplinary Research and Growth Evaluation*, *4*(1), 823–831. DOI: 10.54660/.IJMRGE.2023.4.1-823-831

Okosieme, O. O., Okosieme, O., Amewonor-Etsey, W. K., Oyeyemi, D. O., & Biriku, K. (2025). The Role of Strategic Communication in Translating Labor Market Analytics into Workforce Policy. *International Journal of Scientific and Management Research*, *8*(11), 39–56. DOI: 10.37502/IJSMR.2025.81104

Olawale, H. O., Isibor, N. J., & Fiemotongha, J. E.Habeeb Olatunji OlawaleNgozi Joan IsiborJoyce Efekpogua Fiemotongha. (2024). A cultural conduct risk assessment model for embedding ethical governance in financial and insurance sales practices. *International Journal of Scientific Research in Science and Technology*, *11*(2), 1033–1045. DOI: 10.32628/IJSRST251222712

Oliver, R. L. (1980). A Cognitive Model of the Antecedents and Consequences of Satisfaction Decisions. *JMR, Journal of Marketing Research*, *17*(4), 460–469. DOI: 10.1177/002224378001700405

Ollif, K., & Patel, J. (2025). *Current US university-industry partnerships: Realignment and opportunity*. The National Academies.

Opderbeck, D. W. (2019). Artificial intelligence in pharmaceuticals, biologics, and medical devices: Present and future regulatory models. *Fordham Law Review*, *88*, 553.

Owolabi, O. R., Olatoye, F. O., Elufioye, O. A., & Okunade, B. A. (2024). Human resources management in healthcare: recruitment, retention, and workforce development: A review [Review of *Human resources management in healthcare: recruitment, retention, and workforce development: A review*]. *World Journal of Advanced Research and Reviews, 21*(2), 950. GSC Online Press. https://doi.org/DOI: 10.30542/wjarr.2024.21.2.0522

Pantelidis, V. S. (2009). Reasons to use virtual reality in education and training courses and a model to determine when to use virtual reality.

Parasuraman, A., Zeithaml, V. A., & Berry, L. L. (1988). SERVQUAL: A multiple-item scale for measuring consumer perceptions of service quality. *Journal of Retailing, 64*(1), 12–40.

Park, D.-H., Lee, J., & Han, I. (2007). The Effect of On-Line Consumer Reviews on Consumer Purchasing Intention: The Moderating Role of Involvement. *International Journal of Electronic Commerce, 11*(4), 125–148. DOI: 10.2753/JEC1086-4415110405

Parker, E. (2024). *The Illusion of Innovation: Escape" Efficiency" and Unleash Radical Progress.* Simon and Schuster. Paul, A. L. Cloud-Based Post-Market Surveillance Platforms: Enhancing Signal Detection and Risk Mitigation in Medical Devices.

Park, S., Kim, H.-K., Lee, H.-J., Choi, M., Lee, M., & Jakovljevic, M. (2023). Strategic management and organizational culture of medical device companies in relation to corporate performance. *Journal of Medical Economics, 26*(1), 781–792. DOI: 10.1080/13696998.2023.2224168 PMID: 37300440

Parween, S. (2024). The significance of employee training and development on enhancing workforce efficiency.

Penchev, P., & Kenarova-Pencheva, I. (2025). Agility, Flexibility, Responsiveness and Competitiveness–the Challenge to Define the Difference. Proceedings of the International Conference on Business Excellence, Post, C., De Smet, H., Uitdewilligen, S., Schreurs, B., & Leysen, J. (2022). Participative or directive leadership behaviors for decision-making in crisis management teams? *Small Group Research, 53*(5), 692–724.

Peng, F., Zeng, X., & Li, Y. (2024). Female stereotype and occupational stigma. *Annals of Tourism Research, 109*, 103837. DOI: 10.1016/j.annals.2024.103837

Pesqueira, A., & Almeida, D. (2026). Breaking Barriers: Redefining Legal and Regulatory Boundaries for a Sustainable Financial Future in Pharmaceuticals and. In *Legal and Regulatory Considerations of Leveraging Sustainable Finance* (pp. 83-110). IGI Global Scientific Publishing.

Pfatteicher, S. K. (2025). *Collaborative Thinking: How to Build and Sustain College Consortia.* JHU Press. DOI: 10.56021/9781421453323

Pham, T. (2025). Ethical and legal considerations in healthcare AI: Innovation and policy for safe and fair use. *Royal Society Open Science, 12*(5), 241873. DOI: 10.1098/rsos.241873 PMID: 40370601

Phares, S., Trusheim, M., Emond, S. K., & Pearson, S. D. (2024). Managing the challenges of paying for gene therapy: Strategies for market action and policy reform in the United States. *Journal of Comparative Effectiveness Research, 13*(12), e240118. DOI: 10.57264/cer-2024-0118 PMID: 39540549

Philip, B., Mathew, G. A., Sebastian, R. T., Eshwari, B., Roopa, M., & Mathews, S. B. (2024). Strategizing Talent Acquisition for Fostering Future Workforce Success: Addressing Millennial Turnover and Hiring Challenges in a Rapidly Evolving Business Landscape. In *Anticipating Future Business Trends: Navigating Artificial Intelligence Innovations: Volume 1* (pp. 357-368). Springer.

Pisano, G. P. (2006). *Science Business: The Promise, the Reality, and the Future of Biotech.* Harvard Business School Press.

Polimerou, R., & Spais, G. S. (2025). Establishing relationships amongst brands and customers via strategic social media chatbots for telecom goods and services. *Journal of Marketing Analytics.* DOI: 10.1057/s41270-025-00396-5

Pontes, B. R. (2021). *Avaliação de Desempenho: métodos clássicos e contemporâneos, avaliação por objetivos, competências e equipes. 14ª Edição.* Editora LTR.

Porter, M. E. (2008). The five competitive forces that shape strategy. *Harvard Business Review, 86*(1), 78–93. PMID: 18271320

Porter, M. E., & Teisberg, E. O. (2006). *Redefining health care: Creating value-based competition on results.* Harvard Business School Press.

Powell, W. W., Koput, K. W., & Smith-Doerr, L. (1996). Interorganizational collaboration and the locus of innovation: Networks of Learning in Biotechnology. *Administrative Science Quarterly, 41*(1), 116. DOI: 10.2307/2393988

Presbitero, A., & Toledano, L. S. (2018). Global team members' performance and the roles of cross-cultural training, cultural intelligence, and contact intensity: The case of global teams in IT offshoring sector. *International Journal of Human Resource Management, 29*(14), 2188–2208. DOI: 10.1080/09585192.2017.1322118

Price, W. N.II, & Cohen, I. G. (2019). Privacy in the age of medical big data. *Nature Medicine, 25*(1), 37–43. DOI: 10.1038/s41591-018-0272-7 PMID: 30617331

Purc, E., & Łaguna, M. (2019). Personal Values and Innovative Behavior of Employees. *Frontiers in Psychology, 10*, 865. Advance online publication. DOI: 10.3389/fpsyg.2019.00865 PMID: 31057470

Puttaraju, K. H. (2024). Accelerating Innovation Through Data-Enabled Agile Stage-Gate Processes: Implications For Business Strategy And Execution. *International Journal of Core Engineering & Management*, *7*(11), 204–216.

Ragsdale, J.Jr. (2024). *Effective Business Strategies to Mitigate Outsourcing Failures*. Walden University.

Rai, B., Srivastava, J., & Saxena, P. (2025). Challenges in translating laboratory findings to drug development. In *Protein Misfolding in Neurodegenerative Diseases* (pp. 319–354). Elsevier. DOI: 10.1016/B978-0-443-18716-2.00009-0

Rajapathirana, R. P. J., & Hui, Y. (2020). Relationship between innovation capability, innovation type, and firm performance. *Journal of Innovation & Knowledge*, *3*(1), 44–55. DOI: 10.1016/j.jik.2017.06.002

Rajpurkar, P., Chen, E., Banerjee, O., & Topol, E. J. (2022). AI in health and medicine. *Nature Medicine*, *28*(1), 31–38. DOI: 10.1038/s41591-021-01614-0 PMID: 35058619

Ramakrishnan, M. (2025). *From Finance Experts to Strategic Partners: Addressing Cross-Functional Preparedness in Higher Education*

Ramesh, H. (2023). A framework for corporate innovation management and managerial innovation in medical devices industry.

Ranbhor, R., & Kulkarni, P. (2025). Evaluating Biosimilar Development Projects: An Analytical Framework Utilizing Net Present Value. *Biologics*, •••, 125–135. PMID: 40165807

Rasmussen, N. (2014). *Gene jockeys: Life science and the rise of biotech enterprise*. JHU Press. DOI: 10.1353/book.29448

Raut, N., Bajaj, K., Matte, P., Vhora, M., Kale, V., Umekar, M., & Harane, S. (2023). Building bridges: Harmonization efforts for enhanced collaboration between developed and developing countries. *Int J Drug Regul Aff*, *11*(3), 68–79. DOI: 10.22270/ijdra.v11i3.622

Ravinetto, R., Henriquez, R., Srinivas, P. N., Bradley, H., Coetzee, R., Ochoa, T. J., Ngabonziza, J. C. S., Mazarati, J.-B., Van Damme, W., & van de Pas, R. (2024). Shaping the future of global access to safe, effective, appropriate and quality health products. *BMJ Global Health*, *9*(1), e014425. DOI: 10.1136/bmjgh-2023-014425 PMID: 38195155

Reich, M. R. (2018). The core roles of transparency and accountability in the governance of global health public–private partnerships. *Health Systems and Reform*, *4*(3), 239–248. DOI: 10.1080/23288604.2018.1465880 PMID: 30207904

Reis, E., Melo, P., Andrade, R., & Calapez, T. (2022). Estatística Aplicada – Volume 2, 6ª edição. Edições Silabo. ISBN: 978-972-618- 986-2

Reis, F. (2010) Como elaborar uma dissertação e mestrado segundo Bolonha. Pactor. ISBN 978- 989-693-000-4

Reis, M. do C. (2009). Comunicação Organizacional e Relações Públicas no Brasil são singulares? *Organicom*. 6.

Reis, E. (2019). *Estatística Descritiva. 7ª edição*. Edições Sílabo.

Rejon-Parrilla, J. C., Epstein, D., Mestre-Ferrandiz, J., & Espín, J. (2025). A Framework for Considering the Requirement of the Public Sector in R&D of Health Technology [Review of *A Framework for Considering the Requirement of the Public Sector in R&D of Health Technology*]. *Pharmaceutical Medicine*. Adis, Springer Healthcare. DOI: 10.1007/s40290-025-00576-9

Rejon-Parrilla, J. C., Espin, J., & Epstein, D. (2022). How innovation can be defined, evaluated, and rewarded in health technology assessment. *Health Economics Review*, *12*(1), 1. DOI: 10.1186/s13561-021-00342-y PMID: 34981266

Relling, M. V., & Evans, W. E. (2015). Pharmacogenomics in the clinic. *Nature*, *526*(7573), 343–350. DOI: 10.1038/nature15817 PMID: 26469045

Richard, O. C., Murthi, B. S., & Ismail, K. (2007). The impact of racial diversity on intermediate and long-term performance: The moderating role of environmental context. *Strategic Management Journal*, *28*(12), 1213–1233. DOI: 10.1002/smj.633

Ridwan, S., Syah, T. Y. R., Kustiawan, U., & Nofierni, N. (2025). Financial planning and investment feasibility analysis based on five-year projections using ROI, NPV, IRR, and financial ratios. *Journal La Bisecoman*, *6*(2), 489–506. DOI: 10.37899/journallabisecoman.v6i2.1970

Riza, M. F., Hutahayan, B., & Chong, H. Y. (2025). Fostering high-performing organizations in higher education: The effect of participative leadership, organizational culture, and innovation on organizational performance and commitment. *Cogent Education*, *12*(1), 2448884. DOI: 10.1080/2331186X.2024.2448884

Roberts, P., & Hamilton Edwards, L. (2023). Portfolio management: A new direction in public sector strategic management research and practice. *Public Administration Review*, *83*(4), 947–959. DOI: 10.1111/puar.13633

Romiti, A., Vecchio, M. D., Cavicchi, C., & Vagnoni, E. (2025). Healthcare organizations in crisis context: Decision-making models and requirements of CEOs. *BMC Health Services Research*, *25*(1), 273. DOI: 10.1186/s12913-025-12420-6

Ross, J. M., Fisch, J. H., & Varga, E. (2018). Unlocking the value of real options: How firm-specific learning conditions affect R&D investments under uncertainty. *Strategic Entrepreneurship Journal*, *12*(3), 335–353. DOI: 10.1002/sej.1275

Roth, L., Bempong, D., Babigumira, J. B., Banoo, S., Cooke, E., Jeffreys, D., Kasonde, L., Leufkens, H. G., Lim, J. C., Lumpkin, M., Mahlangu, G., Peeling, R. W., Rees, H., Ndomondo-Sigonda, M., Stergachis, A., Ward, M., & Nwokike, J. (2018). Expanding global access to essential medicines: Investment priorities for sustainably strengthening medical product regulatory systems. *Globalization and Health*, *14*(1), 102. DOI: 10.1186/s12992-018-0421-2 PMID: 30382856

Rouissi, C. M. (2025). Navigating change: The role of change management strategies and cultural factors in Saudi Arabian organizations. *Frontiers in Psychology*, *16*, 1551902. DOI: 10.3389/fpsyg.2025.1551902 PMID: 40959749

Ryu, J. M., Park, S., Park, Y., Park, J., & Lee, M. (2021). Innovative Culture and Firm Performance of Medical Device Companies: Mediating Effects of Investment in Education and Training. *International Journal of Environmental Research and Public Health*, *18*(17), 8926. DOI: 10.3390/ijerph18178926 PMID: 34501515

Sachs, R., Adler, L., & Frank, R. (2023). A holistic view of innovation incentives and pharmaceutical policy reform. *Health Affairs Scholar*, *1*(1), qxad004. Advance online publication. DOI: 10.1093/haschl/qxad004 PMID: 38756835

Salimimoghadam, S., Ghanbaripour, A. N., Tumpa, R. J., & Watanabe, T. (2025). Core leadership competencies of project managers for enhancing project success in today's fast-evolving world: a systematic literature review. *Smart and Sustainable Built Environment*, 1-40.

Samuel, K. Big Data in Regulatory Compliance: Enhancing Reporting Accuracy and Timeliness for Medical Devices.

Sanders, E. B. N., & Stappers, P. J. (2014). Probes, toolkits and prototypes: Three approaches to making in co-designing. *CoDesign*, *10*(1), 5–14. DOI: 10.1080/15710882.2014.888183

Santra, S., Kukreja, P., Saxena, K., Gandhi, S., & Singh, O. V. (2024). Navigating regulatory and policy challenges for AI-enabled combination devices. *Frontiers in Medical Technology*, *6*, 1473350. DOI: 10.3389/fmedt.2024.1473350 PMID: 39669903

Sari, M., Dahrani, D., & Sagala, N. A. (2023). Determinants of employee performance at public hospitals in Indonesia: Examining the moderating role of organizational culture. *Problems and Perspectives in Management*, *22*(1), 57–68. DOI: 10.21511/ppm.22(1).2024.06

Sarkar, S., Searcy, C., & Fraser, E. D. G. (2022). Strategic partnerships and innovation in healthcare technology ecosystems. *Technological Forecasting and Social Change*, *174*, 121254. DOI: 10.1016/j.techfore.2021.121254

Saura, J. R. (2020). Using Data Sciences in Digital Marketing: Framework, methods, and performance metrics. *Journal of Innovation & Knowledge*, *6*(2), 92–102. DOI: 10.1016/j.jik.2020.08.001

Saura, J. R., Škare, V., & Došen, Đ. O. (2024). Is AI-based digital marketing ethical? Assessing a new data privacy paradox. *Journal of Innovation & Knowledge*, *9*(4), 100597. DOI: 10.1016/j.jik.2024.100597

Savickas, Š., & Užienė, L. (2024). Interplay Amongst Knowledge Management and Digital Transformation: Designing Solutions. *European Conference on Knowledge Management, 25*(1), 735. DOI: 10.34190/eckm.25.1.2592

Scavone, C., Di Mauro, G., Mascolo, A., Berrino, L., Rossi, F., & Capuano, A. (2019). The new paradigms in clinical research: From early access programs to the novel therapeutic approaches for unmet medical needs. *Frontiers in Pharmacology*, *10*, 111. DOI: 10.3389/fphar.2019.00111 PMID: 30814951

Schiavone, F., & Simoni, M. (2019). Strategic marketing approaches for the diffusion of innovation in highly regulated industrial markets: The value of market access. *Journal of Business and Industrial Marketing*, *34*(7), 1606–1618. DOI: 10.1108/JBIM-08-2018-0232

Schindler, M., & Eppler, M. J. (2003). Harvesting project knowledge: A review of project learning methods and success factors. *International Journal of Project Management*, *21*(3), 219–228. DOI: 10.1016/S0263-7863(02)00096-0

Schoemaker, P. J., Heaton, S., & Teece, D. (2018). Innovation, dynamic capabilities, and leadership. *California Management Review*, *61*(1), 15–42. DOI: 10.1177/0008125618790246

Schuhmacher, A. (2024). Pharma innovation: How evolutionary economics is shaping the future of pharma R&D. *Drug Discovery Today*, *29*(12), 104222. DOI: 10.1016/j.drudis.2024.104222 PMID: 39510495

Schuhmacher, A., Brief, E., Gassmann, O., Hartl, D., & Hinder, M. (2025). Benchmarking R&D success rates of leading pharmaceutical companies: An empirical analysis of FDA approvals (2006–2022). *Drug Discovery Today, 30*(2), 104291. DOI: 10.1016/j.drudis.2025.104291 PMID: 39805539

Schuhmacher, A., Gassmann, O., Hinder, M., & Hartl, D. (2024). Comparative analysis of FDA approvals by top 20 pharma companies (2014–2023). *Drug Discovery Today, 29*(9), 104128. DOI: 10.1016/j.drudis.2024.104128 PMID: 39097219

Schweizer, P.-J., & Renn, O. (2019). Governance of systemic risks for disaster prevention and mitigation. *Disaster prevention and management: an international journal, 28*(6), 862-874.

Scullion, H., & Collings, D. G. (2011). Global talent management: Introduction. In *Global talent management* (pp. 19–32). Routledge. DOI: 10.4324/9780203865682

Semedo, N., Calheiros, A., & Carvalho, W. (2014). Especificidades e desafios da implementação de um modelo de avaliação de desempenho numa pequena média empresa em Portugal. Conferência - Investigação E Intervenção Em Recursos Humanos, (4). https://doi.org/DOI: 10.26537/iirh.v0i4.2048

Shah, N. P.Nirali P Shah. (2024). Navigating challenges in new product development: Strategies for reducing failure rates in the medical device industry. *World Journal of Advanced Research and Reviews, 22*(03), 786–795. DOI: 10.30574/wjarr.2024.22.3.1740

Shahzad, M. U. (2024). Core competencies for digital leadership development: A perspective from the lens of paradox theory. *The Bottom Line (New York, N.Y.), 37*(4), 454–472. DOI: 10.1108/BL-10-2023-0278

Shajari, S., Kuruvinashetti, K., Komeili, A., & Sundararaj, U. (2023). The emergence of AI-based wearable sensors for digital health technology: A review. *Sensors (Basel), 23*(23), 9498. DOI: 10.3390/s23239498 PMID: 38067871

Shan, Z., & Wang, Y. (2024). Strategic talent development in the knowledge economy: A comparative analysis of global practices. *Journal of the Knowledge Economy, 15*(4), 19570–19596. DOI: 10.1007/s13132-024-01933-w

Sheehan, M., Garavan, T. N., & Morley, M. J. (2023). The Microfoundations of Dynamic Capabilities for Incremental and Radical Innovation in Knowledge-Intensive Businesses. *British Journal of Management, 34*(1), 220–240. DOI: 10.1111/1467-8551.12582

Shepherd, N., Mooi, E., Elbanna, S., & Lou, B. (2023). Fast and high-quality decision-making: The role of behavioral integration. *European Management Review, 20*(4), 679–697. DOI: 10.1111/emre.12573

Shi, C. R., Anadkat, M. J., Mamo, A., & Ortiz, A. E. (2021). Disparities in telehealth access among minority and underserved patient populations in ambulatory dermatology. *Journal of the American Academy of Dermatology, 85*(6), 1640–1642. DOI: 10.1016/j.jaad.2021.06.011 PMID: 33421478

Shipton, H., Fay, D., West, M., Patterson, M., & Birdi, K. (2005). Managing people to promote innovation. *Creativity and Innovation Management, 14*(2), 118–128. DOI: 10.1111/j.1467-8691.2005.00332.x

Shivakumar, P. (2025). *The role of open innovation in medical device development: challenges of navigating the European regulatory landscape* Kauno technologijos universitetas.].

Shortliffe, E. H., & Cimino, J. J. (Eds.). (2021). *Biomedical informatics: Computer applications in health care and biomedicine* (5th ed.). Springer. DOI: 10.1007/978-3-030-58721-5

Silva, P. (2018). Avaliação de desempenho: perceções de justiça organizacional dos funcionários públicos [Tese de Mestrado em engenharia e gestão industrial no Instituto Superior de Engenharia do Porto] http://hdl.handle.net/10400.22/14115

Simon, F. M. (2024). Artificial intelligence in the news: How AI retools, rationalizes, and reshapes journalism and the public arena.

Simpao, A. F., & Rehman, M. A. (2020). Telehealth, artificial intelligence, and the coronavirus disease 2019 pandemic: A perfect storm. *Anesthesia and Analgesia, 131*(5), 1249–1251. DOI: 10.1213/ANE.0000000000005027

Singh, V. K., & Srivastava, V. (2024). A statistical analysis of strategic leadership qualities in the pharmaceutical sector of India's National Capital Region. International Journal of Experimental Research and Review, 41(Spl Vol), 259–279. DOI: 10.52756/ijerr.2024.v41spl.022

Singh, A., Lim, W. M., Jha, S., Kumar, S., & Ciasullo, M. V. (2023). The state of the art of strategic leadership. *Journal of Business Research, 158*, 113676. DOI: 10.1016/j.jbusres.2023.113676

Singh, V. (2007). Ethnic diversity on top corporate boards: A resource dependency perspective. *International Journal of Human Resource Management, 18*(12), 2128–2146. DOI: 10.1080/09585190701695275

Sinsky, C., Colligan, L., Li, L., Prgomet, M., Reynolds, S., Goeders, L., Westbrook, J., Tutty, M., & Blike, G. (2016). Allocation of physician time in ambulatory practice: A time and motion study in 4 specialties. *Annals of Internal Medicine, 165*(11), 753–760. DOI: 10.7326/M16-0961 PMID: 27595430

Siwicki, B. (2022). Healthcare data breach costs hit all-time high for 12th year in a row, IBM report finds. Healthcare IT News. https://www.healthcareitnews.com/news/healthcare-data-breach-costs-hit-all-time-high-12th-year-row-ibm-report-finds

Smith, B. D. (2019). *Leadership in the Life Sciences: Ten Lessons from the C-Suite of Pharmaceutical and Medical Technology Companies*. Routledge. DOI: 10.4324/9780429022319

Smith, P. R., & Zook, Z. (2011). *Marketing communications: Integrating offline and online with social media*. Kogan Page.

Soltanzadeh, A., Zarei, E., Mahdinia, M., & Sadeghi-Yarandi, M. (2024). An integrated approach to assess safety and security risks in chemical process industries. *Journal of Loss Prevention in the Process Industries, 90*, 105344. DOI: 10.1016/j.jlp.2024.105344

Song, X. M., Thieme, R. J., & Xie, J. (1998). The impact of cross-functional joint involvement across product development stages: An exploratory study. *Journal of Product Innovation Management, 15*(4), 289–303. DOI: 10.1111/1540-5885.1540289

Spais, G. S., & Chryssochoidis, G. (2025). Trends and future of artificial intelligence (AI), machine learning (ML) algorithms, and data analytics and their applications and implications for digital marketing and digital promotions. *Journal of Marketing Analytics*. https://doi.org/DOI: 10.09057/s41270-025-00406-6

Spanos, S., Leask, E., Patel, R., Datyner, M., Loh, E., & Braithwaite, J. (2024). Healthcare leaders navigating complexity: a scoping review of key trends in future roles and competencies [Review of *Healthcare leaders navigating complexity: a scoping review of key trends in future roles and competencies*]. *BMC Medical Education, 24*(1). BioMed Central. DOI: 10.1186/s12909-024-05689-4

Spinelli, C., Wisener, M., & Khoury, B. (2019). Mindfulness training for healthcare professionals and trainees: A meta-analysis of randomized controlled trials. *Journal of Psychosomatic Research, 120*, 29–38. DOI: 10.1016/j.jpsychores.2019.03.003 PMID: 30929705

Sriharan, A., Sekercioglu, N., Berta, W., Boet, S., Laporte, A., Strudwick, G., Senkaiahliyan, S., & Ratnapalan, S. (2024). Addressing the health human resources crisis: Strategies for retaining women health care professionals in organizations. *PLoS One*, *19*(6), e0293107. Advance online publication. DOI: 10.1371/journal.pone.0293107 PMID: 38870169

Stahl, G. K., Maznevski, M. L., Voigt, A., & Jonsen, K. (2010). Unraveling the effects of cultural diversity in teams: A meta-analysis of research on multicultural work groups. *Journal of International Business Studies*, *41*(4), 690–709. DOI: 10.1057/jibs.2009.85

Stevens, B. (2004). The Ethics of the US Business Executive: A Study of Perceptions. *Journal of Business Ethics*, *54*(2), 163–171. DOI: 10.1007/s10551-004-9464-9

Subha, S., Shanmugathai, M., Prasanth, A., Varagi, S. S., & Dhanashree, V. (2024). Digital transformation in the pharmaceutical and biotech industry: challenges and research directions. *Digital twins in industrial production and smart manufacturing: an understanding of principles, enhancers, and obstacles*, 297-324.

Suhag, D. (2024). Regulatory and ethical considerations. In *Handbook of Biomaterials for Medical Applications, Volume 2: Applications* (pp. 355-372). Springer. DOI: 10.1007/978-981-97-5906-4_11

Suleiman, T. A., & Adinoyi, A. (2023). Telemedicine and smart healthcare—The role of artificial intelligence, 5G, cloud services, and other enabling technologies. *International Journal of Communications, Network and Systems Sciences*, *16*(3), 31–51. DOI: 10.4236/ijcns.2023.163003

Sundaram, S. (2025). Innovating for the Future: Sustainable Corporate Strategies for Workforce Upskilling and Reskilling. *International Journal of Research in Entrepreneurship & Business Studies*, *6*(3), 33–46. DOI: 10.47259/ijrebs.2025.633

Sureda, E., Chacón-Moscoso, S., Sanduvete-Chaves, S., & Sesé, A. (2021, August 30). A Training Intervention through a 360° Multisource Feedback Model. *International Journal of Environmental Research and Public Health*, *18*(17), 9137. DOI: 10.3390/ijerph18179137 PMID: 34501727

Suriyaamporn, P., Pamornpathomkul, B., Patrojanasophon, P., Ngawhirunpat, T., Rojanarata, T., & Opanasopit, P. (2024). The artificial intelligence-powered new era in pharmaceutical research and development: A review. *AAPS PharmSciTech*, *25*(6), 188. DOI: 10.1208/s12249-024-02901-y PMID: 39147952

Swoboda, B., Huber, C., Schuster, T., & Hirschmann, J. (2017). Corporate Reputation Effects Across Nations: The Impact of Country Distances and Firm-Specific Resources. *MIR. Management International Review, 57*(5), 717–748. DOI: 10.1007/s11575-017-0313-3

Tagscherer, F., & Carbon, C. (2023). Leadership for successful digitalization: A literature review on companies' internal and external aspects of digitalization [Review of *Leadership for successful digitalization: A literature review on companies' internal and external aspects of digitalization*]. *Sustainable Technology and Entrepreneurship, 2*(2), 100039. Elsevier BV. DOI: 10.1016/j.stae.2023.100039

Takawira, B., Kanyangale, M., & Mutambra, E. (2022). An exploratory study towards business sustainability through strategic leadership in emerging pharmaceutical business of South Africa: A case of Alpha distribution. *International Journal of Research in Business and Social Science, 11*(7), 109–120. DOI: 10.20525/ijrbs.v11i7.2077

Takawira, B., Kanyangale, M., & Mutambra, E. (2023). Competencies of strategic leadership towards business sustainability in emerging pharmaceutical business of South Africa: A case of Alpha distribution. *Cogent Social Sciences, 9*(2), 2275443. DOI: 10.1080/23311886.2023.2275443

Takawira, B., & Mutambara, E. (2023). The Roles of Strategic Leadership in Ensuring Sustainable Competitive Advantage: Empirical Evidence from Pharmaceutical Distribution in Emerging Markets. *Business Ethics and Leadership, 7*(4), 89–107. DOI: 10.61093/bel.7(4).89-107.2023

Tanvir, A., Juie, B. J. A., Tisha, N. T., & Rahman, M. M. (2020). Synergizing big data and biotechnology for innovation in healthcare, pharmaceutical development, and fungal research. *International Journal of Biological. Physical and Chemical Studies, 2*(2), 23–32.

Tarekegn, S. M., Tadesse, D., Argaw, M. D., Semahegn, A., Taddesse, L., Shifarraw, S., Enbiale, W., Muluneh, M. D., Abate, B. B., Tamire, A., & Makonnen, M. (2025). Capacity and performance of primary health care in Ethiopia: A novel mixed methods measurement in low-income country. *BMC Primary Care, 26*(1), 299. DOI: 10.1186/s12875-025-02988-7 PMID: 41023838

Tarique, I., Schuler, R., & Gong, Y. (2006). A model of multinational enterprise subsidiary staffing composition. *International Journal of Human Resource Management, 17*(2), 207–224. DOI: 10.1080/09585190500404424

Tate, K., Penconek, T., Dias, B. M., Cummings, G. G., & Bernardes, A. (2023). Authentic leadership, organizational culture and the effects of hospital quality management practices on quality of care and patient satisfaction. *Journal of Advanced Nursing*, *79*(8), 3102–3114. DOI: 10.1111/jan.15663 PMID: 37002558

Tessema, D. B. (2025). Pillars of organizational transformation and sustainability: Leadership, learning, culture, and knowledge management as key success factors in environmental public health. *Health Economics and Management Review*, *6*(1), 1–21. DOI: 10.61093/hem.2025.1-01

Tham, W. Y. (2023). Science, interrupted: Funding delays reduce research activity but having more grants helps. *PLoS One*, *18*(4), e0280576. DOI: 10.1371/journal.pone.0280576 PMID: 37099515

Thirunavukarasu, A. J., Ting, D. S. J., Elangovan, K., Gutierrez, L., Tan, T. F., & Ting, D. S. W. (2023). Large language models in medicine. *Nature Medicine*, *29*(8), 1930–1940. DOI: 10.1038/s41591-023-02448-8 PMID: 37460753

Topol Review. (2019). Preparing the healthcare workforce to deliver the digital future. Health Education England. https://topol.hee.nhs.uk

Topol, E. (2019). *Deep medicine: How artificial intelligence can make healthcare human again*. Basic Books.

Tsenov, S. (2022). Digital transformation in pharmaceutical industry. *Journal of Pharmaceutical Innovation*.

Tsugita, Y., Ushimaru, Y., Kato, T., Sasaki, M., Hata, T., Hosaka, M., Eguchi, H., Doki, Y., & Nakajima, K. (2023). Efficacy of human resource development program for young industry personnel who will be involved in future medical device development. *Surgical Endoscopy*, *37*(12), 9633–9642. DOI: 10.1007/s00464-023-10474-3 PMID: 37891373

Tummuri, S. S. R. (2025). *Enterprise Integration: Strategies, Technologies And Future Trends*. Academic Guru Publishing House.

Uslu, M., & Özutku, H. (2025). The Transformative Impact of Cultural Values on HRM: Shaping Global Practices. *International Journal of Management and Administration*, *9*(18), 145–162. DOI: 10.29064/ijma.1754176

Vahedi, H., Shivyari, S. R., Soltanmohamadi, S., & Babakhanian, F. (2024). The Role of Leadership Competence as well as organizational Culture in Enhancing Healthcare Service Quality. *Journal of Archives in Military Medicine*, *12*(3). Advance online publication. DOI: 10.5812/jamm-156498

Valdez, J. W., Sharma, S., & Gould, J. (2025). Systemic territoriality in academia: The Gollum effect's impact on scientific research and careers. *One Earth*, *8*(6), 101314. DOI: 10.1016/j.oneear.2025.101314

Vallano, A., & Pontes, C. (2024). Escalating costs of innovative medicines: Perspective and proposals. *Frontiers in Public Health*, *12*, 1449707. DOI: 10.3389/fpubh.2024.1449707 PMID: 39381757

Valluvan, S., Prasanth, S., Subramanian, S. P., Sriranjani, G., Sanjay, J., & Sri Abirami, N. (2024). The impact of performance appraisal on employee motivation. Library Progress International. https://bpasjournals.com/libraryscience/index.php/journal/article/view/3708

Van den Bogaert, S., Declercq, J., Christiaens, T., Jacobs, G., & Bracke, P. (2018). In the land of pharma: A qualitative analysis of the reputational discourse of the pharmaceutical industry. *Public Relations Inquiry*, *7*(2), 127–147. DOI: 10.1177/2046147X18774588

Van Der Zalm, A. J., Barroso, J., Browne, P., Casey, W., Gordon, J., Henry, T. R., Kleinstreuer, N. C., Lowit, A. B., Perron, M., & Clippinger, A. J. (2022). A framework for establishing scientific confidence in new approach methodologies. *Archives of Toxicology*, *96*(11), 2865–2879. DOI: 10.1007/s00204-022-03365-4 PMID: 35987941

van Riel, C. B. M. (1995). *Principles of Corporate Communication*. Prentice Hall.

Van Zee, A. (2009). The promotion and marketing of OxyContin. *American Journal of Public Health*, *99*(2), 221–227. DOI: 10.2105/AJPH.2007.131714 PMID: 18799767

Vayena, E., Blasimme, A., & Cohen, I. G. (2018). Machine learning in medicine: Addressing ethical challenges. *PLoS Medicine*, *15*(11), e1002689. DOI: 10.1371/journal.pmed.1002689 PMID: 30399149

Veldsman, D., & van der Merwe, M. (2022). Promises in action: The role of employer brand, employee value proposition and employee experience in delivering on psychological contract expectations. *EWOP in Practice, 16*(1).

Ventola, C. L. (2014). Social media and health care professionals: Benefits, risks, and best practices. *P&T : a Peer-Reviewed Journal for Formulary Management*, *39*(7), 491–520. PMID: 25083128

Vest, J. R., & Gamm, L. D. (2017). Health information exchange: Persistent challenges and new strategies. *Journal of the American Medical Informatics Association : JAMIA*, *17*(3), 288–294. DOI: 10.1136/jamia.2010.003673 PMID: 20442146

Vial, G. (2019). Understanding digital transformation: A review and a research agenda. *The Journal of Strategic Information Systems, 28*(2), 118–144. DOI: 10.1016/j.jsis.2019.01.003

Villena, V. H., & Gioia, D. A. (2018). On the riskiness of lower-tier suppliers: Managing sustainability in supply networks. *Journal of Operations Management, 64*(1), 65–87. DOI: 10.1016/j.jom.2018.09.004

Visser, B. C.. (2013). Mobile medical applications. *Journal of Medical Internet Research, 15*(3). Advance online publication. DOI: 10.2196/jmir.2380

Vogel, L. (2021). How COVID-19 normalized virtual care. *Canadian Medical Association Journal, 193*(7), E247–E248. DOI: 10.1503/cmaj.1095946

Voigt, P., & Von dem Bussche, A. (2017). *The EU General Data Protection Regulation (GDPR): A practical guide*. Springer. DOI: 10.1007/978-3-319-57959-7

Vudugula, S., Chebrolu, S. K., Bhuiyan, M., & Rozony, F. Z. (2023). Integrating artificial intelligence in strategic business decision-making: A systematic review of predictive models. *International Journal of Scientific Interdisciplinary Research, 4*(1), 01-26.

Wagner, B., & Fain, N. (2018). Regulatory influences on innovation in the public sector: The role of regulatory regimes. *Public Management Review, 20*(8), 1205–1227. DOI: 10.1080/14719037.2017.1350282

Wang, Q., Wang, F., Zhang, S., Liu, C., Feng, Y., & Chen, J. (2023). Effects of mindfulness-based interventions on stress and burnout in nurses: A systematic review and meta-analysis. *Frontiers in Psychiatry, 14*, 1218340. DOI: 10.3389/fpsyt.2023.1218340 PMID: 37599884

Wang, S., Yang, H., & Bai, G. (2025). Construction of intelligent decision support systems through integration of retrieval-augmented generation and knowledge graphs. *Scientific Reports, 15*(1), 35462. DOI: 10.1038/s41598-025-19257-3

Wang, X., Wen, X., Paşamehmetoğlu, A., & Guchait, P. (2021). Hospitality employee mindfulness and its impact on creativity and customer satisfaction: The moderating role of organizational error tolerance. *International Journal of Hospitality Management, 94*, 102846. DOI: 10.1016/j.ijhm.2020.102846

Wang, Y., & Jin, X. (2021). Structural risk of diversified project financing of city investment company in China based on the best worst method. *Engineering, Construction, and Architectural Management, 28*(1), 196–215. DOI: 10.1108/ECAM-05-2019-0249

Wang, Z., Wu, P., Hou, Y., Guo, J., & Lin, C. (2024). The effects of mindfulness-based interventions on alleviating academic burnout in medical students: A systematic review and meta-analysis. *BMC Public Health, 24*(1), 1414. DOI: 10.1186/s12889-024-18938-4 PMID: 38802770

Waruwu, Y. (2024). Opportunities and challenges of results- based performance management in the public sector. *International Journal of Science Academic Research, 5*(1), 6806–6812. http://www.scienceijsar.com

Weaver, S. J., Lubomksi, L. H., Wilson, R. F., Pfoh, E. R., Martinez, K. A., & Dy, S. M. (2013). Promoting a culture of safety as a patient safety strategy: A systematic review. *Annals of Internal Medicine, 158*(5 Pt 2), 369–374. DOI: 10.7326/0003-4819-158-5-201303051-00002 PMID: 23460092

Weill, P., & Ross, J. W. (2004). *IT governance: How top performers manage IT decision rights for superior results*. Harvard Business School Press.

Weintraub, P., & McKee, M. (2018). Leadership for innovation in healthcare: An exploration. *International Journal of Health Policy and Management, 8*(3), 138–144. DOI: 10.15171/ijhpm.2018.122 PMID: 30980629

Willie, M. M. (2025). Perspective Chapter: Strategies for Successful Cultural Change during Strategy Implementation. In *Business, management and economics*. DOI: 10.5772/intechopen.114935

Wizemann, T. (2010). Public Health Effectiveness of the FDA 510(k) Clearance Process: Balancing Patient Safety and Innovation: Workshop Report. Washington (DC): National Academies Press (US). 4, The Medical Device Industry Innovation Ecosystem. Available from: https://www.ncbi.nlm.nih.gov/books/NBK209786/

Woolley, S. M. N., & Currie, G. (2023). The Practices and Processes of Strategic Leadership. In *Organizational behaviour in health care* (p. 131). Springer International Publishing., DOI: 10.1007/978-3-031-24212-0_7

World Health Organization. (2019). *WHO guideline: Recommendations on digital interventions for health system strengthening*. WHO. https://apps.who.int/iris/handle/10665/311980

World Health Organization. (2020). *Global strategy on digital health 2020–2025*. World Health Organization.

World Health Organization. (2021). Global strategy on digital health 2020–2025. WHO Press. https://www.who.int/docs/default-source/documents/gs4dhdaa2a9f352b0445bafbc79ca799dce4d.pdf

Wright, T. A., & Cropanzano, R. (2004). The Role of Psychological Well-Being in Job Performance: A Fresh Look at an Age-Old Quest. Organizational Dynamics, 33(4), 338 351. DOI: 10.1016/j.orgdyn.2004.09.002

Wu, J., & Gu, N. (2025). New orientation of interdisciplinarity in medicine: Engineering medicine. *Engineering (Beijing)*, *45*, 252–261. DOI: 10.1016/j.eng.2024.09.009

Wujarso, R., & Dameria, R. (2023). *Human capital management as a resource in achieving competitive advantage*. Asadel Publisher.

Wu, P., Yeh, G., & Hsiao, C. (2011). The effect of store image and service quality on brand image and pur-chase intention for private label brands. *Australasian Marketing Journal*, *19*(1), 30–39. https://doi.org/10.%201016/j.ausmj.2010.11.001. DOI: 10.1016/j.ausmj.2010.11.001

Xi, Y., Zhou, L., & Wang, H. (2025). Ambidextrous leadership and innovation: A process perspective and an experimental approach. *Humanities & Social Sciences Communications*, *12*(1), 612. Advance online publication. DOI: 10.1057/s41599-025-04922-9

Yadav, B., et al. (2012). CRM in pharmaceutical marketing.

Yang, Z., Dong, M., Guo, H., & Peng, W. (2025). Empowering resilience through digital transformation intentions: Synergizing knowledge sharing and transformational leadership amid COVID-19. *Journal of Organizational Change Management*, *38*(1), 59–81. DOI: 10.1108/JOCM-07-2023-0303

Yi, Y., Chen, Y., & He, X. (2021). CEO Leadership, Strategic Decision Comprehensiveness, and Firm Performance: The Moderating Requirement of TMT Cognitive Conflict. *Management and Organization Review*, *18*(1), 131–166. DOI: 10.1017/mor.2021.10

Young-Babb, T., Hall, L. F., Kuhn, A., & Pryor, C. (2025). Professional Development: Enhancing Adaptability for a Future-Ready Workforce. *International Journal of Advanced Corporate Learning*, *18*(3), 89–102. DOI: 10.3991/ijac.v18i3.52541

Yusof, A. N. M., & Ahmad, M. F. (2024). Unlocking HR's Hidden Treasure on Innovation Capability: The Mediating Requirement of Knowledge Management Capacity. *Information Management and Business Review*, *16*(3S(I)a), 282–298. DOI: 10.22610/imbr.v16i3S(I)a.4211

Zaiter, F., & Azouz, M. (2025). Digital Companies: Smart Decision-Making and Knowledge Management for Adapting to Rapid Changes. *Accounting & Finance/ Oblìk ì Fìnansi, 107*(1).

Zajac, S., Woods, A., Tannenbaum, S., Salas, E., & Holladay, C. L. (2021). Overcoming challenges to teamwork in healthcare: A team effectiveness framework and evidence-based guidance. *Frontiers in Communication*, *6*, 606445. DOI: 10.3389/fcomm.2021.606445

Zayed, A., & Farghly, R. (2023). Analyzing the expected role of strategic leadership and supportive culture in executing business strategies: The mediating role of employee engagement. *The Academic Journal of Contemporary Commerical Research*, *3*(2), 18–42. DOI: 10.21608/ajccr.2023.304706

Zeleke, L. W., Guyo, W., & Moronge, M. (2025). Adaptive Leadership Styles as well as organizational Performance: Evidence from Local NGOs in Ethiopia. *Innovation Journal of Social Sciences and Economic Review.*, *59*(2), 68–75. Advance online publication. DOI: 10.36923/ijsser.v7i2.323

Zhang, Y., Dare, P. S., Saleem, A., & Chinedu, C. C. (2022). A sensation of COVID-19: How organizational culture is coordinated by human resource management to achieve organizational innovative performance in healthcare institutions. *Frontiers in Psychology*, *13*, 943250. Advance online publication. DOI: 10.3389/fpsyg.2022.943250 PMID: 36248478

Zhang, Y., & Griffith, M. D. (2023). Human Resource Management Systems and Firm Innovation: A MetaAnalytic Study. Economic and Business Review, 25(4), 202-215. https://doi.org/DOI: 10.15458/2335-4216.1327

Zhao, Y., Qu, Y., Xiang, Y., Uddin, M. P., Peng, D., & Gao, L. (2024). A comprehensive survey on edge data integrity verification: Fundamentals and future trends. *ACM Computing Surveys*, *57*(1), 1–34. DOI: 10.1145/3680277

Zheng, X., Zhu, W., Zhao, H., & Zhang, C. (2015). Employee well-being in organizations: Theoretical model, scale development, and cross-cultural validation. *Journal of Organizational Behavior*, *36*(5), 621–644. DOI: 10.1002/job.1990

Zhou, J., & Duan, Y. (2026). Blockchain-enabled product life cycle assessment information management system. *Ain Shams Engineering Journal*, *17*(2), 103993. DOI: 10.1016/j.asej.2026.103993

Zhou, Y., & Coplin, A. E. (2022). Innovation in a Science-based Sector. *China Review*, *22*(1), 39–76.

Zhu, L., Liu, C., & Xu, X. (2025). Unlocking synergy of knowledge in the digital era: Inter-team collaboration, network position, and knowledge creation. *Journal of Knowledge Management*, *30*(1), 1–29. DOI: 10.1108/JKM-07-2024-0801

Zhu, Z. (2025). Intelligent information management enables quality-by-design in pharmaceutical production. *Scientific Reports*, *15*(1), 44201. DOI: 10.1038/s41598-025-27879-w

Zivnuska, S., Kacmar, K. M., Ferguson, M., & Carlson, D. S. (2016). Mindfulness at work: Resource accumulation, well-being, and attitudes. *Career Development International*, *21*(2), 106–124. DOI: 10.1108/CDI-06-2015-0086

About the Contributors

Stéphanie Monteiro is a senior quality and regulatory affairs professional with extensive experience across the pharmaceutical, medical device, and medical technology sectors. Her professional background encompasses quality management systems, regulatory compliance, risk management, and product lifecycle governance in highly regulated healthcare environments, including pharma, MedTech, and medical device innovation contexts. She has built her career at the intersection of quality, innovation, and operational excellence, contributing to the development, validation, and continuous improvement of products and processes in accordance with international regulatory frameworks and standards. Her expertise includes quality assurance, compliance strategy, process optimization, and cross-functional collaboration with R&D, clinical, regulatory, and executive leadership teams. Stéphanie is actively involved in academic and applied research initiatives related to medical technology, healthcare innovation, and organizational performance, and has contributed to several academic publications and edited volumes in these domains. Her professional and academic interests focus on how quality systems, human capital, and leadership practices enable sustainable innovation and performance in regulated industries.

***

Luís Miguel dos Santos Abreu is a senior Environmental Health professional with extensive experience in public health, environmental protection, occupational safety, and health education. He holds a degree in Environmental Health from the Escola Superior de Tecnologias da Saúde de Coimbra, a Master's degree in Food Technology, postgraduate training in Safety Engineering and Ergonomics and postgraduate in Health Unit Management. With a career spanning nearly three decades in the Portuguese public health system, he has worked in several Public Health Units, currently serving at the Local Health Unit of the West. His professional activity focuses on environmental health surveillance, water and food safety, pollution control, waste management, occupational health, school health, and health promotion. In addition to his technical duties, he has significant experience as a trainer, lecturer, and internship supervisor in environmental health and occupational safety, contributing to the education and qualification of professionals in these fields. His work is guided by a strong commitment to public service, risk prevention, and the promotion of healthy and sustainable environments.

atrícia Cardoso is a university lecturer, consultant, and certified trainer in management, marketing, and human development. She holds a degree in Economics and a Master's in Financial Economics and is currently pursuing a PhD in Business Management. With over 20 years of professional experience in management, marketing, and human resources, she is also the co-founder of ECKM – European Consulting on Knowledge and Management and author of scientific publications in marketing and management.

Swati Dagar is a research scholar in the fields of Human Resource Management and Organizational Behaviour. She has actively engaged in academic writing and is working toward publishing her research in peer-reviewed and Scopus-indexed journals. Her broader academic interests include employee engagement, digital transformation in HRM, and human-centered AI applications in organizations.

Bablu Kumar Dhar is an Associate Professor of Business Administration at Mahidol University International College, where he teaches and conducts research in management and sustainability. He holds a PhD in Human Resource Management and has completed postdoctoral work in sustainability, corporate social responsibility, and emerging technologies. His research focuses on business ethics, environmental management, and organizational performance, particularly in emerging markets. With an extensive publication record in international journals and broad academic impact, his work integrates management, sustainability, and digital transformation perspectives, contributing to both theory and practice in global business environments.

Pedro Manuel do Espírito Santo is a Portuguese academic and consultant with over 20 years of business experience. He holds a PhD in Management – Applied Decision Science (2015) and an MBA in Business Strategy. Since 2023, he has been a researcher at the Polytechnic University of Leiria, where he also teaches management and marketing courses.

Deepak Gupta is a distinguished academician with over 20 years of teaching experience and expertise in Computer Science and Engineering. He holds a Ph.D. in

Computer Engineering and has an extensive research portfolio, including many international journal papers, multiple conference proceedings, and several books. His research interests span machine learning, artificial intelligence, and data mining. Currently, Dr. Gupta serves as an Associate Professor and Head of Department of CSE (Emerging Branches) at ITM Gwalior, MP, India. He has also contributed significantly to the field through patents and copyrights and actively engages as a reviewer, conference chair and editor.

Jyoti Kumari is an Assistant Professor in the Department of Computer Science and Engineering, specializing in Machine Learning and Artificial Intelligence. Her research primarily focuses on AIML (Artificial Intelligence and Machine Learning), data analytics, and related cutting-edge areas. She has authored and published numerous research papers, chapters, patents, copyrights and books in the field of AIML, contributing valuable insights to the academic and scientific community. Dedicated to shaping the next generation of technologists, she is committed to preparing students for successful careers in technology and research. Through her teaching, she instills a strong foundation in core concepts, emphasizes hands-on practical experience, and cultivates an innovative mindset. Her pedagogical approach goes beyond traditional instruction by inspiring students to explore novel ideas, adopt emerging techniques, and stay aligned with the latest industry trends and technological advancements.

Ricardo Marcão is a university professor at ISLA Santarém, where he directs several academic programs in management, strategy, and international relations, including the Master's in Business Management, the Master's in Project Management, and the Executive Master in Competitive Intelligence and International Management. He also directs the cTeSP in SME Management and several MBA programs focused on economic-financial diplomacy, quality management, and project management. An engineer and PhD in Management, he is a researcher at NECE – Research Center in Business Sciences at the University of Beira Interior, where his work consistently focuses on sustainability and examines the impact of strategy, innovation, and artificial intelligence on organizations and society. He is currently pursuing a Graduate Certificate in International Relations and Grand Strategy at Harvard University. He is the author of several technical and scientific books published in Portugal and the United States, an international speaker, and Chairman of the SCIP – Strategic Consortium of Intelligence Professionals – in Portugal. Alongside his academic career, he serves as an international project manager at Feedzai, a technology unicorn headquartered in New York (of Portuguese origin) specializing in the prevention of banking fraud.

Domingos Martinho is President and Coordinating Professor at ISLA Santarem - Polytechnic University. He holds a PhD in Information and Communication Technologies in Education and has an extensive academic and leadership career in higher education. His work focuses on computer science, digital technologies, and innovation in education. Domingos Martinho is actively involved in national and international academic and institutional bodies, contributing to the development of higher education systems and policies. He is also a researcher affiliated with NECE – Research Unit in Business Sciences and has authored numerous scientific publications, including journal articles, books, and conference papers.

|**Filipa Martinho** is an Executive Board Member and Adjunct Professor at ISLA Santarem - Polytechnic University. She holds a degree and a master's in Psychology and a Specialist Title in Management and Administration. Her work combines academic teaching with executive leadership, focusing on human resource management, organizational behavior, and applied management practices. Filipa is actively involved in research in the fields of management and organizational psychology, contributing to the development of interdisciplinary approaches that bridge academic knowledge and practical application. Her professional and academic work emphasizes people-centered management, organizational development, and performance improvement.

Rui Martins is a Professor in ISLA-Santarem, Department of Management and Economics, Portugal and collaborator of the Management Unit of the ISLA Santarem Research Unit and Student of a PhD in Management from the University of Beira Interior, Portugal. His research focuses on the Born Globals, Clusters, strategies of Internationalization of SMEs, business and cooperation networks, entrepreneurship and innovation.

Rupa Rathee is an associate professor at the Department of Management Studies, DCRUST, Murthal, Haryana (India). She has more than twenty years of teaching experience to her credit. Her teaching and research areas include Marketing and HRM. She has written three books with renowned publishers like Lambert Academic Publishing, PHI Learning and CRC Press (Taylor and Francis). She has over fifty publications to her credit in reputed international and national journals of publishers like Emerald, Sage and Elsevier. She has contributed more than ten book chapters to the books of IGI Global, McGraw Hill Education, and Palgrave Macmillan publishers. She has attended more than 30 FDPs at various prestigious institutes like IIM-Bangalore, IIM-Calcutta, IIM-Kozhikode, MDI-Gurgaon, IITM-Gwalior etc. She has contributed papers in over fifty international and national conferences. She has completed seven consultancy projects and one UGC (University

Grants Commission) sponsored major research project. She was awarded "The Best Teacher Award" instituted by the Sonepat Hindu Educational and Charitable Society for outstanding performance. She has been awarded four "Best Paper Award" at various prestigious International Conferences. Three scholars have been awarded Ph.D. degrees under her guidance. She is the department's research coordinator, cultural coordinator, NEP coordinator, and Assistant training and Placement Officer. She is a soft-skill trainer and motivational speaker. She has organized many cultural/ technical events, professional development programs, and workshops. She has delivered many expert lectures in various institutions.

Vasco Santos is the CEO and Founder of VRS Hospitality Consulting and a Professor at ISLA Santarem - Polytechnic University. He has extensive experience in hospitality management, business strategy, and international consulting, supporting organizations in improving operational efficiency and strategic positioning. Vasco combines executive leadership with academic involvement, contributing to the development of future professionals in management and business. As an author and speaker, his work focuses on strategic management, service innovation, and organizational performance across global markets.

Karimov Rashid Salayevich is affiliated with the Department of Accounting at Mamun University, Khiva, Uzbekistan. His academic interests focus on accounting systems, financial reporting, auditing, and financial management. He is actively involved in teaching and academic activities aimed at strengthening students' understanding of accounting principles and modern financial practices. His work emphasizes transparent financial reporting, the application of international accounting standards, and the use of contemporary analytical tools in accounting and finance. Karimov Rashid Salayevich also contributes to academic discussions related to corporate finance, business management, and financial regulation. Through his teaching and scholarly engagement, he aims to enhance accounting education and support the development of competent professionals capable of addressing modern financial and organizational challenges.

Index

H

I

K

M

O

P

Q

R

www.ingramcontent.com/pod-product-compliance
Lightning Source LLC
LaVergne TN
LVHW080909300926
849162LV00003B/616